MULTIVERSITIES, IDEAS, AND DEMOCRACY

GEORGE FALLIS

Multiversities, Ideas, and Democracy

UNIVERSITY OF TORONTO PRESS
Toronto Buffalo London

© University of Toronto Press Incorporated 2007
Toronto Buffalo London
Printed in Canada

Reprinted 2007

ISBN 978-0-8020-9240-3 (cloth)

Printed on acid-free paper

Library and Archives Canada Cataloguing in Publication

Fallis, George, 1947–
    Multiversities, ideas, and democracy / George Fallis.

    Includes bibliographical references and index.
    ISBN 978-0-8020-9240-3

    1. Education, Higher – Aims and objectives. 2. Research institutes.
3. Universities and colleges – Research. 4. Education, Humanistic.
I. Title.

LB2324.F34 2007   378′.012   C2007-901198-5

University of Toronto Press acknowledges the financial assistance to its
publishing program of the Canada Council for the Arts and the Ontario
Arts Council.

University of Toronto Press acknowledges the financial support for its
publishing activities of the Government of Canada through the Book
Publishing Industry Development Program (BPIDP).

Contents

Acknowledgments vii

1 Introduction 3

Part One: The Emergence of the Multiversity

2 The Idea of a University 17
3 The Uses of the Multiversity in Postindustrial Society 48
4 The Multiversity and the Welfare State 84
5 A Social Contract: Tasks, Autonomy, and Academic Freedom 111

Part Two: The Character of Our Age

6 The Constrained Welfare State 145
7 The Information Technology Revolution 178
8 Postmodern Thought 222
9 Commercialization 260
10 Globalization 297

Part Three: Renewing the Social Contract

11 The Multiversity and Liberal Democracy 339
12 A Liberal Education for Our Age 381

Notes 421
References 445
Index 465

Acknowledgments

The idea of writing a book about the future facing multiversities emerged while I worked on academic planning as dean of the Faculty of Arts at York University. Several colleagues, including Doug Freake (who suggested I read Martha Nussbaum), Anne Simone, Peter Victor, and especially Michael Wayne encouraged me as I began, in ways they might not have recognized. On stepping down as dean, I was especially fortunate, through the kind of initiative of James Carley, to spend my sabbatical leave as the first York Fellow at Massey College, Toronto. John Fraser, the Master of Massey College, and all the Massey community were most welcoming and provided an ideal environment for reading, reflection, and writing. Based on some of the ideas in this book, I wrote an essay 'The Mission of the University' that, through the support of Ian Clark, president of the Council of Ontario Universities, was posted on their website (http://www.cou.on.ca). Many people provided helpful reaction to this essay, and it led to an invitation to visit and present a public lecture at the University of Victoria. Mary Ellen Purkis and her colleagues at Victoria were both gracious hosts and stimulating in their comments. Many colleagues commented on portions of the manuscript or provided help and encouragement in other ways. They included Paul Axelrod, Ron Bordessa, Avi Cohen, David Goldbloom, Allan Greer, John Fraser, Michiel Horn, Dan Lang, Bernie Lightman, Bryan Massam, Ken McRoberts, David Palfreyman, Ross Rudolph, Mohit Sahni, Michael Skolnik, and Adrian Shubert. My greatest debt is to two remarkable women – Sheila and Zoe – who were my companions on the long journey to publication.

MULTIVERSITIES, IDEAS, AND DEMOCRACY

1 Introduction

This is a book about multiversities, a particular type of university that emerged in the second half of the twentieth century. It is about their role in society and the future they face.

The book focuses on multiversities in the Anglo-American world – particularly in the United States, England, and Canada. At the heart of postindustrial societies, the multiversities are sprawling conglomerates providing undergraduate liberal education, graduate education, and professional education. They are the core of society's research enterprise, the source of innovation and ideas. Often called research universities, the multiversities average more than 20,000 students each and have become the dominant institutional form for universities in the Anglo-American world and powerfully influential institutions in our society.

This is also a book about ideas: the ideas we have about the university and the ideas that define the character of our age. The ideas of our age are changing the multiversity and revolutionizing its role. The multiversities of the future will be measured by how they respond now. At present, multiversities are drifting away from their core ideals under pressure from the ideas of our age.

And finally, this book argues that multiversities must be conceptualized in a new way. It offers a new idea of a university: the university must be conceptualized not just as a place of teaching and research, but also as a fundamental institution of our democracy. I will argue that democracy in our postindustrial society requires multiversities whose mission includes a role in democracy and that are held accountable for their contribution to democratic life. Recognition of this role for multiversities will help to anchor against their drift away from core ideals.

The book addresses many questions. Why do we have universities? Why are liberal learning and research important? Why should society support the multiversity? And the answer is always the same – because ideas matter. Ideas matter to our economy, to our democracy, to our culture, and to our understanding of what it means to be human.

We are living in the postindustrial society so presciently forecast by Daniel Bell some forty years ago.[1] It is a knowledge-based society – an ideas-based society. Employment shifts out of manufacturing and into services such as finance, government, education, and health; manufacturing itself is transformed. Professional and technical jobs expand while blue collar and semiskilled jobs contract. An industrial society is organized around machines producing goods, and sources of power for the machines (steam, oil, gas, and electricity); whereas a postindustrial society is organized around the application of knowledge and new ideas, and the systems for generating and communicating knowledge and ideas. Although every society has been animated by knowledge and its dissemination by word, text, or image, what is decisive about postindustrial society is the development of self-conscious research programs and 'the centrality of theoretical knowledge as the source of innovation and policy formation.'[2] The foundation of the industrial society is a mechanical technology; the foundation of postindustrial society is an intellectual technology.

Theoretical knowledge becomes the axial principle of the economy, technology, and the occupational structure: an axial principle is 'the *organizing* frame around which the other institutions are draped, or the *energizing* principle that is a primary logic of all the others.'[3] The university – a place where theoretical knowledge is codified, enriched, disseminated, and authenticated – becomes an institution at the heart of society. In 1967, Daniel Bell wrote: 'if the business firm was the key institution of the past one hundred years, because of its role in organizing production for the mass creation of products, the university will become the central institution of the next one hundred years because of its role as the new source of innovation and knowledge.'[4]

The mission of the multiversity in such a postindustrial society is well-recognized: we need advanced research and highly educated graduates.

We also live in a democracy, however – a democracy of a particular sort and with particular needs at the beginning of the twenty-first century. Since the Second World War, in the Anglo-American world liberal democracy and capitalism have combined into what we call the welfare state. Under the social contract between citizens and their government, the government assumes a certain responsibility for the welfare of its citizens through a number of interventions in the market economy. Under this social contract, governments have funded the expansion from elite to mass university education: undergraduate study is available to all who are qualified and motivated. Accessible university education is necessary for equality of opportunity and an avenue to full participation in society. Democratic society supports an undergraduate liberal education, in part, for the purpose of making more intelligent, capable, and active citizens. The university is a place where our culture is preserved, redefined, critiqued, and disseminated. The multiversity is funded to provide professional degrees, the gateways to the professions such as law, medicine, architecture, and engineering. Society needs competent professionals possessed of knowledge and expertise; but it also needs ethical professionals with a commitment to the public good as well as to a private career. Democratic governments have allowed the professions to be self-regulating, with the reciprocal obligation of attention to the public good. Our postwar democracies finance the research enterprise of the university. Governments provide research grants and contribute to buildings, laboratories, libraries, computer systems, and most vital of all, to faculty positions that allow the time to do research. Both basic and applied research are supported, but with the presumption that the research will lead to the betterment of society: to the enhancement of our economy, our health, our national security, and our culture. In postindustrial society, politics requires deliberation on complex questions and visions of alternative futures. The multiversity is home to independent experts, critics, and public intellectuals; it protects us against the tyranny of majority ideas. We have come to realize that democracy means more than just elections: democracy requires that citizens have the ability and opportunity to participate in the deliberations that lead to collective decisions.

Thus, not only does the multiversity contribute advanced research and highly educated graduates to the postindustrial economy, we must also recognize that, across all its activities, the multiversity is vital to democratic life in the twenty-first century.

The multiversity developed through the second half of the twentieth century as a response to two great transformations: an economic transformation into a postindustrial economy and a political transformation into a welfare state. Clark Kerr, writing in 1963, labelled this new sort of university, this great sprawling conglomerate, the multiversity.[5] He called multiversities a uniquely American institution, but they are no longer. The same forces that created the multiversity in the United States have made the multiversity the dominant institutional form in other nations. The focus of the book will be on publicly supported institutions, but much of what is said applies to private multiversities. It is an analysis of the Anglo-American world, with particular emphasis on the United States, England, and Canada – all postindustrial societies with broadly similar liberal democratic cultures.

But what lies ahead? How is our world changing and how will these changes affect the multiversity? Reflections on these questions are the heart of the book. The university is being buffeted as it has been many times in history. Old values are challenged, seem uncertain, and may disappear. Reflecting on ten years as president of the University of Michigan, James Duderstadt observed: 'The most predictable feature of modern society is its unpredictability. We no longer believe that tomorrow will look much like today. Universities must find ways to sustain the most cherished aspects of their core values, while discovering new ways to respond vigorously to the opportunities of a rapidly changing world. This is the principal challenge to higher education as we enter a new century.'[6]

Today, even as the responsibilities of multiversities increase, public support diminishes, criticisms mount, and misunderstanding persists. The real value of government support per student declines. Senior civil servants see the multiversity as recalcitrant and unresponsive to new realities and government priorities. Critics claim that professors neglect undergraduate teaching in favour of their own research and that knowledge has become fragmented and esoteric, unconnected to the needs of students or society. Many voters understand the university simply as a place where students go to prepare for a job and demand that this be the focus of undergraduate education. There is a loss of confidence within the multiversity as well, which is reflected in the writing about universities by professors. There is a pervasive sense that universities are drifting away from their core mission: a list of recent books includes *The Research University in a Time of Discontent* (1994), *Bankrupt Education: The Decline of Liberal Education in Canada* (1994), *The University in Ruins* (1996), *Failing the Future: A Dean Looks at Higher Education in the Twenty-First Century* (1998), and *The Postmodern University? Contested Visions of Higher Education in Society* (1997).[7] Politicians, voters, and professors are frustrated, believing the others do not understand and have violated long-established fundamental principles.

Thus, the position of the multiversity is something of a paradox. It is an enormously powerful institution, having great influence upon society. Higher education and advanced research are high priorities. Usually, the multiversity enjoys great respect and considerable deference. Yet often, the society that supports the multiversity is impatient and frustrated. It wants the multiversity to change. The multiversity in turn feels overwhelmed by outside pressures, unsure of its mission.

This book is written out of a passionate commitment to the idea of a university and for those who care about its future, whether professor or university president, parent or citizen, politician or civil servant. It looks forward and will be useful to those who want to understand the future of our multiversities. It is a scholarly book, written to be accessible to the informed, curious reader. It deals with the United States, England, and Canada, where similar forces are shaping their multiversities. It is intended for readers in these countries.

Most readers will have attended a university and perhaps on their travels walked the precincts of the great and famous universities like Oxford or Harvard. Your children or your friends' children will attend one; the doctor, lawyer, or architect you use will have been trained there; and what you read will often quote a professor past or present. But most of us (including many professors) have a hazy picture of the multiversity, influenced more by nostalgic memories of undergraduate days and current movies than by informed reflection on the reality of the twenty-first century. This book dispels some of the haze. It tells some of the history of the university, how it has grown and adjusted, and describes its ideals and inner workings. It analyses the ideas of our age that now challenge and threaten the multiversity, in the hope that we can better appreciate the role of the multiversity and better participate in the process of readjustment.

The multiversity is only as strong as the public's support for it. The multiversity and society are connected through an unwritten social contract. Informed reflection and a vigorous civic conversation are required as we renew our understanding and commitment to universities. This book wants to provoke and contribute to the conversation. A conversation has dozens of voices, including the words of writers past and present who have thought about universities. We discover and listen to their voices because they are insightful and because this is the beginning of learning. This book presents many of these voices and includes them in the conversation.

The book is divided into three parts. Part One examines the history of universities and the emergence of the modern multiversity. Part Two looks at the future of the multiversity and examines five characteristics of our age that challenge the multiversity. Part Three looks at the renewal of the social contract between the multiversity and society. It looks at how society's support for the multiversity might be renewed, and argues that we need a renewed focus upon a liberal undergraduate education and that multiversities, among their many missions, should be recognized as institutions of democracy.

We cannot understand today's multiversity without understanding its history, and the ideals that it embodies. Eric Ashby, in his monumental study of higher education in the British Commonwealth, wrote: 'An institution is the embodiment of an ideal. In order to survive, an institution must fulfill two conditions: it must be sufficiently stable to sustain the ideal which gave it birth and sufficiently responsive to remain relevant to the society which supports it. The university is a medieval institution which fulfills both these conditions.'[8] A look at the history of the university helps us to understand its ideals and also helps us to understand how, in each era, it has responded to the society that supports it.

The multiversity has developed by taking on many, often conflicting, functions. The multiversity is defined by these functions: it is a place of teaching – undergraduate education, graduate education, and professional education – and it is a place of research. But a multiversity is also defined by its institutional form and governance. All these functions are best fulfilled in a spirit of free inquiry. Multiversities have certain tasks and in return are financially supported by government grants, tuition fees, contracts with corporations, and by private philanthropy. But to ensure the free inquiry necessary for their tasks, multiversities are autonomous institutions. Their professors and students have academic freedom. And, they operate, on academic matters, with a system of collegial self-governance. This relationship between the multiversity and the society that supports it is complicated and fraught as never before. The ideas of our age pull the multiversity closer and closer to government and business, shrinking its autonomy and academic freedom.

The authors of a recent book about Canadian universities, in discussing their methodology, noted that many books about universities, especially books like this written for the non-specialist, 'rest on careful reading, long observation of universities in action, and personal experience within universities.'[9] My methodology is in this tradition and the outcome, no doubt, is shaped by my observation and experience. In no sense, however, is the book a personal memoir.

I come to writing about universities, not as a research specialist in higher education, but as a professor and former dean of the Faculty of Arts. For the past twenty-seven years, I have been a professor of economics and social science at York University in Toronto. York is Canada's third-largest university, with a large graduate school and many professional schools. Most of my research and previous publications have dealt with issues of public policy. My research on universities began during my time in academic administration, during my seven years as dean. The Faculty of Arts at York University is very large (over 17,000 students), and unusual in that it included not only the humanities and social sciences, but also mathematics and statistics, and kinesiology and health science. As dean, I was involved in the issues of the humanities, social sciences, and sciences.

One fundamental responsibility of a dean is to lead the process of academic planning. I was always trying to analyse what was driving our world and what lay ahead for my faculty and my university. Like most academic administrators, I was intensely involved in day-to-day responsibilities and had little time to read about the university. Despite being an academic, I could not approach my responsibilities as a university administrator as an academic – I could not study the literature about my field. On stepping down as dean, I decided to confront these questions again but now as an academic: what is driving the world of the multiversity and what lies ahead? What does the literature have to say about these topics, what are people writing? One hope in writing this book, and in choosing this methodology, has been to encourage a deeper engagement with the literature about universities. Most of us within the academic community are remarkably poorly read about this world we live in. The hope is that those who care about the university can use this literature to better understand what is going on around them and to better prepare for the future.

The first task was to understand the nature of the multiversity and its history. This is the focus of Part One. The second task was to ask what lies ahead, what is the character of our age, and by doing so to identify the most significant issues challenging multiversities over the next decade. After much reading, after conversation with other deans and professors, I selected five characteristics of our age, and they are the topics of chapters 6 through 10, and form Part Two of the book. Part Two is entitled The Character of our Age.

In our age, the welfare state, which was so influential in creating the multiversity, expands no longer; the welfare state is constrained (chapter 6). Ours is the age of the information technology revolution (chapter 7). In some quarters, there is a new attitude, a new way of seeing the world, which can be labelled postmodern thought. It brings a profound sckepticism about authority, received wisdom, and cultural norms, as well as a radical critique of the existing western social order (chapter 8). In our age, postindustrial society continues to evolve, but with a particularly intense belief that research is crucial to the wealth of nations and that we must focus upon commercialization of this research (chapter 9). We live in an era of globalization (chapter 10).

Each characteristic of our age is transforming the multiversity. The constrained welfare state limits government expenditure, forcing higher tuition fees and increased reliance on external fundraising. University education is going through its greatest technological change in 400 hundred years; online teaching could replace the lecture hall and revolutionize the processes of teaching and learning. The postmodern critique rejects the grand narratives of progress and enlightenment, and even the idea of objective knowledge, the foundations upon which the multiversity has been built. Governments are shifting from supporting basic research towards supporting applied research and are asking that commercialization of research become a fundamental responsibility of the multiversity. Globalization diminishes the sovereignty of the nation state, disconnects the multiversity from its national cultural mission, and sets multiversities in competition across nations. These issues are the future that multiversities face, and posterity will judge the multiversities by how they respond. Running throughout is a special worry about the place of the humanities that once so defined the essence of the university.

This list, of course, is not exhaustive of the issues that lie ahead, and many crucial issues with which the multiversity must grapple and that may reshape multiversities are thus omitted. Some authors would emphasize the need for fundamental reform in the governance of multiversities; others the difficulties in recruiting and retaining faculty, with the coming wave of retirements; still others the rise of a bureaucratic/managerial class of administrators and their importation of business models into academic life. Others identify the rise of unionization and the increasing use of part-time, lower-paid instructors rather than tenured faculty. Some would emphasize the impact of the genomic revolution and advances in neuroscience upon the nature of biological and medical research at multiversities, and the attendant ethical issues.

Equally, of course, this list is not unique. Each topic included on the list, appears on many other lists, although often the same themes are gathered together in different ways or under different names.

This book does, however, have a unique approach. It sets out to examine the critical issues that will shape the multiversity over the next decade. It approaches these issues as driven by the ferment of ideas. Multiversities are being challenged by the ideas of our age. The challenges to multiversities are analysed as intellectual forces, forces that are changing both society and the multiversity – and these forces arise in part from the dynamic of multiversity research. Thus, the book analyses the multiversity in a manner that exemplifies its raison d'être: ideas matter. Each chapter of Part Two begins with an exploration of the bundles of ideas, before analysing their implications for the multiversity. Also by focusing on ideas, on intellectual forces, the book both illustrates and analyses the influence of the multiversity on society. Each bundle of ideas is presented to illustrate the dynamic of multiversity research. A theme running throughout the book is the profound effect of multiversity research upon society. Through its teaching and research, the multiversity is an extraordinarily powerful institution.

Much recent writing has emphasized multiversity research in the sciences, engineering, and medicine. I have given equal emphasis across the humanities, social sciences, and sciences. Ideas from social science are explored through the welfare state, ideas from science and engineering through the information technology revolution, and ideas from the humanities are explored through postmodernism. Each academic domain is powerfully reshaping society in its own way.

This book draws upon diverse literatures. Of course, it draws upon the literature on multiversities and on liberal education. But it also draws upon literatures not usually connected to writing about universities, including recent literature about deliberative democracy, about citizenship, and particularly about the evolution of the welfare state. I believe there is an extraordinarily productive terrain opened up by bringing together the literature about the liberal democratic welfare state and the literature about the multiversity.

One of the pleasures of being a dean is reading about and seeing the research of faculty members. This book is written out of the excitement of seeing new professors hired, new research projects begun, and new ideas taking shape at the university. These ideas challenge and disrupt ways of thinking and operating, both in the university and in society – which is as it should be and what makes the university such a precious institution.

Another of the pleasures of being dean is the involvement with undergraduate students and the responsibility to provide the best possible undergraduate education. Yet, it is and will be a difficult time for undergraduate education: undergraduate education does not receive the priority it deserves, and the curriculum is drifting away from its commitment to liberal learning. Likewise, the concept of citizenship, which has always been central to a liberal education, now receives little attention. In our age, as in every age, we must struggle to define what it means to be liberally educated and what should be in the curriculum of a liberal undergraduate education. Throughout the long traditions of liberal learning, study in the humanities has always had a special role. Today, however, the humanities are marginalized as never before. This book is written with the conviction that undergraduate education was, and remains, the central task of the multiversity. Also, undergraduate education must always be a liberal education, and must include study in the humanities and be an education for citizenship – although even as we draw upon these fundamental ideas of liberal learning, we must reinterpret them for our age.

This book is also written out of a tormenting worry that we risk squandering our inheritance, partly through inattention, partly through intransigence, and partly through prodigal adaptation to the ideas of our age. Our times are unpredictable and perplexing; our ways of thinking and ways of living shudder. The postwar balance of citizen, market, and state is not stable; new communications and information technologies penetrate our economy, our culture, and our homes; the postmodern critique challenges the meaning of truth and exposes the connection of knowledge to power; advanced research has become crucial to economic prosperity; liberal education is pushed aside; globalization promises a more prosperous, less parochial world, even a global village of universal humanity, but globalization could disguise a western hegemony or reveal irreconcilable differences.

Many in the multiversity are convinced that the ideas of our age will revolutionize the multiversity, so radically changing its functions that the unbroken history with universities past will be severed. The modern multiversity has many of functions, often conflicting and always given shifting emphasis. If the tormenting worry had to be summarized in a single sentence it would be: in postindustrial society of the twenty-first century, the economic functions of the multiversity will flourish and its democratic functions will wither. We must not allow this to happen.

PART ONE

The Emergence of the Multiversity

2 The Idea of a University

The multiversity, a vast conglomerate, emerged in the decades after the Second World War. How are we to comprehend this new type of university, this multiversity? We cannot comprehend it without understanding its history, particularly the ideals that it embodies. This fact is crucial to comprehending the multiversity. It makes the multiversity unusual among modern institutions: its history and its ideals are essential to what it is today.

Clark Kerr in his book *The Uses of the University* has famously written: 'About eighty-five institutions in the Western world established by 1520 still exist in recognizable forms, with similar functions and unbroken histories, including the Catholic church, the Parliaments of the Isle of Man, of Iceland, and of Great Britain, several Swiss cantons, and seventy universities. Kings that rule, feudal lords with vassals, and guilds with monopolies are all gone. These seventy universities, however, are still in the same locations with some of the same buildings, with professors and students doing much the same things, and with governance carried on in much the same ways.'[1]

One interpretation of this extraordinary fact would be that universities are isolated, conservative institutions – ivory towers – that have persisted in their sixteenth-century ways despite the industrial revolution, the transition to liberal democratic government, and the creation of the postwar welfare state. A corollary conclusion might be that eventually, likely very soon, this inflexible institution will be so out of sync with society that it will be washed away or restructured out of all recognition. Another interpretation would be that the tasks of the university, the tasks of teaching and learning, are the same today as they were in 1520, and therefore professors and students could and should be doing much the same things and going about their business in much the same ways. A corollary conclusion might be that, because teaching and learning will always be needed, universities will dominate the list, compiled one hundred years from now, of institutions with similar functions and unbroken histories.

Neither interpretation is entirely correct. Universities have not been ivory towers; throughout history they have been remarkably attentive to the needs of the society that supported them. They have evolved and taken on new tasks as society required, particularly in the past fifty years when they accommodated mass university education, established and expanded professional schools, and became research institutions in service of the nation. Nevertheless, they have always had core tasks and core ideals and core ideas about their governance that persist and allow us to recognize them as universities, despite their transformation.

There are many ways to understand the complex history of the multiversity. In this chapter, I characterize four 'ideas' of a university: the university as a place of undergraduate liberal education for the elite; the university as a place of graduate education and basic research; the university as place of professional schools; and the university as a place of accessible education and applied research. Each idea can be taken as an archetype in the several meanings of the word: each embodies an ideal form; each is an original model or prototype; and each is a recurring motif in writing and thinking about universities. One way to comprehend the multiversity is to recognize that it combines all four of these ideas.[2] And then there follows another crucial fact about multiversities: they combine conflicting ideas.

Regardless of its type, the central task of a university has always been undergraduate education.[3] This remains true today for the multiversity, for all its many tasks. To illustrate, American multiversities together awarded 426,000 bachelor's degrees in 1997–8 compared with only 36,800 doctoral degrees.[4] As we set out to comprehend the multiversity, it is fitting to begin with the idea of the university as a place of undergraduate study. Every age throughout the history of the university has struggled with two questions: what is the purpose of an undergraduate education and what should be included in the curriculum? The answer to the first question has always been: an undergraduate education should be a liberal education, although how a liberal education is defined varied tremendously. And, of course, what should be studied also varied tremendously. These two questions remain just as important, and just as vexing, for multiversities today. Running through this chapter's presentation of the four archetypes of a university will be an exploration of the various ideas of a liberal education. The questions about undergraduate education recur through the chapters of Part Two in discussions about the five characteristics of out age and their implications for the multiversity. In chapter 12, I will return to these themes. One of the great challenges for the multiversity in our age is to re-examine the meaning of a liberal education.

The University of Cardinal Newman

In our age, as in every age, we must ask: what is the mission of a university? What is the purpose of an undergraduate education? What does it mean to be liberally educated? No one has answered these questions better than Cardinal John Henry Newman. For Newman, *the* mission of a university is undergraduate liberal education: 'The view taken of a University in these Discourses is the following: – That it is a place of *teaching* universal *knowledge*.'[5] This sentence begins the most influential book ever written in the English language about universities: Cardinal Newman's *The Idea of a University*. He continues: 'Knowledge is capable of being its own end. Such is the constitution of the human mind, that any kind of knowledge, if it be really such, is its own reward.'[6] For Newman, humankind is innately curious; we want to know and to understand. Because of this basic human characteristic, knowledge is its own reward.

A liberal education is the 'process of training, by which the intellect, instead of being formed or sacrificed to some particular or accidental purpose, some specific trade or profession, or study or science, is disciplined for its own sake, for the perception of its own proper object, and for its own highest culture.'[7] If a 'practical end must be assigned to a University course, I say it is that of training good members of society. Its art is the art of social life, and its end is fitness for the world.'[8]

> It is a great point then to enlarge the range of studies which a University professes, even for the sake of the students; and, though they cannot pursue every subject which is open to them, they will be the gainers by living among those and under those who represent the whole circle. This I conceive to be the advantage of a seat of universal learning, considered as a place of education. An assemblage of learned men, zealous for their own sciences, and rivals of each other, are brought, by familiar intercourse and

> for the sake of intellectual peace, to adjust together the claims and relations of their respective subjects of investigation. They learn to respect, to consult, to aid each other. Thus is created a pure and clear atmosphere of thought, which the student also breathes, though in his own case he only pursues a few sciences out of the multitude. He profits by an intellectual tradition, which is independent of particular teachers, which guides him in his choice of subjects, and duly interprets for him those which he chooses. He apprehends the great outlines of knowledge, the principles on which it rests, the scale of its parts, its lights and its shades, its great points and its little, as he otherwise cannot apprehend them. Hence it is that his education is 'Liberal.' A habit of mind is formed which lasts through life, of which the attributes are, freedom, equitableness, calmness, moderation, and wisdom.[9]

For Newman, a liberal education should be devoted to knowledge for its own sake; it should not be preparation for a job, nor to gain mastery of one discipline. Rather, it should prepare for membership in society, and it should be a broad education. At Cardinal Newman's university, the responsibility of professors was to teach. For undergraduate students, their years in college were a time of both learning and character formation. There was close connection between professor and student; instruction was in small tutorials; and both teacher and student lived and dined in college.

Newman's book is deservedly at the centre of any discussion of the university. The book does two remarkable things: it defines a university and it defines a liberal education. Nowhere else do we have such an uncompromising articulation and written in such self-confident, elegant prose as could flow from the pen of this nineteenth-century Englishman. No doubt, Newman is influential in part because he happened to write during the mid-nineteenth century, a formative era in the development of modern universities. But his ideas still have a deep resonance today. They are invoked by university presidents in their convocation addresses to graduating students and their parents. Just as often, paradoxically, Newman is invoked by critics who argue that our universities (and their presidents) have lost their way and betrayed Newman's idea of a university, allowing themselves to become beholden to corporations and the labour market. If we are to think about multiversities, Newman is a good starting point, although as we read *The Idea of a University*, we discover Cardinal Newman is not quite the champion that presidents and critics thought.

John Henry Newman was born in 1801 to a middle-class Church of England family, went up to Oxford in 1817, and was elected a Fellow of Oriel College in 1822. Two years later, he was ordained into the ministry of the Church of England and shortly after became vicar of St Mary's, the Oxford University church. Across all the transitions and tumult of his life, Newman would always remain a man of Oxford – the Oxford of the early nineteenth century. The idea about which he would write so eloquently was the Oxford of his youth.

England was being transformed economically, politically, and socially by the industrial revolution and the intellectual aftermath of the French Revolution. Once an agricultural nation stratified under a landed aristocracy, England was becoming industrial, urban, and democratic. The new middle class grew, working in commerce, industry, and trade; the Protestant dissenters outside the established Church of England exemplified the emerging social order. The Scottish universities and the new University of London were accommodating themselves to industrialization and democracy; Oxford was not. Astonishing as it seems, admission to Oxford in the mid- nineteenth century was restricted to men, and among men, to men of the (established) Church of England.

An admirer of tradition and authority, Newman moved closer to the Roman Catholic Church. In 1843, Newman resigned as vicar of St Mary's, continued his figurative and literal journey towards Rome, and soon thereafter was ordained as a Roman Catholic priest. Late in life, he was named a Cardinal. In 1851, the Archbishop of Dublin invited Newman to found a Roman Catholic university in that city. As he worked to create this Catholic university, Newman delivered a series of lectures (discourses) and published a series of essays, finally gathering them together into a volume published in 1873 – *The Idea of a University*.

How curious that a work with this genesis should prove to be so seminal, so frequent a referent in discussion of modern universities. Newman's first task in addressing the Catholics of Dublin was to explain why a specifically Catholic university was needed. The first four discourses in *The Idea of a University* are devoted to why Christian theology belongs within 'universal knowledge' and why theology integrates and is superior to other branches of knowledge. Certainly today, it would be a rare president at convocation who would begin by proclaiming the centrality of religious truth in a liberal education.

The curiosities continue. Newman was sexist, seeing no place for women in his university. His liberal education was to create a *gentleman*, with a 'cultivated intellect, a delicate taste, a candid, equitable, dispassionate mind, a noble and courteous bearing in the conduct of life; – these are the connatural qualities of a large knowledge; they are the objects of a University.'[10] He was perhaps racist, certainly Eurocentric. He could write of humanity outside Europe: 'There are indeed great outlying portions of mankind which are not, perhaps never have been, included in this Human Society; still they are outlying portions and nothing else, fragmentary, unsociable, solitary and unmeaning, protesting and revolting against the grand central formation of which I am speaking.'[11] And how much of Newman's opposition to applied or professional learning should be ascribed to his defence of the status quo and his Church? Applied learning was associated with the new middle class in commerce and trade, and with the Protestant dissenters demanding greater democracy. Newman had little place for the learning sought by such people. His vision ignored the university's potential in the emancipative transformation of the nineteenth century. His university had no special place in the slowly emerging liberal democracy.

We should not be too smug or too critical of Newman, in self-righteous hindsight. Each is of his or her era. We might pause to speculate how what we write today will be read in 150 years – if it will be read at all. Newman articulated an ideal of undergraduate liberal learning, an ideal which remains at the essence of any university, and against which every university in every era will be judged. His prose has gone forth into western culture, 'his language has established the style and essential mode of discourse with which to speak and write of the academic life. Virtually everything else written about universities has lacked his harmony and style and the capacity of his ideas to resonate with the desire that the educational process, whatever else it may do, rise above the humdrum of everyday existence and transform the immature into the mature, the unformed into the formed, the unreflective into the reflective, the youth into the adult.'[12]

Sheldon Rothblatt, a leading historian of universities, draws our attention to another remarkable aspect of Newman's book: 'not any particular idea of a university, however interesting it may appear, but the very idea of an idea of a university.'[13] It is remarkable that the university should have an 'idea' at all.

Part of 'the lovely treachery of words'[14] is that they can take different meanings in different contexts. The word 'idea' means the object of thought, as in: 'Keynes's ideas about monetary policy were formed as he observed the long recession of the 1920s.' This will be a common usage of the word 'idea' in this book. But 'idea' can also mean, as it especially did in Newman's day, a pure form or archetype as distinguished from its realization in the world. For Newman, the 'idea' of a university is its essential purpose, embedded in the institution and in its history.

Today, we might use the word 'ideal.' Newman chose to write about the *ideal* of a university. Sheldon Rothblatt concludes: 'But such continuities as universities enjoy, such aspirations as they have to be a moral force in modern society, or at least a unique force, are attributable to the odd and special history of the idea of the idea of a university.'[15] The genius of Newman was not in his specific idea but in his 'desire to elevate the university to the moral centre of modern culture and to do so by freeing the university from the grip of utilitarian and hedonistic schools of thought.'[16] Our multiversities confront this same struggle to escape from utilitarian and hedonistic schools of thought, and they do so by holding to certain ideas of the university.

Cardinal Newman defined a university as a place of liberal learning and by so doing claimed for the university the idea of liberal learning, an idea that is much older than the university itself. Our ideas of liberal learning originate in Greek and Roman thought, but the first university did not arise until the medieval era. Newman articulated one particular idea of liberal education, but there were many others. Because its history reaches back into the richly variegated thought of antiquity, the idea of liberal learning has taken many forms. Scholars of liberal education are quite clear: 'Contrary to the conventional perception, the tradition of liberal education is not uniform and continuous, but full of variety, discontinuity, and innovation.'[17]

Greek and Roman thought contains many different ideas about liberal education. One strand in Greek thought, not the strand picked up by Newman, developed liberal learning as a reaction against education intended to pass on traditional practices and traditional values. This strand is the philosophical tradition of Aristotle and Socrates. For Socrates, liberal learning emerged through sceptical questioning, through the application of reason, and through dialogue. All our knowledge, all our ways of seeing and of doing, both individual and collective, should be subjected to the scrutiny of reason. Through civil dialogue, question-and-answer, give-and-take, true knowledge emerges. Students should challenge orthodoxy and tradition; students should not accept thoughts, rather they should have responsibility for their thoughts. Tradition was a cage from which we must escape. Socratic questioning is not mere scepticism or rebelliousness, because the question is posed: What should we do? What is virtuous? What is just? What is good – for an individual, for a family, for a society? Socrates believed that to be free to exercise one's own thought was the essence of being human and so much of human essence that 'the unexamined life is not worth living.'

The liberal education of Newman's university was not grounded in Socratic, sceptical reason; Newman's purpose was the cultivation of a Christian gentleman. But his idea of liberal education, too, could find origins in Greek and Roman thought, in the traditions of the orator. Oxford was educating young men to become leaders in the clergy, Parliament, or civil service; they were to be leaders in the English nation state. Newman wanted the same for Catholics in Ireland. Reform of the political order was not on his agenda. The priority was responsible, wise, virtuous leadership of the existing order.

From all the variation of classical thought, there emerged a Roman synthesis regarding the liberal arts, and a consensus on the ideal form of education. Bruce Kimball in his masterful book *Orators and Philosophers: A History of the Idea of Liberal Education* calls this consensus the *artes liberales* ideal. He associates it with the oratorical, as opposed to philosophical, theme in classical thought. Kimball sets out the key characteristics of the ideal. The first is that liberal learning has the goal of training good citizens – virtuous and competent to lead society. 'This goal necessarily implies the prescription of values and standards for character and conduct,' and requires respect for these values and standards. 'A body of classical texts [both Greek and Latin] provides the means to identify and agree upon them.' Through this liberal education, an elite is identified 'who achieve greater merit by adopting the personal and civic virtues expressed in the texts.' Pragmatic rather than analytic, the oratorical tradition believed truth could be known and expressed and 'that the task of liberal education is to inform students of the virtues rather than, as the Socratic tradition held, to teach the student how to search for them.'[18] Cardinal Newman's liberal education is in this *artes liberales* tradition.

In classical thought, ideas of liberal learning, of both the orator and the philosopher, were inextricable from ideas of freedom, citizenship, and democracy. Liberal learning in antiquity was inherently civic. An informed citizenry was essential to Athenian democracy and to the

Roman Republic, and equally essential was a tradition of reasoned debate. Wars of words, bombastic assertion, or the alchemy of 'spin doctors' could not ensure democracy – a lesson we have forgotten. Liberal learning in classical thought 'addresses the human longing for wholeness and its relation to the principles of a just and satisfying political order ... Human nature comes fully to light only when man's relation to the political community is elaborated. According to classical thinkers, human life is incomplete apart from membership in a civic association, and cannot be adequately grasped on individualistic grounds.'[19] The concept of citizenship is central. In the chapters ahead, particularly as I situate the modern multiversity as part of democracy and the welfare state, the concept of citizenship will reappear again and again.

The Medieval University

However hard we might try, we cannot trace an unbroken institutional history from the Roman synthesis about liberal education to Newman's Oxford. Indeed, the first universities were very unlike Newman's Oxford. The first universities – the medieval universities – were not devoted to knowledge for its own sake. Rather, the medieval universities arose to meet the needs of the economy of Europe, marked by a revival of town life and the expansion of continental trade. The establishment of the medieval university was 'inextricably bound up with utilitarian values. They evolved as institutional responses to the pressures to harness educational forces to the professional, ecclesiastical and governmental requirements of society ... Their essential purpose was to increase educational opportunity for students of ability destined for professional employment within the ecclesiastical hierarchy or civil government, or in some legal or medical capacity.'[20]

The early universities sometimes emphasized one field, acquiring a continental reputation. Three great prototypes were Bologna, known for law; Salerno, known for medicine; and Paris, known for theology. During the thirteenth century, universities proliferated, new faculties were added, and gradually a typical structure emerged with four faculties: arts, law, medicine, and theology. Study in the arts faculty was preparatory to study in the latter three, which were regarded as the higher faculties. Here in the medieval university we have a second idea of a university: a university that gives pre-eminence to the professional schools. This idea has clearly been incorporated into the multiversity, for one distinguishing characteristic of multiversities is the number and importance of professional schools within them.

The arts curriculum of the medieval university was in the *artes liberales* tradition. The curriculum was broad and comprehensive; it required study of the seven liberal arts: grammar, logic, and rhetoric (the *trivium*) and arithmetic, geometry, music, and astronomy (the *quadrivium*). Medieval scholarship, especially as it incorporated Aristotelian thought, overlaid the seven liberal arts with study of 'the three philosophies' – natural, moral, and metaphysical. Natural philosophy examined sensory experience and the physical world; moral philosophy examined human affairs; and metaphysical philosophy examined the nature of being. Although using terminology archaic by today's lights, this medieval conception still stands, in the minds of many today, as the ideal undergraduate curriculum – comprehensive across the humanities, social sciences, and sciences, and concerned with values and citizenship.

Thus, these first universities had two components, two missions: liberal education and professional education. These are with us still. And these medieval universities contained an irreconcilable conflict that is also still with us: the university pursues knowledge for its own sake, particularly through the liberal arts, but it also pursues knowledge to meet the economic needs of society. Although we often forget, from the very outset, universities connected academic study and career.

Newman's university has a certain similarity to the medieval university: it has the four faculties of arts, law, medicine, and theology. But Newman grants primacy to the arts, noting approvingly that 'even down to this day, in those academical corporations which have more than others retained their medieval origin – I mean the Universities of Oxford and Cambridge – we hear little of Theology, Medicine or Law and almost exclusively of Arts.'[21] Newman's beliefs – that nineteenth-century Oxford was similar in structure to medieval universities and that medieval liberal education had no regard for the professional destination of its students – were commonly held in his day but they were poor history.

At the turn of the nineteenth century, 'the historian and theologian Hastings Rashdall challenged and overturned this long-standing conclusion regarding the origins of the university. He argued – and his viewpoint has prevailed – that professional education had always been the distinguishing characteristic of the university. In his monumental study of the European university and in lectures he gave around the kingdom, he publicized his findings in an obvious effort to promote support for a university ideal'[22] that differed from Newman's; an alternative that matched the needs of late nineteenth-century society. 'No longer was it improper for universities to relate their education directly to careers or to train their students for specific professional occupations, as in fact they had long been doing.'[23]

Humboldt and the University of Berlin

Although the university's institutional origins are medieval, the intellectual origins of today's multiversities are later – in early modern world. The intellectual origins of the modern idea of a university are found in Renaissance humanism, the Scientific Revolution, and the Enlightenment. Today, many postmodern writers call these intellectual traditions 'the project of modernity.' The multiversity is rooted in the project of modernity.

The Renaissance humanists began the separation of man from God, giving birth to what Robert Proctor, in his penetrating analysis of the humanities, *Education's Great Amnesia: Reconsidering the Humanities from Petrarch to Freud*, called 'the autonomous self.'[24] Human reason and human experience could be relied upon and humanity could advance by its own efforts.

The Scientific Revolution was the culmination of changes in the fundamental structures of European thought. Reason was replacing deference to authority. Nature was closely observed and categorized. Explanations were being tested against empirical observation. The world was approached neither as chaotic nor as the working of God's conscious hand; rather the world was being approached as a mechanism that conforms to laws that can be expressed mathematically. The great and emblematic text of the Scientific Revolution was Isaac Newton's *Principia (Philosophiae naturalis principia mathematica – the Mathematical Principles of Natural Philosophy)*, published in 1687. In this, he analysed the properties of light and optics, set out laws of motion, and presented a theory of gravity to explain the motions of the planets. The universe could be understood through theory expressed in mathematics; the observations of reality could be explained by the theory; and theory could, and should, be tested against observation.

The advances of science were wondrous; their contributions to improving daily life monumental. Enlightenment thinkers in eighteenth-century Europe sought to apply the Newtonian approach – the scientific approach – to understanding the economic and political spheres. The writers of the Enlightenment – Voltaire, Kant, Hume, Adam Smith – believed that knowledge came from reason and observation, not from revelation or from tradition. All knowledge, especially knowledge based on religion or tradition, must be challenged. Their goals were material progress and human emancipation. Both could come through improved knowledge of the world, by overcoming ignorance and religious superstition, and by the creation of new forms of government. The scientific approach was the way to knowledge in all spheres. They believed most of the horrific suffering in human history had been brought in the name of religion, and therefore religious tolerance must be a cornerstone of any governmental order. Freedom and the equality of all men are fundamental. Ultimate authority in politics rests with the free and equal people; governments derive their authority only through a social contract with the governed.

A new idea of a university emerges with this intellectual character of modernity: the modern university is concerned with research and the discovery of new knowledge. Cardinal Newman, in *The Idea of a University*, has surprisingly little to say about the discovery of new knowledge. Research is so much a part of a modern university professor's work, and so much the focus of public policy towards multiversities, that we might think new knowledge had always been a raison d'être for universities. But this is not the case; certainly Newman believed otherwise. His university was for teaching and for students, and most emphatically not for research. For Newman, the object of the university 'is the diffusion and extension of knowledge rather than the advancement. If its objects were scientific and philosophical discovery, I do not see why a University should have students.'[25] Newman believed the search for new knowledge is better done outside the university in specialized literary and scientific academies. He recommends the 'division of intellectual labour between Academies and Universities. To discover and to teach are distinct functions; they are also distinct gifts, and are not commonly found united in the same person.' We look elsewhere to discover the origin of the research mission of the university – to Germany, also in the nineteenth century. Here we find another idea of a university, the idea of a university devoted to research, as well as to teaching.

Germany, in the early nineteenth century, was very different from England. England had been a nation state for centuries; Germany remained a fragmented and fractious collection of principalities. Napoleon had crushed the Prussian army at Jena in 1806. Such humiliation to the greatest of the German 'states' could only be countered by the creation of a 'modern' German nation state. It was a matter of urgent national necessity that Prussia establish a new university in Berlin as part of building a modern nation. King Friedrich Wilhelm III commissioned his head of the Civil Cabinet with the task. Leading academics were invited to offer proposals for the design of the new university. Implementation fell to Wilhelm von Humboldt, and the University of Berlin was founded in 1809. We find in Berlin another idea of a university, the first modern university.

We associate the University of Berlin with Humboldt, but its vision and structure owe much to the proposals made by German academics and to the Enlightenment philosophy of Immanuel Kant, who had been a professor of logic and metaphysics at the Prussian University of Konigsberg in the late 1700s. For Kant, knowledge (*wissenschaft*) came from the 'scientific' (*wissenschaftlich*) inquiry into philosophical questions. 'Scientific' inquiry was inquiry governed by reason, and philosophy was the discipline governed by reason. Therefore, the faculty of philosophy (overarching and encompassing all the liberal arts) should be more important in a university than the faculties of law, or medicine, or theology. The university should be dominated by reason and free inquiry, that is, by philosophy, and not by the needs of the professions.

In the German university of research, professors were not generalists responsible for teaching diverse aspects of the curriculum; instead there was a division of labour into the fields of knowledge. Professors taught and examined in their own fields. There is a perpetual conflict between tradition (established knowledge) and rational inquiry; each discipline advances by re-examining its established knowledge under the light of reason. Knowledge progresses through this perpetual conflict between reason (embodied by the faculty of philosophy) and tradition (embodied by the other faculties and fields). This dialectic requires that professors be free to study and to teach according to the dictates of their curiosity and their application of reason. This ideal of professorial free inquiry, known as *lehrfreiheit*, has profoundly influenced the modern university. In Germany the professor as researcher was a high calling; austere and deeply cultured, a disinterested seeker of truth, unaffected by concerns of utility. The work required long study, patience and arduous labour, but also passion for knowledge and total honesty following where logic and evidence would lead.[26]

Using the *wissenschaftliche methoden*, the German professor, an accomplished leader in his chosen discipline, worked with students who had chosen this discipline and would take their learning to the most advanced level. Pedagogical methods were designed to simultaneously create new knowledge and fully realized individuals. Lectures and seminars rather than tutorials became the mode of instruction. In lectures, professors were not simply to offer explications of existing knowledge, but also critiques, and to discuss recent advances in knowledge. The curriculum emphasized, and examinations rewarded, both original thought and the understanding of basic philosophical principles. The German research university also provides the idea of the university as a place of advanced study, a place of graduate education.

Humboldt's Berlin was a university where both teaching *and* research were regarded as primary duties of its professors. This now defines a university. Humboldt believed 'research and instruction were naturally inseparable. They were also endless processes. Just as a student could never complete his education because intellectual (or spiritual) development was endless, so too was research a never-ending story.'[27]

Humboldt's special genius was his ability to transform philosophical ideas into institutional arrangements for a university. His university was organized and administered around disciplinary specialization. He greatly enhanced the rigour of research and allowed new professorships and disciplines to be added as knowledge advanced and expanded. German universities led the world in introducing new scientific disciplines, such as chemistry, into universities. Humboldt understood that the new university must serve the project of building a modern German nation. Prussian universities were creatures of the state; professors were paid as civil servants. The university must prepare lawyers, civil administrators, doctors, and scientists, and enhance the knowledge that each could apply. Together, these tasks would help to realize the German nation. Humboldt embraced these tasks. And the German universities prospered as the modern German nation state was created during the industrial boom of the later nineteenth century. But nonetheless, Humboldt argued, universities must be autonomous. In the dynamic application of reason, which produced new knowledge, only scholars could judge the work of students and other scholars. More profoundly, 'all educational development has its sole origin in the inner psychological constitution of human beings, and can only be stimulated, never produced by external institutions.'[28] The government 'must demand nothing of them [universities] which directly concerns itself or its own operations, but must hold fast to an inner conviction that if the higher institutions reach their ultimate aim, its own aim, too, will be thereby fulfilled, and from a much loftier point of view than any that could have been arranged directly by the state itself.'[29] Humboldt created a rationale and structure for government support of universities coupled with university autonomy – another defining characteristic of the modern multiversity.

The combination of ideas and structures represented by the University of Berlin has been enormously influential in the evolution of universities of England, the United States, and Canada, and elsewhere around the world. By the late nineteenth century, Berlin and other German universities had become world-leading centres of scientific research and graduate education – much admired and much emulated.

The Scottish Universities

The present high renown of Oxford, its long history and frequent appearance in famous English lives, might seem to imply an equally long history of intellectual leadership – if not across Europe at least in the British Isles. However, Oxford (and Cambridge) suffered a long period of decline during the seventeenth and eighteenth centuries, not truly recovering until the later nineteenth century. The curriculum remained steadfast in its medieval conception, often degenerating into a pedantic scholasticism and resisting the introduction of the new knowledge in science and technology. Most English leaders of Enlightenment and scientific thought worked outside these established universities – their new learning was not welcome there – and found homes in new scientific societies such as the Royal Society of Arts, founded in 1754 for the encouragement of the arts, manufactures, and commerce in Great Britain or in the new academies established by Protestant dissenters excluded from Oxford and Cambridge. At the ancient English universities, fees rose, enrolments fell, and scholarships once available for students of modest background were taken by sons of wealthy gentry and clergy. 'The rise in costs was not owing to the basic cost of living but to the competitive extravagance of gentlemen undergraduates in wining and dining, in acquiring fine clothes and furniture, in keeping horses, and in living high.'[30] The universities became bastions of gentlemanly privilege. Perhaps less than gentlemanly, one caustic critic wrote: 'In no places of education are men more extravagant; in none do they learn to drink sooner; in none do they more effectively shake off the firm sensibilities of shame and learn to glory in debauchery.'[31]

Real dynamism and academic leadership in this period were found in the Scottish universities, whose leadership predates and presages the University of Berlin. The Scottish universities provide another idea, another archetype, of a university. We hear far less of the University of Edinburgh than we hear of Oxford or Berlin, despite the Scottish universities being internationally acknowledged centres of knowledge. Perhaps this is because institutions of the periphery will always be less regarded than institutions of the centre. Or perhaps, there was no one to write *The Idea of a University (in Scotland)*, or no imperial patron to solicit plans for a new university. But the Scottish universities contribute as much to our ideal of a multiversity as does the University of Berlin. A recent popular history, *How the Scots Invented the Modern World* by Arthur Herman, has given the Scottish contribution new prominence: 'the Scots created the basic ideals of modernity.' 'When we gaze out on a contemporary world shaped by technology, capitalism and democracy, and struggle to find our place in it, we are in effect viewing the world through the same lens as the Scots did.'[32] The multiversity is a product of this modernity, this world of technology, capitalism, and democracy.

The four 'ancient' Scottish universities were Edinburgh, Aberdeen, Glasgow, and St Andrew's. The Scottish universities, unlike Oxford and Cambridge, always had close associations with government, often the town council, and with the broader society. The Scottish Reformation, especially the writings of John Knox, emphasized universal public education. The Scottish universities 'were part of an educational system and tradition whose ideal was to reach all classes of society and not merely the privileged ... Any boy who could do the work was welcome; the money necessary for the relatively small tuition fees and lodgings in town could usually be scraped together somehow.'[33] Accessibility was the virtue, not gentlemanly manners. Scotland shows us the university as a public institution of opportunity and social mobility.

The Scottish universities, long before Oxford, opened themselves to the new scientific learning. Following the Dutch example, Scottish universities established new chairs in natural philosophy (physical science) and moral philosophy, from which came the field of political economy and later the social sciences such as economics, political science, and psychology. Specialist chairs were appointed within the traditional fields of mathematics, astronomy, and medicine (notably in biology and chemistry). Pedagogy was reformed. General tutors who dealt with the entire curriculum were replaced with tutors in each discipline. Lectures replaced tutorials. Laboratory demonstrations were introduced, revolutionizing scientific and medical education. Instruction was in the vernacular (English) rather than Latin.

These ideas and accomplishments of Scottish universities were recognized widely: 'By the middle of the eighteenth century the Scottish universities were distinguished among the institutions of higher education in Europe by their strong commitment to utilitarian social service and their concern for educational progress and reform. These utilitarian and reform emphases were clearly manifest in three areas: first, the attention devoted by universities to curricular and pedagogical reform; second, the rise of Scottish medical schools and the introduction of a wide range of scientific subjects into the curriculum; and third, the involvement of the universities and their professors in the economic and industrial development of the country.'[34]

Accessible, reformist, and socially engaged, Scottish universities were admired for their contributions to Scotland's robust industrialization and 'national' development. Wherever industrialization and nation-building were interconnected national priorities, as in the United States and Canada, the Scottish idea of a university was influential. As medieval universities responded to the social and economic needs of their time, so too did Scottish universities in the eighteenth century, offering avenues of opportunity to the growing middle class and advancing knowledge in science and technology to propel the process of industrialization. Although seldom given the acknowledgment they deserve, the Scottish universities provided an ideal that helps to define today's multiversities in the Anglo-American world.

By early in the nineteenth century, the four ideas of the university had been set out: Newman's university of undergraduate liberal education; the medieval university of professional schools; the German university of graduate education, research, and pure science; the Scottish university of undergraduate accessibility and applied science. Gradually the university was being connected to the nation state, its economy, and its culture. All this history, these four archetypes, came together in the second half of the twentieth century to form the multiversity. These four ideas shape our modern thinking about the mission of a multiversity. And the tensions of the nineteenth and early twentieth centuries – between elite education and accessible education, between teaching and research, between withdrawal from the world and engagement, between knowledge valued for its own sake and knowledge valued for its utility, between specialized learning and generalized learning, between the humanities and the sciences – are with us still.

During the mid-nineteenth century, while John Henry Newman was writing *The Idea of a University*, there was a fierce debate in Great Britain about the nature of a university and the nature of a liberal education. The controversy centred on how to accommodate the new scientific knowledge and the role of the humanities in liberal learning.

The best-articulated alternative to Newman came from Thomas Huxley, a leading Victorian scientist and foremost supporter of Charles Darwin. Huxley became Rector of the University of Aberdeen, one of the ancient Scottish universities. In his inaugural address, 'Universities: Actual and Ideal,' Huxley declared there should be 'a duly organized Faculty of Science in every university. The establishment of such a Faculty would have the additional advantage of providing, in some measure, for one of the greatest wants of our time and our country. I mean the proper support and encouragement of original research.'[35] Like Humboldt, Huxley organized the university by discipline and institutionalized the research ideal; and the research that Huxley advocated was very much concerned with application in the real world.

Huxley rejected Newman's classical liberal education and championed a different ideal, an ideal recognizing and celebrating scientific knowledge. The old and still-dominant belief was that 'culture is obtainable only by a liberal education; and a liberal education is synonymous, not merely with education and instruction in literature, but in one particular form of literature, namely, that of Greek and Roman antiquity.' Scientific knowledge was rejected as narrowing and indeed even unnecessary.

Huxley mocked the champions of the classical literary curriculum, and openly declared: 'I hold very strongly by two convictions – The first is, that neither the discipline nor the subject-matter of classical education is of such direct value to the student of physical science as to justify the expenditure of valuable time upon either; and the second is that for the purpose of attaining real culture, an exclusively scientific education is at least as effectual as an exclusively literary education.'[36]

The essence of culture, for Huxley and also for the humanists, was to examine life. 'It implies possession of an ideal, and the habit of critically estimating the value of things by comparison with a theoretical standard. Perfect culture should supply a complete theory of life, based upon a clear knowledge alike of its possibilities and of its limitations.'[37] The classical texts might have been sufficient for the Renaissance, but not for a culture in Huxley's scientific and industrial world. 'This distinctive character of our own times lies in the vast and constantly increasing part which is played by natural knowledge. Not only is our daily life shaped by it, not only does the prosperity of millions of men depend upon it, but our whole theory of life has long been influenced, consciously or unconsciously, by the general conceptions of the universe, which have been forced upon us by physical science.'[38]

Bruce Kimball in *Orators and Philosophers: A History of the Idea of Liberal Education* argues that during the seventeenth and eighteenth centuries another ideal of liberal education emerged that he calls the liberal-free ideal, in contrast to the *artes liberales* ideal. The liberal-free ideal, like the *artes liberales*, could find origins in Greek and Roman thought, especially the philosophical Socratic tradition. But its vital roots are in the Enlightenment, with its sceptical stance towards tradition and authority, especially religious and monarchial authority, and in the scientific revolution of Galileo, Descartes, and Newton. Huxley is an exemplar of this liberal-free tradition.

Although associated with no single writer or group of writers, Kimball identifies a coherent cluster of ideas that make up the liberal-free ideal. Foremost is 'an emphasis on freedom, especially from a priori strictures and standards,'[39] including those of religion and tradition. 'The desire for freedom is particularly linked to an emphasis on intellect and rationality' because use of the intellect requires freedom and freedom is maintained by use of the intellect. 'The liberal-free ideal incorporates a critical skepticism,' which properly leaves even the most basic of science's generalizations and certainties open to empirical refutation. 'As "certainty is the mother of intolerance," so tolerance became a [fourth] characteristic of the liberal-free ideal.' This was a new virtue because 'the notion of tolerance had previously implied weakness or cowardice, that is, lack of commitment to one's professed beliefs.' The rejection of traditional authority, the ideal of a free, reasoning individual, sceptical and tolerant, all conjoined to give this liberal education an egalitarian spirit and an 'emphasis upon volition of the individual rather than upon the obligations of citizenship found in the *artes liberales* ideal.' Man was born free and by nature free; education must both awaken the motivation to learn and be a project of personal development. The search for truth shall set you free.

Debates about the nature of a liberal education continue within the multiversity today. Are there texts that every liberally educated person should read? Should the curriculum for an undergraduate education be specialized or broad, should the curriculum be tightly prescribed or a cafeteria of choices? Should every student study some science, some social science, and some humanities in order to be liberally educated, or can a liberal education be realized in specialized study? Every age must ask and answer these questions; so must we in our postindustrial age.

The Special Role for the Humanities

Until the middle of the nineteenth century, the university curriculum for a liberal education, whether at Oxford or Berlin or Harvard, required reading the great writers of antiquity in the original Greek and Latin. This 'literature' of the ancients was not just literature as we use the word today. It included the writings of historians, the speeches of orators, the analysis of philosophers, as well as plays and verse. Today, we use the word literature to refer to imaginative writing, to distinguish between fiction and non-fiction. Then, the distinction was between the vernacular and the refined, the everyday and the polite, the untutored and the learned. The refined, the polite, and the learned constituted literature and were worthy of study.

The famed course of study at mid-nineteenth century Oxford – *literae humaniores* – began with study of Greek and Latin. This was followed by 'a second part, familiarly known as "Greats," in which the Greek and Latin classics, whether studied as imaginative literature, history, philosophy, or political economy, became models to set against subsequent developments.'[40] By reading the classical texts, the student would learn values and standards of conduct, and discover lives to emulate.

The continued study of Greek and Roman literature into the nineteenth century might seem to demonstrate the inertia of which the university is so often accused – in this exhibit, a monumental inertia lasting the 600 years since universities began. But this interpretation is superficial. To accept it would obscure an understanding of our current dilemma in conceptualizing the curriculum for a liberal education

The special role for the humanities began in the fourteenth century through what Robert Proctor, in *Education's Great Amnesia*, calls 'the humanist transformation of classical antiquity.'[41] In classical antiquity, there was no separation between the humanities and the sciences. Everything was part of the universe, and all was to be studied. The individual human is part of this whole – as Cicero wrote, man is 'some little part of the perfect.'[42] For Proctor, the Renaissance humanists fragmented the harmony and unity of the classical world-view. Humanists could no longer accept a virtuous, harmonious universe encompassing nature, man, and the skies. They were living with contingency, anxiety, and grief. Theirs was the world of the Black Death. Gratuitous violence could befall travellers between towns. Nature's whims wrecked ships and ruined crops. The humanists could not see man as 'some little part of the perfect' and shifted towards 'the creation of a unique autonomous self.'[43] The self must live in this alien world. And how was one to live? To live in a world of contingency and anxiety, to live morally and virtuously, the humanists concluded, would require the nourishing and shaping of oneself through disciplined study. Guidance would come through knowledge of others who had been challenged, and overcome the challenge. The classical texts were being 'rediscovered,' and it was to these the humanists turned. What emerged was the concept of the 'humanities as a program of education with three distinguishing characteristics: (a) the concept of a unique, autonomous, personal self, to be shaped through (b) the study of the language and literature of ancient Greece and Rome, (c) according to the perspectives of a group of primarily literary academic disciplines.'[44] Renaissance humanists drew away from, and some even disparaged, the study of mathematics and natural science because these offered no guidance about the virtuous life.

This recognition that the humanities became the custodians of the civic purposes of the liberal education, and that these purposes were served by reading the classical literature, should not be allowed to camouflage how classical and Christian texts were inextricable until well into the nineteenth century. Their separation in the exploration of virtue was inconceivable. Most universities had explicit religious affiliation. One of the narratives in the history of the university is the passage from a religious to a secular institution. So complete is this passage that today's professors can scarcely comprehend the religious heritage of universities. But one hundred and fifty years ago, religion was part of the walls, part of the library, and part of the air that academics breathed.

Today, our students will have read (or realize they should have read) the plays of Shakespeare or the novels of Dickens, but will not have read (and see no reason why they should have read) the poetry of Virgil. In the early nineteenth century, the situation was the reverse. Indeed, English literature, as opposed to classical literature, was not even a formal subject of study at the university.

For the high classicists of the mid-nineteenth century, Greek 'was the most lovely and subtle instrument of expression ever devised,'[45] the Latin of Virgil was 'pure sensuousness.' Literature written in English could not compare. However, 'few students of the classics ever reached the stage where languages became works of dazzling art or even "subtle instruments of expression,"' and gradually, grudgingly, vernacular English literature was recognized and acknowledged as containing works equal to the classics. The 'moderns' entered the curriculum propelled by the robust self-confidence of the Victorians and the desire to ensure culture in a slowly democratizing society. The new middle class was less familiar with Greek and Latin. Latin ceased being the language of instruction in universities. Society became more secular and less inclined to see religion as essential to the undergraduate curriculum. However, the humanities still retained their role as the civic and moral centre of liberal learning, but a new rationale had to be found.

The great new role for the humanities was most famously articulated by the literary critic, Matthew Arnold, in his essay *Culture and Anarchy*. Together with Cardinal Newman, Matthew Arnold is the most quoted and most influential of the Victorian men of letters in the development of English-language universities.

We know Arnold as a literary and cultural critic, and as one of the great English poets of the mid-nineteenth century. His poem, 'Dover Beach,' appears in many anthologies of English verse.[46] The closing lines, revealing a Christian romantic's profound disquiet at advancing modernity, speak to us still and in a way that science and social science cannot:

> Ah, love, let us be true
> To one another! for the world, which seems
> To lie before us like a land of dreams,
> So various, so beautiful, so new,
> Hath really neither joy, nor love, nor light
> Nor certitude, nor peace, nor help for pain;

And we are here as on a darkling plain
Swept with confused alarms of struggle and flight,
Where ignorant armies clash by night.

But Arnold is more than poet and literary critic. He is hard to classify: his famous *Culture and Anarchy* is subtitled *An Essay in Political and Social Criticism*, and his writings have shaped our thinking about the relationships among politics, government, literature, and culture. Although he is now remembered as a high Tory of culture, Arnold's views were a rebuke to the Victorian establishment.

Matthew Arnold was an inspector of English schools, especially the Protestant (dissenter) schools outside the established Anglican Church. As part of his duties, he toured the schools of France and greatly admired the role of the French state in building a national culture. For Arnold, the French Revolution 'was the greatest, most animating event in history.'[47] This is scarcely the sentiment of a high Tory. But Arnold also believed that democracy had a dilemma in its essence. 'The difficulty of democracy,' he declared, 'is how to find and keep high ideals.'[48]

For Arnold, culture starts in curiosity, but has its true 'origin in the love of perfection; it is *a study of perfection*. It moves by the force, not merely or primarily of the scientific passion for pure knowledge, but also of the moral and social passion for doing good.'[49] The enemies of culture are English liberalism and the middle class's belief in 'doing as one likes.' This leads to anarchy. Freedom is too much worshipped in itself 'without regarding the ends for which freedom is to be desired.'[50] Arnold was caustic in his ridicule of the Victorian middle class: self-satisfied worshippers of machinery; he called them Philistines. Arnold's social criticism retains its bite today.

Humans want a source of authority, and the right source is our own best self. 'It then becomes of vast importance to see whether or not the things around us are, in general, such as to help and elicit our best self, and if they are not, to see why they are not, and the most promising way of mending them.'[51] The solution for Arnold is the study of 'the best that has been thought and said,' including the 'great' English literature. Study would occur through state-sponsored and state-directed education. Arnold viewed the state as 'what [Edmund] Burke called it: *the nation in its corporate and collective character*. The state is the representative acting power of the nation; the action of the state is the representative action of the nation.'[52] The study by citizens of the great works of literature will animate a democratizing, industrializing nation and allow culture to prevail against anarchy.

Matthew Arnold's words on culture, on the love of and search for perfection, recall the orator's ideal of a liberal education and the classical idea of a harmonious order. But now the great project of liberal education seeks to preserve a community against the fragmentation of individualism and industrial capitalism. The reading of the great works of philosophy, literature, and political theory achieves these purposes. This is the great new role for the humanities, with a special place for the reading of imaginative literature and the appreciation of art.

The Romantic movement of Arnold's time exalted emotion over reason, the senses over the intellect, and turned inward to examine the human personality with its passions and potentials. It sought a deepened appreciation of nature. Arnold held that there are different ways of knowing the world, and that each gives us access to things that the other cannot. Study of literature and the fine arts can offer what science cannot. Most Romantics retained the moral purposes of the humanities. The Romantic William Ruskin, in his *Modern Painters*, entitles one chapter 'Of the Open Sky.' 'Those attentive to the history of taste know that sky-awareness is a fairly late development. There is little of it, for example, in the eighteenth century, which felt no pressing need for such emblems of infinity as sky and sea.' 'Here Ruskin asserts that hitherto no one has paid sufficient attention to the sky, and that we have thus missed much of what Nature has to tell us for our moral benefit.'[53] For Ruskin, 'the great exponent of the sky's moral work is the painter J.M.W. Turner ... The painter of such effects is a master artist whose achievements in light and color imitate those of God himself in His most earnest pedagogic moments.' Arnold incorporated these aspects of Romanticism into his rationale for the humanities in education.

The mid-Victorian university in England, the United States, and Canada was a university of undergraduate teaching and learning. It was an institution of culture, of the word, of the orator, firmly in the *artes liberales* tradition of liberal education. During the later nineteenth century change came rapidly. The Anglo-American university became also an institution of science, of the mind, of the philosopher, accommodating the liberal-free ideal of liberal education.

The liberal-free ideal did not displace the *artes liberales* ideal during the late nineteenth century; rather the two ideals coexisted in uneasy balance, because to be liberally educated is to be both orator and philosopher. Even today, the two ideals are often invoked by the same speaker, sometimes in contradictory ways. With the rise of science, engineering, and medicine, and the liberal-free ideal, the late nineteenth-century university was shifting its centre. But the vision of Arnold offered a counterbalance; it gives us the university as a centre of culture, and this culture is connected to the nation state and national development. Without culture, there is too much 'doing as one likes,' and there will be anarchy.

The reading of English literature and study in the humanities still retained a special role in liberal learning one hundred years after Arnold, well into the 1950s and 1960s. An elegant sentence of Lionel Trilling, written in the 1960s, captures the sentiment: the reading of English literature is uniquely effective 'in opening the mind and illuminating it, in purging the mind of prejudice and received ideas, in making the mind free and active. The classic defence of literary study holds that, from the effect which the study of literature has upon the private sentiments of a student, there results, or can be made to result, an improvement in the intelligence, and especially the intelligence as it touches the moral life.'[54]

Since then, the Arnoldian project of nation-building through public education and a collective reading of 'the best that has been thought and said' has been harshly criticized, and justifiably. The project sustained an ethnocentric nationalism, which in Victorian England fed colonialism and imperialism. And who is to determine 'the best that has been thought and said'? Under Arnold's banner, the writings of dead white males have been chosen by a self-perpetuating group of living white males.

Nonetheless, Arnold's social criticism is as germane today as 150 years ago. He criticized the stunting, suffocating philistinism of commercial and industrial societies. He recognized democracy's problem of finding and keeping high ideals. He championed the literary and the imaginative; he allowed contemporary literature a place with classical literature; he proclaimed that both literary and scientific study fulfil our human needs; he argued that culture has a moral purpose. Arnold's notion of national self-awareness had a benign consequence, if somewhat belatedly, in former British colonies when his vision was invoked to support the study of one's own history and one's own literature (rather than the history of England and literature of England). His university was a university of culture, and in countries like Canada, universities became an essential institution in the development of independence and national identity, through nurture of Canadian literature and Canadian history.

Recent jeremiads about today's undergraduate education, which decry the liberal-free curriculum and call for return to the study of the great books – to the study of Plato and Aristotle, Cicero and Thucydides, Chaucer and Shakespeare – sound like the wails from an old fogey. But in a deep sense, these jeremiads are correct, at least in their diagnosis if not their remedy. A liberal education for citizenship requires a set of values and standards for conduct. For most of history they were found in the classical and Christian texts and in English literature. Without these texts, the values and standards are gone. The absence of values and standards in today's curriculum, it is argued, perforce requires a return to great books. We may agree with the diagnosis, but reject the remedy. The questions for us are: can anything replace the classical texts and English literature to ensure the liberal education fulfils its civic aspirations? Without these purposes, why study the humanities? These questions become especially troubling in light of the postmodern critique, which holds that most literature, far from being the best that has been thought and said, is rather a product of the dominant powers in society.

Throughout the twentieth century, universities have struggled with how to address these questions in a curriculum, and we still have no clear answers or consensus regarding the curriculum of a liberal undergraduate education. However, unambiguous answers and consensus are false gods. The responsibility of each era is to ask the questions. The questions remain as apt for us as they were for Newman, or Humboldt, or Huxley. More important for us today than consensus is to ask the questions. And a central question must be: what is the role of the humanities in a liberal education for our age? Part Two of the book examines the character of our age and reveals powerful forces, especially postmodern thought and commercialization, which erode the special role for the humanities. Chapter 12 in Part Three of the book takes up the question again in examining a liberal education for our age.

Universities and Democracy

One theme of this book is that today's multiversities should be conceptualized in a new way: multiversities should be recognized as fundamental institutions of our democracy, and their mission should be expanded to include an explicit responsibility to contribute to democratic life. This requires a change in how we think about universities; even well into the twentieth century, universities certainly could not be considered institutions of democracy. None of these four archetypes, these four ideas of the university, has a particularly close identification with democracy, except the Scottish model. Universities at the beginning of the twentieth century stood apart from the development of democracy – and on many occasions resisted it.

It was more through the connection to Greek and Roman thought and classical ideas of liberal learning that nineteenth-century universities had an association with democracy, rather than any connection to the politics of their day. Robert A. Dahl, one of the most distinguished scholars of democracy, recently published a marvellously accessible book: *On Democracy*. It begins with a brief history of how democracy began and developed. Around 500 BC in classical Greece and Rome, 'systems of government providing for popular participation by a substantial number of citizens were first established.' In the case of Greece, the sovereign states were city states; and 'it was the Greeks – probably the Athenians – who coined the term *democracy*.'[55] In the case of Rome, the beginning was also a city state, although Rome soon expanded its territory across Italy and beyond. The Romans called their system of popular government a republic. In both cases, the major rival to democratic ideas was 'the claim that government should be turned over to experts deeply committed to the common good and superior to others in their knowledge of how to achieve it – Guardians Plato called them ... Advocates of Guardianship attack democracy at a seemingly vulnerable point: they simply deny that ordinary people are competent to govern themselves.'[56] The answer from ancient democrats to such arguments was to provide a liberal education for all citizens: a liberal education would ensure the civic competence of citizens. In classical thought, liberal education, citizenship, and democracy were inseparably connected. These classical ideas have always been included within the painting of the university landscape, but for most of the university's history they have been a shading, a coloration, rather than fundamental to the composition of the picture. The ideas of democracy have only truly shaped the university landscape in the later twentieth century.

The first universities arose in the medieval era, hardly a time of flourishing democracy. The universities, through their arts faculties, retained the connection to classical ideas of liberal learning, but the democratic spirit was subdued. This remained true for hundreds of years. Sheldon Rothblatt in his essay on the liberal education in the English-speaking world notes 'that from the earliest times it is mainly wealthy families that furnish sons with a liberal education.' Only they could be free from the necessity of earning a living and had the leisure to undertake education for its own sake. 'Consequently over the centuries, there exists an explicit connection between high social standing and liberal education ... Liberal education historically is associated with privileged elites, especially elites in government, at princely courts, in the great State churches, universities, and the leading professions. It is associated with leisured classes and those aspiring to high social position.'[57] Indeed, until well into the twentieth century, the liberal learning of universities was much more associated with such gentlemanly privilege than with democracy.

Rather than connected to democracy, universities until the twentieth century were more characterized by a connection to religion and moral education. Julie Reuben in *The Making of the Modern University: Intellectual Transformation and the Marginalization of Morality* convincingly argues that American university reformers, even late in the nineteenth century, still accepted the ideal of the unity of truth, 'the unity of moral and intellectual purpose,'[58] even as they accepted the research ideal, promoted the methodology of science, created graduate schools, and added professional schools. The same was true in Canada and England.

A history of democracy combines both the evolving and changing ideal and its actual institutional practices. Great signposts of both are the English Bill of Rights of 1689, the American Declaration of Independence (1776) and the first ten amendments to the American Constitution known as the Bill of Rights (1789), and the French Declaration of the Rights of Man and of the Citizen (1789). The English Bill articulated the rights of Parliament as against the Crown; the American Bill of Rights articulated the rights to freedom of speech, press, religion, peaceable assembly, and to petition the government (First Amendment); and the French Declaration articulated the equality of all men and the right to equal opportunity: 'men are born and remain free and equal in rights' (Article I) and 'all the citizens, being equal in the eyes of the law, are equally admissible to all public dignities, places, and employments, according to their capacity and without distinction other than of their virtues and their talents' (Article VI).

These defining proclamations of democratic ideals were the product of Enlightenment philosophy, preceded by its necessary antecedents of

Renaissance humanism and the Scientific Revolution. These same intellectual movements, of course, also created the modern university. Democracy and the modern university share many fundamentals. But they have not developed in parallel or in mutually supporting fashion.

The practices of democracy developed slowly and with much struggle throughout the nineteenth century. Even at the beginning of the twentieth century, democracy was still not as we understand it today. True, the fundamental ideas and structures of representative democracy were in place – but they were terribly incomplete. Women could neither vote nor stand for election. Male suffrage was not complete: even by 1914, only 30 per cent of Great Britain's population over the age of twenty was eligible to vote.[59] Certain principles of democracy were widely accepted: that ultimate authority rests with people and that governments rule with the consent of the governed. But the relationship between citizens and their government was nothing like it became after the Second World War. At the turn of the century, government expenditure was very limited – there was little government spending on health care or education, there were no old age pensions or income security programs.

In the late nineteenth century, universities were small. Only a tiny percentage of the population went to university and among the select group there were few women. The universities neither led nor encouraged the inclusion of women. For example, Oxford and Cambridge had established colleges for women by the late nineteenth century, but even in 1910, women had to obtain permission to attend lectures and were not allowed to take degrees. In all, although the universities were important to national development in the nineteenth and early twentieth centuries, they could not be considered crucial to the development of democracy, and indeed, in their admissions policies even resisted its development.

Although the modern university and liberal political thought share much in their philosophical foundations, liberal political thought has surprising little to say about universities. Edward Shils, the distinguished sociologist of the University of Chicago and Cambridge University, explores this in his 1989 essay, 'The Modern University and Liberal Democracy.' He begins: 'The first thing to be said is that the university as a particular type of institution is not a creation of liberal-democratic society.' Some of the distinctive features of universities – 'instruction at an advanced level, the pursuit and transmission of fundamental truths, institutional autonomy, and financial support by external powers' – were fixed 'long before the emergence of the liberal-democratic order which took root over the past two centuries.'[60]

The universities of the Anglo-American world in the eighteenth century, and well into the nineteenth, were not intended to serve a liberal democracy, even as those societies were evolving into liberal democracies. Universities received little or no financial support from the state. The colleges of Oxford and Cambridge were independent foundations, required religious affiliation, and trained an elite for life in the clergy or high civil service. Shils notes that American universities and American colleges, although founded in a country built upon liberal ideas, 'were not intended to serve a liberal democracy. They were intended to instruct young men who would enter the clergy or who might play a part of significance in oligarchical colonial societies.'[61] The same was true in Canada.

Shils goes on to note that 'liberal thinkers did not have an especially high opinion of universities, nor did they think that they had any great part to part to play in liberal society.'[62] Certainly, many liberal political philosophers recognized the centrality of education in a democracy, most famously Jean Jacques Rousseau in *Emile*, but their attention was directed to primary and secondary education.

Edward Shils's essay does explore some complementarities between liberal democracy and universities: 'One motive for the establishment and expansion of universities in the United States was an aspiration to realize one of the ideals of liberalism, namely to introduce rationality and soundly based knowledge into the management of the affairs of society.'[63] The same motive helped found and expand universities in Canada and England. Another complementarity – a complementarity between liberal democracy and research – has been noted. Robert Merton's famous article 'The Normative Structure of Science' was published originally as 'Science and Technology in a Democratic Order.' In that paper, he stated that scientists had come to recognize 'their dependence on particular types of social structure.' The ethos of science – universalism, communism, disinterestedness, and organized scepticism – was more complementary, he argued, with democracy than with other political systems.[64] And certainly, freedom of speech and freedom of thought, so necessary to democratic life, are closely connected to the concept of academic freedom so necessary for the university.

The most one could claim, however, of the relationship between universities and democracy is a certain sharing of philosophical origins and complementarities. Universities in the early twentieth century could not be conceived as institutions of democracy.

The four ideas that would create the multiversity had been set out by the end of the nineteenth century. However, change in the universities was slow – though inexorable and cumulative. Universities could not be considered axial institutions in the first decades of the twentieth century. Change accelerated after mid-century. Then, writing in the 1960s, Christopher Jencks and David Riesman, surveying the evolution of American universities from the late nineteenth century, declared there had been a profound transformation: an academic revolution – 'the rise to power of the academic profession.'[65] With its commitment to mass higher education, research, professionalism, and meritocracy, the university assumes a prominent place in the life of the nation.

In the second half of the twentieth century, elaborations on nineteenth-century ideas moved further and took a very specific institutional form: these several ideas and diverse purposes for the university came to be combined in one institution – the multiversity. It is to this we now turn.

3 The Uses of the Multiversity in Postindustrial Society

The universities of Oxford and Bologna, Berlin and Edinburgh, represent four ideas of a university – four archetypes. These ideas and traditions evolved across the late nineteenth century and through the twentieth amid industrialization, urbanization, and democratization. After the Second World War, a distinctive new form of university emerged in the United States, one labelled by Clark Kerr as 'the multiversity.' The multiversity combines all four archetypes. It combines multiple tasks and conflicting ideas.

Although the multiversity does not have a Cardinal Newman, in Clark Kerr it has a witty and insightful friend. He first discussed the multiversity in the Godkin Lectures on the Essentials of Free Government and the Duties of the Citizen, delivered at Harvard University in 1963. The lectures were published in book form as *The Uses of the University*. At roughly ten-year intervals thereafter, Kerr added new chapters, updating his analysis and looking ahead, culminating in the final edition in 2001. The title of the book signals immediately the character of the postwar twentieth century: Kerr writes about the *uses* of the university, whereas in the nineteenth century Newman wrote about the *idea* of a university.

The multiversity is not the small community of professors and students so beloved by Newman. The multiversity is large, diverse, and complex. James Duderstadt, the recently retired president of the University of Michigan, characterized this university as:

> a very complex, international conglomerate of highly diverse businesses. To illustrate, imagine how one might characterize the business lines of the 'University of Michigan Inc.' With an annual budget of $3 billion and an

additional $3 billion of investment assets under active management, the U of M, Inc., would rank roughly 470th on the Fortune 500 list. The university educates roughly fifty thousand students on its several campuses at any given moment – an educational business amounting to about $1 billion per year. The university is also a major federal R & D laboratory, conducting over $500 million a year of sponsored research, supported primarily by federal grants and contracts. The University of Michigan operates a massive health care company. University-owned hospitals and clinics currently treat almost a million patients a year, with a total medical centre income of $1.2 billion ... The university is already too big and complex to buy insurance, so we have our own captive insurance company, Veritas, incorporated in New Hampshire ... And, of course, the university is involved in public entertainment, the Michigan Wolverines, characterized by roughly $250 million in commercial activities a year.[1]

Clark Kerr identifies the multiversity as an American institution. But this is no longer true. The Anglo-American world shares the same ideas of a university – the medieval professional schools, the traditions of Cardinal Newman's undergraduate liberal education, the ideas of the German research university, and the Scottish ideas of accessibility and applied research. Over time, Canada, England, and many other countries combined the four archetypes into a single institution. This conglomerate, this great unwieldy bundle, has become an identifiable institutional form of university in the English-speaking world and dominates its systems of higher education. The multiversity is the distinctive adaptation of 'the university' to the later twentieth century.

The multiversity is not however a new *idea* of a university, because it lacks any unifying theme or vision. Indeed, as Clark Kerr has remarked, the multiversity 'is so many things to so many people that it must, of necessity, be partially at war with itself.'[2] It is a pluralistic institution – 'pluralistic in several senses: in having several purposes, not one; in having several centres of power, not one; in serving several clienteles, not one.'[3] And because of this pluralism, multiversities are vulnerable to mission drift. They can drift away from core ideals in times of stress, as they are doing now in our own age.

Multiversities differ much among themselves, but they do share a number of characteristics.[4] They are large conglomerates. Multiversities offer undergraduate liberal education; they provide professional education at both the undergraduate and graduate levels; and they provide many graduate programs through to the doctorate. Faculty members usually teach at both the undergraduate and graduate levels, but the multiversity has an especially strong commitment to graduate education. All faculty members are expected to do research and to submit their work to referees for assessment, leading to publication in books and academic journals. The multiversity is particularly research intensive: research promise and accomplishment are the principal criteria used in the hiring and promotion of faculty members. The multiversity supports the research mission with modest teaching loads for faculty members and substantial investments in libraries, laboratories, and computer systems. The research mission is also supported through grants and contracts from governments, businesses, and foundations. The research is both basic, which pursues knowledge for its own sake, and applied, motivated by the desire for usable knowledge.

Postindustrial Society and the Multiversity

To better understand the multiversity, let us first examine its emergence in the United States. Clark Kerr explains the American multiversity as the combination of several strands of history and as a response to a knowledge-based society.

In the nineteenth century, the United States had many colleges along the Oxford model. Often with Calvinist origins, they were committed to the liberal education of gentlemen, after which their students would enter the learned professions. In 1876, Johns Hopkins University opened, adopting the Berlin ideal of research and focusing on graduate education. Soon other universities, which until then had been undergraduate colleges, added graduate schools; among these were Cornell, Michigan, Harvard, Columbia, Stanford, the familiar elite of American higher education. The expanding state universities also added graduate schools. (Important exceptions were some colleges which continued as liberal arts colleges specializing in undergraduate education.)

The other strand of history was the land grant movement. Under the Morrill Act of 1862, the U.S. federal government provided land to the states for new universities. These new state-owned universities, very like the Scottish universities, would serve regional interests for social and economic development, by offering educational opportunities to the children of farmers and industrial workers, as well as of the middle class, and by offering degree programs in applied fields such as agriculture, business, engineering, and home economics. Land grant universities soon added liberal arts faculties.

The United States did not create distinct and separate institutions for undergraduate education, graduate education, research, and professional education; rather these coalesced to become the multiversity.[5] American universities, both existing and newly created, proved to be flexible, responsive, and entrepreneurial, taking on new tasks, expanding their enrolments, establishing new departments, new graduate programs, new research centres, and new professional schools all within the same institution. There was no national government policy dictating the structure of universities. The environment was decentralized and competitive. The unwieldy conglomerate which resulted – the multiversity – was once described as 'a series of separate schools held together by a central heating system.'[6]

The societal imperatives that combined the strands of history into the multiversity arose in the twenty years after the Second World War, the period examined in Clark Kerr's first lectures. In his Preface in 1963, he noted: 'Although it is one of our oldest social institutions, the university today finds itself in a quite novel position in society. It faces its new role with few precedents to fall back on, with little but platitudes to mask the nakedness of the change.' By understanding the society's imperatives that created the multiversity, we better understand the multiversity today. These imperatives have not changed, indeed have become sterner. They appeared first in the United States, but now are present across the Anglo-American world, indeed across the entire world.

> The basic reality, for the university, is the widespread recognition that new knowledge is the most important factor in economic and social growth. We are just now perceiving that the university's invisible product, knowledge, may be the most powerful single element in our culture, affecting the rise and fall of professions and even of social classes, of regions and even of nations.
>
> Because of this fundamental reality, the university is being called upon to produce knowledge as never before – for civic and regional purposes, for national purposes, and even for no purpose at all beyond the realization that knowledge eventually comes to serve mankind. And it is also being called upon to transmit knowledge to an unprecedented proportion of the population.[7]

In the 1990s, business commentators breathlessly announced the arrival of the new economy – a knowledge-based economy. Even allowing for the commentators' constant need to discover 'new' trends, such proclamations show remarkable myopia: Clark Kerr was writing about the knowledge-based economy in 1963.

In 1973, Daniel Bell culminated ten years of thinking and writing on the subject of a knowledge-based economy with the publication of his seminal book *The Coming of Post-Industrial Society*. He describes his analysis as a venture 'in social forecasting,' dealing with the future of advanced industrial societies, and forecast the emergence of postindustrial society around the world, albeit in different forms suited to different political and cultural contexts. His analysis focused on the United States, because there the postindustrial society had already arrived.

Bell's analysis divides society into three parts: the social structure, the polity, and the culture: 'The social structure comprises the economy, technology, and the occupational system. The polity regulates the distribution of power and adjudicates the conflicting claims and demands of individual groups. The culture is the realm of expressive symbolism and meanings.'[8] These separate parts each have their own dynamic, but changes in one pose challenges to the others.

A postindustrial society emerges from changes in the social structure – changes in the economy, technology, and occupational system. Bell identifies five dimensions of change: an economy dominated by goods production becomes an economy dominated by services; the professional and technical class rises to pre-eminence; theoretical knowledge becomes central to innovation and to policy formation; the society becomes future-oriented, raising issues of the control of technology and technology assessment; and the mode of decision-making creates a new intellectual mindset.

The term *service economy* can be misunderstood. Services include the familiar personal services of the retail, travel, and entertainment industries; but the term also includes business services (such as banking, finance, real estate, and insurance) and other categories like communications, utilities, government, health, education, and research. It is all these services – the other-than-personal services – that are decisive in the postindustrial society. Workers in the service industry manipulate symbols and ideas, rather than physical objects. They are the knowledge workers.

Bell points out forcefully that 'knowledge has of course been necessary in the functioning of any society. What is distinctive about the post-industrial society is the change in the character of knowledge itself. What has become decisive for the organization of decisions and the direction of change is the centrality of *theoretical* knowledge,'[9] and a new relationship between theory and application, between abstract learning and real world phenomena. The new relationship between theory and application is most evident in a new relationship between science and technology. The postindustrial society, as no society before it, engages in self-conscious research programs to advance theoretical knowledge and to solve applied problems: 'Theoretical knowledge increasingly becomes the strategic resource, the axial principle, of a society. And the university, research organizations and intellectual institutions, where theoretical knowledge is codified and enriched, become axial structures of the emergent society.'[10] For Bell, the university is the primary institution of postindustrial society. It is one of the chief innovative forces of the society, one of the chief determinants of social opportunity and social stratification, and a focus of intellectual and cultural life. The multiversity is the distinctive adaptation of 'the university' to postindustrial society.

Let me now consider each component of the multiversity in greater detail, particularly as shaped by trends in the United States. Later in the chapter, I will discuss how similar trends have emerged in England and Canada, also creating multiversities.

Research

Many writers prefer to label the multiversity as the 'research university.' The titles of many books and articles contain the words 'the research university'; however, the labels 'research university' and 'multiversity' describe the same group of institutions.[11] The highlight placed on research does capture something of the essence of the multiversity, because the commitment to research is as close as possible to a single animating idea within the multiversity. An institution's prestige, in the long run, depends heavily upon the research achievements of its faculty members. Highlighting research also serves to emphasize the historical evolution of certain universities from teaching-focused to research-focused institutions.

The label 'research university' seems to imply that modern universities might be divided into research and non-research institutions; or phrased alternatively, divided into research-oriented and teaching-oriented institutions. However, no such division is possible. This is vividly revealed if you talk with faculty members from universities implicitly designated as 'non-research': they bridle at such a designation. In reality, all modern universities have research as part of their mission, even those exclusively devoted to liberal arts undergraduate education. Attendance at any international scholarly conference makes this clear: those attending the conference and presenting the papers come from all across the university system. The only difference across universities is the relative priority given to research and graduate education. The multiversity is marked by its *especially intense* commitments to research and to graduate education.

The research/non-research designation is more appropriately used to distinguish between universities and 'non-universities' within the system of higher education. Universities have research as part of their core mission; 'non-universities' do not. The mission of these non-university institutions of higher education is to prepare students for the labour force through vocational training.

Most importantly, use of the label 'research university' leaves in shadow two core responsibilities of the multiversity: liberal education for undergraduates and professional education. The research label obscures the fundamental heterogeneity of the institution. Clark Kerr's label, 'the multiversity,' while less ennobling than 'research university,' is more insightful and more revealing of the essence of the institution. Nonetheless, understanding the research mission, and that it is accorded a top priority, is essential to understanding the nature and growth of the multiversity. Fundamental to the emergence of the multiversity in the United States is a major commitment by government to support advanced research at universities.

The research enterprise of the American university had its beginning in the late nineteenth century with the formation of graduate schools, the transformation of medical education, and in the agricultural and engineering research of the land grant universities. Research was strengthened during the 1920s and 1930s by funding from major organizations such as the Carnegie and Rockefeller foundations.

Research truly flourished after the Second World War, with massive and sustained federal government support for research at universities. During the war, government/university collaborations under the Office of Scientific Research and Development (OSRD) made notable discoveries related to radar, penicillin, computing, DDT, and of course, the atomic bomb. Towards the war's end, Vannevar Bush, director of OSRD and former dean of Engineering at MIT, produced a report at the request of President Roosevelt setting an agenda for how the federal government should support scientific research after the war. The recommendations of Bush's report, *Science – The Endless Frontier*, were not all adopted and by no means universally supported, but the main pillars of Bush's recommended approach prevailed: most crucially, that government must continue to support basic research and that the support for basic research be directed to universities, rather than to government laboratories or private industry.

Vannevar Bush argued that scientific progress is essential for the war against disease, for economic prosperity, and for national security. Progress requires 'continuous additions to knowledge of the laws of nature, and the application of that knowledge to practical purposes.' 'New knowledge can be obtained only through basic scientific research.'[12] Drawing an analogy to the pioneering spirit that settled the west, Bush advocated a national strategy to settle the endless frontier of science. It would require increased and sustained federal support. There should be federal funds to support the education of men and women in science and to support basic research. For Bush, basic research was the wellspring of technological progress. Basic research should be conducted where scientists are free to pursue the truth without concern for its application. Universities are such places and federal funds should be directed there. This contrasted with a European approach of supporting basic research in government laboratories or specialized research institutes. Government agencies and industrial laboratories are more concerned with practical objectives, Bush believed, and should be the institutions for applying new knowledge to practical ends. The distribution of federal funds, while recognizing the legitimate interests of politicians, should be at arm's length from government and ruled by the principles of scientific merit and peer review. This was the best way, Bush asserted, to ensure scientific progress.

There was widespread support for Bush's desire to continue federal support for scientific research through a new agency – the National Science Foundation. However, there was much disagreement about how this should be accomplished. Immediately after the war, the disagreements prevented the establishment of a single agency and federal departments stepped into the gap. Federal support for research moved through four main channels: military research programs, the Atomic Energy Commission (with responsibility for all research using radioactive materials), the National Institutes of Health (NIH), and the Office of Naval Research (which supported a broad spectrum of basic research). State governments also supported research, most notably agricultural research. Eventually, the National Science Foundation was established in 1950 'to promote the progress of science; to advance the national health, prosperity, and welfare; to secure the national defense.'[13]

Explicit support for the humanities did not begin until the establishment of the National Endowment for the Humanities in 1965, and would remain modest. The social sciences never had a dedicated granting agency, but in 1968 were included explicitly within the National Science Foundation. Social scientists received substantial support from the federal and state governments, under contracts to study social problems and social policies. Some social scientists, especially psychologists, received funds from the NIH.

The magnitude and rapid expansion of U.S. federal commitments to university research are, in retrospect, astonishing. From 1953 to 1968, federal funding jumped ninefold, adjusted for inflation.[14] That fifteen-year interval has been dubbed 'the golden age'; some have even called it the 'glided age.' Nonetheless, federal commitments continued to expand thereafter. In 1980, funding stood at U.S. $4.1 billion and rose to U.S. $13 billion by 1995. The real value of federal research support rose by 57 per cent from 1980 to 1995.[15]

The main contours of this federal support for university research have remained from the early postwar era to the present. The level of support has expanded at times, contracted at others (especially in certain fields), and levelled off sometimes. But overall, the government support for university research has been sustained. This support has been concentrated on relatively few universities, and thus the multiversity became differentiated from other universities. Clark Kerr entitles one of his chapters about the multiversity: 'The Federal Grant University.' The government's significant financial support secured the position of the multiversity at the heart of society's research enterprise. The twentieth century tells a remarkable story of success: as it began, few American universities could be seen as the world's best centres of advanced research or as a model to emulate, but by the century's end American multiversities were both world leaders in advanced research and widely emulated.

Governments in England and Canada also supported basic research at universities, although the level of support was far below that in the United States. Over the past twenty years, their research support to universities has increased significantly, with the result that certain large English and Canadian universities have taken on the character of multiversities.

Today, and looking forward, all countries struggle with the same questions: Is the level of support sufficient and will it continue to grow? What is the balance between scientific and political control, between basic and applied research? What is the balance between the humanities, social sciences, medicine, and the sciences? And, who should own the patents from the research results? There is always the tension between those who would allocate funds solely on merit (which favours the established well-endowed multiversities) and those who would favour building the research capability in newer multiversities and in all regions of the country. And, of course, we must ask: what research questions should be tackled and who will benefit from the findings? Because the research is supported by democratic governments, we must also ask: new knowledge for whom?

One of the most important ideas of our age is that multiversity research has been linked to economic prosperity, with the result that support for multiversity research has become part of economic policy, and multiversity professors are asked to commercialize the results of their research. This has profound implications for the multiversity, taken up in chapter 9.

Graduate Education

Another distinguishing feature of the multiversity, complementary to its especially intense commitment to research, is an especially intense commitment to graduate education: a multiversity has a large graduate school, with many programs proceeding to the doctoral level.

A special task of the multiversity is to train the next generation of advanced researchers. Graduate students are involved often in the research projects of faculty members; in many areas of science, engineering, and medicine, graduate education uses a research-apprenticeship model, although this is less so in the humanities and social sciences. In most laboratories, the graduate students are an essential part of the research enterprise, and the research could not be done without them. As Vannevar Bush recognized, if federal research money had gone to government labs or to industry, the interpenetration of research and graduate education would be lost.

The growth of U.S. graduate school enrolments after the Second World War was rapid and continuous, if not quite matching the spectacular growth of federal research funds. In 1950, U.S. universities awarded 6,000 doctorates. By 1970, 30,000 were awarded, and by the late 1990s over 46,000 annually. This expansion was supported by substantial federal money for student assistance, as Vannevar Bush had recommended. Fields of doctoral study proliferated: early in the twentieth century there were 150 fields of study, now there are well over 500, with dozens of doctorates besides the PhD, for example, a doctor of social work, a doctor of education, or a doctor of business administration. Most of these doctorates are awarded by the multiversities. Many of the graduate students came from abroad; some returned home and others stayed on. This international character of graduate education has been a significant component of globalization in the postwar period.

Graduate education also expanded in Canada and England, although not to the same extent, and the rapid growth began later. But there too, graduate education is an integral part of the multiversity. Looking forward, in the Anglo-American world, it is difficult to forecast the pattern of future graduate enrolments. Certainly, the economy will need more people with advanced research training, and the coming wave of retirements of current university professors means there will be many academic jobs. But attempts to forecast graduate enrolments by forecasts of the labour-market demands have had only mixed success. A prudent forecast would be for steady, but not spectacular, growth of graduate education.

For all the expansion of research funding and graduate education, however, research universities have huge responsibilities in undergraduate education. Research and graduate education are only part of the bundle in a multiversity, and doctorates represent only 8 per cent of the degrees awarded by U.S. multiversities.[16]

Undergraduate Education

Another factor fundamental to creating the American multiversity was the U.S. government's commitment to financing mass higher education. The presidents of multiversities are well aware that undergraduate education is their central task, although their professors often need to be reminded. President Frank Rhodes of Cornell wrote, in a 1994 volume entitled *The Research University in a Time of Discontent*:

> I believe it is time to state clearly and firmly that, while research and teaching both contribute to the strength and vitality of the U.S. research university, it is undergraduate teaching and learning, that is the central

task. Undergraduate education is fundamental to the existence of the university: it occupies more time, involves more people, consumes more resources, requires more facilities and generates more revenue than any other activity. Almost everything else universities do depends on it ... It is through undergraduate education that the public encounters the university most directly, and it is on undergraduate education that the health of the research university will stand or fall.[17]

The commitment to mass higher education, like the commitment to university research, had its genesis in the Second World War. The great postwar expansion of higher education began with the commitment to assist the veterans' return to civilian life. Having risked their lives, veterans were offered assistance towards higher education by their grateful country. The GI Bill of Rights of 1944 provided tuition and money for books, housing, and counselling for veterans to continue in school or college. Stephen Graubard, a distinguished historian of American higher education, comments: 'that single piece of federal legislation, perhaps as much as any other act passed in this century, changed U.S. higher education.'[18] The veterans came from all walks of life, all races and social classes, all regions and states, forcing the universities and colleges to open up to this diversity. Soon thereafter, the democratic spirit of time would urge that higher education be made available to all who were capable and interested. Such education not only gave access to new perspectives that could enrich one's life; it also ensured a better job, a higher salary, lower unemployment, faster promotion, not to mention a certain measure of social prestige. It improved both one's quality of life and one's standard of living. Therefore, equality of opportunity required equality of access to higher education, regardless of class, race, or gender. Fortunately, the labour market, propelled by robust growth and the economic transformation to a postindustrial society, required more and more graduates. Growing democratic aspiration and a growing economy were synchronized.

The American system of higher education can be divided into two sectors: the university sector, which includes universities and colleges offering bachelor's degrees and higher degrees through to the doctorate, and the two-year junior colleges, often called 'community colleges,' offering associate in arts and associate in science degrees and other diplomas. The community colleges are extraordinarily diverse. Most draw their students from their immediate community and provide some mix of collegiate education (after which one can transfer to the university sector), vocational/technical education, and remedial education. Many also provide adult continuing education.[19]

The participation rate in higher education can be measured in different ways. One widely used way is to look at the people of the age at which they would attend higher education, and see how many are attending school (the available data from the past do not allow determination of what sort of school). In 1950, in the United States, 9 per cent of the population between the ages of 20 to 24 years was in school, by 1980, it was 22 per cent, and in 2000, it was 32.5 per cent. More detailed data are available since 1965, when 27.6 per cent of those aged 20 to 21 were enrolled in school; by 1995, the percentage had risen to 44.9.[20] This growth was accommodated across the entire American system of higher education, across the multiversities, the other universities, and the community colleges. Although the transition from elite to mass higher education was accomplished more extensively through the community colleges, the entire university sector also made the transition from an elite to a mass system.

Within the university sector, undergraduate enrolments, once dominated by arts and science departments, expanded much faster in the professions: in the short period from 1969 to 1976, undergraduate enrolments in the professions went from 38 to 58 per cent of total undergraduate enrolments. The student body changed as accessibility improved. Women were 31 per cent of the student population in 1960, but 51 per cent in 1980. Minorities increased from 10 per cent (in 1968) to 17 per cent of enrolments in 1980. The expansion of enrolment was backed by a massive increase in federal student aid – from U.S. $300 million to U.S. $10 billion (in 1980 dollars).[21]

Martin Trow, in his 1973 essay, *Problems in the Transition from Elite to Mass Higher Education*, emphasizes how different in character a system of mass higher education will be from an elite system. He defines an *elite system* as educating about 5 to 10 per cent of the eligible age cohort. An elite system can expand to about 15 per cent, without changing its character, through growth of the original institutions. Thereafter, there will be a great transformation. Many of the original institutions must grow so large as to alter their essential character. New institutions, also large, must be created. A system of mass higher education enrolls about 15 to 50 per cent of the age cohort; and beyond that level, the system may be characterized as one of universal access.[22]

When a country shifts from an elite to a mass system of higher education, the purpose of an undergraduate education shifts as well.

Martin Trow has argued that an elite system is 'concerned primarily with shaping the mind and the character of the ruling class, as it prepares students for broad elite roles in government and the learned professions. In mass higher education, the institutions are still preparing elites, but a much broader range of elites that includes the leading strata of all technical and economic organizations of society. And the emphasis shifts from the shaping of character to the transmission of skills for more specific technical elite roles.'[23]

More profoundly, with mass higher education, the university becomes connected to democracy, and this was the intent. In 1947, President Truman appointed the Commission on Higher Education to prepare for the postwar period; its report was titled *Higher Education for American Democracy*.

The role of universities changes when a country commits itself to mass university education. The university system becomes the institutional embodiment of the political commitment to equality of opportunity. Any system of mass university education, regardless of its tuition regime, will be sustained by government funding. Publicly funded universities will predominate. The university becomes an institution for social justice, for changing the class structure of a nation, for including the previously excluded. The movement from elite to mass university education is surely one of the great successes of the democratic project in the postwar era. This new role helped create the multiversities and was welcomed by them.

The forces of the democratic ideal and the research ideal, of expanded university education and of knowledge specialization, wrought a profound change in undergraduate education. Students no longer studied the *artes liberales* curriculum; rather, they specialized in one discipline of the liberal arts. For example, they might specialize in chemistry, or political science, or English literature, or art history. This discipline of specialization is often called the student's 'major.' In the twentieth century, the liberal arts were relabelled as the natural sciences, social sciences, humanities, and fine arts. These liberal arts stand in distinction to what might be called the 'applied arts,' or vocationally oriented fields, such as education, law, or engineering. But did this discipline-focused education fulfil all the purposes of an undergraduate education? Did it remain a liberal education?

In 1943, amid the Second World War, Harvard University embarked upon a remarkable reflection on the nature of an undergraduate education, culminating with the report *General Education in a Free Society*, published in 1945. The report it is often referred to as the Redbook – for its cover rather than its politics. It chose the term *general education*, rather than liberal education, acknowledging that for some the terms would be synonymous. The starting premise was that something was fundamentally changing: 'today, we are concerned with a general education – a liberal education – not for the relatively few, but for a multitude,'[24] and that the purposes of undergraduate study are connected not to educating an elite, but to educating citizens in a democracy.

Daniel Bell, in a review of general education, has written of the paradoxical assumptions of American culture: 'a desire for cultivation along with a utilitarian purpose to education; a populist spirit in the classroom (are students ever deferential to professors?) and a respect for learning; a training for citizenship, yet a skepticism about laws; a deference to *humanitas* and an emphasis on technique and training for the purposes of a career.'[25] The postwar curriculum had lost balance. It addressed one side of each paradox, but not the other. Lost were cultivation, respect for tradition, citizenship, and *humanitas*. Also, the curriculum, like knowledge itself, became fragmented. The broad relationships across different types of knowledge were not incorporated or even discussed.

Everyone recognized that specialization was necessary and desirable, most particularly in a system of mass university education. The question then became whether there is still room within the degree program for a structured program of liberal learning in the *artes liberales* tradition. The debates about liberal learning focused on the structure of these courses outside the specialization. And this was what the Harvard Redbook addressed. In the report, *general education* was defined as 'that part of a student's whole education which looks first of all to his life as a responsible human being and citizen; while the term, special education, indicates that part which looks to the student's competence in some occupation'[26] (or academic discipline). Of course, the parts are neither separable nor independent, and both are valuable; but the report emphasizes the need for general education and its connection to democracy: 'Democracy is the view that not only the few but that all are free, in that everyone governs his own life and shares in the responsibility for the management of the community. This being the case, it follows that all human beings stand in need of an ampler and rounded education. The task of modern democracy is to preserve the ancient ideal of liberal education and to extend it as far as possible to all members of the community.'[27]

A theme running throughout the Redbook is 'a sense of heritage.' The report does not shrink from identifying common beliefs and core values. It deems inescapable the conclusion that societies rest on common values and beliefs and that a major task of a general education is to pass them on. The Redbook argues that a general education requires knowledge of the three branches of learning: the natural sciences, the social sciences, and the humanities, most importantly because they represent different methods of knowing. The method of science is to describe, analyse, and explain. Logic and mathematics provide the theoretical structure; observation and experiment test the theory. The method of the humanities is to appraise, judge, and criticize: 'The humanities explore and exhibit the realm of value. For example, in literature the student is presented with various ways of life, with the tragic and the heroic, or with the merely pathetic and ridiculous. His imagination is stirred with vivid evocations of ideals of action, passion, and thought, among which he may learn to discriminate. The intelligent teacher will explore the great arts and literatures in order to bring out the ideals toward which man has been groping, confusedly yet stubbornly.'[28] The social sciences, argues the report, combine the methods of both science and the humanities, using both explanation and evaluation.

The Redbook acknowledged the necessity of specialization through a major, but called for courses that were common to all students and that were designed explicitly for the aims of general education. One course in humanities and one in social science would be taken by all students, and provide the common core: 'the body of learning and ideas which would be a common experience of all Harvard students.' The humanities course would be 'Great Texts of Literature' and the social science course 'Western Thought and Institutions.'

Many critics thought the Redbook either hopelessly elitist and nostalgic, or naive in attempting to reconcile the irreconcilable – the reality of diversity in a democracy with the need for shared heritage and common values. It was, in the end, never fully implemented at Harvard. Nonetheless, the Redbook exemplifies the democratic liberal thought that sustained the ideal of a liberal undergraduate education after the Second World War. Notions of citizenship, responsibility to others, and common values were paramount. Although never invoking Cardinal Newman or Matthew Arnold's dictum of 'the best that had been thought and said,' the report shared their spirit and retained the special role of the humanities in moral education.

Curiously, in England, the land of Newman and Arnold, the shift to specialization was much more complete in the postwar period than it was in North America. Undergraduate students are admitted, not just into a college or one faculty of the university, as in the United States and Canada, but also directly into their chosen academic discipline. The first year provides foundations in the discipline, and later years offer more specialization and advanced study. Debates about a structured program of general education to accompany this specialization have not been a significant part of the British experience in the postwar period. This may in part be the result of the late transition to mass higher education and the later appearance of multicultural diversity in the student body; but with these changes, the question of liberal education will likely arise again.

The experience of Canadian universities after the Second World War was very like the American one, shaped by much the same values and forces. Canadian degree programs became specialized, but many universities had a structured program of general education to accompany the student's major. At mine, York University in Toronto, the Redbook's ideals were very influential in the design of our general education program.

In Canada, the universities were given the additional task of nurturing a national culture and creating a national identity as part of the project of mass university education. The most influential government initiative concerning universities in early postwar Canada was the 1951 report of the Royal Commission on National Development in the Arts, Letters, and Sciences (the Massey Commission), a national attempt to chart the future of postwar Canada. The Order in Council creating the commission begins: 'it is desirable that the Canadian people know as much as possible about their country, its history and traditions; and about their national life and common achievements.'[29]

A.B. McKillop concludes his encyclopedic *Matters of Mind: The University in Ontario, 1791–1957* by examining the Massey Commission. He writes: 'the commissioners concluded that the universities were essential to the nation's future as never before. They were the "nurseries of a truly Canadian civilization and culture." ... "All civilized societies," the commissioner's report asserted, "strive for a common good, including not only material but intellectual and moral elements."'[30]

'Such deeply held sentiments marked the mid-twentieth century expression of an Anglo-Canadian moral imperative that had first been given force and direction generations earlier in evangelical Christianity and in the desire to cultivate the life of the mind in the face of inhospitable colonial circumstance. It had been given academic shape by the rise of the Victorian liberal arts curriculum, and had been propelled into the twentieth century by idealist intellectual sympathies linked to a cultural disposition that was kindred in spirit to the thought and sentiments of Matthew Arnold. Philosophical in its underpinnings, it was secular but moralistic in its twentieth-century ambience.'[31] As in the United States, the Arnoldian vision for liberal education and the humanities survived well into the postwar period.

Over the later twentieth century, however, in both the United States and Canada, the tradition of liberal learning and general education would evolve and reshape itself. Eventually, the commitment to a structured program of general education and the special role for the humanities withered in an increasingly arid soil under a glaring sun of criticism. The pressures of diversity and choice overwhelmed the desire for heritage and common values. The undergraduate curriculum is now conceived almost entirely as the student's major, perhaps with a loose collection of distribution requirements.

Most multiversities seem unable, and unwilling, to look again and attempt to redefine the content of a liberal education. However, the original worries about a specialized undergraduate education remain and cannot be escaped: the lack of emphasis on cultivation, on citizenship, on common values, and on the humanities. Knowledge is still fragmented and the need for integration is great. The multiversity cannot slough off these worries; after all, the central task of the multiversity is undergraduate teaching and learning. At the beginning of the twenty-first century, multiversities have a fundamental responsibility: to re-examine the rationale for the liberal education in a postindustrial democratic society.

Perhaps the character of our age will demand new answers to these questions. As the ideas of our age are examined in the chapters of Part Two of this book, these questions about undergraduate education will be ever present, hovering about the analysis. For example, what are the implications for undergraduate education of the revolution in information technology, or of postmodern critique, or of globalization? Part Three of this book looks at renewal of the social contract between the multiversity and society. A liberal education for our age, a top priority in renewal of the social contract, is taken up in chapter 12.

The Professional Schools

In the great bundle that is the multiversity – research, graduate education, undergraduate liberal education, and professional education – the least-emphasized and least-analysed component is professional education. This is all the more surprising because the professional schools played a crucial role in the emergence of the multiversity, and they will increase their influence in years to come.

The place of the professional schools in universities is as old as the university itself. The first universities – the medieval universities – might even be described as collections of professional schools linked with a subordinate arts faculty. But the place of the professional schools began truly to rise with the development of the concepts of career and professionalism among the middle class. Burton J. Bledstein, in *The Culture of Professionalism: The Middle Class and the Development of Higher Education*, argues that these concepts are essential to understanding the development of modern universities. In nineteenth-century America, the middle class 'appeared as a new class with an unprecedented enthusiasm for its own forms of self-expression, peculiar ideas and devices for self-discipline.' 'Ambitious individuals in America were instrumental in structuring society according to a distinct vision – the vertical one of career. The most emphatically middle-class man was the professional, improving his worldly lot as he offered his services to society as ascending stages of an occupation.' 'With the creation of the university in America ... the middle class succeeded in establishing an institutional matrix for its evolving types of behavior. By and large the American university came into existence to serve and promote professional authority in society.'[32]

An analysis of the role of professional schools in the multiversity surely requires a definition of a *profession*. A precise and unambiguous definition, however, would elude us, whatever methodology we adopted, whether proceeding from abstract principles, or by examining histories of what we now call professions such as law or medicine, or by examining the motivations of members of professions. Nonetheless, professions can be taken to have certain characteristics, as the word is used in this analysis. A profession is an occupation based upon a well-defined body of specialized knowledge and upon skills and expertise that are developed through practical experience. The specialized knowledge is not a blueprint; its application requires discretion. The client of the professional does not have this specialized knowledge and experience, and therefore has difficulty assessing the quality of service provided. Governments recognize the need for competent, ethical practitioners, and recognize the inequalities and complexities of the client/professional relationship. This might suggest the need for government regulation of the professions in order to protect the public interest and the client, but an alternative means has been adopted to these ends. Organizations of professionals are granted self-regulating status by governments: the professional organizations determine who can practise the occupation, especially through control of how people are trained to qualify for their 'licence'; the professional organizations establish the standards of practice; and the organizations discipline members who fail to meet the standards of the profession. The government's grant of self-regulation carries a reciprocal obligation to society. Membership in the profession carries the obligation of concern for both the client's interests and the public interest. The professional association has been granted the right to regulate on behalf of the public interest and is responsible for encouraging, among its members, awareness of the public interest and a motivation to attend to it.

Professionals and their organizations, historically, were quite independent of universities, and often held the view that a university education had little to offer, except the liberal arts preparation. The professions favoured a practice-based apprenticeship as the educational preparation to enter them, this education being controlled by practising professionals. Gradually, however, preparation became based in the university and, eventually, a general model emerged: university study in a professional school, to be followed by practice-based apprenticeship, overseen by a professional association that would grant the right to practise.

Entrepreneurial and socially responsive, American universities added professional faculties and schools, and the land grant movement accelerated the process. Law and medicine were joined by faculties of education, engineering, architecture, and veterinary science.

An analysis of professional schools in the multiversity should be expanded to include those faculties/schools known within the multiversity as professional schools, whose graduates have many of the characteristics of a professional, although not the self-regulating powers of a professional association. The most important example is the business school. Other examples are schools of public administration and journalism. These schools are occupationally defined. Their curricula cover a specialized body of knowledge, and they recognize the importance of apprenticeship and practical experience in developing professional competence. In almost every respect, these schools behave in the same way as the schools for the self-regulating professions and therefore should be included among the professional schools of the multiversity.

Daniel Bell identifies the pre-eminence of the professional class in the occupational structure to be part of what defines the postindustrial society. The professional class requires advanced, university-level training and immersion in the ethos of abstract reasoning and research. Demand for professionals grew faster than the total demand for labour. The number of professions multiplied. The multiversity and postindustrial society suited each other. In both new and old professions, the university-based portion of professional education came to dominate. Michael Burrage, in his study of professional education, concludes: 'practitioner-controlled professional education has not been entirely displaced. As internship, it remains an integral part of medical education.'[33] It is similarly important in education, law, engineering, and architecture. However, in the contemporary consensus, 'it is the university or professional school diploma, rather than the practitioner's say-so, that certifies professional competence and provides the decisive qualification for professional practice and status. Nowadays, would-be professionals invariably acknowledge the fact by seeking, above all else, to have their future entrants certified by a university qualification.'[34] The multiversities have happily obliged.

The historian Harold Perkin offers an analysis of middle-class professionals similar to Bledstein's in his wonderful social history *The Rise of Professional Society: England since 1880*. Perkin argues that, whereas Victorian England had emphasized the entrepreneur and industrial capital, over the twentieth century England came to emphasize the professional ideal 'based on trained expertise and selection by merit.'[35] England became a professional society: dominated by professionals, permeated by the professional social ideal, and whose wealth depended upon human capital not industrial capital. Human capital was important in the past, 'but only in post-industrial society have the professions as a whole been able to establish human capital as the dominant form of wealth.'[36] And English professional society needed universities: 'The universities, particularly Oxford and Cambridge, were to become among the main articulators of the social ideal of the professional class.'[37] The rise of professionalism in Canada similarly shaped the growth of its universities.[38]

The long history of professional schools in American universities and the needs of postindustrial society are widely recognized, yet the dominance of professional education within the multiversity still comes as a surprise. Each professional school operates autonomously, and no single professional school is dominant (except perhaps the medical school), but collectively the professional schools are so large that the liberal arts, including both undergraduate and graduate activities, are now a minority in many a multiversity.

Harvard University has always had a position of special leadership in American undergraduate liberal education. Yet in 2000, less than one half of its 1,940 faculty members (excluding the Faculty of Medicine) were in the Faculty of Arts and Sciences. The majority were in the faculties of Design, Education, Law, Business, Divinity, Government, and Public Health.[39] Harvard is not an exception. Arts and science professors now make up about half of all professors within the entire group of American multiversities.[40]

The forces encouraging new professional schools in the multiversity will no doubt continue. Also, the relative importance of professional schools in the multiversity will continue to rise because many of the current forces shaping universities – such as increasing tuition fees, the revolution in information technology, the increased reliance on external contracts and gifts, and the increasingly vocational orientation of students – are far less threatening to professional education than they are to other parts of the multiversity.

The Multiversity Model

The multiversity developed in the United States in the years following the Second World War. Some authors, joining a river of writing on American exceptionalism, still argue that the American multiversity is unique. But the multiversity has now emerged in England and Canada and throughout the Anglo-American world. It has become an equally influential and strategically dominant model in their systems of higher education. There is much evidence that the multiversity model is rising to dominance across the world, but it is beyond the scope of this book to consider the role of the multiversity beyond the Anglo-American countries.

In several respects, however, the American multiversities do remain unique. Many American multiversities provide public entertainment to regional and national audiences through intercollegiate athletics.

Some provide patient care to the general public through university hospitals. In most countries, sports entertainment and health care are not university responsibilities. These domains are beyond the purview here and will be set aside. It should also be noted that the United States is unique in being a military superpower, and its multiversities are unique in their role in supplying the science and technology demanded by a military superpower. Finally, the United States is distinct in the significant share of university education provided by private institutions.

Writers, especially American writers, have emphasized the differences in the American tradition of higher education from the traditions in Europe, especially continental Europe. Derek Bok, the former president of Harvard, cites 'the remarkable freedom from government control that [American] institutions of higher education have enjoyed'; 'the extent to which colleges and universities compete with one another – for faculty members, for students, for funds'; and their responsiveness, 'the independence and competition that characterize American universities cause them to pay close attention to a number of constituencies – students, faculty, alumni, foundations, corporations, governments, and even local community groups.' The American system of higher education is felt to be unique because of its 'decentralization, market competition, and institutional pluralism ... a product largely of historical happenstance and constitutional pluralism.'[41] Subtexts of most international comparisons have been a contrast between the 'planned' European model and the 'competitive' American approach, and a contrast between the elitist European heritage and the democratic American heritage.

Writers about English universities likewise treat the English experience as unique, distinct from both the American and the European. Indeed, there are many differences between the English and American experience. The United States has nothing comparable to the dominance and traditions of Oxford and Cambridge. Government in England, in the first decades after the Second World War, neither financially supported university research to the same extent nor financed an expansion to mass university education. This has now changed, but certainly English writers do not use the term *multiversity*.

International comparisons are inherently problematic, and especially when made of institutions like universities, which are so rooted in their particular histories and national culture. Most writers about national higher education systems presume, implicitly or explicitly, that their national system is culturally specific and distinct in significant respects from that in other countries, perhaps even sui generis. However, if we do not focus upon contrasts between the United States and Europe, but instead restrict our gaze to the Anglo-American world, we gain a different perspective and similarities appear. Perhaps as a Canadian, whose university system has been influenced by both English and American traditions, I can better recognize the underlying commonality.

The American model was highly successful in the postwar period and, of course, would be emulated. Moreover, although each nation has its own tradition of university education, all are connected to similar strands of history. Even more significantly, these nations have all become postindustrial societies. They are subject to the same societal imperatives. The governments of the Anglo-American world have made similar commitments to support research through universities. They have made similar commitments to mass university education, and their students now come from all classes, genders, religions, and walks of life. Their middle classes are indistinguishable in their faith in merit, competence, discipline, and career. Their professions proliferate and seek the same model of accreditation and social prestige: university followed by practice-based apprenticeship. The United States, England, and Canada share similar views about the importance of universities to the individual, and to society, the economy, and their culture. They have similar political cultures and practices of democratic politics, and all became welfare states in the second half of the twentieth century.

In rest of the Anglo-American world, too, just as in America, universities enjoy considerable freedom from close government control. Their systems of higher education are all characterized by a diversity of institutions and pluralism. Their universities compete with one another for students, faculty, and funds – both public and private. They are not ivory towers, but seek to respond and adapt, forcing themselves to pay close attention to a number of constituencies. Planned or unplanned, elite or democratic, they have ended up in the same place. The Anglo-American nations have all created a group of universities within their systems of higher education that can be labelled 'multiversities.'

To provide context for the chapters that follow, it is useful to define and name the multiversities in each country. To begin, one must characterize the whole domain of higher education, and then identify the place of the multiversity within it. It is important to remember that universities are one part of the system of higher education, and multiversities but one group among all universities.

The United Nations Educational, Social, and Cultural Organization (UNESCO) has developed an International Standard Classification of Education (ISCED), revised most recently in 1997. National education systems are divided into seven levels, from 0 to 6. The first four are relatively easy to categorize: pre-primary (level 0), primary (level 1), lower secondary (level 3), and upper secondary (level 4). Primary and secondary education, in contrast to higher education, are generally free, compulsory, and government controlled. Higher education is divided into levels 5 and 6.

The first level of higher education (level 5) is divided into two separate streams. ISCED 5A programs 'are largely theoretically based and are intended to provide sufficient qualifications for gaining entry into advanced research programmes and professions with high skill requirements. Level 5A programmes have a minimum cumulative theoretical duration (at the tertiary level) of three years full-time equivalent, although they typically last four or more years.'[42] Level 5A programs include both the bachelor's and the master's degree, in most English-speaking countries. 'The content of ISCED level 5B programs is practically oriented / occupationally specific and is mainly designed for participants to acquire the practical skills and know-how needed for a particular occupation or trade or class of occupations or trades ... They have a minimum of two years' full-time equivalent duration.'[43]

ISCED level 6 programs 'lead to the award of an advanced research qualification. The programmes are therefore devoted to advanced study and original research and are not based on course-work only ... It typically requires submission of a thesis or dissertation of publishable quality which is the product of original research and represents a significant contribution to knowledge ... It prepares graduates for faculty posts in institutions offering ISCED 5A programmes, as well as research posts in government, industry, etc.'[44] Level 6 programs award doctoral degrees.

Within the university sector, certain universities offer both level 5A and level 6; they offer degrees through to the doctorate. Among this group, there is a further subdivision, into multiversities and other doctoral/research universities. Among the doctoral universities, multiversities have a *particularly intense* commitment to research and a *particularly intense* commitment to graduate education. The difficult task in specifying the multiversities is to identify them from among all the doctoral universities.

The Carnegie Foundation's Classification of American Institutions of Higher Education (as revised in 2000) can be used to see the place of the multiversity in American higher education. The Carnegie classification closely resembles that of the ISCED and identifies six categories of institutions: doctoral/research universities; master's colleges and universities; baccalaureate colleges; associate's colleges; specialized institutions; and tribal colleges. The university sector includes the first three categories. The associate's colleges typically offer two-year programs and do not offer bachelor's degrees. These are the institutions providing level 5B education, and are known as junior colleges or community colleges.

The university sector has about 56 per cent of higher education enrolments; the associate's colleges about 40 per cent.[45] The non-university sector is large indeed and all too often forgotten in discussions of higher education.

The university sector comprises 261 doctoral/research universities, 611 master's colleges and universities, and 606 baccalaureate colleges. The 261 doctoral/research universities are divided into two groups: extensive and intensive.[46] The extensive doctoral/research universities are the multiversities, the subject of this book.

The Carnegie Foundation defines extensive doctoral/research universities as those awarding fifty or more doctoral degrees per year, across at least fifteen disciplines. In an earlier version of this taxonomy, the Carnegie Foundation had a second criterion: a certain level of research had to be undertaken in order to qualify as a multiversity – this was proxied by a certain minimum value of federal research grants. Unfortunately, the data required were no longer available. The Foundation is planning an overhaul of its classification, including comprehensive new measures of research activity.[47] The 2000 Carnegie classification identifies 151 universities in the extensive doctoral/research category; these are America's multiversities. The names of the 151 multiversities are too many to list but are available in the Carnegie publications; they include the famous private universities like Harvard or Stanford, and the equally famous state universities like Michigan, Wisconsin, or Berkeley. There are forty-nine private multiversities and 101 public multiversites; many of the public ones began as land grant universities. When Clark Kerr first wrote about 'the federal grant university' in 1963, he identified twenty universities that received 79 per cent of research funds, and these were heavily concentrated in the northeast and California. Now, both the number and location have expanded: the 151 multiversities are spread across forty-six states.

Although these 151 multiversities make up only 10 per cent of the university sector institutions, they dominate university education. James Duderstadt has described American higher education as an ecosystem: 'At the top of the evolutionary ladder in the higher education ecosystem – at least in terms of prosperity and prestige – is the research university.'[48] These American multiversities (the doctoral/research extensive universities) are large – with average enrolments of about 20,000 students, and make up 37 per cent of total university sector enrolments and award 36 per cent of all bachelor's degrees. (Other types of university are much smaller; for example, master's colleges and universities average 5,300 students and baccalaureate colleges average 1,700.) The multiversities award 80 per cent of the doctorates and 57 per cent of the first-professional degrees. The multiversities are diverse: they award degrees over a wide range of arts, sciences, and professional fields. It is difficult to measure the research intensiveness of institutions, their research output, or their share of the entire national research enterprise. However, a rough proxy is available in science and engineering; these fields require major research grants to pay for the laboratories, equipment, computer systems, and technicians necessary to do the research. In these fields, research activity can be approximated by the value of research grants received. In the United States, about 80 per cent of federal support for research in science and engineering goes to multiversities. The average multiversity receives U.S. $71 million in federal science and engineering support each year. In the humanities, social sciences, and professions, proxy measures of research activity are harder to find, but the dominance of multiversities is likely similar.[49]

The most controversial part of this taxonomy is the separation of doctoral/research universities into the extensive and intensive categories. There is a middle group of about thirty universities that might go either way. The Carnegie categories, however, are clearly different on average. The extensive doctoral/research universities (the multiversities) average slightly over 20,000 students, and the intensive category about 10,000; on average extensive universities receive almost $72 million in federal funds for science and engineering annually, while the average intensive university receives about $10 million; and extensive universities award nearly 250 doctorates per year, while intensive universities award about one-fifth as many. The extensive doctoral/research universities have a *particularly intense* commitment to graduate education and research.

An examination of the systems of higher education in Canada and England reveals that the multiversity has emerged as a distinct institutional type atop their ecosystems as well. Both have a group of doctoral/research universities, and within this group, there are universities with a particularly intense commitment to graduate education and research – the multiversities.

Canada's university system evolved under the shaping influences of the British, Scottish, French, and American traditions. Like the United States, Canada is a federal country, and university education is a provincial, rather than a national responsibility. Unlike the United States, where the leading universities were national institutions, in Canada the leading universities remained as regional institutions, attracting almost all their students from nearby, until very recently. Canada was very similar to the United States in offering university education to the returning war veterans and in moving to mass university education in the thirty years after the Second World War. Also similarly, many occupations became professions, and the professions affiliated themselves with universities.

The Canadian government's involvement with research began with the establishment of the National Research Council (NRC) in 1916. The government's strategy at the time was to support research in this national institution, rather than in universities. The NRC offered advice to government on science and technology, funded fellowships at Canadian universities, and conducted its own research, principally industrial and applied research. During the Second World War, the NRC expanded significantly, working on diverse projects from weapons and synthetic fuels to food packaging and medicines. After the war, it began to support universities more extensively and established the principle that its external grants would match its internal budget. Gradually however, the strategy of the Canadian government shifted towards supporting research at universities, rather than in special-purpose national institutions. The Medical Research Council (MRC) was founded in 1966, and the National Science and Engineering Research Council (NSERC) was formed in 1978; both functions had previously existed as committees of the National Research Council. The Canada Council for the Arts, Humanities and Social Sciences was established in 1957, following the recommendations of the Massey Commission. In 1978, the Social Sciences and Humanities Research Council (SSHRC) was spun off as a separate entity.[50] Throughout this evolution, the emphasis shifted to supporting university and hospital-based research. The federal government in Canada, until recently, had not made the same commitment as its U.S. counterpart to university research. However, in the past ten years, there has been an enormous increase in federal research support, backed by the belief that advanced research is necessary for economic prosperity.

A recent chapter on the history of the postwar Canadian university begins: 'Universities have steadily expanded the scope of their activities and assumed many new roles. The result of this expansion of functions and ambition is the "multiversity," a complex and powerful institution that embraces several different educational philosophies within its walls.'[51]

Canada has no formal classification analogous to the Carnegie Foundation's, but a roughly similar taxonomy can be developed. Like the United States, Canada has two distinct parts to its first level of higher education: universities (offering level 5A) and community colleges (offering level 5B education). There are seventy-six universities with 58 per cent of the enrolment in higher education, and 206 community colleges with 42 per cent of the enrolment.[52] Just as in the United States, this non-university sector of higher education is large indeed, and too often forgotten.

Statistics Canada's Register of Postsecondary Institutions divides Canada's seventy-six universities into six categories: medical/doctoral, comprehensive, primarily undergraduate, First Nations and Metis, and special-purpose. The medical/doctoral and comprehensive universities grant bachelor's, master's, and doctoral degrees; the others focus on undergraduate education (level 5A only). There are twenty-seven medical/doctoral and comprehensive universities, analogous to the Carnegie's doctoral/research category.

Canada's multiversities come from among the twenty-seven medical/doctoral and comprehensive universities. Again, the problematic (and controversial) task is to identify the multiversities, those *particularly* research-intensive and *particularly* graduate-intensive institutions within this group. For about the past ten years, a self-selected group of ten research-intensive universities – known as the G10 – have met regularly, though informally, to discuss 'their similar challenges and opportunities.' The group was selected on the basis of the value of federal research grants received and the number of PhDs awarded.[53] Using the group's own cut-off criteria of grants and PhDs, two other universities should be added.[54] For this analysis, let us assume Canada has twelve multiversities. The names of these are listed in the endnotes.

Canada's multiversities comprise 16 per cent of the country's universities, but they have over 46 per cent of the enrolment. They have on average about 22,000 students and they award almost 75 per cent of all doctorates. A good proxy for the research at universities in Canada is the allocation of Canada Research Chairs. These research chairs have been funded by the federal government as endowed professorships, allocated to universities on the basis of their share of the research grants awarded by the three national granting councils – the Social Sciences and Humanities Research Council, the National Science and Engineering Research Council, and the Canadian Institutes for Health Research. The twelve multiversities will receive over 68 per cent of the Canada Research Chairs (and the percentage would have been higher but for a special allotment for small universities). In Canada the multiversities are indisputably the dominant research institutions.[55]

As in the United States, although there is ambiguity around whether a few doctoral/research universities should or should not be in the multiversity group, the split between the multiversities and the other doctoral/research universities is very clear. In Canada, the multiversities average about 22,000 students, whereas the other doctoral/research universities average 13,400. The multiversities on average award 241 doctorates per year, the other doctoral/research universities average sixty-six. The multiversities on average will receive 113 Canada Research Chairs, the others twenty-nine. The two groups are very distinct. The second group does not have the same *particularly intense* commitment to graduate education and research.

Higher education policies in England have been very different from those in North America.[56] Scholars writing about the English system of higher education since 1950 do not tell the story of the emergence of the multiversity. Indeed, the term *multiversity* is seldom used. Nonetheless, I would argue, the multiversity has emerged there as well. It emerged rather later because of the later commitment to mass university education and the later emphasis on linking research at universities to economic prosperity. The similarity across the Anglo-American world has been masked recently because of the turbulence in the United Kingdom regarding the introduction and increase in tuition fees, the increasing emphasis on a more managerial style of senior administration, and changes in the governance structures of universities. U.K. writers focus on these when they consider the crucial issues for the future. The ferocity of the current controversies is unique to the United Kingdom, but all of these are part of the emergence of the multiversity. Also, the U.K. system of public funding is different, with a clear separation of funding for teaching versus research. Nonetheless, from the perspective of across the Atlantic and taking a long-term view, I would argue that in the English experience we can see that the same forces have been at work as across the Anglo-American world in the past – and will be in the future.

The great ancient universities, Oxford and Cambridge, with their traditions of liberal learning, were founded before the Scientific Revolution and the Enlightenment. Although their colleges were independent foundations, collectively they were intimately connected to the established Church of England. Since the nineteenth century, an essential context of English higher education is the struggle to overcome established power and tradition.

The opening up to a new type of student, and to science and technology, began with University College, London, and gained momentum with the creation of the civic and 'redbrick' universities, such as Leeds, Bristol, Sheffield, Manchester, and Birmingham, in the later nineteenth and early twentieth centuries. Many of these had been initiated and supported by local businessmen to develop science and engineering for local industry. European industry, especially in Germany and France, was closing the gap with Britain, and even surpassing her in certain fields. The new universities were intended to provide both skilled manpower and new research for British industry.[57] Both in their intended students and their subject matter, the civic/redbrick universities were not so different from the American land grant universities of the same time.

The next great opening came in the 1960s, when seven new universities were created: East Anglia, Essex, Kent, Lancaster, Sussex, York, and Warwick. All were to help accommodate the expansion of university education in England, and although the vision and pattern of development differed across institutions, all are committed to the research ideal, to graduate education across many fields, and to becoming national and international institutions. Reflecting their era, many had a liberal arts rather than professional or science orientation, but over time they have diversified. Despite this expansion, the

English university system remained elite in orientation, and had not yet moved to mass university education as occurred in the United States and Canada. That transition did not come until the last decades of the twentieth century. All of these universities, from Oxford and Cambridge, through the civic/redbricks, to York and Warwick, have now become doctoral/research universities. The English multiversities come from this group.

Where the English system differs from North America is not in the research/doctoral category but in the other parts of the university sector and in the rest of the system of higher education. England does not have a group of universities focused on undergraduate education and offering bachelor's degrees in the liberal arts and sciences, as in the United States and Canada. Also, and more significantly, England does not have a group of institutions primarily offering higher education programs of one or two years, providing the occupational and technical skill for direct entry into the labour market (level 5B higher education). Instead, England developed a system of polytechnics.

Following Lord Robbins's *Report on Higher Education* of 1963, which called for an expansion of the system of higher education, the new Labour government announced in 1965 a 'binary policy' in higher education. The system of higher education in England (and Wales) would be divided into two parts: the universities and the polytechnics. The government would establish twenty-eight (later thirty) polytechnics as the leading institutions of the non-university sector in higher education. By 1973, thirty polytechnics had over 150,000 students.

The polytechnics were an important part of increasing accessibility to higher education, especially for working people and their children. They were to meet the need for vocational, industrial, and professional courses not being offered by the university. Their primary purpose was to prepare students for the labour force upon graduation. They focused on their regional communities and developed close ties with industry. Their faculty members were to emphasize teaching. The description, thus far, would suggest that the polytechnics would focus on level 5B education, much like the community colleges in Canada and associate's colleges in the United States, but this is not the case. The polytechnics did, indeed, offer many one- and two-year vocational programs (level 5B). But they also offered degree-level programs; a national agency, the Council for National Academic Awards (CNAA), accredited their programs and was the vehicle through which degrees could be awarded. Their faculty members engaged in applied research. In very sharp contrast to the North American experience, the polytechnics also offered post-undergraduate courses. In 1992, 18,000 students were in such programs in polytechnics.

When first formed, the polytechnics' students were mainly part-time, and most were taking non-advanced courses. By the 1990s, they were mainly full-time, and most of them were taking degree-level courses. Perhaps not surprisingly, in 1992, the government allowed the polytechnics to acquire the title of 'university' and to award their own degrees, without the CNAA.

Higher education in England now is made up of seventy-seven universities, fourteen general colleges, and forty-one specialist institutions. The universities (including the former polytechnics) have the vast majority of the higher education enrolments. There is no non-university (level 5B) group of institutions as in the United States and Canada.

This particular experience in England has perhaps masked the emergence of English multiversities. Under the English binary policy, universities were seen as autonomous from government, discipline-based, engaged in pure research that sought knowledge for its own sake (unsullied by close connections with industry), and as exclusive institutions, catering to the academically gifted. In contrast, the polytechnics were seen to be under government control, responsive to society's needs, problem-oriented rather than discipline-oriented, engaged in applied research with close connections to industry, and accessible institutions catering to the needs of working-class students. This view of the binary system, however, sets up a false dichotomy. It suggests that, over the postwar period, universities were remaining independent institutions, moved by the dynamics of academic disciplines, unchanged by the needs of an industrial democratic society. In fact, this was not the case and had never been the case: the civic/redbrick universities, which were and remain the backbone of the university system, had always been places of applied research, connected to industry, and relatively accessible. All English universities have been changing since the 1960s. When the polytechnics became universities in 1992, more than one observer commented that the issue was not that the polytechnics had become universities, but rather that the universities had become polytechnics. The English universities over the past forty years have been reshaped by all the same forces that reshaped the universities in the United States and Canada.

A symbolic point for the change in English universities was the speech by Labour Prime Minister James Callaghan, delivered at Ruskin College, Oxford, in 1976. A recent overview of the period concluded: 'the Ruskin speech and the so-called "Great Debate" which followed represented a symbolic indication of central government's desire to influence the nation's education in certain ways.' 'Callaghan made explicit the relationship between education and the nation's well-being, particularly its economic prosperity. This was to dominate much government thinking on education.'[58] The dominance of these ideas transcended party lines – a Labour prime minister spoke them, they continued through the Thatcher revolution and Tory years, and they continue under 'New Labour.'

The combined effects of two factors – the belief that universities are crucial to economic prosperity and the inevitable, but long-delayed, transformation from an elite to mass system of higher education – were enormous. A recent essay concludes: 'Today, Britain much more closely approximates the U.S.A.'s experience of higher education as a "normal" phenomenon than it did even twenty years ago, although the effects of this on wider social relations are, as yet, only imperfectly understood.'[59]

The institutions of higher education in England can be roughly divided into two parts: the doctoral/research universities and others, principally the former polytechnics and specialized institutions. Within the English doctoral/research universities, there has emerged a group of multiversities. Just as in Canada and the United States, it is a problematic and controversial task to specify the group exactly; but the doctoral/research universities do fall into two groups. In the United Kingdom, an informal and self-selected group of research-intensive universities has been meeting, the Russell Group, so-called because the meetings take place in the Russell Hotel. There are nineteen universities in this group, sixteen from England. The Russell Group is made up of research-intensive, graduate-intensive universities. These sixteen are the English multiversities, and they are named in the endnotes.[60]

The Higher Education Funding Council for England allocates money for teaching and research to 144 higher education institutions. The Russell Group universities include fifteen of the top sixteen English universities in terms of research funding received in 2003–4. The group receives about 65 per cent of the research grants to universities. The one anomaly in the Russell Group, whose research funding is not in the top sixteen, is the London School of Economics and Political Science, an atypical institution. The Russell Group universities also have very large programs of graduate education. The group includes the thirteen largest universities in terms of graduate education (measured as full-time postgraduate enrolment) and all are in the top twenty. These universities also cover many areas of study, as indicated by the fields submitted for the Research Assessment Exercise.[61]

These English multiversities are large, averaging about 22,300 students, respresenting about 21 per cent of English higher education enrolments. As in the other English-speaking countries, the English multiversities, on average, are clearly distinct from the other English doctoral/research universities. The multiversities have the *particularly intense* commitment to research and graduate education.

The transformation of the English university system to include multiversities can be no more dramatically illustrated than by looking at Oxford, so beloved of Cardinal Newman. Oxford is now a multiversity; it has medicine, engineering, and even a business school. In size (over 21,000 students) and range of subjects across undergraduate and graduate programs, Oxford is comparable to North American multiversities. It has an enormous continuing education department. As a research university, Oxford proudly announces that it 'has more academic staff working in world-class research departments than any other university in the U.K.' The university's website celebrates the employment success of its graduates, and Oxford's ranking compared with other universities. With a click of the mouse, the viewer can move along to where donations are solicited – and accepted. Oxford proclaims its contributions to the economy, reporting on its website that 'Isis Innovation, the University's technology transfer company, files on average one new patent application a week and spins out a new company from University research every two months.' Like every multiversity, Oxford presents itself to the world on its website,[62] which in topic and tone resembles every other multiversity's website.

The similarities across the three countries are truly striking, having identified the multiversities in each. Their multiversities are about the same size, about 20,000 students. They award about the same number of doctorates, about 230 per year. Absolute levels of research money cannot be compared, because the amount of government money available differs, but in each country the multiversities receive over 65 per cent of the research funds available to universities. Also, in each country, the multiversities as a group differ significantly from the other doctoral/research universities.

The multiversity now sits atop the ecosystem of higher education, but what lies ahead? Will it remain a dominant model? How will the multiversity adapt to the ideas of our age, which are bringing tumultuous change? Part Two of this book examines five characteristics of our age and how they may reshape the multiversity.

Before proceeding to Part Two, however, I want first to continue to examine the emergence of the multiversity in the second half of the twentieth century. The second half of the twentieth century was marked not just by a great economic transformation, the transformation into a postindustrial society, but also by great political transformation. Anglo-American liberal democracies were transformed into welfare states, and the multiversity is intimately connected with the development of the welfare state. This is the subject of chapter 4.

4 The Multiversity and the Welfare State

The multiversity flourished in the postindustrial society after the Second World War. The economy required new knowledge, skilled graduates, and professionals as never before, and the multiversity obliged.

Most of the writing about multiversities explains their emergence in this transformation of our economy, in the transformation from an industrial to a knowledge-based economy. Daniel Bell calls it a postindustrial society. In his analysis, Bell divides society into three parts: the social structure, the polity, and the culture. The social structure he defines as the economy, the technology, and the occupational structure of a society. Changes in the social structure brought the postindustrial society. This economic lens through which to understand the nature of our society has been well-used, and the role of universities is well-understood. Postindustrial society requires both highly educated workers and advanced research. Today, this connection of the multiversity with the knowledge-based economy has become even more intense and it dominates current discussions about multiversities. (This characteristic of our age is discussed in chapter 9.)

We should recognize, however, that after the Second World War there was an equally significant transformation of the polity. In Bell's typology of society, the polity regulates the distribution of power and adjudicates the conflicting demands of individual groups. However, writers about universities have paid very little attention to how this political transformation helped to create the multiversity.

After the Second World War, there emerged a new social contract between citizens and their governments in Anglo-American liberal democracies. The nature and meaning of a democracy changed fundamentally into a new synthesis of democracy and capitalism that can be labelled 'the welfare state.' This transformation of our democracies into welfare states was just as significant for the emergence of the multiversity as was the economic and technological transformation into a postindustrial society.[1]

After the war, liberal democracies assumed new responsibilities for the welfare of their citizens, hence the term *welfare state*. Rather than allowing private markets to fully determine the outcomes, governments intervened to stabilize the market economy and to pursue full employment. Governments created programs to reduce insecurities from sickness, old age, and unemployment, and to ensure minimum standards of income, health, housing, and education. The government-protected minimums were provided to everyone by right as a citizen, not as charity. The welfare state was intended to protect not only the poor and the vulnerable from the extremes of unfettered capitalism; it was directed as much to the middle as to the extremes. The pursuit of full employment and the provision of social insurance and social services were intended for the middle class, indeed, for all citizens. And there was no conflict between economic needs and social justice, because by protecting against the uncertainties and inequalities of capitalism, the welfare state was also intended to make capitalist economies more productive. The multiversity is the distinctive adaptation of 'the university' to this transformation of democracy, to the creation of the welfare state.

The previous chapter discussed the two great financial commitments of government that created the multiversity in the United States – the support for research and the support for mass university education. They reflect long-standing government concerns about economic growth and equality of opportunity. However, these new financial commitments can also be analysed as part of the transformed role of government, the welfare state. Recognizing this profound change in the polity after the Second World War gives us a new lens through which to understand the nature of our society. Through this lens, the tasks and responsibilities of the multiversity can be seen in new ways.

In the thirty years after the Second World War, the welfare state was put in place. The role of government expanded, built upon a remarkable consensus about the objectives of government and the means to achieve them. Not coincidentally, this expansive period is often identified as the golden age for the multiversity. The welfare state supports the multiversity financially: it provides operating grants and capital grants; it often regulates tuition fees; and it provides research grants and contracts. Also it calls upon professors as advisers, uses the multiversity's research, and hires many of its graduates. The multiversity flourishes or struggles as the welfare state itself flourishes or struggles.

Beginning in the mid-1970s, the consensus supporting the welfare state fragmented and the intellectual pillars of the welfare state were challenged. Almost all of the challengers recommended a rollback of the role of government in the economy and society, a shift in the balance of public versus private. Again, not coincidentally, the past twenty years have been tumultuous and troubled for the multiversity. Looking ahead, the future of the multiversity depends upon the future of the welfare state. This future is taken up in Part Two, chapter 6. The nature of the welfare state in the twenty-first century – what I will label 'the constrained welfare state' – is the first characteristic of our age examined in Part Two.

In this chapter, I examine the postwar establishment of the welfare state and its profound influence on the emergence of the multiversity. This was the era when public universities rose in prominence in the Anglo-American countries. Canada's universities are now virtually all public, but both England and especially the United States have always had private universities and they have made up a disproportionate share of the elite universities. The private universities – like Oxford and Cambridge, Harvard and Stanford – remain influential leaders, and such is their influence that much of the writing about multiversities still draws disproportionately upon writers from these institutions speaking on behalf of the whole. (This book is no exception.) But, this should not mask the reality that in our liberal democracies, the public multiversities are the majority. This exploration of the intimate connection between the welfare state and the multiversity not only helps us to better understand what created the multiversity; it serves other purposes as well. It looks at the multiversity not through an economic lens, but through the lens of politics and public policy. It emphasizes how the multiversity emerged and is evolving as a result of changes in our liberal democracies. This chapter begins to establish the argument that multiversities should be analysed as institutions of democracy and have a responsibility to democratic life.

Another theme of this book is that multiversities have become central institutions in our society. They are influential in part because of their research, because of the power of ideas. This chapter begins to demonstrate the new place of multiversities in society by illustrating the power of multiversity research. In this chapter, we see the influence of the ideas of social scientists upon society. Later chapters will illustrate the power of ideas from the sciences and from the humanities.

Defining the Welfare State

The term *welfare state* is used and understood in many different ways, both in academic writing and in public discussion. Here, I use the term to describe the new role of government, the new social contract between citizens and their government, that emerged in liberal democracies of the Anglo-American world after the Second World War. These liberal democracies were capitalist market economies, based on private ownership and free enterprise. The welfare state established a new and more expansive role for government in society; it established a new balance between the government, the market, and the individual. The core idea is that governments assume new responsibility for the welfare of their citizens. In such liberal democracies, the well-being of citizens is not left entirely to the outcomes of the private market economy, or to the privileges and deprivations of birth and social class, or to the vagaries of natural contingency.

In the welfare state, the concerns of citizens and the commitments of government are several. Foremost, the government is recognized to have a role in reducing the level of unemployment. The bedrock for the well-being of a citizen is to have a job. Prior to the war, one of the greatest problems of capitalism in the Anglo-American world was chronic high unemployment, most catastrophically manifest in the Great Depression. A closely related government responsibility is to provide the framework for economic growth to ensure jobs and an improvement in well-being in the future. Second, the government is recognized to have a role in providing certain social insurance: it has a role in seeing that people have adequate income in old age and have some form of insurance against lost income due to unemployment, illness, or disability. Third, the government is recognized to have a role in providing certain social services and in seeing that all have 'adequate' education, health care, food, and shelter. The exact role of government and the definition of *adequacy* and the means to meet the government's commitments will vary; but that government has some responsibility, there is no doubt. And finally, the government is recognized to have a role in reducing inequalities of income and wealth, and in securing some greater equality of opportunity and life chances.

The term *welfare state* was first used in Britain during the Second World War, to contrast with the 'power state' of Nazi ideology.[2] The term came to represent the social benefits that democratic governments would provide their citizens after the war. The term is a commonplace in Great Britain, used less in Canada, and still less again in the United States. North Americans often restrict the word 'welfare' to mean government payments to the very poor (this is decidedly not the way the term is used here) and prefer the more anodyne terms of economic and social policy when discussing the new role of government. In the United States, the transformed role of government is associated with the New Deal of Franklin D. Roosevelt's presidency. Whatever the terminology, however, there was an extraordinary consensus, over the postwar period in the Anglo-American world, regarding the new responsibilities of democratic governments for the welfare of their citizens.

In recent years, some American scholars have begun to use the term *welfare state*, for example, in the 1988 collection of essays edited by Amy Gutmann, *Democracy and the Welfare State*. That volume deals mainly with the United States, and the authors clearly understand the United States as a welfare state. Gutmann begins the introduction: 'Every modern industrial state is a welfare state. None permits natural or social contingencies fully to determine the life chances of its members. All have programs whose explicit purpose is to protect adults and children from the degradation and insecurity of ignorance, illness, disability, unemployment and poverty.'[3]

My usage of the term welfare state is similar to that of Ramesh Mishra, who has written extensively on welfare states. He defines a *welfare state* as 'a liberal state which assumes responsibility for the well-being of its citizens through a range of interventions in the market economy, e.g. full employment policies and social welfare services. The term includes both the idea of state responsibility for welfare and the practices through which the idea is given effect.'[4] In my analysis, I consider the welfare state as founded on four intellectual pillars: (1) government policies dealing with unemployment; (2) government social insurance and social expenditures; (3) the concept of social citizenship; and (4) the system of progressive taxation to finance the welfare state.[5] As we shall see in this and later chapters, each pillar has important implications for the multiversity.

Much writing on the welfare state focuses solely on explicit expenditure related to social insurance and social programs. These social expenditures are direct government expenditure on education, health services, housing assistance, pensions/social security, unemployment compensation, and other income maintenance programs. (The remaining categories of government expenditure are administration, defence and foreign affairs, law and order, transportation, environment, economic programs, and interest payments on the public debt.) It is understandable to focus upon social expenditures, because government social expenditures are at the heart of the welfare state and are its most evident manifestation. Social expenditure is also the easiest to measure, and therefore data on social expenditures are the most effective measure to demonstrate the establishment and growth of the welfare state.

The beginnings of the welfare state actually came well before the Second World War.[6] Government social expenditures reached 5 per cent of gross domestic product (GDP) in the United Kingdom in 1920, although they did not reach this level in North America until 1931. The social programs, however, were modest, did not cover the whole population, and did not provide a very high level of support. The huge transformation in the role of government occurred after the war.

During the golden age of the welfare state, from 1960 to 1980, social expenditures rose dramatically and came to represent more than one-half of all government spending. Social expenditures grew much faster than the economy, with the result that they almost doubled their share of GDP. The pattern was similar in Canada, the United Kingdom, and the United States. By 1981, social expenditures accounted for 22 per cent of Canada's GDP, 24 per cent of the GDP of the United Kingdom, and 21 per cent of that of the United States.[7] The majority of social expenditures were on health, education, and pensions/social security, and these were the most rapidly growing categories. With social expenditures at more than 20 per cent of GDP, the welfare state was, indeed, a major transformation of the social contract between citizens and their government.

There is, of course, more to the welfare state than social expenditures. The welfare state includes policy regarding unemployment and economic growth, the concept of citizenship, and the tax system used to finance government expenditures. We must understand all of these if we are to fully comprehend the connection between the welfare state and the multiversity, and more importantly, if we are to understand the implications of changes in the welfare state for the future of the multiversity. Nonetheless, the data on social expenditures do provide a quantitative measure of the new social contract.

Before exploring how this transformation of the polity contributed to the emergence of the multiversity, let us examine briefly how the role of government changed leading up to the later twentieth century and the place of universities in that evolution.

The Role of Government and Universities

People have been reflecting on the appropriate role for government in a market economy since capitalism replaced feudalism, and certainly since the eighteenth century, when moral philosophers asked whether the acquisitive ethics of capitalism could be compatible with the traditional virtues of sociability, sympathy, and justice. A great legacy of the Scottish universities during the Enlightenment is the discipline of political economy, founded by their moral philosophers. Adam Smith was appointed professor of logic at the University of Glasgow in 1751, and the next year he was awarded the chair in moral philosophy. His research and lectures led first to the publication of *The Theory of Moral Sentiments* in 1759, and culminated in *An Inquiry into the Nature and Causes of the Wealth of Nations* in 1776. Together, these created the discipline of political economy.

Political economy studies the interconnections of the market economy and government, exploring the appropriate roles of the public sector and the private sector. It consists not just of description and analysis, but also of prescription. It asks: What is the appropriate role for government? What should government do? How should government programs be designed? Who should pay for government services? Embedded within these general questions are specific questions such as: What is the role of government in providing education and who should pay for education?

These general questions are really no different than questions that have been at the heart of liberal learning since Greek and Roman times. Liberal learning in classical thought asked: What are 'the principles of a just and satisfying political order?' Political economy updates this question for a capitalist economy with representative government. Every society must address these questions. In every era, they must be asked and answered anew. The answers profoundly shape the multiversity.

The political economy of Adam Smith grants governments a far more limited role than we see in the modern welfare state. Smith was reacting against Mercantilism, the dominant political economy of his age. Mercantilism recommended a very large role for government in economic life. Mercantilists measured a nation's wealth by how much precious metal it possessed. To generate a favourable balance of trade and thus to accumulate gold bullion, Mercantilism recommended national self-sufficiency, high tariffs, special protection for agriculture, and highly regulated domestic industry. Mercantilism called for an activist government, regulating and managing the economy. In contrast, Smith recommended a laissez faire approach.

Smith placed industry and commerce, not agriculture, at the fore in the economy, and said the wealth of a nation depends upon its production of goods, and the ability to trade its goods for other goods, not the accumulation of gold bullion. It is the output of the economy and the ability to trade some of this output for the output of other nations that measures the wealth of nations. He recognized how the division of labour could increase output, argued in favour of freer trade and against the regulation of industry, and emphasized the importance of individual enterprise.

For Smith, the principal duties of government were three. The first was national defence. The second was 'protecting as far as possible, every member of society from the injustice or oppression of every other member of it ... [that is] establishing an exact administration of justice.'[8] The third duty was 'erecting and maintaining those public institutions and those public works, which though they may be in the highest degree advantageous to a great society, are, however, of such a nature, that the profit could never repay the expense ... and which it therefore cannot be expected that any individual or small number of individuals should erect or maintain.'[9] Public works included roads, bridges, harbours, and water works. Public institutions included most notably public education, at least to the primary level. These roles for government were significant, but did not constitute a welfare state.

Smith mentions universities only briefly, but speaks highly of broad learning, which freedom from a routine occupation can bring. However, he is ambivalent about government support for universities. He does assert that 'the expense of the institutions of education ... [is] beneficial to the whole society, and may, therefore, without injustice, be defrayed by the general contribution of the whole society.'[10] But he cautions it might be better to charge tuition fees, because education is so directly beneficial to the individual student. Smith favoured government support for education at the primary level for 'the common people,' believing 'people of some rank and fortune' can take care of themselves.

Smith was a harsh critic of the old endowed universities, Oxford and Cambridge, because they did not teach science; they taught only classics and 'very negligently and superficially'[11] at that. Furthermore, 'the discipline of colleges and universities is in general contrived, not for the benefit of the students, but for the interest, or more properly speaking, for the ease of the masters.'[12] Many a modern observer would ruefully comment that little has changed.

The political economy of Adam Smith complemented the political philosophy of liberalism developing in his time and into the nineteenth century especially through such writers as John Stuart Mill, Voltaire, and Thomas Jefferson. Classical liberalism was a political doctrine emphasizing liberty, the rights of individuals, the right to private property, and limited constitutional government. Smith's political economy is so complementary that often it is subsumed under the title of classical liberalism. Classical liberalism, with its belief in a limited role of government, dominated the Anglo-American world throughout the late eighteenth and much of the nineteenth centuries. Classical liberalism gave little prominence to universities; and universities were not central institutions in society.

The beginnings of a larger role for government and the origins of the welfare state are found in Germany with the social insurance programs of Otto von Bismarck. The long process of German nation-building had culminated with the creation of the German Empire in 1871, superseding a loose confederation of German states. King Wilhelm I of Prussia became emperor and Bismarck the chancellor. Their task was to consolidate the new nation. Bismarck established national, compulsory sickness insurance for industrial workers in 1883, followed immediately by accident insurance, and then by pensions in 1889. Workers could become poor (and unproductive) through no fault of their own because of sickness, accident, or old age, but these risks could be mitigated by social insurance provided by the government. The German initiatives drew international attention immediately. Government commissions in many nations analysed the principles of social insurance and drafted legislation for their own countries.[13]

The design, implementation, and administration of national social insurance plans were complex tasks requiring civil administrators, lawyers, actuaries, and demographers. These were supplied by the flourishing German universities, a role acknowledged and accepted by their leaders. This role in nation-building had been anticipated by Wilhelm von Humboldt at the founding of the University of Berlin in the early nineteenth century.

The German social insurance initiatives were not the political decisions of a liberal democracy; they were the decisions of an emperor and chancellor about national priorities. Social insurance did reduce hardship among citizens and improve economic performance, but this was not the prime motivation. Bismarck's intent was to blunt the growing socialist movement and to capture the loyalty of the working class.

Industrialization and capitalism, under the umbrella of the nation state and classical liberalism, were remaking Europe – enriching many and impoverishing others. Urban industrial workers lived in poverty and squalor, devastated by typhus, tuberculosis, and cholera. Polite society was not unaware of this. Clergymen, novelists, and even government reports offered graphic portrayals. Nor were the polite and powerful unaware of workers organizing for radical change – some workers were organizing for greater democratic rights, but others to overthrow capitalism entirely. 'There is a spectre haunting Europe – the spectre of communism,' begins the preamble of *The Manifesto of the Communist Party* published in 1848. The Communist League, an international association of workers, asked Karl Marx and Friedrich Engels to write a detailed theoretical and practical program for the party. Their analysis was clear and the remedy incendiary:[14]

> The history of all hitherto existing society is the history of class struggles.
>
> The modern bourgeois society that has sprouted from the ruins of feudal society has not done away with class antagonisms. It has but established new classes, new conditions of oppression, new forms of struggle in place of the old one.
>
> Our epoch, the epoch of the bourgeoisie, possesses, however, this distinct feature: it has simplified class antagonisms. Society as a whole is more and more splitting up into two great hostile camps, into two great classes directly facing each other – bourgeoisie and proletariat.
>
> Constant revolutionizing of production, uninterrupted disturbance of all social conditions, everlasting uncertainty and agitation distinguish the bourgeois epoch from all earlier ones. All that is solid melts into air, all that is holy is profaned, and man is at last compelled to face with sober senses his real condition of life and his relations with his kind.
>
> The Communists disdain to conceal their views and aims. They openly

declare that their ends can be attained only by the forcible overthrow of all existing social conditions. Let the ruling classes tremble at a communist revolution. The proletarians have nothing to lose but their chains. They have a world to win.

Workers of all countries, unite!

The Communists proclaimed they would abolish private property, nationalize industry, banking, and transportation, and allocate resources according to an explicit, rational plan: from each according to his ability, to each according to his need. They would levy a progressive income tax and provide free education for all children. The individualist private market would be overthrown and replaced by the collectivist government plan.

Classical liberalism and communism opposed each other from opposite ends of the political spectrum for the next 140 years. One favours the private, the other favours the public; one defends private property, the other abolishes it; one has decentralized markets, the other has central planning; one minimizes the role of government, the other maximizes it. Both combine elements of ideology and utopia. The battle between them profoundly shaped our world and the political economy of the welfare state until the late 1980s.

Neither classical liberalism nor communism much discussed the role of universities in society: universities were marginal private institutions for nineteenth-century political economists, although the implications for universities of each ideology are obvious. In *On Liberty* (1859), John Stuart Mill states: 'if the roads and railways, the banks, the insurance companies, the great joint stock companies, the universities and the public charities were all of them branches of the government ... not all the freedom of the press and popular constitution of the legislature would make this or any country free otherwise than in name.'[15] Classical liberalism recognized the need for autonomous universities. Under communism, universities are creatures of the state and, among other things, teach the ideology of the party.

Classical liberalism and communism offer diametrically opposed answers to the questions of political economy. The Anglo-American nations rejected the extremes of the spectrum, and their welfare states developed as a middle alternative, although always tugged by visionaries from the two ends. For most of the twentieth century, the tug was greater from the left than from the right. The means – a workers' revolution and the abolition of private property – might not have been convincing, but the utopianism, the advocacy of equality, social justice, freedom, and prosperity for all, held broader appeal across the political spectrum. A desire for a more just society and a deep commitment to public service and social change were widely shared, especially among the educated middle class. These progressive social reform movements profoundly reshaped universities in the late nineteenth and twentieth centuries.

Some reformers, like the Fabians in England, accepted the communist/socialist vision for society, but not the revolutionary means. In 1938, the Fabian Society declared: 'The Society consists of socialists. It therefore aims at the establishment of a society in which equality of opportunity will be assured, and the economic power and privileges of individuals and classes abolished through collective ownership and democratic control of the resources of the community. It seeks to secure the ends by the methods of political democracy.'[16] The Fabians believed that the cause of socialism could be furthered by education and research, as well as through political organization. The Fabian Society was instrumental in founding the London School of Economics and Political Science, a university committed to public involvement and public service.

Formal socialist movements were much less important in the United States and Canada, but the utopian vision, the urge to democratic reform, the conviction that education and research could bring about social improvement, animated many in the mainstream parties. These convictions were strong in the Protestant evangelical traditions, especially the Social Gospel movement, itself a vital political force. In the United States, progressivism was a powerful, if eclectic, political movement urging democratic reform and that government take active responsibility for the welfare of its people. Science, engineering, and the 'new' social sciences were crucial to social progress. The Progressive movement championed the introduction of these disciplines into American university curricula, against those who wanted to retain an emphasis on mathematics, the humanities, and moral philosophy. In both countries, such progressive forces helped to move the universities towards greater involvement in the economy and involvement in public service.

The Intellectual Foundations of the Welfare State

There are many ways to understand the growth of the welfare state and its different development in different countries. Many writers, particularly those who focus upon the redistributive activities of the welfare state, emphasize politics and the mobilization of political interests. One recent study concluded that 'partisan politics was the single most important factor that shaped the development of welfare states through time and accounts for the variation in welfare state outcomes across countries.' These partisan politics are coloured by the dominant political culture and structural features of the nation, particularly the strength of organized labour and religious cleavages.[17] Certainly, such political analysis must be at the core of understanding the growth of the welfare state.

Here in this chapter, I emphasize the role of ideas in the establishment of the welfare state. This methodology is not a substitute for the political and structural explanations, but a complement to them. It emphasizes the role of social thought in explaining social change.[18] It also helps illuminate the interconnections between the multiversity and the welfare state; each intellectual pillar of the welfare state has important implications for the multiversity.

An examination of the intellectual foundations of the welfare state is also an examination of the power of university research – in this example, research in the social sciences – to reshape our world. As John Maynard Keynes famously remarked about academic scribblers: 'the ideas of economists and political philosophers, both when they are right and when they are wrong, are more powerful than is commonly understood. Indeed the world is ruled by little else. Practical men, who believe themselves exempt from any intellectual influences, are usually the slaves of some defunct economist. Madmen in authority, who hear voices in the air, are distilling their frenzy from some academic scribbler of a few years back. I am sure the power of vested interests is vastly exaggerated compared with the gradual encroachment of ideas.'[19]

Earlier in the chapter, I characterized the welfare state as having four pillars: employment policy, social expenditures, social citizenship, and progressive tax policy. The ideas that provide the intellectual foundations of the welfare state emerged from many voices and out of long traditions, but in the mid-twentieth century the crucial intellectual foundations were articulated by university professors. The intellectual foundations of the first three pillars are especially associated with the writings of three British academics: John Maynard Keynes on full employment policy, William Beveridge on social policy, and Thomas H. Marshall on social citizenship. All were professors who moved back and forth between the worlds of government and the university.

John Maynard Keynes was born in 1883, raised in a comfortable Victorian academic family, and died in 1946. His biographer Skidelsky observed: 'He was born into a world which assumed peace, prosperity, and progress to be the natural order of things, and lived long enough to see all these expectations toppled.'[20] Keynes was educated on scholarship at Eton, then Cambridge, where he studied mathematics and philosophy. On graduation in 1906, he took the Civil Service Examination and entered the India Office as a junior clerk, but soon won his fellowship at King's College, Cambridge, which became and remained his academic home. Keynes's life is a narrative of the new role of government in the twentieth century and of the birth of the welfare state. At the same time, his life is a narrative of the changing role of professors, the changing role of social science research, and the changing role of universities in the life of a nation.

After 1914, the world for many Europeans was descending into chaos. Skidelsky writes: 'Civilization, Keynes acknowledged in 1938, was a "thin and precarious crust." The men of power took over [Stalin, Mussolini, Hitler] to impose their versions of order on chaos.'[21] Keynes's great contribution to the welfare state was his conviction – and demonstration – that human thought could understand the world and human agency could make it better. 'Uncertainty could be managed, not by brute force, but by brains, by the exercise of intelligence, and gradually the harmonies might be restored. This was his ultimate credo, his message.'[22] This was also the ultimate credo, the message of the welfare state. And it became the credo of the multiversity. Vannevar Bush subscribed to this same credo in *Science – The Endless Frontier*, arguing that new scientific knowledge was needed to improve health and economic well-being.

Keynes developed his economic ideas as he reflected upon the overwhelming economic problem of his era: persistent mass unemployment. The inflationary boom of 1919–20 was followed by a long recession in the United Kingdom, and even after prices settled down, unemployment remained stuck over 10 per cent and then soared during the Great Depression. In the United States, unemployment reached 24 per cent by 1932 and remained above 14 per cent until 1941. Keynes rejected classical economic analysis, which held that the market economy was self-regulating and would always tend towards full employment. Classical economics did acknowledge there could be frictional unemployment, as the economy adjusted to unforeseen changes, but full employment would be restored (relatively) quickly.

Keynes's economic writings, especially *The General Theory of Employment, Interest and Money*, demonstrated that the capitalist market economy could become stuck at an underemployment equilibrium because of a deficiency in aggregate demand. Moreover, misguided government policy could sustain this underemployment equilibrium. Fortunately, judicious government policy, by increasing aggregate demand, could move the 'stuck' economy back to the full employment equilibrium. Monetary policy (discretionary changes in the supply of money) and fiscal policy (discretionary changes in tax rates or public expenditures) could move the economy back to full employment. Keynes's analysis also showed that government monetary and fiscal policy could stabilize the fluctuations in unemployment and prices.

The first great intellectual pillar of the welfare state was in place: governments accepted the goal of full employment and took responsibility for stabilization of the economy. So important is this pillar that the postwar welfare state is often referred to as the Keynesian welfare state. The British commitment to full employment and stabilization was contained in the White Paper on Employment Policy of 1944 and the American commitment in the Employment Act of 1946. The government would 'manage' the economy. Keynes's ideas offered a solution to capitalism's gravest ill: unemployment. The communist model, it seemed, at least offered full employment. Now, managed capitalism made socialism and public ownership unnecessary. Keynes admired much about socialism, notes Skidelsky, 'its passion for justice, the Fabian ideal of public service, and its utopianism,' but he 'emphatically rejected socialism as an *economic* remedy for the ills of capitalism.'[23]

We must be careful to remember, however, that the crucial commitment under the new social contract of the welfare state was not Keynesian policy per se, but that governments had some responsibility to pursue employment for all. This commitment arose from the belief that the foundation for the welfare of citizens – for their personal dignity, personal security, and indeed, even personal freedom – was to have a job. Citizens would not allow governments to leave employment levels entirely to the operation of the private market. Unemployment might be addressed through Keynesian policies, or it might be addressed with other policies, the substantive point was a government commitment to address the problem. The government should also be concerned with economic growth, because only with growth could there be jobs for the growing population.

Keynes's ideas were taken up, clarified, and formalized by other professors. Academic papers flowed, classical economists responded, mathematical models were set down and put to the test of data, the test in Keynes's phrase of the 'facts from experience.' The scientific method was applied. Around the world, professors and graduate students read the papers. Alvin Hansen, the Lucius N. Littauer Professor at Harvard University, published *A Guide to Keynes* in 1953, 'to assist, and induce, the student to read *The General Theory*.' University research and the transmission of these ideas through the international scholarly community changed our understanding of the economy and the role of government. What happened in a Cambridge seminar room changed seminars in the United States and Canada; and eventually changed government policy in London, Washington, and Ottawa. In 1972, President Richard Nixon declared: 'We are all Keynesians now.'[24]

Keynes, the Cambridge professor, was also Keynes the public intellectual and Keynes the government adviser. He wrote regularly in the *Times*, edited twelve supplements in the *Guardian* criticizing the international financial arrangements that followed the First World War, and published widely read pamphlets on economic policy. So often was his advice sought that he became as influential as any Whitehall civil servant.

Keynes's theories provided the analytical foundation of national income accounting and the rationale for the collection of national data on consumption, investment, prices, and unemployment. Economic forecasting and the analysis of fiscal and monetary policy became the work not only of politicians and civil servants, but also of bankers, manufacturers, home builders, and of political parties, newspapers, and voters. Daniel Bell's postindustrial society 'lives by innovation and the social control of change, and tries to anticipate the future in order to plan ahead.'[25] Bell cites economic forecasting as a major example. The universities provided both the ideas for the social control of change and the practitioners to carry it out.

Keynes's credo, that social concern and intelligence could make the world a better place, was shared by all the intellectual founders of the welfare state, most particularly by William Beveridge, author of the blueprint for Britain's postwar welfare state: *Social Insurance and Allied Services: Report by Sir William Beveridge*, published in 1942. 'The report was designed, Beveridge asserted, not merely to abolish physical want, but to give a new sense of purpose to democracy, to promote national solidarity and to define the goals of the war.'[26] The Beveridge Report established a framework of comprehensive government programs for progress against what he called 'the five giants on the road to reconstruction – Want, Ignorance, Squalor, Idleness, and Disease.'[27]

Beveridge, like Keynes, had a privileged late-Victorian upbringing. He was born in India, son of a high-ranking civil servant, and returned to England for his education, reading mathematics and literature while completing 'Greats' at Balliol College, Oxford. Beveridge graduated with no career in mind, but a growing desire to be involved in social reform. He worked at a university settlement house[28] in East London for a time, then as an editorialist and later as a civil servant at Westminster directing rationing and price controls during the First World War. In 1918, Beveridge was named director of the London School of Economics and Political Science, a position he held for eighteen years.

Between the first and second wars, social assistance programs, both from the government and voluntary sectors, had grown haphazardly: with overlap, inconsistency, and inequities between programs and regions. Several major studies of poverty, notably Seebohm Rowntree's 1941 report, *Poverty and Progress*, established the reality of widespread poverty and that its causes were not fecklessness or indolence, but unemployment and old age. The Beveridge Report built upon a growing public commitment to comprehensive social reform and upon public recognition that voluntarism and piecemeal government programs were not enough. The Great Depression had proven their inadequacy beyond all doubt. 'The report set out the long series of proposals that Beveridge had devised over the previous twelve months – for a national health service, family allowances, full employment and a comprehensive system of social insurance designed to cover the whole community.'[29] Social insurance would cover accident, unemployment, and old age (pensions/social security). Beveridge was transformed 'overnight from a rather obscure and academic figure, best known as a broadcaster on "thought-raising subjects," into a much-feted national hero.'[30] The report sold over one hundred thousand copies and became the vision for life after the war.

The second great intellectual pillar of the welfare state was in place: government took responsibility for the provision of social services and social insurance. And again, the universities supplied both the ideas and the graduates to implement the ideas. Although neither had a Beveridge Report, Canada and the United States were moving in a similar direction, propelled first by the experience of the Great Depression and later by obligations to war veterans: 'If, as our Constitution tells us, our Federal Government was established among other things, "to provide for the general welfare," then it is our plain duty to provide for that security upon which welfare depends,' Franklin Delano Roosevelt declared in 1934.[31] Within the next five years, the U.S. Congress passed measures for unemployment insurance, social security for old age and disability insurance, and aid to dependent children. The American welfare state was established.[32]

During the early 1960s, social research in all three countries demonstrated that poverty and racism remained widespread and inequalities persisted, despite the postwar economic boom. Ramesh Mishra, in his comparative analysis of welfare states, concludes: 'If the decade following the war showed a seesawing of ideas around market and state welfare, the early 1960s saw the weight of argument shift in favour of the welfare state. It is against such a background that North America (both the United States and Canada) moved further towards developing state welfare provision. The paradox of "poverty in the midst of plenty," together with the political pressures generated through the civil rights protest and urban race riots, made it clear that a steady, annual increase in GNP was not by itself going to solve social problems.'[33] Americans declared a War on Poverty and envisioned a Great Society; Canada set its objective as a Just Society.

The accomplishments of science were well known. By the early 1960s, economics seemed to come of age as a science, able to manage the economy using Keynesian theories formalized into mathematical and quantitative models. Mishra observes: 'Other social disciplines, for example, sociology and psychology, it was believed, could emulate economics and in due course emerge as sciences, and generate well-tested theories which would enable social phenomena to be understood and controlled with scientific precision.'[34] A rational science of society, a social engineering, could bring the amelioration, even solution, of social problems. Harold Perkin, in *The Rise of Professional Society: England since 1880*, strongly connects the rise of professionals with the implementation of the postwar welfare state. Faith in the new social science was especially strong in the United States. The social sciences at universities grew spectacularly, fed by student demand, government research money, and the government's need to hire the graduates – all testament 'to the willingness of society to underwrite the development of social knowledge as well as the hopes pinned on it.'[35] The faith of Keynes and Beveridge in the ability of human thought and action to create a better world continued in the social sciences. This faith powerfully contributed to the growth and influence of the multiversity and to the government's willingness to support it.

The third pillar of the welfare state was an extension of the concept of citizenship. Sociologist Thomas H. Marshall, in his lectures 'Citizenship and Social Class' delivered at Cambridge in 1949, articulated the intellectual framework. Like Keynes and Beveridge, Marshall came from an upper-middle-class family. 'His father was a successful London architect, with a house in Bloomsbury and country retreats. By the time he was 19, Marshall's education had followed the familiar path from preparatory to boarding school (Rugby) to Cambridge, with a Foreign Service career as the predictable destination.'[36] Instead, strongly influenced by his time during the First World War in a German civilian internment camp, he turned to academic work on comparative social institutions and joined the LSE where he later held the Martin White Chair, England's premier professorship of sociology. Like the other intellectual founders of the welfare state, 'Marshall's views were strongly shaped by a critical reaction to Marx and Marxism. Marshall wanted to defend the claims of reformist socialism as contrasted to its bolder and violent cousin, revolutionary communism.'[37]

Marshall submits that citizenship has three elements: civil, political, and social. 'The civil element is composed of the rights necessary for individual freedom – liberty of the person, freedom of speech, thought and faith, the right to own property and to conclude valid contracts, and the right to justice.'[38] The institutions most associated with civil citizenship are the courts of law. Political citizenship, for Marshall, means 'the right to participate in the exercise of political power, as a member of the body invested with political authority or as an elector of the members of such a body. The corresponding institutions are parliament and councils of local government.'[39] Social citizenship means 'the whole range from the right to a modicum of economic welfare and security to the right to share to the full in the social heritage and to live the life of a civilized being according to the standards prevailing in the society. The institutions most closely connected with it are the educational system and the social services.'[40]

Civil citizenship was established during the eighteenth century with the emergence of the middle class. Political citizenship was established during the nineteenth and early twentieth centuries, accommodating the working class and extending the suffrage to all men, and belatedly, after much struggle, to all women. Social citizenship is the citizenship of the twentieth-century welfare state, the citizenship of postwar democracies. The benefits of the welfare state are due, not as charity, but to citizens. Social citizenship is inclusive, granting full membership for all.

Education becomes a core public commitment for social citizenship, because full membership requires equality of opportunity, which education can help to provide. Also, civil and political rights are designed for reasonable and intelligent persons, and therefore, education is a necessary prerequisite to civil and political freedom. Education is so necessary that primary and secondary education should be free – and compulsory. Universities, though not compulsory, would become increasingly important to social citizenship, until in postindustrial society, accessible university education has become a necessary component of social citizenship. It is the combination of the postindustrial society and the concept of social citizenship that led to mass university education.

Marshall speaks only briefly about universities, but his remarks are always clear-headed. He realizes that expanded higher education would mean universities must be closely linked with the economy and a student's future occupation; but not because the economy demanded that universities prepare skilled workers, rather because higher education linked to occupation is a move away from hereditary privilege, towards equality of opportunity and a means to social justice. And he foresaw an inescapable problem with the welfare state. The achievement of equality of opportunity brings a contradiction: equality of opportunity is 'the equal right to display and develop differences or inequalities.' 'Through education in its relations with occupational structure, citizenship operates as an instrument of social stratification.'[41] A welfare state must always seek a compromise between equalization and the right to legitimate differences. University education works both for and against an egalitarian outcome, a dilemma that is with us still.

There is a fourth, almost unrecognized, intellectual pillar of the welfare state. It had no particular spokesperson. This fourth pillar is related, not to government expenditures, but to taxation and how the government should raise money to pay for the welfare state. The fourth pillar is that most services should be financed by taxes rather than user fees and that taxation should be based upon ability to pay. There should be progressive taxation: the fraction of income paid in taxes should rise as income rises. The fourth pillar dictates that universities should be largely supported by government grants with low tuition fees (or even no fees, as in England for much of the postwar period).

That the fourth pillar should be so little recognized presages a weakness of the welfare state: the founders of the welfare state did not analyse, explicitly enough, the level of taxation needed to pay for the new government expenditures and who would pay these taxes. In the welfare state today, the fourth pillar – how high should taxes be and what the role of user fees should be – has become crucial to the future of multiversities.

The welfare state, constructed on these four pillars, is a new type of government. Despite differences in rhetoric and detail, there has been consensus across the Anglo-American world about the four pillars, and the countries implemented very similar welfare states. Political discourse in the United States has not provided the same legitimacy for the welfare state as in Britain or Canada. American discourse places greater weight on individualism and equality of opportunity, and less on collectivism and equal outcomes. But America has always lived with the cognitive dissonance between public ideology and democratic legislative reality. The rhetorical differences should not mask the fundamental similarities in government commitments and programs across the three countries. As noted above, the share of social expenditures in GDP did not differ that much between the countries in 1981. All three recognized the role of universities – through their teaching, research, and service to society – in realizing the promise of the democratic welfare state. All three dramatically expanded their university systems as part of the implementation of their welfare state.

Nonetheless, there are differences between welfare states in the Anglo-American world. In the United States, the range of programs is not as comprehensive, the benefit levels are sometimes lower, and there are gaps: most notably in health care, where a sizable minority of citizens has neither public insurance nor private insurance. It may seem a paradox, but in this least comprehensive welfare state, university education is best-supported. The United States has had the highest participation rates in university education and supported its universities more widely and deeply. It has also provided the highest level of support for research. Furthermore, it was in the United States that the multiversity first developed. The American welfare state always placed greater emphasis on equality of opportunity and economic growth and, therefore, has been very supportive of universities, while being less supportive of some other welfare state programs. Over the past twenty years, the English and Canadian welfare states have been shifting to a greater emphasis on higher education and in this respect moving closer to the American model.

The expanding welfare state of the decades after the Second World War could be sustained because of a remarkable economic context: unprecedented economic growth, combined with low unemployment and modest inflation. Economic prosperity seemed assured; an affluent society was arriving. Keynesian macroeconomic policies could stabilize the economy. Social policy and economic policy were regarded as mutually supportive, not in conflict; social policy was making the economy more productive and more just. Rapid economic growth coupled with a progressive tax system meant government revenues soared, reducing overt competition among claims on the public purse and obscuring the trade-offs in the welfare state. The age allowed improving public services *and* rising after-tax incomes. This age called forth the multiversity and allowed it to flourish.

Political Culture and Education

The analysis of this chapter, which connects the multiversity to the implementation of the welfare state, is an application of a tradition of analysis that connects political culture and education.

The term *political culture* has been used in many different ways. David Bell in an article titled 'Political Culture in Canada,' offers one definition: 'political culture consists of the ideas, assumptions, values, and beliefs that condition political action. It affects the way we use politics, the kinds of social problems we address, and the solutions we attempt. Political culture serves as a filter or lens through which political actors view the world ... .[It] is the language of political discourse, the vocabulary and grammar of political controversy and understanding.'[42]

All countries must decide upon and implement the relationship of state, market, civil society, individual, and family that best provides for the satisfaction of basic human needs.[43] Civil society is defined to comprise those institutions outside the market, the state, and the family; institutions such as universities, or churches, or other non-profit groups. For example, all countries must decide what should be provided by the public sector versus the private sector, and what should be the role of the institutions of civil society. What should be the responsibility of government and what should be the responsibility of the individual and her or his family? Countries must decide what sort of education system they want, just as they must decide what sort of health care system, or pension system, or income security system they want. The answers are shaped by the political culture of the particular country.

There is a deep and fundamental connection between educational institutions and democracies, a connection so close that the study of educational regimes can be a route to the study of democracy. This is the premise of Ronald Manzer's comparative study, *Educational Regimes and Anglo-American Democracies*. He writes about primary and secondary education, but with the move to mass university education in the postindustrial society, his work could apply equally to the study of universities: Schools 'are means by which people in a democratic polity collectively strive for civic virtue, economic wealth, social integration, and cultural survival ... Schools are expressions of the fundamental beliefs, attitudes, values, and principles that underlie Anglo-American democracy. In how they are governed and what they teach, schools express conceptions of human needs, make statements of moral principles, and convey visions of individual and collective development.' [44] In these sentences, we could replace 'schools' with 'universities.'

Most writing about education and democracy has focused on primary and secondary education. In this book, of course, the focus is on university education. I have chosen to examine the multiversities of the Anglo-American world because a similar institutional form has emerged in these countries and in the conviction that their multiversities emerged because of similar forces (and in the future will be similarly pressured by the ideas of our age). This decision to examine universities in the Anglo-American world is further supported by the fact that the Anglo-American world shares much beyond a common language: England, the United States, and Canada broadly share the same liberal democratic political culture. It seems highly likely that their educational institutions would evolve in similar ways.

When political scientists compare forms of democracy in all the nations of the world, they identify a particularly Anglo-American form. They identify a common political tradition, a common liberal pluralist culture, in Australia, Canada, New Zealand, the United Kingdom, and the United States. Neil Nevitte and Roger Gibbins, for example, in their book on Anglo-American democracies write: 'Perhaps no other five countries in the industrialized world are more alike; they share not only roughly comparable economies, social structures, and cultural environments, but also the same political tradition.'[45] The Anglo-American multiversities of this book exist in similar liberal pluralist political cultures.

The welfare state developed at different rates and with different specifics in western liberal democracies, but certain countries have developed in similar ways. When scholars make comparisons of welfare states across the world, they identify a particularly Anglo-American welfare state. Gosta Esping-Andersen, in *The Three Worlds of Welfare Capitalism*, identified three types of welfare regime: a liberal regime, associated with the Anglo-American states; a social democratic regime, associated with the Nordic states; and a conservative regime, associated with the countries of continental Europe, especially France and Germany.[46] The Anglo-American multiversities of this book exist in similar welfare states.

The Multiversity's Democratic Roles

At the beginning of the twentieth century, the structures of liberal democracy were far from complete in England, Canada, and the United States, but by mid-century, this was no longer the case. All citizens enjoyed freedom of speech, thought, and faith, and were equal before the law. All citizens could vote and hold public office. There was still a great struggle to overcome the barriers of social class and family background, race, and gender. Much remains to be done, but the principles were established. To use Marshall's terminology, people enjoyed civil and political citizenship and, finally, during the second half of the twentieth century, the meaning of citizenship was extended to include social citizenship.

With the two great transformations of the postwar period – the coming of postindustrial society and the implementation of the welfare state – the multiversity moved to the centre of society. Multiversities are many and large. They are open to all. They are sprawling conglomerates providing undergraduate liberal education, professional education, and graduate education. They have become the centre of society's research enterprise. The multiversity is now a powerful institution whose teaching and research exert enormous influence on both individual and national well-being.

As we examine the emergence of the multiversity and, at the same time, examine the evolution of liberal democracies in the postwar period, we can begin to see how the multiversity has many roles in a democracy. Each component of the bundle that is the multiversity – undergraduate liberal education, the professional schools, graduate education, and research – has a crucial role in the liberal democracy of postindustrial society.

The multiversity's primary democratic responsibility is that all of its education – undergraduate, professional, and graduate – must be accessible. The multiversities collectively must be open to all who are capable and willing to undertake university study. In our postindustrial economy, higher education is crucial for one's job and career. In our liberal democracy, social citizenship requires equality of opportunity. Together, they require accessible university education.

We want the students at the multiversity to be representative of the entire society; and we measure this accessibility in various ways. The most basic measure of accessibility is the participation rate: the percentage of the eligible age cohort that attends university. A more accessible university system will offer education to a higher percentage of the eligible age cohort. As the welfare state was implemented, we moved from elite to mass university education. Accessibility is also measured by the family background of students. It is expensive to attend university – for tuition, books, living expenses, and foregone income from not working – but equality of opportunity requires that family or personal income not be a barrier to participation. As participation rates have risen, the percentage of students of all income backgrounds attending university has risen, but it still remains that students from higher income backgrounds are more likely to attend university. Accessibility is also measured by whether men and women are equally likely to attend university. Accessibility is further measured by whether visible minorities, persons with disabilities, and Aboriginal peoples attend. Some countries or regions have a commitment to providing education in several languages. For example, several provinces in Canada have a commitment to ensure that university study is available in both French and English. Accessibility is also connected to whether there are opportunities for adults, for part-time study, and for distance education.

In a democracy, each multiversity and the entire system of universities must be accountable for their contributions to accessibility. This does not mean a retreat from high academic standards. Indeed, the commitment to high standards becomes even more important. We might recall Matthew Arnold's observation: 'The difficulty of democracy is how to find and keep high ideals.' We need not agree with

Arnold's solution to this difficulty, but we should acknowledge its truth. Universities in liberal democracies must remain committed to the pursuit of knowledge and to assessment: to distinguishing deep understanding from shallow understanding, to distinguishing significant contributions to knowledge from modest contributions, to distinguishing profound reflections from superficial. Accessibility means that all should have the opportunity to participate in this pursuit.

The multiversity's second democratic responsibility concerns its primary task: undergraduate education. Undergraduate education has always been, in part, a liberal education and liberal education has always included education for citizenship. Multiversities have a responsibility to prepare undergraduate students for citizenship in today's democracy.

Undergraduate education in a democracy raises the question of curriculum – what is to be studied? The curriculum question is especially controversial in the humanities. The university is the place where our culture is preserved, redefined, critiqued, and disseminated. Should all students study the humanities, and if so, are there books that all should read? Might the chosen curriculum be a barrier to full inclusion of all members of society? The multiversity in a democratic society has a special obligation to reflect on these questions. This does not require a retreat from standards, from a desire to study 'the best that has been thought and said.' It does, however, require that the content of the curriculum be open to sustained critical analysis in light of the university's democratic role.

The professional schools also have democratic roles. They are the gateways to the professions and, therefore, like all forms of university education, must work to see that their student bodies are representative of the entire society. But their democratic role goes further. Democratic governments have allowed the professions to be self-regulating; this carries a reciprocal obligation that professionals be attentive to their clients' interests and to the public good. The multiversity shares the responsibility to educate professionals for this attentiveness, on behalf of our democracy.

Finally, the multiversity as a research institution, financed by our democratic governments, is crucial in the dynamic of generating new ideas that so influence our society. Multiversities are powerful institutions, and their research is immensely influential. In a knowledge-based society, knowledge is power, and this means that multiversities are part of the power structure. The multiversities have a democratic obligation to ask what questions are being studied, why these questions are chosen, and to assess the impact of the new knowledge.

In our knowledge-based society, political choices require assessment of complicated issues. Sometimes, the assessment requires scientific knowledge: for example, what are the environmental risks of automobile pollution and what technology might reduce that pollution? At other times, the assessment can involve social science: for example, how will new information technologies influence the practice of democratic politics? The assessment can also involve knowledge of the humanities: for example, the history of Islam can help us to evaluate proposals for peace in the Middle East. The professors of the multiversity can contribute this scientific, social scientific, and humanistic knowledge to democratic political deliberation. They have an obligation to be public intellectuals and social critics.

None of these democratic roles is really new. They are inherent in the nature of the modern university. However, they have been treated as indirect implications of the multiversity's mission of teaching, research, and service to society, and they have not been brought together to demonstrate how all of the multiversity's tasks involve a responsibility to democracy. The time has come to make such democratic roles explicit: the multiversity's responsibility to democracy should be an explicit part of its mission and the multiversity should be accountable for its achievement. Part Two of this book asks what lies ahead, asks what is the character of our age, and explores issues challenging multiversities over the next decade. Under pressure from the character of our age, the multiversity is suffering mission drift. I believe that giving the multiversity an explicit mission to contribute to democratic life will help to stop its drift away from core ideals. This argument is the focus of Part Three of this book, which discusses renewal of the social contract between the multiversity and the society that supports it.

Before finally proceeding to Part Two, there is one further task: to explore more closely the social contract between the multiversity and society and, in particular, the role of institutional autonomy, academic freedom, and collegial self-governance.

5 A Social Contract: Tasks, Autonomy, and Academic Freedom

To fully comprehend the multiversity, we must understand its relationship to the society that supports it. The multiversity has emerged as a vital institution of postindustrial democracies, taking on many tasks for society. The public, through its governments and through tuition fees, provides huge sums of money to the multiversity and demands accountability about how those sums are spent.

How, then, should multiversities be governed, to best fulfil these public purposes and to ensure their accountability? Should multiversities be under the direct control of governments? Should their professors be supervised as civil servants? The answer has always been unequivocal – no. Instead, it has been concluded that to best fulfil its responsibilities to society, the multiversity must be an autonomous institution. Also, professors must have academic freedom in their work. To protect this institutional autonomy and academic freedom, universities should operate under a system of collegial self-governance. So essential is this institutional arrangement that the very definition of what constitutes a university includes both a specification of its tasks and of its governance.

The previous chapters have explored the tasks of the multiversity: undergraduate liberal education, professional education, graduate education, and research both basic and applied. To this list of tasks that define a multiversity, there should be added another necessary characteristic: a multiversity is an autonomous institution, whose professors and students have academic freedom, and which operates on academic matters with a system of collegial self-governance.

The justification for university autonomy and academic freedom is that this form of governance is necessary if the university is to fulfil the responsibilities given to it by society. The multiversity's independence, the principles of academic freedom, and the right to self-government are set out in the statutes that create the university. However, ultimately, the public and their government must decide, in each era, how much they want to control multiversities. Eric Ashby, in his overview of university governance, concludes 'that academic freedom and university autonomy are more effectively protected by unwritten conventions than by charters and statutes ... They both in the last resort depend on public opinion which understands what universities are for and is prepared to respect them.'[1]

Inevitably, however, there is a conflict between public funding and institutional autonomy. This is always a fundamental tension between the multiversity and the democratic society that supports it.[2] Every age must tend and renew the relationship between the university and society. Every age brings special tensions in the relationship. Ours is no different. Informed reflection and a vigorous civic conversation are required as our age renews its commitments to the multiversity.

A Social Contract

The relationship between the multiversity and the society that supports it can be spoken of in various ways. Clearly, the nature of this relationship has changed through history and this nature is fundamentally different today because of the public funding of multiversities and their research and because of the power and centrality of the multiversity in our society. Often today we say that multiversities must be accountable to the government and the general public. Or, multiversities must be responsive to their various stakeholders and constituencies. It is an elusive and multifaceted relationship. I believe that a useful and powerful metaphor to describe the relationship, and the most appropriate way to describe the relationship, is that there is a social contract between the multiversity and liberal democratic society.[3] Borrowed from political theory, the metaphor of a social contract emphasizes the democratic role of the multiversity, recognizing that the multiversity helps to meet the needs and aspirations of democratic societies and that it is ultimately accountable to its citizens.

The relationship is like a contract – setting out the responsibilities of the multiversity, the financial support to be given to the multiversity, and granting the multiversity autonomy and freedom in fulfilling these responsibilities. But it is not a written formal contract, specifying deliverables in return for money. It is more fluid and open, in part because the deliverables cannot be specified in advance.

The concept of a social contract embodies more than an unwritten arrangement between parties. In political philosophy, social contract theory is used to conceptualize the founding of democratic societies. It asserts that political structures and the legitimacy of democratic governments are derived from an implicit agreement, a social contract, under which individuals surrender certain of their rights and agree to obey the laws in return for the protection and stability of an effective government. The *social contract* is the basis of political legitimacy and of political obedience in a democratic society. This was how the term was used in chapter 4 in dealing with the welfare state: the welfare state constituted a new social contract between citizens and their government.

To say that multiversities and government (and thus also the public) are in a social contract is not a precise use of the political philosophical concept, but it is an illuminating metaphor. Ultimate authority to create universities, to sanction their degrees, and to determine how much money to give to universities, rests with the government (and the public). The government has assigned certain tasks to the multiversity and provides it with (relatively) stable long-term support. To better fulfil these tasks, the multiversity is granted autonomy from government and its professors have academic freedom. The multiversity and professors agree to fulfil these tasks with disinterest and integrity. But the ultimate legitimacy of the multiversity – for its many tasks and its privileged standing – comes from the people in a democratic society.

The social contract is formulated over time and shaped by history. A government of the day, backed by public opinion of the moment, does have authority to change universities; but the history of autonomy and the history of the social contract dictate that the essence of universities, the idea of a university, not be changed. Like a written constitution, a social contract establishes basic principles and is above easy or abrupt change. But like constitutions and constitutional practice, there must be responsiveness through time. Continuous reflection and dialogue are required between the multiversity and society, as each era renews the social contract according to its needs.

In a recent paper, 'The Limits of Academic Freedom,' Louis Menand writes: 'freedoms are socially engineered spaces in which parties engaged in specific pursuits enjoy protection from parties who would otherwise naturally seek to interfere in those pursuits. One person's freedom is therefore always another person's restriction ... Since freedoms are socially constructed and socially maintained, their borders are constantly patrolled on both sides. Those on the inside are vigilant about external threats of interference; those whose interests naturally impel them toward intervention are keen to find some means of influencing behavior inside the protected space.'[4]

There have been recent border skirmishes, even border wars, between those on the inside and those on the outside of the multiversity. Some observers within the multiversity describe the recent past as consisting of devastating invasions and claim that the social contract has been abrogated. The war between the British government and British universities in the late 1980s and early 1990s, following what the universities regarded as an attack crippling their autonomy, led Conrad Russell in his 1993 book, *Academic Freedom*, to conclude: 'Perhaps never since the Parliamentary visitors entered Oxford in 1647 to enforce the rule of the victors in the English Civil War, have we had a regime so alienated from its Universities.'[5] In the United States, the Council for Aid to Education titled its 1996 report: *Breaking the Social Contract: The Fiscal Crisis in Higher Education*.[6] Multiversities everywhere feel themselves under siege and lament the lack of public support and understanding.

Many observers foresee devastating violations of the social contract in the years ahead – overt violations by government and by corporate donors, or covert violations as a utilitarian ethos, antithetical to the social purposes of the university, nonetheless prevails. There is no question that governments are asking for greater accountability from universities and in many instances are taking more explicit control. In some cases, governments have created performance indicators and tied financial support to these measures of performance. Unfortunately, the performance indicators measure only a minor part of the multiversity's activities and have focused on assessing the economic contribution of universities. Not everyone sees the same threatening future, but there is no doubt the social contract is under great stress.

The social contract is not well understood. Neither party seems to understand the other. Certainly, universities feel misunderstood and that their autonomy is under threat. But universities enjoy more deference and independence than they are prepared to admit. The civic conversation to renew the social contract will require more critical self-reflection by multiversities and their professors than has usually been exhibited. A recent examination of Canadian universities concluded:

'debate about Canadian universities is episodic, seldom probing or philosophical. Its terms are increasingly dominated by universities themselves, which skillfully argue their case ... As a result, university priorities are seldom challenged or even debated. Universities, more so than any other powerful Canadian institution, sail on seas of unwarranted deference.'[7] Such countervailing candor is needed.

In this climate of misunderstanding, there is an obligation on all parties to articulate, explore, and affirm the social contract. There is a special obligation on the part of the leadership of the multiversity to engage in continuous dialogue with the society that supports the multiversity – articulating, explaining, and defending the ideals of the university – and also listening and responding to the concerns of the society.

The very first universities were autonomous institutions; and ever since, the nature of this autonomy has been refined and reinterpreted in each age and in each case where autonomy was contested. The idea of academic freedom for professors has likewise evolved, but its origins are more recent; academic freedom is really a twentieth century idea. Thus, the interconnected story of university autonomy and academic freedom begins with university autonomy.

University Autonomy

Those medieval universities most influential in the Anglo-American tradition were established as guilds of professors/masters, albeit under the patronage of either Church or state. Medieval guilds were associations organized for mutual aid and protection, most frequently of people in a similar trade. The guilds controlled who could enter the trade and the training/apprenticeship needed for entry. Universities negotiated considerable autonomy for themselves, as guildlike corporations controlling the process of apprenticeships. The guild of professors had authority to determine who would enter the university, what they would study, and who would be certified, and therefore, who could become a professor. Guilds also were self-governing, holding their own assemblies, making their own rules, and electing their own heads; and professorial guilds did likewise. The colleges of Oxford and Cambridge were self-governing foundations, independent of both church and state. Our current ideas of autonomy and collegial self-governance in multiversities are as old as the university.

The ideal of university autonomy established in the medieval university has prevailed even into today. Through much of its history, the university struggled to ensure independence from the church; in the nineteenth and twentieth centuries, the struggle was against the influence of government and of business. Autonomy did not necessarily imply withdrawal from society, although autonomy is certainly easier to achieve in an ivory tower. Wilhelm von Humboldt understood that the research and teaching of the University of Berlin were very much in service of the state – there could be no withdrawal – but he argued successfully that these state purposes could best be served by autonomous universities.

Today's multiversity is no ivory tower, and the meaning of its autonomy must be negotiated amid its many social tasks and external connections. As these responsibilities to society and external connections have multiplied, so the complexity of the social contract has increased, and the difficulty of retaining appropriate autonomy increases. Most fundamentally, the multiversity exists because of government financial support – the threat to autonomy arises because of the power of the purse. This cannot be dismissed lightly, because as Russell notes, 'the principle that public money ought to be accounted for is at the heart of democratic principles. Taxes are voted by consent, and that consent must rest on some understanding about how they are to be used.' 'Neither academics nor indeed anyone else has a natural right to receive public money.'[8]

Under our current understanding of autonomy, an autonomous university can determine the standards for entry, the curriculum of study, the assessment of students, and who is awarded a degree. The university is responsible for academic standards, and the government cannot be allowed to interfere with these standards. An autonomous university can determine which professors it will hire, which it will grant tenure, and which it will promote. The autonomous university has the obligation to protect the academic freedom of professors in research and teaching and to ensure the highest ethical and professional standards in research and teaching. Also, although in this aspect there is less similarity and consensus across nations, the autonomous university should be free to allocate as it sees fit the resources assigned to it through government grants and student tuition fees. For example, the university should be free to make the choice between spending money on professors' salaries versus student assistance, between which departments to support, or between computing and libraries. Finally, the university must permit public scrutiny of its affairs, be transparent in how choices are made to achieve its academic mission, and be accountable to government and to the public about how public funds have been spent. Of course, the autonomous university is subject to the laws of the land, and its professors, staff, and students have all the rights and responsibilities of other citizens.

This autonomy is circumscribed, however, as it must be for such an institution, fulfilling so many social purposes, and receiving so much financial support from the government and the public. The government has responsibility for broad policy direction in higher education: determining the amount of public funds to be allocated to multiversities and research granting councils; setting tuition fees or establishing the discretion allowed universities in setting fees; and determining the allocation of public funds for student assistance, and whether the funds will be dispersed as grants or loans, and how the loans will be repaid. However, as these broad policy directions become more specific, the terrain is contested. Most observers agree that the social contract allows governments to determine whether to open a new medical school or engineering faculty; but most observers would argue that the social contract would be violated if government policy were to cut back, say, the English department and expand the biology department. Broad policy direction is fine, micromanagement is not; the controversial question is where to draw the line. This controversy has become intense in our age, as government seeks to make multiversity research serve the economy directly (chapter 9).

The autonomy of the multiversity is an extraordinary privilege. It also brings an extraordinary responsibility. As the multiversity is buffeted by the ideas of our age, reforms will be needed as well as resistance to change. To serve democratic society, the multiversity must be both responsive and steadfast. The primary responsibility to manage this adaptation rests with the multiversity, its presidents, and its professors.

The autonomy granted universities as part of the social contract carries with it certain further obligations beyond ethical practice. The first of these is institutional neutrality. Derek Bok, former president of Harvard University, emphasizes this in his analysis, *Beyond the Ivory Tower: Social Responsibilities of the Modern University*: 'Universities insisted on the greatest possible freedom from outside interferences with their teaching, research and educational policies. But neither professors nor administrators could expect to receive such protection unless they were willing to have the university refrain from taking official stands.'⁹ This neutrality does not prevent the multiversities from trying to influence government policy regarding universities and research, but it does require that the university, *as an institution*, refrain from pressing for specific social or ideological goals. For example, the institution can lobby for more funds for universities, but not against a war in Iraq. Individual professors can oppose a war in Iraq, but not the institution.

To maintain its autonomy, the multiversity must make a commitment to dialogue – a continuing and public dialogue – about its tasks and the role of the multiversity in society. The social contract implies an obligation on the multiversity and its leadership to reflect upon these tasks, to think and to write about them publicly, to articulate their value in society; to defend them when they are threatened, but also to reconsider them in light of criticism and evolving social needs. The multiversity must lead the civic conversation, as we renew the social contract in our age. It must constantly search for new ways to converse and interact with society. The revolution in information technology (discussed in chapter 7) offers many new opportunities, if we have the vision and commitment to pursue them. Within the social contract the multiversity must be accountable – a term that carries two meanings. The multiversity is accountable in the sense that if it does not fulfil its responsibilities, sanctions can be imposed, most likely the withdrawal of resources. But the multiversity must be accountable in the sense that it must give an account – it must report clearly and fully to society of its activities, how decisions are reached, how resources are deployed, and how outcomes are assessed.

The final obligation, perhaps the deepest obligation, of the autonomous multiversity is to ensure the academic freedom of its own professors.

Academic Freedom

Free inquiry is the raison d'être of the modern multiversity. It is integral to all the responsibilities of the multiversity. Free inquiry is the essence of the liberal-free tradition of liberal education. The theory of knowledge inherent in the research mission assumes free inquiry: knowledge is best advanced when professors are free in their pursuits and when knowledge is subjected to tests based in free inquiry. Free inquiry encourages a diversity of opinions and allows the multiversity to fulfil its democratic functions of social criticism and preparing future citizens. Free inquiry values knowledge for its own sake, escaping the distortions that can arise when there is concern with how the knowledge will be applied or with who paid for the inquiry.

The Academic Freedom amendment to the Education Bill of 1988 in England claimed for professors 'the freedom within the law to question and test received wisdom, and to put forward new ideas and controversial or unpopular opinions without placing themselves in jeopardy of losing their jobs or privileges they may have at their institutions.'[10] All multiversities today would make a similar claim for their professors. The rectors of eighteen European universities declared at Bologna in 1988: 'The university is an autonomous institution at the heart of societies ... To meet the needs of the world around it, its research and teaching must be morally and intellectually independent of all political authority and intellectually independent of all political authority and economic power.'[11] Yet although the principle of academic freedom is universally accepted, in the multiversity today, professors are expressing deep concern about the threats to academic freedom. Every age brings new challenges to academic freedom.

Of fundamental consequence for the development of the idea of academic freedom, especially because of the ecclesiastic connections of universities, were religious tolerance and religious liberty. Later, the political and philosophical thought of the Enlightenment, which challenged the church and the monarchy, and the methodology of science, which married scepticism, free inquiry and empirical verification, were also crucial in the history of academic freedom. It is no mere coincidence that these same forces of religious tolerance, the Enlightenment, and the Scientific Revolution nurtured the modern university.

The formalized origins of academic freedom are to be found in the United States in the late nineteenth and early twentieth centuries. There, a series of developments within the universities culminated in the foundation of the Association of American University Professors (AAUP) in 1915 and the 'Declaration of Principles' issued by its committee on academic freedom and tenure: 'The purpose of this statement is to promote public understanding and support of academic freedom and tenure and agreement upon procedures to assure them in colleges and universities. Institutions of higher education are conducted for the common good and not to further the interest of either the individual teacher or the institution as a whole. The common good depends upon the free search for truth and its free expression.'[12] In other English-speaking countries like England and Canada, the discussion of academic freedom was not so explicit and the provisions for academic freedom not so formally codified as in the United States.[13] Nonetheless, the same forces shaped academic freedom; academic freedom is similarly crucial to their multiversities; and today, the same forces threaten academic freedom.

The developments most influential in shaping the idea of academic freedom in the United States were the attenuation of religious authority in science precipitated by the acceptance of Darwin's ideas of evolution; the adoption of the German ideals of research and *lehrfreiheit*; and the firing of professors because of their public criticism of laissez-faire capitalism.[14]

Charles Darwin's *On the Origin of Species by Means of Natural Selection* was published in 1869. The revolutionary import of his ideas – that species were not fixed in form but rather evolved by a process of natural selection, and that the theory applied to man as it did to all other animals – was apparent immediately. Yet the reverberations are still rumbling through our consciousness. The initial scepticism of American scientists to Darwin's ideas was overcome quickly by numerous independent empirical confirmations. But even as the science was confirmed, opposition grew. Some professors of Darwinian persuasion were not hired, others were not renewed, and some were fired. Certain academic texts were proscribed. The narrative conveys a tale of science versus religion, theory and evidence versus scriptural revelation and faith, and offers the lesson that free scientific inquiry must be protected against the dogma of religion.

Walter Metzger, in the second essay in *The Development of Academic Freedom in the United States*, draws further lessons. The fight against Darwinism was in part religious belief against science, in part ignorance against evidence. But 'at the core of the religious resistance, making it hard and bitter and giving it desperate strength, was not so much ignorance as fear. "Nothing is more evident," wrote the Andover theologian William J. Tucker, "than that a certain sense of fear ... has begun to seize the heart of our generation. We are literally afraid of the world in which we live." The fact was that while Darwin laboured to make the natural world intelligible and pellucid, to many of the men of his generation he had rendered that world cold and repellant, and they fought to keep it safe from his negations.'[15] The sense of fear – that science, even as it attempts to understand the world, brings danger – is with us still, perhaps more haunting, as we struggle with the implications of new genetic technologies. Fear can restrict academic freedom just as much as faith can. Today, people are often afraid – afraid of genetic technologies, afraid of global terrorism, afraid of feminist ideas. These fears bring pressures on academic freedom.

This attenuation of religious authority in science answers two questions at the heart of academic freedom: who is competent to judge the work of professors and what shall be the criteria for judgment? The now-legendary riposte of Thomas Huxley in a debate with Bishop Wilberforce over Darwinism in 1860 gives the answer. Bishop Wilberforce had inquired: 'Is it on his grandfather's or his grandmother's side that the ape ancestry comes in?' Huxley replied: 'If there were an ancestor whom I could feel shame in recalling, it would be a man ... who, not content with success in his own sphere of activity, plunges into scientific questions with which he has no real acquaintance.'[16] If there were to be academic freedom, the clergy could not judge the work of scientists, and by analogy, nor could trustees of the university nor, indeed, even the president or the dean. A professor's work must be judged by peers and by the criteria of science. 'The evolutionists' formula did not level every opinion to equal value. It held that every claim to a discovery of truth must submit to open verification; that the process of verification must follow certain rules; that this procedure is best understood by those who qualify as experts. Hence, academic freedom does not theoretically justify all kinds of intellectual nonconformity, but only that kind of nonconformity that proceeds according to rules; not any private belief, but that kind of private belief that allows itself to be publicly tested.'[17]

This 'freedom' to be judged by one's peers complements the research ideal, institutionalized in the organization of the university as disciplinary departments. Departments have fundamental authority over who to hire, who to grant tenure, and who to promote. As part of their deliberations about hiring and promoting, the professor's work is submitted to external peers for review and assessment. This academic freedom makes professors like a profession (for example, doctors and lawyers) in their right to self-regulation; a point not lost on the founders of the AAUP, who sought to achieve for professors the independence, dignity, and prestige of the professions.

This freedom carries the obligation to conduct research in an ethical and professional manner and to submit results to the review of peers. An important heritage of the Darwinian controversy is that the 'rationale of academic freedom has been endowed with certain fundamental values, values not original to science, but implicit in scientific assumptions and inherent in scientific activity. Such values as tolerance and honesty, publicity and testifiability, individuality and cooperativeness have all been part of the scientific bequest.'[18] The obligation of science to reliably assess the work implies that who you are – your gender, class, religion, nation, caste, or sexual orientation – have no place in the judgment. There is also a commitment to neutrality and disinterestedness. From this scientific tradition, Metzger concludes, 'academic freedom has come to stand for the belief that science must transcend ideology, that professors must renounce all commitments that corrupt the passion for truth.'[19] Our age brings a new challenge to this requirement for academic freedom. Governments ask that multiversities commercialize their research findings (chapter 9). Many professors now become investors in the companies that implement their ideas. No longer do professors renounce all commitments that might corrupt their passion for truth.

The German idea of *lehrfreiheit* was influential in conceptualizing academic freedom in the United States. Many American academics in the middle to late nineteenth century had been trained in or had visited German universities. They returned with the idea of a 'true' university as a research institution, and vigorously set about establishing graduate schools and adding research to the mission of their universities. The research mission implied not just graduate education and libraries and laboratories but an ethos as well. The research at universities was to be pure research; it sought knowledge for its own sake, it was disinterested, indifferent to career or application. Its pursuit was a high calling, an almost spiritual quest. Although German universities were government institutions and the professors were civil servants, the universities enjoyed considerable autonomy. There was no board of governors or senior administration interposed between the professors and the government. The faculty (the professors) ran their own affairs, electing a rector regularly from within their own number. Professors searching after knowledge enjoyed *lehrfreiheit*. Unencumbered by bureaucracy and controlling their domain, *lehrfreiheit* meant that 'the university professor was free to examine bodies of evidence and to report his findings in lectures or published form – that he enjoyed freedom of teaching and freedom of inquiry.'[20] This freedom, an academic freedom, was the special prerogative of professors as searchers after truth, and it defined the true university.

Research at American universities was both theoretical and applied, especially after the establishment of the land grant universities.

Research and expertise were needed in agriculture, engineering, management, and the social sciences to provide 'the better ways of doing' that American progress relied upon. The search for knowledge could be progressive and pragmatic – to serve the needs of a dynamic urbanizing industrializing society. The German professor would be theoretical and withdrawn; the American professor could be pragmatic and engaged. This gave a particular American twist to one rationale for academic freedom. Professors would be asked to give advice regarding the complex problems of government and business – the best advice would come from those whose conclusions and recommendations were the product of disinterested, free inquiry, from those with academic freedom. One might wonder whether today's professors, with investments in start-up companies or with large consulting practices, are sufficiently free of conflicts of interest.

The third decisive influence on the concept of academic freedom in America was the reaction to the power of 'big business' over universities, especially via donations and via membership on the board of governors. During the second half of the nineteenth century, American universities were transformed from small liberal arts colleges into large universities with graduate schools, faculties of engineering, agriculture, medicine, law, and so on. As the institution changed so did its board of governors: clergymen as the majority were replaced by businessmen and lawyers. The universities needed new expertise in finance and property, as well as new donations. Some of the gifts were enormous even by today's standards. For example, the estate of Leland Stanford provided U.S. $24 million to create Stanford University and the University of Chicago received U.S. $34 million from the founder of the Standard Oil Company.

In the late nineteenth and early twentieth centuries, business influence went much beyond shaping the direction of institutions through donations. A number of professors were dismissed, either directly by the board of governors or by the president at the board's instigation, for making comments critical of the social order and advocating reform. Many of those dismissed were economists who spoke against laissez-faire capitalism, condemning the excesses of monopolies, the huge income inequalities in America, and recommending that governments regulate monopolies and redress the inequalities. These were scarcely radical prescriptions from our perspective today, but enough to cause dismissal at the time. The dismissals attracted national media attention, the most high profile being the dismissal of Edward A. Ross, then secretary of the American Economic Association, by the president of Stanford University at the direct behest of Mrs Stanford, widow of the great benefactor. She wrote to the president saying that Professor Ross, through his statements, goes beyond the proper role of a professor, 'to associate himself with the demagogues of the city, exciting their evil passions, drawing distinctions between man and man, all laborers and equal in the sight of God, and literally plays into the hands of the lowest and vilest elements of socialism, it brings tears to my eyes. I must confess I am weary of Professor Ross, and I think he ought not to be retained at Stanford University.'[21] The president resisted, at first, but came to agree with Mrs Stanford.

These dismissals, the fierce resistance of big business to any reforms curbing laissez-faire capitalism, and the populist spirit of the age created a conviction that business was inimical to the university, most especially the university's ideal of academic freedom. The conviction was supported by another line of argument, most familiar from the acerbic, turn-of-the-century critic Thorstein Veblen. The university should be an institution of disinterested, free inquiry; a community of scholars that operates in an egalitarian fashion through collegial self-governance. Business firms are the antithesis of such institutions. Business-dominated boards of governors, actively if unwittingly supported by the president and other senior administrators, were imposing a business model on the university. Hierarchies and rules were being introduced, power centralized, administrators proliferating, with the emphasis on standardization, managerialism, and efficiency, reducing professors to the status of wage-employees. All of which, in subtle and myriad ways, was suppressing creative thought, encouraging conformity, and ultimately subverting academic freedom.[22] English universities have had a much longer and stronger tradition of collegial self-government than North American universities and only recently have shifted towards the more managerial model of North America. Veblen's critique has enormous relevance today in England, but still resonates in Canada and the United States as well.

The dismissal of professors who criticized laissez-faire capitalism and concerns over the influence of big business on the university reveal another strand of the tradition of academic freedom. This strand is connected not to research and a theory of how knowledge is best advanced, but rather to social criticism and free speech. It is related to political life in a democracy and to how democratic freedoms are best protected. Professors must be free to follow their curiosity and analysis where ever it may lead and to criticize established thought or authority – whether in government or in business. This view of academic freedom has been central to the British tradition, and therefore also important in Canada. It was significant even before the adoption of the research ideal. A.H. Halsey and M.A. Trow, discussing academic freedom in their volume, *The British Academics*, conclude: 'As regards freedom to follow and express political and social views in opposition to government or convention there has never been any serious question.'[23] This aspect of academic freedom is also important in the United States, but it has been largely based upon the right to free speech enjoyed by all citizens rather than a special right within universities.

At the beginning of the twentieth century, professors were being dismissed for espousing controversial ideas. Academic freedom had not yet been secured. A small group of leading American scholars gathered to consider how professors could be better protected and in 1915 founded the American Association of University Professors, with its famous 'Declaration of Principles.' Soon thereafter, the national association of university presidents, called the Association of American Colleges (AAC), and the AAUP began a collaboration to define academic freedom, establish procedures for its protection, and seek wider public support for the ideal and procedure. In 1940, the AAUP and the AAC issued a joint 'Statement of Principles on Academic Freedom and Tenure,' which now has been endorsed by virtually every governing board, presidential association, and faculty group in the United States.

So great is the consensus on these issues across the world today that the United Nations Educational, Scientific and Cultural Organization (UNESCO) adopted in 1997 a Recommendation Concerning the Status of Higher-Education Teaching Personnel, which is very similar to the Statement of Principles and now endorsed by most member states.

With such consensus, we like to think that the time is past when the board of governors or president of a multiversity would try to dismiss a faculty member for questioning received wisdom or for putting forward controversial ideas. Every president and board has endorsed the principle of academic freedom. But academic freedom can never be taken for granted; free enquiry cannot flourish without support. The years since 1940 are filled with attempts to restrict freedom; presidents, boards of governors, and professors have not always been stout defenders of the ideal. Each era brings forth its own attempts to limit academic freedom, and the attempts never go away.

The menace to academic freedom evolves, but people always want to suppress critical thought. An economist who argues that monopolies should be regulated is no longer threatening, but a feminist who argues that families are part of the patriarchal power relations of capitalism is threatening. Communist thought is no longer threatening, but the infamous Senator McCarthy and the House Un-American Activities Committee of the Cold War eerily reappears as Vice-President Cheney in the war on terrorism. The president of the United States declares, if you are not for us, you are against us.

There are other threats as well. The professor's right to control the content of the curriculum and to free speech within the classroom seemed secure and uncontroversial until the canon wars erupted and speech codes were adopted. Passionate critics decried 'political correctness' as the antithesis of free inquiry. Donors, both individual and corporate, are actively encouraged by the university to become engaged in the university's work and to choose which activities to support. Phrased less sympathetically, fundraising is a process by which we encourage donors to shape the direction of the multiversity. The increased reliance on external donations subtly encourages that most insidious limit on free inquiry: self-censorship. If you have worked hard to secure a corporate donation for your lab, have become involved with senior corporate executives through the solicitation of the donation, the planning of the lab, and stewardship of the donors afterwards, and have got to know them and respect them – are you not less likely to embark on a research program whose results could undermine the products of that company?

The principle of academic freedom is now accepted, but how do professors use this freedom? Within the university, the responsibilities of professors are summarized under the headings: teaching, research, and service. All professors must teach, usually at both the undergraduate and graduate levels. All professors must undertake research, submit it to their peers for review, and seek to have it published and so become available to the international scholarly community. All professors must provide service – both to the university itself and to the society outside. The balance among these three responsibilities will differ among professors and at different times in a professor's career. Moreover, all professors are not equally good at each of the three tasks. But, all have these three responsibilities.

Academic freedom brings these academic duties. Outsiders are first surprised, and then puzzled, by how little authority the senior administration has over professors. The traditions of collegial self-governance and academic freedom mean that professors have enormous latitude to manage their time and to select the tasks and topics that interest and animate them, with only modest responsibility to report their activities. They have no 'boss' to direct their activities save which classes they must teach. There is very little monitoring of their activities, although there are frequent complaints about inattention to undergraduate education, of too little time on campus, and of withdrawal from participation in university governance. University professors have fought for and secured academic freedom, but regrettably, they have not fulfilled the reciprocal responsibility to articulate academic duties and to instruct the next generation in these duties. There is an embarrassing lack of accountability for how a professor spends his or her time and lack of clarity around what are full-time responsibilities to one's university. Henry Rosovsky, a clear-eyed observer of university life, wrote in his 1991 report to the Harvard Faculty of Arts and Sciences that the faculty 'has become a society largely without rules, or to put it slightly differently, the tenured members of the faculty – frequently as individuals – make their own rules. Of course, there are a great many rules in any bureaucratic organization, but these largely concern less essential matters. When it concerns our more important obligations – faculty citizenship – neither rule nor custom is any longer compelling ... as a social organism, we operate without a written constitution and with very little common law. That is a very poor combination, especially when there is no strong consensus concerning duties or standards of behavior.'[24]

This lack of accountability and lack of clarity are a stain on the tradition of academic freedom and the rationale for tenure. But the public and their government, justifiably, are demanding greater clarity and accountability. After stepping down as president of Stanford University, Donald Kennedy wrote, in his book *Academic Duty*, that there has been an 'internal failure to come to grips with responsibility in the university. Having been given a generous dose of academic freedom, we haven't taken care of the other side of the bargain. The struggle about universities has little or nothing to do with Right and Left, or with cultural relativism, or with race relations, or with any of the particular matters which earn us media attention. It has to do with how we see our duty and how our patrons and clients see it. If we can clarify our perception of duty and gain public acceptance of it, we will have fulfilled an important obligation to the society that nurtures us.'[25]

Although primary fault must rest with the professors, senior administrators are not blameless. Henry Rosovsky observed that the first step towards discharging duties is to know what they are and 'that we often accomplish in unforgivably casual fashion. Most professors have little sense of social contract – after all, who or what will give them that sense?' They receive little from the administration beyond statements of the responsibility to do teaching, research, and service. 'Universities also show administrative lack of will, and that is a more damaging weakness. Faculty behavior (e.g., little teaching and frequent absences) has been rational and understandable, given the absence of constraints. For this, administrations should assume a major share of the blame because of a manifest unwillingness to set clear tasks and clear limits.'[26]

In renewing the social contract between the multiversity and society, the multiversities – their senior administration and their professors – have no task more important than to develop an explicit code of professorial responsibilities and conduct.

Collegial Self-Governance

The autonomy of the multiversity is embedded in a social contract; it is circumscribed and the external influences are many, but the autonomy is real. How, then, are multiversities to be governed to ensure their autonomy and to preserve academic freedom? How are they to make plans, to make decisions? Much has changed, especially for multiversities in the postwar era, since the time when professors could be said to run the university. Multiversities are huge complex conglomerates, sustained by government commitments to mass university education and to research. They have created a similarly complex structure for governance. However, despite considerable differences in detail, there has emerged a remarkable consensus across jurisdictions around certain fundamental structures of governance.

The university is established by a charter or statute of the government. Universities owe their legitimacy to an action of government; no new university, even one funded entirely privately, could be established to grant degrees without the approval of the government. This government charter gives the university the right to grant degrees and establishes the governance structure for the multiversity. In most cases, there is a two-tier structure. The upper tier is the board of governors (or board of trustees; in the United Kingdom also known variously as the council or court), and the other tier is the senate (or academic council or academic board). The board of governors has 'final responsibility' for the university and is charged to serve the best long-run interests of the institution. The board both interprets the needs of society to the university and represents the university to society. The board has special responsibility for finances and property and a duty to ensure the long-run fiscal soundness of the university.[27] The senate is responsible for all academic matters of the university, including admissions, curriculum, grading, and the awarding of degrees.

The board of governors is made up of representatives of society – mainly business persons and professionals, but also representatives of religious communities, of labour, non-profit groups, and the arts community. The board also includes representatives of the faculty, staff, students, and alumni of the university, but the university representatives are a small minority.

The senate is made up primarily of professors, but it also includes members of the university administration, also usually student representatives, and occasionally board members or staff. Each faculty within the university and each department within the faculty will also have its own academic council equivalent to the senate, dominated by professors, with responsibility for academic programs and policy in their domain. These councils derive their authority by delegation from the senate.

The board of governors may have de jure responsibility for the university; but the board chooses a president (vice-chancellor), after consultation with the senate, and then delegates most of its authority to him or her, who then has de facto responsibility for the university. Governors have full careers and lives of their own, and no special expertise in academic matters. The operations of the university are managed by the officers of the university, typically known as 'the university administration' or 'the senior administration,' headed by the president. The president selects his or her vice-presidents and the deans of the various faculties, after consultation with the academic council of the faculty.

Although only having authority by delegation, the president and senior administration are so influential that they should be identified as a third tier of university governance.[28] The reasons for their power are many. Although formally they only 'implement' and 'administer' the academic decisions of the senate and academic councils, in practice, they are responsible for the budget and have authority to allocate resources. They are full-time managers, whereas the faculty members on the senate devote only a small portion of their time to administration. The staff of the university report to the senior administration, in the manner of employees in business or government. These staff employees provide analytical support to the president and senior administration. All these reasons combine to provide the president (and by delegation, the vice-presidents and deans) with de facto authority and responsibility for management and leadership of the multiversity, albeit within a complex environment of shared governance.

Whatever the formal governance structure, and despite the significance of presidential power, the dominant ethos within all universities remains that faculty members should rule supreme on all academic matters – there should be collegial self-governance. This ethos is captured in the common, if somewhat nostalgic, image of the community of scholars. Professors are more akin to independent professionals or entrepreneurs than to employees. The president, as leader and manager, must continuously consult faculty opinion, and secure faculty support for his or her decisions. There is intense competition among multiversities for the best faculty, and this reinforces the role of faculty in multiversity governance, especially the influence of 'stars' in high-demand disciplines or disciplines selected as strategic priorities. Clark Kerr once spoke of the multiversity, saying he 'sometimes thought of it as a series of individual faculty entrepreneurs held together by a common grievance over parking'.[29]

Faculty supremacy and collegial self-governance are easiest to achieve at the department level within the multiversity. Within their own departments, professors do indeed control the requirements for the degree, what is taught in the courses, the assessment of students, who is hired, and who is given tenure. They prepare academic plans and determine the evolution of their discipline. Collegial self-governance is realized through department meetings and a committee structure – hiring committees, tenure committees, curriculum committees, and so on. Although professors complain fiercely about the time required by committees, they even more fiercely defend their autonomy. These departmental committee responsibilities integrate relatively easily into the rest of their work: their own background, teaching, and research have a natural application in the task at hand. Their authority is matched with responsibility to implement the decisions within their own department (although without budgetary authority). Most professors define themselves first as members of a discipline, and many professors care more about the 'quality of the department' than about the faculty or the whole university.

Collegial self-governance is very hard to achieve, and has little reality, at the university-wide level, despite the numerical dominance of professors in the academic council or senate. Multiversities are bewildering, complex, and diverse institutions; few professors understand the whole or have the experience and expertise to analyse the tasks at hand. Planning at this level requires a detailed knowledge of not only academic issues, but also the financial structure of the multiversity and the policies of governments and research-granting agencies. To acquire this knowledge means foregone attention to teaching and research. Often decisions must be made quickly, leaving little time for consultation with the senate. Most importantly, the senate has neither budgetary authority nor responsibility to ensure fiscal soundness. James Duderstadt, former president of the University of Michigan, provides an unusually candid assessment: 'the university-wide faculty governance bodies are generally advisory on most issues, without true power. Although they may be consulted on important university matters, they rarely have any executive role. Most key decisions are made by the university administration or governing board. The history of higher education in America suggests that, in reality, the faculty has had relatively little influence over the evolution of the university.'[30] The same is true in the multiversities of other countries. This creates a tension within the governance of the multiversity: the ethos of collegial self-governance clashes with the reality of governance by the senior administration.

This tension runs very deep. Presidents have not always defended academic freedom; on occasion, they have tried to suppress or release the 'troublesome' professor, in the 'long-run best-interests' of the institution. Academic freedom is inseparable from governance: academic freedom requires that professors participate in the governance of the multiversity.[31]

The dominance of the senior administration in governance means that the board, the president, and the senior administration have a special responsibility to maintain the social contract – they must take the lead in the continuous dialogue with society. In recent years, too much time has been spent managing, cheerleading, and fundraising, and not enough time nurturing the social contract. The administration must lead the dialogue about the meaning of liberal learning, about the value of free inquiry, and defend them against the misunderstandings and threats of our age. This senior leadership should be judged by how well it contributes to this dialogue, and not just by how well it manages, raises the multiversity's profile, and raises money.

A recent review of this leadership in England concludes that performance has been less than stellar: 'One striking characteristic of British higher education in the present era is its seeming passivity, despite the energy which universities today invest in political lobbying and public relations. The offices of vice-chancellors and managers of corporate communications are clogged with press statements and fliers proclaiming the achievements of their students in obtaining employment, how effective their institutions are in inculcating "enterprise skills" into their graduates, how successful in their co-operation with industry, how energetic in their contribution to the wealth-creating resources of the nation. Where one speaks of passivity, no suggestion is being made of a lack of energy or initiative. But there is a marked reluctance to articulate a motivating purpose, to address questions about the raison d'être of higher education.'[32] Similar laments can be heard in Canada and the United States.

The multiversity is home to many competing interests; it is little wonder that the governance is complex and cumbersome. The oft-repeated phrase – leading a university is like herding cats – rings true. The important question is not, is it messy, but rather, does it work? A fair observer would conclude that it has worked, at least up to now. The pace of change quickens, however, just as resources become more constrained. The core ideals of the multiversity are being threatened, and it will have to change its governance to cope. This diagnosis and conclusion is pervasive in the recent writings of university presidents, especially in the United States.

Donald Kennedy, president emeritus of Stanford University, wrote: 'Universities, like other organizations, must make choices, and now the choices are becoming more painful ... How, under such circumstances, can universities keep what matters most, and discard other things that matter less? And who decides what matters?' 'Major changes in direction will be required of the research universities, and sharp differences in quality and prestige will develop between the institutions that respond well and those that fail to make the turn.'[33]

One response to the pressure for change could be a more centralized administration; another could be a continued reliance on the present democratic, but stubbornly conservative, mode of decision-making.

But neither will succeed, Kennedy argues: 'Instead, the successes will be marked by a special kind of institutional leadership – one that forces administrations to form new alliances with faculties in order to achieve major shifts in direction, away from traditional academic norms.'[34]

James Duderstadt made 'the challenge of change' the overarching theme of his book, *A University for the 21st Century*. He concluded: 'it is simply unrealistic to expect that the governance mechanisms developed decades or even centuries ago can serve well either the contemporary university or our society more broadly. It seems clear that the university of the twenty-first century will require new models of governance and leadership capable of responding to the changing needs and emerging challenges of our society and its educational institutions.'[35]

I will not be able in this book to analyse this question of whether multiversities will require changes to their governance if they are to prosper in the years ahead, but it cannot be far from mind. As each characteristic of our age is analysed in Part Two, and the challenges to the multiversity it presents are discussed, the question of whether the multiversity is capable of responding cannot be far away. Part Three discusses the renewal of the social contract, and I will return there briefly to the question of leadership and multiversity governance.

Critic and Conscience

Thus far, my treatment of the social contract – tasks are given to the multiversities by society and public resources are provided, with the tasks to be conducted within a structure of institutional autonomy, academic freedom, and collegial self-governance – has followed the traditional literature. These special freedoms are required, it is argued, because they are required for the pursuit of knowledge: teaching and research are best done in a spirit of free inquiry. The fundamental rationale for institutional autonomy and academic freedom is that they are required for the pursuit of knowledge. It is recognized that academic freedom also allows social criticism without risk of losing one's job; but, social criticism is regarded as an indirect implication of academic freedom, not an explicit responsibility of the university to political life.

T.B. Bottomore, in his *Critics of Society: Radical Thought in North America*, explores the origins of social criticism: 'The real beginnings of social criticism as a major influence on human affairs are to be found in Western Europe and North America in the eighteenth century.'[36] He describes the influences that created the traditions of social criticism.

They are the same ones that created the modern university and the tradition of academic freedom: the development of religious freedom and tolerance, the rationalist spirit of the Enlightenment and its critiques of church and monarchy, and the Scientific Revolution with its empirical, experimental methods. Industrialization and urbanization brought massive economic, political, and social change. A new middle class, engaged in commerce and industry, sought greater power in the political process. Democratic movements demanded the extension of political rights. 'The growth of industry broke down old barriers and restrictions but at the same time created new problems: over-crowding, poverty, and unsanitary conditions in the rapidly growing towns, changes in the family through the employment of women and children in factories.' 'It is hardly surprising, therefore, that in the latter part of the eighteenth century there should have appeared movements of social protest and social criticism on a scale hitherto unimagined.'[37]

The pragmatic, socially engaged Scottish universities became centres of the new scientific analysis of society and its institutions. Adam Smith's *An Inquiry into the Nature and Causes of the Wealth of Nations* is the most famous example. By the nineteenth century, social criticism was firmly established as part of the civic conversation of Anglo-American societies. Sometimes the critics offered an overarching theory of society and social change, for example, Marx and Engels in *The Communist Manifesto* and hundreds of subsequent communist and socialist writers. Overarching critique was not always connected to an economic or political ideology – Matthew Arnold's *Culture and Anarchy*, though dealing with literature and culture, was subtitled: *An Essay in Political and Social Criticism*. Other critics eschewed broad theories to focus on a specific issue such as the state of prisons or the right of women to vote.

The nineteenth-century universities were not the sole, or even predominant, source of social theory and social criticism. More social criticism came from independent intellectuals, newspapers, pamphlets, labour organizations, and church pulpits. Novelists, poets, and artists could be trenchant social critics, as realists, as dreamers of utopia, or as prophets of distopia. Nonetheless, the universities were an important source of social criticism. Indeed, social criticism is inherent in the research enterprise of the social sciences and branches of philosophy such as political, legal, or moral philosophy. The work by the scholar to describe and explain the world is often undertaken with the hope that this knowledge will lead to the betterment of society – will allow society to replace what is with something better. And ultimately society's support for this research is given in the belief that the new knowledge will be of benefit. Certainly, the massive government support for social science research, which helped create the multiversity in the postwar period, had such a motivation.

Social criticism is not the sole purpose of the social scientist or political philosopher. Nor do social scientists and political philosophers always address issues of right and wrong, justice, and equity. Certainly, many social scientists in the university have been political radicals or ardent reformers. But many, indeed most, professors in these fields see themselves as impartial, neutral scientists providing objective documentation and analysis of social phenomena. Yet, Bottomore asserts that 'it is difficult to separate entirely social science and social criticism ... Even the most disinterested and objective description when it deals with certain aspects of social life implies or encourages a critical view. To depict faithfully and clearly, though dispassionately, gross inequalities, oppression, misery and suffering, is already a kind of criticism or an incitement to it. To point to the causes may also be to show how they can be removed, and by whom. Thus whether they will or not, the social sciences, social criticism and social reform have proceeded hand in hand.'[38]

It is rare that the role of the multiversity in social criticism is made explicit. However, there is at least one example in the Anglo-American world where this role is made explicit, indeed, is made part of the definition of a university. During the 1980s, New Zealand was in political turmoil. The economy was shrinking; government deficits and debt were rising. The Labour Party, which formed the government, concluded that government programs of social democracy required radical redesign. Universities were not exempt, indeed, were often the focus, because higher education was to be part of the redesign of economic policy. What followed was a 'decade-long war' between the university and the government – the universities felt betrayed by what they saw as a crippling assault on institutional autonomy and academic freedom. During this war, the Education Amendment Act (1990) was passed. The act is an extraordinary document because it reaffirms unequivocally the core ideals of academic freedom and institutional autonomy, even amid political turmoil and radical redesign of the welfare state. There are lessons here for other countries.

The objective of the act was to give universities 'as much independence and freedom to make academic, operational, and management decisions as is consistent with the nature of the services they provide, the efficient use of national resources, the national interest and the demands of accountability.'[39] Then the act defines a university as an institution having certain essential characteristics: '(1) They are principally concerned with more advanced learning, the principal aim being to develop intellectual independence; (2) their research and teaching are closely interdependent and most of their teaching is done by people who are active in advancing knowledge; (3) they meet international standards of research and teaching; (4) they are repositories of knowledge and expertise.' These first four characteristics reaffirm the long-established nature of universities. What is extraordinary is the fifth essential characteristic of universities: (5) 'they accept a role as critic and conscience of society.'[40]

Here we see a democratic function of universities made explicit. Most people within the university acknowledge that sometimes professors act as critic or conscience. But seldom is this role included as an *essential characteristic* of universities. Most writing about universities acknowledges it only as an *indirect outcome* of free inquiry, but the New Zealand Education Amendment Act makes the expectation of social criticism explicit. I believe that in our age this role should be clearly articulated in the mission of all multiversities. Furthermore, as an explicit responsibility, we can then ask universities how well they fulfil it, and judge them accordingly. Universities should be accountable for this. This responsibility of the modern university to democratic life is connected to its responsibility for research, under the guarantees of autonomy and academic freedom. Unlike other democratic institutions such as political parties or the media, the university is committed to research; it is an institution that allows sustained critical reflection and analysis and, therefore, can play a unique role in democratic life.

The New Zealand act says universities 'accept' a role as critic and conscience of society – the choice of verb acknowledges this is not a role to be welcomed by everyone. Although many professors and students see themselves as activists and do welcome the role, most professors and students are uneasy, as are boards of governors, presidents, and senior administrators. They would prefer that social criticism remain an indirect implication of autonomy and academic freedom, rather than an explicit responsibility to society. The university requires the support of the centres of political and economic power; the role of critic and conscience would bring it into conflict with the powerful.

The dangers to the university of this role are evident and many.

Research and teaching, which should be founded upon curiosity and tolerance, might become advocacy and intolerance. It might be that social criticism, like participation in partisan politics, spoils the habits of good scholarship. Social criticism can become political protest, which in turn can slide into antidemocratic politics.

In accepting the role of critic and conscience, the multiversity risks betraying its essential character of disinterested free inquiry, civil debate, and institutional autonomy. This risk is real, and multversities must guard against it vigilantly, but it must be taken. The risk will be mitigated if critical ideas and alternatives are developed through academic research and if they are advanced according to the scholarly canons of respectful, evidence-based exchange. As this task becomes explicit, we will need thoughtful articulation of the corresponding academic duties. This responsibility may also preclude some sorts of social criticism. I believe that this democratic task arises because of the university's autonomy and commitment to disinterested research. The role of critic and conscience should be related to the expertise of the faculty member and would preclude involvement in partisan politics. There will need to be careful separation of an individual's role as a professor at a multiversity and her or his role as a private citizen.

Public Intellectuals

These reflections on democracy in a knowledge-based society lead towards an additional democratic responsibility of professors: their role as public intellectuals. The multversity is a place of advancement and dissemination of knowledge, a place of research and teaching. Universities are the core of society's research enterprise, the source of innovation and ideas. New knowledge is disseminated in the classroom through the teaching of undergraduate and graduate students, through continuing education, and through the publication of research. But, dissemination must not end there. The public has financed this research, and therefore professors have a responsibility to discuss their research with the public.

The concept of a 'public intellectual' is elusive, if commonly invoked. Writers use the term to mean widely different things. Many writers use the term *intellectual* or *public intellectual* to refer to the role of critic and conscience discussed in the previous section. There is a large literature about the role of the intellectual in this tradition. John McGowan uses the term in this way in his marvellously titled book *Democracy's Chil-*

dren: Intellectuals and the Rise of Cultural Politics: 'Intellectuals are democracy's children insofar as they are called into existence in plural societies in which freedom of speech and the press combines with wide-open debate among competing visions of the good life, the good polity and good art (among other things).'[41] Edward Said, in his 1993 BBC Reith Lectures, published as *Representations of the Intellectual*, declares that the true intellectual is 'someone whose place it is to publicly raise embarrassing questions, to confront orthodoxy and dogma ... to be someone who cannot be easily co-opted by governments or corporations.'[42] 'All of us live in a society, and are members of a nationality with its own language, tradition, historical situation. [But], how powerless one often feels in the face of an overwhelmingly powerful network of social authorities – the media, the government and corporations, etc. – who crowd out the possibilities for achieving any change ... Thus in my view the principal intellectual duty is the search for relative independence from such pressures. Hence my characterizations of the intellectual as exile and marginal, as amateur, and as author of a language that tries to speak truth to power.'[43] Professors, hired by an autonomous institution and who can think, write, and speak with academic freedom, surely have a democratic obligation to be such public intellectuals. Not every professor must be one, but the multiversity as a whole must accept the role of critic and conscience.

I shall use the term *public intellectual* in its broadest interpretation; I include the role of critic, of the outsider speaking truth to power, but much else. As a starting point to our understanding, and to explaining how I will use the term, let me explore what it means to be 'an intellectual.' An intellectual is 'generally understood as someone seriously and competently interested in the things of the mind.'[44] Intellectuals are interested in ideas, both as generalists and as specialists. Their interest goes beyond that required of their occupation, and in this sense their labours are disinterested. Their labours are not to achieve a specific task or to advance the body of expert knowledge. They get pleasure from working with ideas. To be an intellectual is not the same as having cultivated tastes, or to being intelligent, although intellectuals usually have both cultivated tastes and intelligence. It is more an attitude of mind; intellectuals like to read and think and to theorize; 'perhaps every true intellectual is bookish, though not all bookish people are intellectuals.'[45]

C.P. Snow, in his famous 1959 Cambridge Rede Lecture, 'The Two Cultures and the Scientific Revolution,' argued that the intellectual life of western society was split between two cultures – at one pole were the literary intellectuals and at the other pole were the scientists. (In a later lecture, he thought a third culture might be emerging, among what we might label the social scientists.) Snow noted that the literary intellectuals 'while no one was looking took to referring to themselves as "intellectuals" as though there were no others.' He went on to recall how G.H. Hardy, the great Cambridge mathematician, 'once remarked to me in mild puzzlement, some time in the 1930s: "Have you noticed how the word intellectual is used nowadays? There seems to be a new definition which certainly doesn't include Rutherford or Eddington or Dirac or Adrian or me. It does seem rather odd."'[46]

My usage of the term *intellectual* includes the literary, the scientific, and the social scientific. An intellectual is not confined to literary or philosophical or artistic pursuits. Intellectuals can be bookish about science or engineering or pure mathematics, as well. An intellectual becomes a 'public' intellectual when her or his writing or speaking is intended for the curious, educated general public.

One sort of public intellectual contributes to discussions about public affairs, sometimes being critic or conscience, as discussed in the previous section. Jeffery C. Goldfarb has explored this role in *Civility and Subversion: The Intellectual in Democratic Society*. He argues that 'intellectuals have played crucial roles in the making of democracy and in the ongoing practices of democratic life.'[47] Furthermore, 'the diminution of intellectual activity presents a major threat to democracy in our times. Intellectuals are central democratic actors, and when they leave the political stage, democratic performance ends in failure ... Intellectuals are particularly able to address one of the most pressing needs of democracies: the need to deliberate about common problems. Intellectuals help societies to talk about their problems. They contribute to democratic life when they civilize political contestation and when they subvert complacent consensus.'[48] University professors should be among the most important public intellectuals of a democratic society. Goldfarb's words are wonderfully chosen: public intellectuals have a role to *civilize* debate and to *subvert* consensus. To do this well is very difficult, but the discipline of academic life should be an excellent preparation. This sort of public intellectual can play a Socratic role in society, questioning assumptions, asking about the larger context, challenging us to think about how we think.

A professor is also a public intellectual, in my usage, if his or her academic writing, produced according to the canons of scholarship in their discipline and intended as a contribution to scholarly knowledge, happens to be accessible to the educated public. Such writing is more and more rare, but can be found most often in the work of historians. It can also be found in the work of some literary and cultural critics, and some political scientists, sociologists, and philosophers. Reviews of their scholarly books can be found in the book sections of newspapers in large metropolitan areas.

Alternatively, professors are also public intellectuals if they write and speak to explain their discipline and their research to the educated public. The research need not be related to public or cultural affairs. The research might help us understand why the sky is blue, or be a new biography of Elizabeth I, or be an economic analysis of trade along the Silk Road in Han dynasty China. The new knowledge is valued for its own sake. Often described as 'popularizing' academic research, I believe this is too pejorative a characterization. I believe it is better seen as inviting the public to join in the life of the mind, to join in the world of ideas. This life and these ideas are valued for their own sake. Such public intellectuals contribute to liberal learning, not in the classroom, but in the wider public. To be such a public intellectual is to contribute to lifelong liberal learning.

It is in all these various possible ways that the professors of a multiversity, because the multiversity is an institution of democracy, have a responsibility to society to be public intellectuals.

Renewing the Social Contract in Our Age

This chapter concludes Part One of the book, which has looked at how four ideas of a university were combined into one conglomerate and how the multiversity is connected to society in a social contract. These chapters have also developed the theme that multiversities now have many democratic responsibilities and should be regarded as institutions of democracy. However, here at the beginning of the twenty-first century, I must acknowledge that multiversities are not conceptualized as institutions of democracy. I shall return to this theme, articulating further the multiversity's democratic responsibilities, in Part Three, Renewing the Social Contract.

We now turn, in Part Two, to what lies ahead for the multiversity. We look into the future for many reasons, not least of which is our intellectual curiosity, our desire to understand the unfolding world. Also, we want to be sure we can both preserve our inheritance and change to make things better. Such reflections are necessary in the civic conversation, as we renew the social contract for multiversities. If we have diagnosed the future correctly, we can acquire a checklist to measure our own multiversity and the multiversities of our country. Are they adapting well to the ideas of our age?

Part Two examines five characteristics of our age, five bundles of ideas, and their implications for the multiversity. The five characteristics of our age that are analysed are: the constrained welfare state, the information technology revolution, postmodern thought, commercialization, and globalization. As each bundle of ideas is explored, we shall see the influence of the ideas coming from multiversity research upon our society. The multiversity is, indeed, a powerful institution in our age.

In Part Three (chapters 11 and 12), I return to the renewal of the social contract. There I will argue that the two highest priorities in renewing the social contract are the explicit extension of the mission of the multiversity to include a responsibility to democracy and a renewed attention to undergraduate education, especially liberal education. These are required to meet the challenges of our age.

Clark Kerr began his reflections about the multiversity in 1963. His book *The Uses of the University* has been republished at regular intervals since, updating his reflections. Looking back to the 1960s, he believes that it was easy to identify the three great forces acting upon universities and their implications. These three great forces were the advent of mass university education, the federal government's support for research at multiversities, and the enhanced availability of resources. He felt he 'was dealing with certainties, not making predictions.'[49] Looking forward in 2001, Clark Kerr sees no such certainties. He confesses to a certain apprehension as he contemplates the future of multiversities. But amid his somber reflections, in a typically wry aside, he admits that writers about universities inevitably mourn a lost glorious past, and anticipate the future with alarm. Forewarned, we can escape this genre. Aware of our inheritance, let us examine the future.

PART TWO

The Character of Our Age

6 The Constrained Welfare State

Part One set out the nature of the multiversity and explored its history and how it came to be the dominant institutional form for universities in the Anglo-American world. Today, early in the twenty-first century, our age brings new forces of change. How will multiversities adapt to the character of our age? What are the crucial issues that will shape the multiversity over the next ten years? These are the questions of Part Two.

Looking Ahead: The Future of the Multiversity

After discussion and reflection, and after surveying the current literature about universities, I have selected five characteristics of our age that will crucially shape the multiversities of the Anglo-American world. Each is explored as a chapter in Part Two. Of course another observer could select his or her own list,[1] and unpredictable events such as a worldwide recession, an outbreak of war, or an environmental crisis, would render anyone's list irrelevant. The list is not exhaustive, but there is no doubt that each item is going to exert powerful influence on the multiversity.

In preparing my list, my first question was: what lies ahead for the welfare state? The implementation of the welfare state was one of the great transformations that created the multiversity – as the welfare state flourishes or struggles so the multiversity flourishes or struggles – and therefore, as we look ahead, we must ask: is the welfare state likely to change?

Despite furious criticism, the welfare state continues. The postwar social contract between citizens and their government remains, but there will be fundamental changes. We will live in what I shall call 'a constrained welfare state.' The constrained welfare state is a defining characteristic of our age. It is the first item on my list and the subject of this chapter.

The second question I asked was: What lies ahead for postindustrial society? This was the other great transformation that created the multiversity. Will there be changes in the economy, technology, and occupational structure? Will the centrality of theoretical knowledge and the engagement in self-conscious research programs to solve applied problems continue? Like the welfare state, postindustrial society continues but with fundamental change. The evolution of postindustrial society is now being driven by the computing, communications, and information technology revolution and by the even greater emphasis on advanced research as crucial to economic prosperity. The information technology revolution and the pressure to commercialize research are also defining characteristics of our age. These are the subjects of chapters 7 and 9.

One of the most influential intellectual ferments of our time comes from postmodern ideas; postmodern ideas help define the character of our age. Postmodern thought is a critique of the western rationalistic tradition and is thus also a critique of the foundations of the multiversity. There is a fierce clash between the modern and the postmodern within the multiversity. One of the great challenges ahead for the multiversity is how it will deal with postmodern ideas. This is the subject of chapter 8.

The fifth item on my list of the characteristics of our age is globalization. The university has always belonged to the borderless world of ideas; but it has also always been connected with the nation state. Globalization diminishes the sovereignty of the nation state, leaving governments less able to influence the economy and culture within their own borders, leaving multiversities with a correspondingly diminished national role. The multiversity is both a force of globalization and reshaped by globalization; it is both a national institution and a cosmopolitan institution. This is the subject of chapter 10.

Part Two examines these characteristics of our age. They are approached as intellectual forces of change, as bundles of ideas. Ideas are driving change. Often, they originate in multiversity research, and even if they do not originate there, the ideas are always considered, disseminated, modified, and advanced in the multiversity. Ideas are transforming society. Any one bundle could radically alter the multiversity. Will the multiversity be sufficiently stable to sustain its core ideals, yet sufficiently responsive to remain relevant to the society that supports it?

Each chapter in Part Two is organized into two segments. In the first, the characteristic of our age is analysed. Each characteristic is approached as a bundle of ideas – to understand our age we must understand the ferment of ideas. The second segment of the chapter analyses the implications for the multiversity of this characteristic of our age. There are, of course, many implications; I will focus on a selected few.

Each chapter both illustrates and analyses the influence of the multiversity on society. A running theme of Part Two is the profound effect of multiversity research – in the social sciences, in the sciences, and in the humanities – upon society. This, too, is a characteristic of our age.

Chapter 6 examines the constrained welfare state, which imposes limits on public sector spending, favours deregulation and market competition over state intervention, and brings higher tuition fees and increased reliance on external fundraising. Chapter 7 discusses the technological revolution in computing, communication, and information technologies, a revolution which could replace the lecture hall and library, revolutionizing the processes of teaching and learning. Chapter 8 explores postmodern thought, the probing inquiries in the humanities that advance a powerful critique of disinterested inquiry, and posit the inescapable link of knowledge to power. The postmodern critique rejects the grand narratives of progress and enlightenment, and even the idea of objective knowledge, the foundations upon which the multiversity has been built. Chapter 9 examines new ideas about the nature and causes of the wealth of nations and the new emphasis on innovation in government economic policies. Governments are shifting from supporting basic research towards supporting applied research and are asking that commercialization of research become a fundamental responsibility of the multiversity. Chapter 10 analyses globalization and how it diminishes the sovereignty of the nation state, brings new conceptions of belonging that threaten the university's traditional connection to national culture, and sets multiversities across nations in competition with one another.

The very essence of the multiversity may become different in this period of rapid change, under pressure of these new ideas. The ideas of our age raise fundamental questions, and posterity will judge the multiversities by how they adapt and how they answer them. But multiversities are not prisoners to this future, nor do they simply adapt. Despite all the conventional rhetoric 'about sailing on stormy seas, blown by hostile winds,' multiversities are powerful institutions that can influence the future and the government policies under which they operate.

The Welfare State in Our Age

The first characteristic of our age to think about is the welfare state, that synthesis of liberal democracy and capitalism that was implemented in the second half of the twentieth century. The welfare state is committed to social citizenship and accessible education; it supports the multiversity financially, calls upon its professors as advisers, uses its research, and hires many of its graduates. There is no greater influence on the multiversity today than government policy with respect to universities. On top of the list of concerns of any president or vice-chancellor is government policy: Will the operating grant be increased? Will there be support for new buildings and the maintenance of existing buildings? How much can tuition fees be increased? Will there be improvements in financial aid for students? Will there be more support for research? The senior administrators of multiversities spend countless hours trying to influence government policy – explaining what the multiversity does, arguing its importance to society, and above all, trying to secure better funding for the multiversity.[2]

From one perspective, our age should be a very good time for multiversities. Our age remains a postindustrial society, albeit one evolving rapidly and in new ways. More than ever before, governments recognize the importance of education and innovation in this postindustrial society. A highly educated workforce and advanced research are seen as crucial to economic prosperity, and governments want to increase participation in higher education. If these are the dominant ideas, we would expect governments to fund multiversities very well. Another golden age could lie ahead. However, government policy towards the multiversity – the decisions about how much to support it and in what form – is not determined solely by ideas about the worth of university education and research. Indeed, government policy towards universities is not shaped primarily by thinking about educational issues. Rather, government policy about universities is shaped by a much larger debate about the appropriate role of government in our society. It is shaped by debate about the welfare state itself. To understand the challenges facing the multiversity, we must first understand the debates about the future of the welfare state. With this understood, we can analyse the implications for the multiversity.

Legitimacy Contested

The postwar consensus around the welfare state was sustained by rapid economic growth and by ideas supporting the welfare state articulated by 'academic scribblers' – notably, Keynes, Beveridge, and Marshall. They set out three intellectual pillars of the welfare state: the commitment to reduce unemployment; the commitment to provide social insurance and social services; and the commitment to social citizenship. The fourth, less-articulated, pillar was the commitment to finance the welfare state through progressive income taxation and low user charges. By the 1980s, the consensus collapsed, as economic growth declined and as countervailing ideas were put forward by other 'academic scribblers.' Each of the four intellectual pillars became contested. Critics, many of them academics, challenged the expanded role for government, calling for a rollback in government responsibilities and spending. The welfare state had always been positioned between classical liberalism and socialism and, during the consensus, the welfare state was tugged more towards the left than the right. During the criticism, the tug from the right grew stronger than the tug from the left. Debate raged – within the university and without. The political economy of the welfare state changed fundamentally. Thus, too, the climate for the multiversity changed fundamentally. For a time, it appeared as though there might be a radical rollback of the role of government, and therefore as well, a radical rollback of government support for the activities of the multiversity.

The welfare state was not radically rolled back however. Instead, a new form of it emerged out of this criticism: the constrained welfare state of our age. Let us first examine the critique of each of the four pillars of the welfare state. Then we can see what prevailed.

The first pillar of the welfare state is the government's commitment to reduce unemployment. During the consensus period, the chief means to reduce unemployment was Keynesian macroeconomic policy. But economic performance deteriorated during the 1970s and after. Before the 1970s, we had high growth, low unemployment, and low inflation; after the mid-1970s, we had slow growth, rising unemployment, and rising inflation. The Keynesian paradigm postulated a basic trade-off between unemployment and inflation: lower unemployment could be achieved by accepting higher inflation. After 1973, the facts of experience told a different story, one of stagflation: simultaneously increasing unemployment and increasing inflation. Inflation kept rising, with expectations of future price increases fueling higher wage demands; but wages never seemed to catch up. In 1980, a year of recession, annual inflation reached a staggering 13.5 per cent in the countries of the Organisation for Economic Co-operation and Development (OECD).[3] Stories of hyperinflation began to appear; inflation was out of control. Unemployment grew steadily, despite government efforts to stimulate aggregate demand. The Keynesian prescriptions to reduce unemployment were no longer working.

As economic growth slowed, social spending growth was cut back to more closely match the growth of the economy. Taxes were increased, but there remained a structural imbalance: government expenditures were greater than government revenues. Government deficits grew, public debt accumulated, and interest payments on the debt ballooned. Interest on the debt grew so rapidly that it took an increasing share of total expenditures and crowded out other claims for government spending. The public finances were in chaos. This fiscal crisis was not due, as many critics have argued, to a continuing expansion of the welfare state, because no major social programs were implemented after the mid-1970s. The crisis was the result of the economic slowdown, rising expenditures on existing commitments, and voters' unwillingness to pay the taxes needed to maintain the existing commitments. This radically altered economic context brought forth new macroeconomic ideas, challenging the Keynesian pillar of the welfare state: the commitment to reduce unemployment and to discretionary macroeconomic policy.[4]

Monetarism, associated with the writings of Milton Friedman of the University of Chicago (who later would be awarded the Nobel Prize in Economics for his work), was sceptical of discretionary stabilization. Monetarists highlighted the long and variable lags between the diagnosis of a problem, the implementation of a response, and the eventual effects on the economy. Government intervention intended to stabilize economic fluctuations could just as often make the fluctuations worse. Monetarists recommended rules for monetary policy, rather than discretion.

Following the pioneering work of Nobel Laureate Robert Lucas of the University of Chicago, the rational expectations revolution created a new classical macroeconomics and forever altered our understanding of the relation between policymakers and the economy: 'In the Keynesian structure, the policy-maker has superior knowledge and, by pulling certain levers, is able to have a predictable effect on the economy. In the world after RE [rational expectations], actors in the economy are smart and forward-looking. They attempt to forecast what the government is going to do, just as the government tries to forecast what the economy is going to do. Policy-making in this context becomes a complex dynamic "game" in which credibility and commitment suddenly have great significance.'[5] If the private market anticipates the government's policy, any government actions may be fully offset by private adjustments. The early new classical macroeconomic analysis came to the radical conclusion that discretionary fiscal policy by government will have no effect on the real economy, and thus government was impotent in attempts to reduce unemployment. Although we now recognize this implication only prevails in models with very restrictive assumptions, the thrust of the analysis eroded confidence that governments could fine-tune the economy.

Neo-Keynesians responded with their own critique of monetarism and the new classicism. They argued that the new classicism could not fully explain economic reality either. The neo-Keynesians acknowledged rational expectations, and constructed models of the economy incorporating rational maximizing agents who anticipated government actions, but which nevertheless suggested a role for government, if more limited, in discretionary monetary and fiscal policy.

Substantial numbers of economists argued that the unemployment of the 1980s was not amenable to Keynesian remedies. Unemployment can be caused by deficient aggregate demand; in such a situation, Keynesian remedies can work. However, there can be other causes – frictional unemployment and structural unemployment. This results as markets adjust to unexpected events and to structural changes, and Keynesian increases in government spending will not cure such unemployment. These economists argued that the unemployment of the 1980s and 1990s was principally structural, much of it precipitated by globalization. Debate raged in university seminar rooms, academic journals, and public forums. The first intellectual pillar of the welfare state was severely critiqued. No longer could it be said: 'we are all Keynesians.' Indeed, Keynesians were a lonely few.

The second intellectual pillar of the welfare state – the government commitment to social insurance and social services – faced the fiercest and most prolonged assault. The assault was on both philosophical and pragmatic grounds. The critique is often called neoconservatism; but in the tradition of political economy it can also be called neoliberalism.[6] This is the term I will use. Like classical liberalism, neoliberalism advocates a limited role for government. After twenty-five years of expansion of the welfare state, neoliberals called for a radical rollback of government activity.

On a philosophical level, the critics returned to the age-old questions of political economy and upon reflection agreed with the answers found in classical liberalism and the political economy of Adam Smith. In the critics' view, liberty is to be valued above all. Limited constitutional government best achieves liberty. Governments should limit their activities to national defence, the maintenance of law and order and the courts, the provision of certain public infrastructure, primary and secondary education, and minimal social policy to prevent destitution – the same list as Adam Smith's.

This philosophical position was reinforced by pragmatic criticism of the actual welfare state programs that had been implemented. The neoliberals declared that the government programs of the welfare state had failed. Social problems had not been solved, or ameliorated, and had often become worse. The caustic remarks, in 1993, by Thomas Sowell of the Hoover Institution at Stanford University capture the neoliberal critique: 'Much of the social history of the Western world, over the past three decades, has been a history of replacing what worked with what sounded good. In area after area – crime, education, housing, race relations – the situation has gotten worse after the bright new theories were put into operation. The amazing thing is that this history of failure and disaster has neither discouraged the social engineers nor discredited them.'[7]

Although cloaked in the language of 'practical men,' much of the neoliberal critique drifted into its own ideological fundamentalism. In their ideology, the public sector does not work, only private markets work; and therefore the state should be rolled back to let the private market work. This market fundamentalism was often applied with no regard for the specifics of the situation or for evidence. It was a matter of faith.

Another complementary thrust of neoliberal thought explained why, despite its evident failure, the welfare state continued and expanded. This explanation came from a new theory of politics called 'public choice' theory, sometimes called an economic theory of politics. In this theory, everyone – politician, voter, and civil servant – is a rational decision-maker pursuing his or her self-interest. Politicians seek re-election, voters support the party that makes them best off, and civil servants promote the programs that improve their well-being. Political parties develop platforms that concentrate the benefits of specific programs on selected marginal voters and spread the costs (the tax increase) across the entire electorate. This dynamic of voters and politicians produces an ever-expanding government sector. Organized interest groups reinforce the dynamic. Civil servants facilitate the expansion because extra government spending increases their power and income. 'Collectivists, such as Keynes and Beveridge, assumed a benevolent and disinterested bureaucracy.' But in the neoliberal critique, 'the state and its institutions become the vehicle for furthering the private interests of public employees and others whose livelihood depends on the perpetuation and expansion of the government. Under the cloak of public interest, then, the government may in fact be serving private interest.'[8] Not all criticism of the welfare state in this vein came from neoliberals: many on the left argued that the welfare state was overly bureaucratic, and some feminists argued it was patriarchal. The welfare state did not serve those it was intended to serve.[9]

The final critical thrust alleged that the social policy of the welfare state, whatever its efficacy, had become a drag on economic performance; the sluggish and inflation-prone economy could be blamed on the expanding welfare state. The implication was clear. We could no longer afford the social programs. Only a rollback of the welfare state could secure economic prosperity.

The terms of the debate about the proper role of government were also shifting because the radical alternative to the welfare state was failing: the communist world could no longer be offered as an example of a productive and just society. The abject failure of communist nations to meet the democratic and material aspirations of their peoples during the 1970s and 1980s was a constant reminder of how well-intentioned government planning could go terribly, terribly wrong.

The neoliberal critique, like the new macroeconomic ideas, struck at the ultimate credo of the welfare state: that human thought could understand the world and human agency could make it better. The neoliberal critics claimed that our attempts at social engineering were bound to fail. Therefore, there was much less need for government intervention; and, as a corollary, there was much less need for the social science research and the social science graduates of the multiversity. There was much less need for the multiversity itself.

The third pillar, Marshall's social citizenship, attracted strident criticism from the neoliberals, as part of their larger critique of the welfare state. They attacked Marshall's notion of social rights, for example, to education and economic security, which flow from citizenship. A survey of recent writing on citizenship concluded that 'whereas Marshall had argued that social rights enable the disadvantaged to enter the mainstream of society and effectively exercise their civil and political rights, the New Right argues that the welfare state has promoted passivity among the poor, without actually improving their life chances, and created a culture of dependency. Far from being the solution, the welfare state has itself perpetuated the problem by reducing citizens to passive dependents who are under bureaucratic tutelage.'[10] This critique argued that citizenship also meant responsibilities, including the responsibility to take care of yourself and your family. The state, it was argued, should pull back and allow individuals to be more responsible for their own well-being and to free them from the controlling bureaucrats.

The fourth pillar of the welfare state – that it should be financed by progressive taxation – emerged for full scrutiny. Shaken by stagnant incomes and economic insecurity, voters had to confront the tax burden necessary to finance the welfare state. They began to ask themselves: How much tax am I willing to pay? Or more politely, what should be the split between public expenditures and private expenditures? The tax burden of the welfare state became the burning political issue. Voters resisted tax increases – as politicians became acutely aware. Government expenditure was restrained because taxes could not be increased, and all of the public sector felt the pinch.

For nearly thirty years, the debate has raged. For a time, neoliberalism dominated the terms of the discussion. Neoliberal governments were elected in Canada, the United States, and the United Kingdom. The growth of government spending slowed and there were major cutbacks in many areas, particularly of programs benefiting the poor and the marginalized. Radical change seemed possible: the welfare state might be replaced by a neoliberal state. The rhetoric from both right and left became overblown and apocalyptic. Neoliberal true believers called for accelerated reductions in the role of government. Supporters of the welfare state, in their alarm, vastly overstated the actual cutbacks occurring in the public sector. Soon, they declared, to rally the opposition to neoliberalism, we would be back in the nineteenth century.

The multiversity was engulfed in the raging debate. To contest the legitimacy of the welfare state was to contest the role of the postwar multiversity. As governments restrained their expenditures, the multiversities suffered. In many jurisdictions, government expenditure per student declined significantly.

Legitimacy Confirmed: The Constrained Welfare State

What lies ahead for the multiversity? Will the debates continue, and might the welfare state be radically rolled back and support for the multiversity radically diminished?

For true believers, on both the left and right, the great struggle continues. But a close reading of the record reveals that although the four pillars of the welfare state have been contested, the legitimacy of each pillar has been confirmed. Much, however, has changed. In our age, the multiversity confronts what I am calling the constrained welfare state. The ideas of our age are the ideas of the constrained welfare state. These are the ideas that will shape the multiversity.

Today, nearly thirty years after the collapse of the Keynesian orthodoxy, no macroeconomic consensus has emerged, but government did not and will not abandon its role in managing the economy. Citizens still expect governments to design policies to reduce unemployment, and governments still accept this responsibility. This fundamental part of the social contract between citizens and their government remains. The Keynesian remedies have been rejected, but not the underlying objectives.

Moreover, despite the academic disagreements about the role of government, there were some stunning government successes in macroeconomic policy: inflation was tamed; public sector deficits were brought under control, and unemployment was reduced. The potentially devastating financial shocks from the Asian financial crisis and the collapse of the technology stock market bubble were handled. A recent survey of the macroeconomic controversies articulated the sentiment that remains: 'High unemployment still threatens lives, so the challenge to comprehend our economic environment is as great as ever. The fact that universal solutions have not been found does not mean that they do not exist. The issues are as important as ever. Macroeconomics is still worth doing ... and worth doing well.'[11] And the multiversities are still needed for their advice, their research, and their graduates.

After the challenge, the legitimacy of the first pillar of the welfare state remains: governments have fundamental responsibilities in the management of the market economy and are still accountable for economic conditions, especially unemployment and inflation. However, attitudes about government are less sanguine. We recognize that government macroeconomic policy can sometimes make things worse and sometimes make things better. Discretionary policies have a place, but fine-tuning is impossible. The benefits of efficient markets, including their self-correcting properties, are more recognized. Less regulation and more flexible labour markets are being pursued. Discretionary stabilization policy is still somewhat important, but what is much more important is that government ensures a stable framework for the economy, especially stable prices and sound public finances. This is the fundamental task of macroeconomic policy.

As nations struggled to get their economic fundamentals correct during the 1980s and 1990s, and eventually did, the diagnosis of the long-run employment problem became clearer. The unemployment problem was not because the economy had become stuck at an underemployment equilibrium. Unemployment was not caused by deficient aggregate demand. Not surprisingly, therefore, the Keynesian prescriptions were not appropriate. The explanation and remedy lay elsewhere. Following the expansion of the 1950s, 1960s, and early 1970s, there had been a long decline in the rate of productivity growth, and there was much structural change in the economy. These were the underlying causes of long-term unemployment. The new economic reality was painful. Expectations formed in the 1960s of continuous strong economic growth were unsustainable. The re-adjustment was traumatic and brought a profound and lasting economic insecurity to the Anglo-American world. Was our future prosperity assured? What must be done to assure it? How can we assure jobs for ourselves and our children?

The first intellectual pillar of the welfare state was being challenged and, by century's end, reconfirmed. A job is still regarded as the bedrock of individual welfare, and government still has a responsibility to design policy to ensure long-run employment. But the emphasis in government policy has shifted from Keynesian macroeconomic policy to the encouragement of productivity growth and to managing structural change. In its reconfirmation, the multiversity emerges with an even more central role in the welfare state, because the multiversity is the pre-eminent institution of higher learning, professional training, and research – and these are what will secure employment for people, not Keynesian macroeconomic policy. (These ideas of our age related to the first pillar, and the implications for the multiversity, are taken up in much more detail in chapter 9.)

In the debates over the second pillar, about whether government should provide social services and social insurance, supporters of the welfare state were initially in disarray, unable to mount a coherent response to neoliberalism. Supporters were slow to acknowledge that much criticism of the welfare state was true and had to be confronted: the public finances were in chaos, some social programs had failed, public workers did have a vested interest in the status quo, and there were some trade-offs between social policy and economic performance. Eventually the debate was joined, however, and in the end, the welfare state was not radically rolled back. Indeed, by many measures the welfare state was not rolled back at all.

This conclusion – the welfare state has not been rolled back – surprises many, especially those, like me, who work in public sector–supported institutions. How could this be possible after Reagan, after Thatcher, after Mulroney, after Bush, after so many neoliberal governments? How could this be possible when we have been living, year after year, in an environment of budget cuts? Much writing about universities is given to extreme statements about the radical cuts to the welfare state. But let us examine the evidence, and in so doing we begin to understand the struggle and paradox that is the constrained welfare state.

The most comprehensive measure of government activity under the second pillar of the welfare state is government social expenditures – public expenditures on education, health, pensions and old age security, housing assistance, unemployment and disability insurance payments, and other social services. This measure is an incomplete assessment of the extent of the welfare state, but is always a starting point for analysis. Using data on social expenditures, we can measure the commitments of our governments in three ways. The first is actual social expenditure each year. Have actual social expenditures been rising or falling? This measure does not fully capture whether governments are doing more or less. Perhaps social expenditures are rising only due to rising costs of providing the same services; we should look at real expenditures, that is, expenditures in constant dollars. Or perhaps expenditures are rising because there are more people in the country; we should look at expenditures per capita to see whether our governments are doing more or less. The second measure combines these concerns and looks at real social spending per capita. A third measure says we should look at how much of our total national income we are devoting to social expenditures in order to determine whether our governments are doing more or less. The third measure is the ratio of social expenditures to gross domestic product (GDP). If the ratio is rising, governments are doing more; if the ratio is falling, they are doing less.

What is the evidence by these three measures? The OECD recently published its social expenditures database for the years 1980 to 2001. This allows consistent analysis over time and between countries.[12] The picture is broadly the same across the Anglo-American world. By the first measure, the welfare state continues to grow. Nominal social expenditures have not declined; they have risen continuously from 1980 to 2001. In Canada, they declined from one year to the next on two occasions in the mid-1990s, but they are now rising, and nominal social expenditures are higher than ever before. In the United Kingdom, they never declined. Similarly, in the United States, nominal social expenditures have risen continuously. By this crudest of measures, there has been no rollback of the welfare state, but rather continued expansion. But, of course, nominal increases may only be due to inflation or to increases in the population.

The much more significant measure is real per capita social spending. But again, the picture is the same. Real per capita social expenditures have also risen nearly continuously, although there have been year-to-year declines. Furthermore, and this is the great surprise, real per capita social spending has never been higher in any of the three countries. Governments have not being doing less; they have been doing more. The welfare state has not been rolled back; it continues to expand.

This clear evidence from the data is hard to square with the rhetoric of savage cutbacks, and also very hard to square with the annual budget cuts experienced in publicly supported institutions. As dean during the 1990s at my university in Canada, my faculty faced a budget cut in every year. How can we understand this paradox? Part of the explanation lies in the fact that per capita expenditures do not capture the changing make-up of the population. Even with a constant population, the need for social expenditures will increase as the share of elderly in the population increases, particularly because of rising health care and pension expenditures. A country will need to have rising real per capita expenditures, just to feel it is staying the same. Also, increasing income inequality and an increasingly diverse and multicultural population will require increasing real per capita social expenditures to feel things are staying the same.

This gives us a basic insight into the constrained welfare state. Real per capita social expenditures are rising, but needs are also rising. The constrained welfare state has not made any new major commitments; the expanding needs arise within existing commitments. In the constrained welfare state, even without new programs, there will be cuts in some programs. And there have, indeed, been wrenching cutbacks in some areas, particularly income support for the poor; many of the most disadvantaged people have suffered greatly, even as real per capita social expenditures rise.

These hardships, these cutbacks cannot be denied. But the continued increase in social spending cannot be denied either. Very soon after the restraint of the late 1980s and early 1990s, voters reasserted that they want good schools, good health care, good pensions, and income security. Governments, people maintained, have a huge role in securing the welfare of citizens. Public services and public infrastructure matter. The renewed emphasis on the role of government was reinforced by some spectacular failures of the private sector, especially the accounting scandals of the high-tech and deregulated utilities sectors. Finally, the last five years of the twentieth century saw the return of robust economic growth and strong growth in productivity. Once again, tax revenues rolled in, and voters could consider reinvestment in government social programs. Voters, although sceptical and angry, would not allow a retreat from the core commitments of the welfare state. Reform and reconstruction were needed, not a rollback to laissez-faire. We are not returning to the world of Adam Smith. This is true of Canada, England, and, to the surprise of many, the United States. Republican president George W. Bush has made more new social spending commitments – in education and health (prescription drugs) – than at any time in the United States since the Great Society programs of the 1960s. The legitimacy of the second pillar of the welfare state – the responsibility to provide social insurance and social services – was ferociously contested, but by century's end its legitimacy was reconfirmed. Citizens still demand that their governments be concerned about education, health care, and pensions / social security.

If we look at the third measure, however – social spending as a share of GDP – the welfare state has been rolled back. In Canada, the United States, and the United Kingdom, social spending as a share of GDP reached a peak in the early 1990s, and since then it has been declining. But the decline is modest; in Canada it has been 4 percentage points, in the United Kingdom 2 percentage points, and in the United States only 1. The GDP share of social expenditures is still well above the so-called golden age of the welfare state in the 1960s and 1970s. It is hard to predict what lies ahead, but the decline appears to have stabilized and perhaps will drift slightly back upward. This third measure reveals a key characteristic of the constrained welfare state: social expenditures are growing, but they are no longer growing as a share of our economy.

The experience of implementing the welfare state and the recognition of its problems has transformed how the role of government is being discussed. There is no appetite for expanding the welfare state – the welfare state is constrained. The naive optimism that sustained the faith in social engineering has vanished. The benefits of consumer choice and market solutions are better recognized. We do acknowledge that the powerful self-interests of public servants can influence the sorts of policies governments actually implement. Manuel Castells characterizes this new time in our approach to government as after 'the collapse of statism.'[13] Market fundamentalism has not disappeared, and in specific policy fields may dominate the choices, but market fundamentalism will not displace the ethos of the welfare state. Indeed, market fundamentalism resulted in some spectacular failures when public services and assets were privatized. One could turn Thomas Sowell's words around and say that the history of neoliberal policy has been a history of replacing what worked (the public sector) with what sounded good (the private sector).

The multiversity is now viewed through this new perspective, as well. Its advice, research, and graduates are still needed, but people are much more sceptical as to whether its social science research can provide solutions to social problems.

The welfare state has proven more robust than expected, perhaps because we often misunderstand its purposes. We too often regard the welfare state as an instrument for redistribution from rich to poor. With cutbacks to programs that helped the poor, we expect to see a significant shrinking of government spending. But the welfare state is mainly about social insurance and social services for all: health, education, unemployment insurance, pensions, and so on. The middle class demand for this insurance and these services has not diminished. Of course, the middle class demand for university education has not diminished either; on the contrary, it continues to increase.

The third pillar of the welfare state – that citizenship includes social citizenship and therefore that citizens have 'the right to share to the full in the social heritage' – has emerged intact. The legitimacy of the rights of social citizenship was never fundamentally eroded in the minds of most voters. There is a simple reality: we live in a diverse society, many are not yet fully included, and we know this must be addressed. This is fundamental to our liberal democracy and perhaps also helps to explain the resilience of the welfare state. Full inclusion is still an unrealized goal. There remains discrimination and exclusion based on class, race, gender, sexual orientation, and ethnicity. Recent immigration is changing the face of Canada, the United, and the United Kingdom. A great challenge for these democracies is to accommodate ethnic, religious, and cultural difference. Diversity is increasing, not decreasing, and must be addressed because, in our liberal democracies, citizenship includes social citizenship. This is not to say there is no struggle. Many forces demonize and marginalize immigrants and ethnic and religious minorities. But the commitment to inclusion has not been abandoned in the mainstream of political discussion.

Marshall recognized the crucial role of education in social citizenship. The commitment to accessible education remains. As before, multiversities should be accessible to students of all backgrounds in order that they enjoy full social citizenship. Furthermore, the multiversity's responsibility to lead in the process of inclusion remains. In the United States, there is still intense concern about whether black and Hispanic Americans are able to attend university. In England, there is still intense concern about whether social class explains educational attainment. In Canada, there is still intense concern about whether family income is a barrier to attending university. In the constrained welfare state, certain affirmative action programs have been ruled out, but the goal of equality of opportunity remains. In all three countries, the ethnic and racial representativeness of both the student body and the professoriate is being scrutinized. Also, the curriculum appropriate for liberal learning and citizenship is being scrutinized. Liberal education remains an education for citizenship, but the meaning of this citizenship must be addressed in a world where some remain excluded.

The constrained welfare state requires a more complex notion of citizenship than Marshall's. The past ten years have seen a huge upsurge of writing about the meaning of citizenship, and the complexities are far from resolved. The complexities multiply with the ideas of postmodernism (chapter 8) and the forces of globalization (chapter 10). This is the world that the multiversity will live in. This theme – of a liberal education and of citizenship for our age – runs through the chapters ahead and returns, to be discussed more fully, in chapter 12.

What of the fourth pillar of the welfare state: that we should pay for social services through progressive income taxation, rather than user charges? In the constrained welfare state, the problem of taxation, ignored during the postwar consensus, is central. There are calls for tax cuts, even when there are demands for improved public services. The constrained welfare state faces limits: it cannot increase taxes very much. A striking fact of the past fifteen years in Canada, the United States, and the United Kingdom is that government revenue as a share of the economy has remained almost constant. For all the neoliberal rhetoric, total government revenues have not declined as a share of GDP. If there were income tax cuts, they were more than balanced by new revenues from value-added taxes, payroll taxes, and user charges. Nevertheless, government revenue as a share of GDP has not increased. We have reached a ceiling on government revenue as a share of the economy; each country because of its history and political culture has a different level, but each has reached a ceiling. This revenue ceiling implies that any new government expenditure commitments, or rapid growth in one area, require cuts in other areas. This ceiling on the share of government revenues in GDP is the most striking feature of the constrained welfare state. New taxes to finance new public services are theoretically possible, but the need has to be clear and extraordinary to overcome the voters' scepticism which has been accumulating and hardening over thirty years.

Unquestionably, the welfare state is also constrained by the forces of globalization. This part of the character of our age is taken up in chapter 10. Many antiglobalization activists attribute the constraints on the welfare state solely to globalization, but this is historically shortsighted. The pressures to limit the welfare state began and found their power well before the current era of globalization.

In the constrained welfare state, there are still demands for more government expenditure in almost every area – from health to national security, from the environment to public infrastructure. The limit to taxation and the competing demands for public funds bring a new discourse to analysis of all government policies, including the programs of the welfare state. Given the limits, what should be our priorities? New and quite fundamental questions are being posed. Should the government continue this activity or should we leave it to the private sector? Would we do better through privatization; or perhaps through a public-private partnership? If the activity remains a priority and remains provided by the public sector, another question is posed: should this public service be financed by taxation or should the people who use the public service pay for it? In recent years, the answer has often been that user fees should be increased. Following this logic, students who attend publicly supported universities are being asked to pay a higher share of the costs through higher tuition fees. Under the same analytical discourse, governments have raised user charges for everything from libraries and parks to public transit and health care.

After all these tough questions there, of course, remain massive social expenditures by governments. But again, a new discourse around public expenditures is occuring. Should we focus expenditures on a few areas or spread them more evenly and more broadly? In many areas of social policy, the welfare state has moved away from universal programs towards programs targeted at the neediest households. This has been particularly true, for example, in Canadian social policy. In all three countries, it is likely that any improvement in financial assistance for university students will be targeted at those with lower incomes. There is much discussion about whether government research support should be targeted upon a few 'flagship' multiversities, rather than being spread across all multiversities. It is argued that research productivity will be higher in clusters with a sufficient critical mass of leading researchers. The new discourse around public expenditures always raises questions of efficiency. Can the existing funds be used more effectively? Finally, the new discourse demands accountability regarding the results of public expenditures. In the constrained welfare state, multiversities will be increasingly called upon to demonstrate that public funds have been used in a focused and strategic manner and have led to demonstrable improvements in accessibility or in the quality of research and learning.

Thus, after the legitimacy of the four pillars was contested but then reconfirmed, a new welfare state has emerged. There is not the consensus of the postwar era, but its broad outlines are accepted by all political parties (likely to be elected). After nearly three decades of furious debate, the outcome is clear: the welfare state remains. The new welfare state has not required a rollback, but it does require learning to live with limits and it does bring a new discourse about the role of government. It is a constrained welfare state. A new political economy has emerged over the past decade and (acknowledging the hubris implied by a forecast) seems likely to operate for decades ahead. This is what lies ahead for the multiversity.

Some aspects of the constrained welfare state are favourable to the multiversity: the greater emphasis on research and human capital in economic policy. Other aspects will hurt the multiversity. The public is more sceptical about the activities of the university. The dreams of a new science of society, of social engineering, are gone. The limits on public expenditures and the competition for public funds will be financially painful.

Confronted with the constrained welfare state, the multiversity is confused, wounded, and deeply troubled. Many in the multiversity refuse to accept the changes, living in an ivory tower of denial, dreaming of the golden age of low tuition fees and rising government grants. Others lash out at politicians and civil servants, calling them philistines in thrall of multinational business. They see a great ideological clash. All must take sides in the battles against neoliberalism. In their turn, politicians and civil servants condemn universities as sluggish and unresponsive, cloaked in a sense of entitlement, unwilling to adjust as everyone else in the private sector and in government has had to adjust. There are yet others in the multiversity who welcome the new political economy with the zeal of converts. They proclaim the necessity for radical change, for new paradigms, and for the overthrow of old ways. They embrace the new discourse, whirling from meeting to meeting, crafting strategic plans, spinning synergies and networks, and unself-consciously adopting the language of business entrepreneurialism.

What multiversities will look like in twenty years will depend upon how they respond to the constrained welfare state. Two crucial places of adaptation will be the pressured space between the rising demand for university education and the limits of public expenditures, and the institutional search for new sources of revenue.

University Life in the Pincers

The limits on the growth of government spending in the constrained welfare state bind all policy fields. Each policy field is forced to lobby vigorously to shape public opinion in the struggle to move up the league table of priorities. Health competes with policing, which competes with education, and on through the list. How will multiversities fare in this competition for public funds?

Health care will command top priority, being so crucial to the well-being and life-chances of everyone, and pressed forward by the health needs of an aging population and the advances in medical technology. Pensions and old age security will be a close second. Across the Anglo-American world, a pension crisis looms. Public security, public infrastructure, and primary and secondary education are not far behind as priorities. Environmental problems, so often ignored until a crisis, could burst forth at any time, especially around climate change and groundwater quality. Government policy towards universities in this age of limits will be moulded by the truth that only one-third of young people receive a university education. University education and research are key items on the economic agenda, but they do not command top priority overall. Multiversities will not fare well in the competition for public funds. In the constrained welfare state, they should not expect increases in real support per student.

The Anglo-American world now faces a decade of increasing demand for university education. Multiversities are caught in pincers: one arm is the public sector spending limit and the other arm is the rising demand for university education. The pincers will squeeze and squeeze and squeeze.

The increase in demand for university education has two sources: the increase in the 'eligible' population of young people and the increase in participation rates (the share of each age group attending university). The first source is much easier to forecast than the second. In the Anglo-American world, the university-age population (20 to 29) will grow between 2000 and 2010. Growth will be particularly large in the United States (13 per cent) and Canada (6 per cent).[14] This is the baby boom echo: the children of the baby boom (born between 1945 and 1965) themselves had children who are now reaching university age.

The increase in demand will be augmented by increases in participation rates, which have risen continuously over the postwar period. One of the great accomplishments of the welfare state has been this increase in participation, especially of women. At the undergraduate level, women students now outnumber men. The democratic commitment to access now extends to other underrepresented groups. The economic benefits of a university education remain high and are rising: incomes are higher, unemployment rates lower, and promotion rates are higher for university graduates compared with people with other types of postsecondary education or with only secondary education. The nonmonetary rewards, though hard to measure, are equally valuable. A wise aphorist, despairing of measurement, declared: the purpose of a university education is to make your mind an interesting place to spend the rest of your life.

If tuition fees increase, all other things being unchanged, the demand for university education should fall; and when tuition falls, participation should rise. Over much of the postwar period, real tuition fees fell, and participation rates increased. Over the past twenty years, however, as governments cut back their grants to universities, real tuition fees have increased. Nonetheless, participation rates have continued to increase, too. Using a narrowly economic calculus, the explanation is clear: although the cost of a university education rose, the benefit of a university education rose faster, so participation rates moved upward. In all likelihood, these trends will continue.

The limits on public expenditures will have even more severe effects because of the cost increases faced by the multiversity. The prices of books and academic journals are rising faster than other prices. Long-deferred maintenance on university buildings is now inescapable. New computing infrastructure adds more expenditure than it replaces. Multiversities face a wave of retirements, which must be replaced, at the same time as more professors must be hired to meet the increasing demand. Professorial starting salaries will increase, particularly in high-demand fields.

As the rising demand for university education confronts the public sector spending limits, the squeeze in the pincers will be intense. The imperative to find new money will be inescapable and increasing. Multiversities, individually and collectively, will lobby politicians, civil servants, and voters to increase operating grants. Tuition fees will increase. Professors will aggressively pursue research grants and contracts. Sophisticated fundraising campaigns will increase private donations. No doubt each revenue source will be increased by these extraordinary efforts. But across the entire system of multiversities, it will not be enough to prevent a decline in real expenditures per student. The casualty will be the quality of education and research.

The budget squeeze will taint every aspect of daily life in all but a few multiversities that can be successful in fundraising and in bending government programs towards their priorities. A very few multiversities will continue to flourish in the constrained welfare state, but the rest will struggle, creating a new hierarchy. The hierarchy will be tremendously reinforced as government research funds are concentrated on a few flagship multiversities. The old, established, and prestigious multiversities start with enormous advantages, and most of them will use these advantages to further separate themselves from other multiversities in the constrained welfare state.

Even the most prestigious multiversities, however, are not immune from the pressures. A 2004 survey at MIT, surely a multiversity well-suited for our age, reports feelings of anxiety, isolation, and deep worries about the budget cuts: 'Every group is feeling that they are working longer hours under greater stress than ever before. For faculty, the work load is seen to be increasing, often crushing, exacerbated by staff reductions in administrative support as positions are cut and remaining staff are spread thinner.' 'The groups who are not directly experiencing layoffs – faculty, research staff, postdocs, and students – are anxious, "waiting for the other shoe to drop," wondering how the cuts will affect them and assuming there will be serious consequences.'[15]

The American system of higher education will confront the greatest demand pressure in the years ahead. A major study for the Council for Aid to Education examined the financial health of America's higher education sector. Its 1996 report, *Breaking the Social Contract: The Fiscal Crisis in Higher Education*, sounded the alarm: 'Our central finding is that the present course of higher education – in which costs and demand are rising faster than funding – is unsustainable. Therefore, we call upon the nation to address the fiscal crisis now, before millions of Americans are denied access to a college education.'[16] The same is true in Canada and the United Kingdom. Indeed, in these countries the fiscal crisis in higher education has arrived long since. There, the squeeze of the constrained welfare state has been unrelenting over the past fifteen years.

In the United Kingdom, during the past two decades, higher education has been transformed from an elite to a mass system, a tremendous, if tardy, accomplishment. Participation rates are now comparable to those of the United States and Canada. Unfortunately, the growth in numbers of students occurred during years of expenditure restraint, with the result that funding per student has fallen dramatically, by nearly 40 per cent in real terms during the 1990s.[17] It is now far below that of Canada and the United States (and the OECD average).[18] Tuition has been introduced, but the revenues do not nearly offset the decline in public spending. Only massive increases in expenditures can restore the student-faculty ratios and research capacity.

The crisis in Canada is similar, if less acute. The decline in public sector support per student was precipitous in the 1990s. Tuition fees rose very steeply early in the decade, but they could not offset the falling government grants. Canada began from a higher level of spending per student than in the United Kingdom, but it, too, requires massive expenditure increases to restore quality and ensure access. In vivid contrast, the United States has so far maintained the government's support for its public universities and, by increasing tuition fees, has even increased real expenditures per student. American expenditures per student are the highest in the OECD; almost triple the U.K. level, and 70 per cent higher than in Canada.[19]

These data remind us of how welfare states differ by country, sometimes in unexpected ways. The United States is acknowledged to have a more limited welfare state than the United Kingdom or Canada, with gaps in health insurance and the social safety net. The spending restraints of the constrained welfare state are more in keeping with American political culture. Yet, this broad characterization of the U.S. welfare state does not apply to university education. The United States supports its universities much better than any other country does, and it has maintained the support in the constrained welfare state – a telling indicator of how highly Americans value equality of opportunity and how much they believe in the benefits of research and innovation.

The prospect of maintaining government support per student as the number of students increases is brighter in the United States than it is elsewhere, but the pressures of increasing demand will be greatest in the United States. Realistically, the prospect of maintaining real support per student is dim in all three countries.

The leadership of the multiversity will be tested to maintain a sense of purpose and optimism across the entire faculty. Some parts of the multiversity are prospering in the constrained welfare state, especially the professional schools and applied sciences, but most are not. Tensions and resentments will grow between waxing and waning parts of the multiversity, and the daily strain of living in the pincers is draining and discouraging. Annette Kolodny has written a first-person report from the humanities in her 1998 book about American universities, *Failing the Future: A Dean Looks at Higher Education in the Twenty-first Century*. Her dispatches tell the tale.

> My friend Marianna is a full professor of English at a public university in the rural south. She has lately begun to complain that she cannot afford to

retire for another eight years, but she is already counting the days. Her litany of grievances is familiar. Due to severe budget cuts, faculty who leave or retire are not replaced, thus increasing the number of students taught each semester by the remaining faculty. With fewer faculty available students have fewer courses from which to choose, and those courses are inevitably overenrolled and overcrowded.

Under the stress of increasing student numbers, poorly prepared students, and the disappearance of money for research, secretarial support, conference attendance, or even copying course materials, Marianna's colleagues have become fractious, their accustomed southern civility fraying jagged. Marianna dreads department meetings and avoids them when she can. And even though she's taken on large numbers of additional students, continued to serve on committees whenever asked, and still managed to publish a prize-winning book, she received only one 3 percent raise in the last seven years.

A gifted teacher, Marianna no longer finds the classroom satisfying enough to make up for shabby buildings, increasing class sizes, edgy colleagues, and a stagnant salary. The approach of each new school year brings on headaches and depression, which Marianna 'treats' by scaling back her expectations for how much this year's crop of students will be willing to read and write.[20]

Marianna's story is both personal and a systemwide story of how the pincers inexorably squeeze the quality of a university education. Class sizes increase. Libraries and laboratories are worse stocked. The demands placed on each student in a course are reduced. Faculty morale seeps away, unable to resist the pressure to dilute the quality of their teaching.

A great challenge for each nation and each multiversity, in the limits of the constrained welfare state, will be to sustain morale and to sustain, much less enhance, the quality of university education.

New Sources of Revenue: Tuition

The economy of the twenty-first century is an economy of ideas and innovation, requiring highly trained people. The demand for higher education is surging because of increased participation rates and demographic changes. The need for increased public spending is inescapable, but the reality of the constrained welfare state forces another conclusion: new sources of revenue must be found.

A university education brings private benefits to the student and also external benefits to society. The private returns can be measured (at least partially) as the increased income earned by the student after graduation, whereas the external benefits are harder to measure. This makes the argument for public support of universities more difficult, although few dispute that the external social benefits are significant. Under the old political economy, when the welfare state was being constructed, the external benefits to society were presumed and government expenditure rose to meet the rising demand for university education. In the new political economy of the constrained welfare state, there is more emphasis on the private benefits to the student. At the same time, in the new economy of innovation and ideas, the economic returns to a university education have risen. University grants, like all claimants for public expenditure, face a new series of questions. What is the justification for public expenditure? Are there other sources of funds? Should user charges be introduced or increased? These questions and the logic of the constrained welfare state lead inexorably towards increased tuition fees as a source for increasing revenue to multiversities.

Nicholas Barr, in *The Welfare State as Piggy Bank*, follows the questions and logic in an austere and clear-headed discussion of several expenditure responsibilities of the welfare state, including health care, primary and secondary education, and university education. The particular situation of universities is better understood after comparing it with these other claims on public expenditures. Barr's strong message is that 'the major vehicle for health finance should be public funding through taxation or social insurance';[21] his message is also that there should be public provision of primary and secondary education, especially 'if we believe that an important task of the school system is to develop social cohesion – a process that is enhanced if children go through a common educational experience.'[22] However, his logic notes the substantial private benefits of a university education and recommends greater use of tuition fees and market forces in university education. Barr points out that although food is essential for our well-being, we rely on market forces in food production – 'paying pensions to the elderly who then buy food in the same shops as the rest of us, and at the same prices.' University education 'is more like food than health care. It is thus completely compatible to oppose excessive reliance on market forces in school education but to support market mechanisms in combination with income transfers to tertiary education and training.'[23]

This recommendation for increased tuition fees slams against our democratic commitment to accessibility and against the idea of social citizenship. We want more participation of students from low-income backgrounds, not less. Social citizenship impels inclusion of underrepresented groups, not exclusion. Higher tuition fees will surely reduce low-income participation and raise barriers against the underrepresented. No reply to these concerns can be completely satisfactory, because the deterrent of high tuition is real.

Nonetheless, two facts of experience must be acknowledged. Because the current student body comes disproportionately from higher-income backgrounds and because the money for government grants comes from general taxation, the current system of financing universities is regressive, not progressive. Second, there is little evidence that low-tuition university systems have a more representative student body than high-tuition university systems. We are left with the conclusion that low tuition is a poor strategy for improving accessibility. There are better, more cost-effective strategies.

The real imperative, if we are to maintain quality and ensure accessibility in the constrained welfare state, is not to lower tuition, but to combine higher tuition with improved student assistance available to those who need it. Nicholas Barr surveys the international experience and presents compelling evidence of what a well-designed system of student assistance would look like: 'A first, and fundamental, characteristic of a well-designed loan scheme is that it should have income-contingent repayments. Secondly, loans should be sufficient to cover all tuition charges and all living costs, so that tertiary education is free at the point of use. Income-contingent loans automatically tailor repayment to ability to pay. A further advantage is that repayment is determined not by where someone *starts* but by where *she ends up*. The third central feature of a well-designed loan scheme is that students should pay an interest rate on their loans broadly equal to the government's cost of borrowing.'[24] Interest subsidies 'are inefficient, expensive and unfair.' If there are to be subsidies, they should take the form of grants to students at the outset, related to their ability to pay.

Postindustrial society demands a high priority for multiversities if we are to meet our economic and democratic aspirations. It becomes a strategic priority in all nations and jurisdictions to implement a sound framework for financing higher education. If we get the framework wrong, we will stunt individual lives and irreparably harm national well-being. The architecture of the framework is obvious: increases in public funds *and* increases in tuition fees *and* improvements in student assistance. If even one is missing, the structure will not hold, and we will not meet our aspirations.

The United States has recognized the need for public sector support and the need for increased tuition fees, but it lacks comprehensive student assistance. England is increasing tuition, and is far advanced in understanding the need for student assistance, but woefully far behind in public sector support. England was late to move to mass higher education and late to move to increasing tuition fees. When the increase in tuition fees became inevitable, it profoundly shocked the system and very nearly brought down the government. Canada has relied heavily on increased tuition fees, with neither a full system of student assistance nor a sustained level of public sector support.

Establishing the framework for financing higher education is a government responsibility. Within this framework, the strategic priority of individual multiversities must be to plan their own growth, tuition fees, and student assistance. Many multiversity-based systems of student assistance remain ad hoc, cumbersome, poorly integrated with government-provided help, and ill-matched to the strategic priorities of the institution. In the constrained welfare state, there will be great advantage to those multiversities with the best system of student assistance. Reforming the mechanics of a system of student assistance is not glamorous work, most of it done in the back office, but the work is vital to ensuring accessibility to higher education in the years ahead.

Older, more prestigious, more selective universities will be able to increase fees more easily. There is a positive feedback loop where quality allows higher fees, and the higher fees maintain and improve quality, which in turn allows higher fees. This loop will create new differences in quality among universities in a jurisdiction, or country, and across the world. Such differentiation has always been part of the American system, although during much of the postwar period many newer universities advanced rapidly to join the upper ranks. The gaps between multiversities will likely widen again. In Canada, there is a long tradition of equal funding of universities. The constrained welfare state introduces a tension and competition among multiversities that did not exist before.

Higher tuition fees will be charged for high-cost degree programs and degree programs with a high economic return for the students, such as business, law, and medicine. Again, there will be a quality feedback loop, this time creating differentiation across departments and faculties in the same university. In the high-fee departments, faculty salaries will be higher, teaching loads lower, and class sizes smaller. The potential for resentment and debilitating internal conflict is enormous.

Once, multiversities were considered national or even simply regional institutions. Increasingly, the leading multiversities are becoming international institutions, competing against each other to attract the best faculty and the best students. (This impact of globalization is discussed in chapter 10.) These universities 'benchmark' themselves against their international competitors, and countries seek to have 'internationally competitive' research universities. The standards of excellence are international, and multiversities are being judged by international standards. This competition across countries forces multiversities to match their competitors' tuition fees in order that they can match their competitors' faculty salaries, teaching loads, and class sizes. The tuition policies of one country now have international repercussions. In England, the so-called Russell Group of research multiversities, which competes against the U.S. research universities, led the lobbying for the right to charge additional tuition fees precisely because of this international competition.

The debates about quality, access, tuition, and assistance will be fierce and divisive, a potent mix of politics and ideology, idealism and pragmatism, ambition for excellence and passion for social justice. These debates will grow more frequent in the years ahead at the national level and within each multiversity. How they play out will do much to determine the nature and place of each multiversity.

New Sources of Revenue: Fundraising

A third source of revenue for the multiversity, after government grants and tuition fees, is private donations. Many hopes are riding on fundraising as an escape from the pincers of the constrained welfare state.

The United States has a long tradition of private philanthropy, and its multiversities have been extraordinarily successful in private fundraising. For example, during 2001, Harvard University raised U.S. $680 million. We associate these efforts with private universities, but American public multiversities are also very successful. During 2001, Indiana University raised U.S. $300 million. The average across all the reporting multiversities was U.S. $72 million. About 30 per cent of the money is raised from alumni and the remainder in about equal portions from other individuals, corporations, and foundations. About one-half of the money raised annually goes to support current operations; 15 per cent goes for property, buildings, and equipment; and 35 per cent is transferred into endowment funds. These endowments are invested with the return, usually about 3 to 5 per cent, transferred to support annual operations. Very often, these endowment revenues are used to provide student assistance.[25]

The success in recent U.S. fundraising, in conjunction with unprecedented high returns on the stock market during the late 1990s, has created huge endowments especially at long-established elite institutions. These endowments astonish. They are truly beyond comprehension for professors and students at most multiversities. Harvard's endowment (even after a 5 per cent loss in 2000) was U.S. $18 billion. Princeton's endowment is U.S. $8.4 billion, and being a smaller institution, its endowment per student is U.S. $1.83 million (almost 80 per cent larger than Harvard's).[26] If this endowment yields 4 per cent per year, there is $73,000 to spend annually on each student – without any tuition fees or government grants!

Many multiversities across the United States, England, and Canada dream of these successes. Fundraising can be glamorous work, courting the rich and the powerful. Certainly, it is more glamorous than reforming the mechanics of student assistance programs and struggling to build the internal political coalition to support higher tuition fees. But the successes of the elite U.S. universities mask the reality at most U.S. universities. Consider the clearest indicator of long-term success in fundraising: the contribution of endowment income to total operating income. At Harvard, endowment income constitutes 28 per cent of operating income. The University of Michigan has the largest endowment of any public multiversity in the United States, and the third largest endowment per student among public multiversities, but endowment income accounts for only 11 per cent of operating income. For all public multiversities together in the United States, endowment income only contributes about 1 per cent towards operating income. The former president of the University of Michigan, James Duderstadt, concludes that 'while endowment income is important for a small number of elite institutions, it is inconsequential to most of higher education in America.'[27] Private fundraising will not, and cannot, be the solution to the fiscal crisis in university education.

There is no realistic prospect of replicating the fundraising success of the small group of U.S. institutions, across the entire system of multiversities in any country, including the United States itself. There are many new claimants on possible donors in the constrained welfare state. All public institutions – hospitals, museums, symphony orchestras, and service organizations – must rely more on private philanthropy. Also, fundraising is an expensive enterprise requiring large upfront expenditures that take a long time to pay off. The average cost of each gift dollar raised by American academic institutions in the 1980s was 16 cents.[28] It is higher today and much higher for institutions relatively new to major fundraising.

Only a small group of institutions can succeed in making endowment revenues a significant part of operating income. Their success will further widen the gap between the elite institutions and the rest of the system. The past decade saw a dramatic increase in the resources available to well-endowed universities because of their success in fundraising and the extraordinary performance of the stock market. The above-normal stock market returns will not continue, but the relative ability to fundraise will gradually and inexorably create a more differentiated hierarchy across multiversities. Each nation and jurisdiction will have to decide whether public policy should reinforce this hierarchy, giving preference to flagship universities, or should remain neutral, or should lean against the tiering process.

Although its contribution is modest, fundraising is now growing as a source of funds in Canadian and English multiversities. However, the different traditions of philanthropy and the late start mean the funds raised are far below U.S. levels. University of Toronto, the most successful Canadian university raised Can $98 million in 2000–1, and its total endowment reached Can $1.2 billion. Its endowments would place it 54th among U.S. universities, and its endowment per student is U.S. $21,500. Compare that with Princeton's U.S. $1.8 million. Furthermore, endowment revenues at the University of Toronto are only one-half of 1 per cent of operating revenues.[29] For most Canadian universities, endowment income makes an even smaller contribution to operating revenues.

Private philanthropy is still less significant in the finances of English universities. The National Committee of Inquiry into Higher Education (the Dearing Committee) of 1997, explored the financing of higher education in fine detail, but gave almost no attention to private donations. The volume summarizing consultations reported: 'Many of the responses quoted examples of successful acquisition of income from private benefactors and from industry but, in general, there was extreme skepticism about the extent to which this can substitute for public expenditure.'[30] This aspect of the report seems dated, as the situation changes rapidly. The London School of Economics recently completed a £100 million capital campaign, and a tour of English multiversity websites reveals how private fundraising now has a prominent place in the public face of universities. In 2004, a task force report to government was entitled *Increasing Voluntary Giving to Higher Education*, and it urged British universities to take a more American approach to fundraising.[31]

Private fundraising is not the answer to the fiscal crisis. Beyond any doubt, however, private fundraising, especially from alumni and friends, will increase in importance at all multiversities. It is one activity where extra organization and extra effort yields obvious rewards: fundraising can make new things happen. Furthermore, fundraising is important not just because it brings in money. It is important also because it is a way to involve the external community in the teaching and research of the university. A strong social contract with society requires familiarity. Fundraising has become a major part of the work of all presidents, vice-chancellors, and deans; it will become part of the work of most department heads and many faculty members.

Fundraising is certainly a part of the response to the fiscal crises, but only a small part, and a part that is being overemphasized. We have been so dazzled by the success of the elite American institutions that it threatens to consume attention out of all proportion. This preoccupation distorts planning and thinking within the university. Presidents, vice-chancellors, and deans are increasingly chosen for their skills in raising money, rather than their understanding of and commitment to the university mission. The image of a university – its 'brand' in marketing parlance – becomes crucial to success in fundraising. With the increased priority given to fundraising, communications and media relations rise in importance, bringing a centralization of authority and decision-making in order to better control the public image. University advertising and promotional materials exhibit a boosterism that would make a small town mayor blush. Donors determine the direction of new initiatives in the university, not the academic senate or the curiosity of researchers. The democratic role of the university and its responsibility to use its academic freedom to offer social criticism become obscured and undervalued. These are the risks in the constrained welfare state.

The reduction in government grants and the increasing importance of tuition revenue and fundraising give a new complexity to the social contract between the multiversity and society. It used to be that the social contract could be defined and maintained through university-government relations. Now, the university gets its support from a greater diversity of sources. Other parties to the social contract are rising in importance, and many do not have a nuanced appreciation of the multiversity's role, of the delicate balance between taking on tasks for others and the need for institutional autonomy and academic freedom. The economic functions of the university are flourishing, but the democratic functions may wither. In the constrained welfare state, the importance of senior leaders who understand and defend the entire mission of the university has never been greater.

7 The Information Technology Revolution

We live in extraordinary times. We are living during a technological revolution. Advances in computing, communications, and information technologies are so rapid, so extensive, and so transforming as to constitute a revolution comparable to the industrial revolutions. This is changing the way things are made, the way institutions are organized, and the way we communicate. The character of our age is defined by the information technology revolution.

The first industrial revolution began in the mid-eighteenth century propelled by the invention of the steam engine, the spinning jenny and other textile machinery, and new techniques of metallurgy. The second industrial revolution, about a hundred years later, was propelled by new sources of power – electricity and the internal combustion engine – by new scientific understandings of chemicals, developments in steel casting, and by mass production of goods using the assembly line.

Michael Dertouzos, an MIT computer scientist who helped create the information technology (IT) revolution, is one of its most astute observers. In 1997, he published *What Will Be: How the New World of Information Will Change Our Lives*. Looking back to the early 1980s, he recalls how unaware we were: 'In a quiet but relentless way, information technology would soon change the world so profoundly that the movement would claim its place in history as a socioeconomic revolution equal in scale and impact to the two industrial revolutions ... Information technology would alter how we work and play, but more important, it would revise deeper aspects of our lives and of humanity: how we receive health care, how our children learn, how the elderly remain connected to society, how governments conduct their affairs, how ethnic groups preserve their heritage, whose voices are heard, even how nations are formed.'[1]

When Michael Dertouzos writes about *information technology*, under this term he includes what are often separately described as computing, communications, and information technologies. Here, I follow his usage and include all three aspects under information technology. The information technology revolution is about the revolution in computing, the revolution in communications, and the revolution in how information is assembled, analysed, and moved around.

Multiversities are in the middle of this revolution. Ideas emerging from university research are helping to create it: many of the technological advances are made in university laboratories; many of the inventors in private laboratories did PhDs at the great multiversities; and most of the skilled personnel who work in the IT industry received advanced degrees in computer science or engineering from a multiversity. Research universities were among the earliest users of computers, and many communication technologies, most particularly the Internet and e-mail, were created to serve universities.

Multiversities are information institutions. The creation, analysis, and communication of information are fundamental tasks at multiversities. Any list of the major forces reshaping multiversities will include the new information technologies. The technology revolution has huge implications for almost every aspect of the multiversity: for how we do research, for conceptions and regulation of intellectual property, for the connection between the university and the outside world. There is not space here to deal with all of these; each would require a book unto itself. In this chapter, therefore, the focus will be on the implications of the revolution in information technology for undergraduate education and the implications for the multiversity as an institution of democracy.

Predictions for the future differ wildly. In 1997, Peter F. Drucker opined: 'Thirty years from now the big university campuses will be relics. Universities won't survive. It's as large a change as when we first got the printed book. Already we are beginning to deliver more lectures and classes off campus via satellite or two-way video at a fraction of the cost. The college won't survive as a residential institution. Today's buildings are hopelessly unsuited and totally unneeded.'[2] Clark Kerr, in 2001, is more circumspect but still certain that momentous changes are under way: 'Higher education is going through its first great technological change in five centuries – the electronic revolution. Late confrontation with fundamental technological change is the main reason why universities are the major institutions in the western world that have changed so little over the past five centuries ... It is too early to tell in detail how the electronic revolution will affect higher education, but it is likely to be dramatic.'[3]

The information technology revolution brings splendid possibilities. What is now available to students and professors on their personal computers is wondrous. On our computers, we can call up and read Adam Smith's *The Wealth of Nations*. As we study the Romantics and read William Ruskin's discussion of the sky's moral work, we can call up an image of J.M.W. Turner's painting *The Starry Night*. As we read of the founding of the University of Berlin by Wilhelm von Humboldt in 1809, we can call up and listen to Beethoven's Emperor Concerto for piano, composed at that time. We can exchange ideas, by e-mail, with other students in our seminars and with people all over the world.

Alone, each is a marvel, but not revolutionary. Considering them together, however, combined with the frantic pace of technological change, futurists are offering apocalyptic prophesies. The undergraduate lecture will disappear; the professor will be transformed from 'the sage on the stage to the guide on the side.' Courses from private corporations (or from the for-profit enterprises of major multiversities like the LSE or Columbia) will be available on the Web, bleeding enrolments from local universities – with catastrophic financial consequences. Industrial mass production will be the model for university courses. Professors will become assembly line workers.

What are we to make of such prophesies? Certainly the IT revolution is real, and there have been enormous transformations in other areas of our society. During the technology boom, the vast fortunes made in the stock market lent a euphoric air to discussions of the impact of information technology on society. Small wonder that we were hearing apocalyptic prophesies for universities. Alan Greenspan, chairman of the U.S. Federal Reserve Board, diagnosed an 'irrational exuberance' in the stock market.[4] After the collapse of the technology stocks, rationality returned to the analysis of stock prices and, one hopes, to the analysis of the impact of new technologies on multiversities. Although no one can be certain of the future, we can try to have our forecasts governed more by scholarly analysis and less by irrational exuberance. But it is not easy – the dynamism of the technology continues to manifest itself in unpredictable ways. Sometimes our bold predictions come true faster than our dreams, while at other times the bold predictions later reveal complete misunderstanding of the implications of the technology. Even the experts get it wrong, a famous example being Thomas Watson of IBM, who declared in 1947: 'I think there is a world market for maybe five computers.' Equally famously, Bill Gates declared in 1981: '640k ought to be enough for anybody.'

As with the previous chapter, this chapter has two segments. In the first, we examine the ferment of ideas that define our age, and in the second segment we analyse the implications of these ideas for the multiversity. Often these ideas come from research at the multiversity. In the previous chapter, we explored the influence of ideas from research in the social sciences. In this one, we explore the influence of ideas from research in the sciences and engineering.

To examine the revolution in information technology is also to examine the impact of science and engineering upon society. The IT revolution is a stunning example of how the scientific research of multiversities, research of the most basic sort, can reshape society. Information technology research began in the most abstract of mathematics, connected with advanced molecular physics, was transformed at the engineer's workbench, and finally became part of everyday life. Daniel Bell identifies this dynamic – this new relationship between basic science and applied technology – as one of the essences of postindustrial society. The information technology revolution exemplifies this. To study the information technology revolution is to study the complex interplay between pure science and technology, and between curiosity and commerce, in postindustrial society.

The multiversity continues to live in a postindustrial society, one evolving in new and more rapid ways during the revolution in information technology. If we wanted to tell the tale of the extraordinary place of the multiversity in society today, of the impact of its research upon daily life, of the new connections between theoretical knowledge and innovation, there is no better example than the tale of the information technology revolution.

From Mathematics and Physics to the World Wide Web

In his book, Michael Dertouzos articulates five pillars of information technology:

1. Numbers are used to represent all information.
2. These numbers are expressed as 1s and 0s.

3. Computers transform information by doing arithmetic on these numbers.
4. Communication systems move information around by moving around these numbers.
5. Computers and communication systems combine to form computer networks.[5]

Consider the first pillar: numbers are used to represent all information. The wondrous things now available to students and professors (or anyone else) on their computers are examples of information. The text of *The Wealth of Nations*, the image of Turner's painting, the sound of Beethoven's Emperor Concerto, and the e-mail message are all information. Word, image, and sound are information – and can be represented as numbers. Every letter in the alphabet, every numeral, punctuation mark, and spacing, can be represented as a number. Therefore, any book can be represented, or transformed, into a list of numbers. *The Wealth of Nations*, or the e-mail message, can be transformed and represented as a list of numbers.

A painting can also be represented as numbers: 'The picture is divided into a grid of perhaps 200 rows and 200 columns, creating 40,000 tiny square cells called *pixels* (picture elements). The cells are so small that within each one the color does not change. The computer assigns three numbers to each pixel that represent the red, green, and blue components of the color in that pixel.'[6] Because there are 40,000 pixels, a list of 120,000 numbers can represent Turner's *The Starry Night*.

The Beethoven piano concerto can also be rendered into numbers. Samples of the sound are taken, which 'if closely spaced, can be used to play back a seemingly perfect replica. In an audio CD, for example, the sound has been sampled 44.1 thousand times a second. The audio waveform (sound pressure level measured as voltage) is recorded as discrete numbers (themselves turned into bits). Those bit strings, when played back 44.1 thousand times per second, provide a continuous-sounding rendition of the original music.'[7]

Dertouzos writes that information can be a *noun* or a *verb*. The examples above are information nouns. Numbers can also represent active things; they can be information verbs when they are computer programs: 'Computer programs are like recipes; they're made of many instructions that tell the computer what numbers to grab, how to change them, and where to store them. The fascinating thing here is that because computer programs are written in characters and symbols, they too are represented by numbers that correspond to these symbols.'[8] This is the first pillar: all information, including nouns and verbs, can be written as numbers.

The second pillar of information technology is that any number can be rewritten as a sequence of 1s and 0s. Our everyday numbering system uses the base 10. Consider the number 29. Moving from right to left, there is the 1s column, then the 10s column (and for larger numbers, the 100s column, the 1,000s column, and so on). When we look at the number 29, we see there is 9 in the 1s column, and 2 in the 10s column. There are 9 ones and 2 tens, which make the number 29. This same number 29 can be written in base 2. Moving from right to left, the first column is the 1s column, the next is the 2s column, the next is the 4s column, the next is the 8s column, then the 16s column, and so on. The number 29 can be written in a base 2 system as: 11101. This shows there is 1 one, no two, 1 four, 1 eight, and 1 sixteen, which make 29. Any number can be rewritten as 1s and 0s, and therefore, all information can be written as 1s and 0s. The column, that contains either a 1 or a 0, is called a *bit*, from the phrase binary digit. Information technology is a world of bits; because all information is represented by binary digits, it is a digital world. When Nicholas Negroponte, director of MIT's Media Lab, wrote a book about the new information age, he chose for his title: *being digital*.

The third pillar is the computer itself. This is where information nouns and verbs reside and where information work is done. The first computers were mechanical devices of cogs and gears, using base 10 numbering. Then, the computer became an electrical device. Electrical devices are suited to base 2 systems because electrical devices can be structured as on/off switches. Off means 0 and on means 1. 'The ingenious, indeed breathtaking, insight that binary mathematics was perfectly suited to electronic computers occurred more or less simultaneously on both sides of the Atlantic to a pair of ingenious, indeed breathtaking visionaries'[9] – John von Neumann of Princeton University and Alan M. Turing, educated at Cambridge. In the 1940s, both men wrote reports for their governments on the possibilities of an electronic computer and both concluded that the best way to analyse information was to use binary numbers, and so turn 'an inert chain of electronic switches into a powerful computational tool.'[10]

This transformation required a logical system, a mathematical system that rendered all computer programs into a series of yes/no decisions. In a wonderful example of the serendipitous nature of scientific advancement, of the unpredictable interaction between pure curiosity and practical application; this mathematics did not need to be developed – it had already been invented more than a hundred years earlier by an obscure and eccentric English clergyman and mathematician George Boole. In the late 1930s, Claude Shannon, an MIT PhD and leader at Bell Labs, took up Boole's algebra and applied it to the design of computing machines. Shannon's work and the subsequent work of others on the mathematical theory of communication gave us the mathematical structures for the information age.

By 1950, the mathematical, logical structure of the digital electronic computer was understood. People dreamed of what electronic computers could do. However, the engineering lagged behind – but not for long. Here we see the new self-conscious research programs of postindustrial society, the new relationship between pure science and applied technology. And the multiversity is crucial to this (along with governments, corporations, entrepreneurial professors, and venture capitalists).

The early electronic computers used vacuum tubes, remarkable devices that can switch on and off 10,000 times per second, but that require considerable power and radiate considerable heat. The University of Pennsylvania's ENIAC computer 'never lived up to its potential because the tubes kept burning out in the middle of computations ... The warmth and soft glow of the tubes also attracted moths, which would fly through ENIAC's innards and cause short circuits. Ever since, the process of fixing computer problems has been called debugging.'[11]

Computing technology improved steadily as it moved from vacuum tubes, to transistors, to integrated circuits, and finally to microprocessors. Each step required major scientific and engineering innovations, and these came either from the professors of the great research universities or from their graduates. Ideas in the multiversity rolled forward into the information technology revolution.

The first step past the vacuum tube was based upon foundational research in semiconductor physics. Some substances, like copper or gold, are conductors of electricity; while other substances, like glass or rubber, block the flow of electricity and are therefore called insulators. Other materials, like silicon, are in between, and they are called semiconductors. The conductivity of a semiconductor can be altered through a process of molecular manipulation called doping. If pure silicon contains a minute amount of arsenic as an impurity, it becomes a conductor; whereas, if the same pure silicon contains a minute amount of boron, it becomes an insulator. Through doping, a sandwich of conductor, insulator, and conductor could be created. This was the transistor, which can perform all the functions of the vacuum tube. Its sandwich of conductor/insulator/conductor creates an on/off switch, but transistors are smaller, use less power, and radiate far less heat. Three scientists – John Bardeen, Walter Brattain, and William Shockley, after completing PhDs at Princeton, Minnesota, and MIT, respectively – came together at Bell Labs, where they invented the transistor. Later, they would receive the Nobel Prize in Physics for their work.

Transistor-based computers were soon beset by the tyranny of numbers. Large computers required thousands of components – transistors, resistors, capacitors – that all had to be interconnected, soldered together by hand. Possessing millions of soldered joints, the machines often failed. As the circuits became longer, the electrons had to travel farther, thereby reducing computational speed. This tyranny was overcome by the integrated circuit, which combined two engineering breakthroughs: integration and interconnection. Integration meant that all the electrical parts – transistors, resistors, capacitors – were made from the same material, silicon, and an entire circuit was constructed on a single silicon chip. Interconnection meant that the wires connecting the parts were printed on a single chip as part of the production process. Hand-wiring, which was both costly and unreliable, was no longer needed. Her Majesty's Science Advisor called the integrated circuit 'the most remarkable technology ever to hit mankind.'[12]

With the invention of the integrated circuit, technological improvement proceeded at a pace never before seen in history. A physical chemist from Johns Hopkins and co-founder of Fairchild Semiconductor Corporation, Gordon Moore, 'was asked in 1964, when the most advanced chips contained about 60 components, to predict how far the industry would advance in the next decade. "I did it sort of tongue-in-cheek," Moore recalled later.'[13] His casual prediction, now known as Moore's Law, proved true: the number of transistors on an integrated circuit would double every eighteen months. It still holds true. Early in the twenty-first century, advanced chips contain over one billion transistors.

Computers have four fundamental parts: input, processor, memory, and output. The first silicon chips were processors. Memory was handled by a system called magnetic core memory, but soon memory also came to be handled through silicon chips. Memory chips, too, began to improve at the rate of Moore's Law. The quest for further integration and miniaturization was relentless. The next destination was reached with the invention of the microprocessor, which placed all the parts of a computer – input, processor, memory, and output – on one silicon chip. And Moore's Law held again.

The microprocessor made possible the personal computer (PC), and with the PC, the socioeconomic revolution truly began. The power and potential of computing were no longer just for the big institutions who had mainframes; computers could be distributed on every desk and in every home. By the late 1980s, the PC was nearly ubiquitous and very visible. There are even more microprocessors that we do not see. They are in cars, household appliances, cell phones, and practically every electronic device. The third pillar – the computer – is now everywhere.

Dertouzos's fourth pillar of information technology is the communication system. Electronic communication began with the telegraph, followed by the radio, telephone, and television. The communication infrastructures evolved, allowing movement first by copper wire, then through the air between towers on the ground, then along coaxial cable; then through the air, from a tower on earth, up to a satellite, and back down to a tower on earth; and finally, through the air on the ground – wireless – using communication cells. Most of these communication systems were in place before digital technology, but digital technology was able to use the same communication infrastructure. Information (text, sound, and image) is converted into bits and sent along wire, or coaxial cable, or through the air. The 1s and 0s are received and then converted back into text and sound and image. Today, the thrust of the IT revolution is to improve and implement wireless communication systems. We want to take our laptops, our cell phones, or our digital organizers anywhere and be able to communicate with anyone.

Each communication system has a different capacity for handling information, called bandwidth, which means the number of bits per second (bps) that can be sent. Different types of information need different bandwidth: text needs less than voice, voice needs less than music, and video needs most of all. Our desires always exceed the capacity of the communication system. We always want more information, sent faster, with the ultimate dream being real-time interactive video. There is a constant search for greater bandwidth – a bigger pipe for the 1s and 0s to flow through. The biggest pipe, so far, is fibre optic cable, which carries bits along light waves down a fibre of pure glass. The installation of new compression technologies, beginning in 1997, has doubled the capacity of fibre optic cables every six to twelve months, so that the capacity of the communication system is improving faster even than Moore's Law.[14] We might call this the Bandwidth Law.

Dertouzos's fifth pillar of information technology is the computer network: individual computers are linked through a communication system to create a computer network. These networks are the infrastructure of the information age, just as the highway system is an infrastructure of the late industrial age.

The personal computer created a distributed computing environment. This was a time of fragmentation. Most users no longer needed a mainframe because there was so much computing power on their desks. However, this meant that they could no longer talk to one another and share information, as they could when their terminals were all wired into a common mainframe. A solution to this problem came from Robert Metcalfe, an MIT PhD working at Xerox's Palo Alto Research Center (PARC). Metcalfe invented the Ethernet: software for connecting computers with in a building, using cables running from machine to machine. Thus, local area networks (LANS) were created. Reconnection had begun.

The next task was to link computers in disparate locations, not in the same building or in the same organization, into a network. The Advanced Research Projects Agency (ARPA) of the U.S. Department of Defense wanted to connect computer scientists working on ARPA-sponsored research projects at different universities. ARPANET, the first computer network connecting widely dispersed sites, went online in 1969, joining computers at the University of California in Los Angeles, Stanford University, the University of California at Santa Barbara, and the University of Utah.

The benefits to university researchers were immediate – but of an unexpected sort. It was not access to the computing power at another university that proved so useful, but rather the communication among scientists through electronic mail. Programs were developed that transferred a message, or an entire document, from one computer to another and placed it in a 'mailbox,' to be retrieved and opened when the receiver wished. 'Email quickly became the network's most popular and influential service,'[15] and changed the way professors could do collaborative research.

Computer science professors at other universities, envious of their ARPA-supported colleagues, established their own computer network, CSNET. Professors in other disciplines soon saw the benefits. The U.S. National Science Foundation established NSFNET for its constituency and later helped to set up BITNET for non-science scholars. Networks of university researchers were established in other countries; and private networks, within corporations and between corporations, were established. Everywhere, individual computers were being connected into networks.

As each network grows, it becomes more valuable because more people are connected to it. When few people have a telephone, it is not a very useful device; but when almost everyone has one, it becomes a necessity. Bob Metcalfe, inventor of the Ethernet, said that the value of a network increases not in proportion to the number of people on it, but in proportion to the *square* of the number of people on it. This has become known as Metcalfe's Law. With the invention of the modem, computers could be connected via the telephone system. Thus, your PC could join a computer network using the telephone network. With each passing day, the value of joining a network rose faster. With each passing day the value and importance of the fifth pillar grew.

These five pillars make up the new information technology. The rate of technological change is exponential, and it feeds on itself. These ideas of our age have truly created a revolution. Computers improve at the rate of Moore's Law. The capacity of the communication system improves at the rate of the Bandwidth Law. The value of the network grows at the rate of Metcalfe's Law. Other pieces of the technology advance at equally astonishing rates. The capacity to store information on a disc doubles every few years – a disc law. New information sources are added to networks at similar rates – a content law. Software brings new and wondrous applications daily, combining the information nouns and verbs. Software companies, from the giants like Microsoft and Google, to small groups writing code, search ceaselessly for the next application – in the lingo of this world, they search for 'the next killer app.'

Computer usage became easier and easier, with the invention of the mouse, the drop-box menu, and graphic icons. Nonetheless, a few final innovations were needed for IT to alter everyday life, and every professor's and every student's life.

LANS and interuniversity networks proliferated around the world, but the networks had trouble communicating with one another. Vincent Cerf, of Stanford University, and others, developed protocols that allowed networks to talk to one another. Finally, one worldwide network, the network of networks, was created – the Internet.

The protocols allowed different networks to talk to one another (to exchange bits), even though the computers were being made by different manufacturers and using different programming languages. Cerf created an Esperanto among computers, now accepted universally. This Internet Esperanto is represented technically as TCP/IP (transmission control protocol/Internet protocol). The brilliance of this construct is that local computers can continue to use their own language, only requiring Esperanto when they speak across networks. With this the world could be connected, electronically, and in a way that overcame the all-too-familiar language barriers among nations. This Esperanto of electronic bits allowed globalization on an unprecedented scale.

By the early 1990s, all universities were connected to the Internet, but the Internet still remained within the university and research communities. The first steps that would move the Internet beyond the research community and into daily life were taken in a most serendipitous way by Timothy Berners-Lee, working at CERN, the European Particle Physics Laboratory in Geneva. There is where the World Wide Web began.

Berners-Lee was working on a way to keep track of all the documents on all the computers at CERN. Scientists would come to CERN from all over the world and often they would bring their own computers, with their own systems; and they would file their documents in their own way. Berners-Lee had a larger vision: *'Suppose all the information stored on computers everywhere were linked*, I thought. *Suppose I could program my computer to create a space in which anything could be linked to anything*. All the bits of information in every computer at CERN, or on the planet, would be available to me and to anyone else. There would be a single global information space.'[16]

In 1965, many years before Berners-Lee was at CERN, Ted Nelson, an eccentric visionary and one of the few pioneers of the information age with a background in the humanities, wrote of 'literary machines,' computers that would enable people to write and publish in a new, non-linear format, which he called hypertext. Hypertext was a series of documents linked to one another, but it was a 'non-sequential' text, in which a reader was not constrained to read in any particular order.

At its simplest, hypertext is a series of linked documents. A document appears on someone's computer screen, with links to many other documents indicated in boldface print. By moving the mouse, the cursor is placed on the bold-printed words. With a click, a link is made to another document, which fills the screen, replacing the first document. This second document also contains bold-printed items, indicating links to still further documents. After visiting them, by clicking the 'Back' icon atop the computer screen, a reverse link is made. With other back clicks, one can return to the original document, and so navigate this web of information. There are a myriad of paths along the web. Ted Nelson thought that, in the future, novels would be constructed this way, with each reader following her or his own path through the material. For Nelson, hypertext is a book with many branches; it allows choices to the reader. Nelson thought these books would be read using an interactive video screen. His vision brought a literary, even poetic, conceptualization of the web of information.

Two parts of the new information technology – the Internet and hypertext – had been around for almost twenty years. It was Berners-Lee's genius to put them together to create the World Wide Web.

Hypertext began as a means to link documents on one computer. Suppose however, we should want to link documents across many computers, computers that are already connected via the Internet. The World Wide Web links documents across computers using hypertext. First, every document has to be identified and located on a specific network and specific computer: this is the URL, the universal resource locator. Then, there has to be a standard computer language for creating hypertext links: this is HTML, hypertext markup language. Finally, there has to be an Esperanto for the hypertext connections across the computers connected via the Internet: this is HTTP, hypertext transfer protocol. With these three – URL, HTML, and HTTP – the World Wide Web was created. And thanks to the vision and tenacity of people like Vincent Cerf and Timothy Berners-Lee, it is a stunningly democratic invention.

No one owns or regulates participation on the Web. Anyone, anywhere, can put information on the Web. Anyone, anywhere, can access that information. A single global information space, a World Wide Web, is created. Berners-Lee's dream has been realized. It is because the Internet had its beginnings in the ethos of science and the university, where knowledge is public and shared, that the World Wide Web could become such an accessible and democratic a technology. These early pioneers were well aware of the commercial potential of what they were working on, but they were motivated by something else – Pekka Himanen has called it 'the spirit of the information age.' He writes that in this spirit 'information-sharing is a powerful positive social good' and that it is the ethical duty of information technology professionals 'to share their expertise by writing free software and facilitating access to information and computing resources wherever possible.'[17] The world owes an enormous debt to their vision and spirit.

During the early 1990s, the U.S. National Science Foundation was 'managing' the Internet. There were numerous commercial networks, but these could not be connected to the Internet because the Internet was restricted to non-profit research and educational uses. However, the logic of connecting private networks to the Internet was inescapable, and the Internet and its management were privatized by 1995. It remained just as democratic, but now the Internet could be used for commercial purposes and all the private networks could join onto this network of networks.

The Internet and the Web were still cumbersome to use, however. A browser is software that allows a person to read hypertext documents. The set of documents interconnected by links is called a web. We navigate a web using our browser, moving from document to document, following the links. Berners-Lee's browser was text-based – easy for computer scientists to use, but hard for the layperson. Soon a better browser was invented. It was not text-based; instead, documents could contain images, and these images could also be used as links to other documents. Then, a search engine was added to the browser. Previous browsers required that users know where they wanted to go; they had to know the URL of the document. A search engine allows the user to type in a name, or a topic, or a group of words, and the search engine will find relevant websites. Navigating the Web became surfing the Web – it was fun and it was easy, easy for anyone.

The new software creating an easy-to-use browser and search engine began with Professor Marc Andreessen and his team at the National Center for Supercomputing Applications at the University of Illinois. Andreessen took it to Silicon Valley, joined with venture capitalists, and created Netscape. In 1995, that company went public. On the first day of trading, shares opened at $12 and closed at $48, and within three months they were at $140.

Netscape typified the conflicting forces in this technological revolution. It began in a multiversity laboratory and was transformed into one of the most famous stories of swashbuckling capitalism. It created billions for its owners but also reinforced an open democratic technology. Netscape made sure that the World Wide Web would continue to be based upon open protocols – TCP/IP, HTML, and so on. None of this would be proprietary to one company. These standards were agreed upon across the world. Anyone, anywhere, and without anyone's permission, could hook themselves onto the Internet, becoming both a receiver of information and a source of information.

In 1985, about two thousand computers had Internet access. By the end of the 1980s, there were 200,000. This is an extraordinary growth rate, but the absolute number was still modest. Then the World Wide Web arrived, commercial uses were allowed, and Netscape made navigation easy. The pace of revolutionary change in IT hardware was more than matched by the pace of innovation in software. Microsoft seemed to power every PC and Google, the most-used search engine, even entered the language as the verb 'to google,' meaning 'to search the Web.' The telecommunications explosion laid fibre optic cable across the world, and wireless connectivity spread equally quickly. The most remote and tiny towns now have Internet cafes. In early 2006, the number of people using the Internet was over one billion and climbing.[18] We live in the information age.

The Information Age and the Multiversity

The information age became possible through the ferment of ideas, ideas from mathematics, physics, computer science, and engineering. Society is being transformed by this revolution in computing, communications, and information technology. We have phenomenal computing power, which is still getting faster, while its devices are still getting smaller. Software allows more and more sophisticated tasks. The content available on the Web multiplies and multiplies. Greater bandwidth allows more to flow, and flow faster. Anyone can connect to this network, and everyone can connect to each other. Wireless technology means access to the network is spreading rapidly through all space. We truly have the World Wide Web of information, as imagined by Timothy Berners-Lee. The next three chapters explore three other characteristics of our age: postmodern thought, the close connection between research and economic growth, and globalization. The IT revolution is so pervasive that each of these three other characteristics of our age is itself shaped by this revolution.

The multiversity is making enormous financial commitments in information technology: for computers, fibre optic cables, servers, routers, Internet connections, software, helpdesks, and technicians. There are commitments in virtually every university activity from teaching to alumni affairs, from research to human resources, from the registrar's office to the library. So important and pervasive is IT that most multiversities have created a new vice-presidential position: the chief information officer. Information technology is now part of the strategic planning of multiversities at the highest level. Those multiversities that plan well will flourish, while those that do not will squander millions of dollars, money that could have been much better spent.

Every multiversity must now ask itself how it is adapting to the information age – how can the information technologies help it to fulfil its basic responsibilities for research, teaching, and service? To answer these questions requires long and deep reflection, and imagination. And because the new technologies bring such opportunities for communication and for sharing information, running through all such reflections should be the question of how the technologies can enable the multiversity to improve its service to society, especially its contribution to democratic life. There will be no one answer for all institutions, and answers will change as technology changes. The questions cannot be avoided, however, and the answers are a continuing challenge for multiversities in the information age. A few of the major implications of the revolution in IT are briefly sketched in this section and the balance of the chapter is devoted to exploring the implications for undergraduate education.

The technology revolution has fundamental implications for the activities of the multiversity. For example, research in every discipline – in the sciences, the professions, the social sciences, humanities, and fine arts[19] – is being transformed by high-speed computation and new software. Two prominent examples are research on the human genome and research on global climate; both require such vast computing power that today's research was impossible even a decade ago. Other examples are computer-based visualization and simulation techniques that take scholars to new frontiers in many disciplines, from psychology to English literature. Professors collaborate across the Internet; new results can be circulated across the globe instantly. No summary of the innovations is even remotely possible. On the whole, the revolution is welcomed: it brings new capabilities and possibilities for research. There are some worries, however, that these developments favour mathematical and quantitative research and are pushing out reflective, synthetic, and qualitative work. But, there is room for diversity, the curiosity of scholars over time encourages balance, and good work of all types can flourish.

New information technology provides dramatic new opportunities to make research more open and more democratic. There are a number of research initiatives worldwide and one suggestion is that each multiversity take responsibility to open-archive the papers published by its professors.[20] A more radical proposal is that research projects be reported on the Web while in progress, in order to allow greater involvement and criticism from those outside the scientific community.[21] The U.K.-based Scientists for Global Responsibility advocate open knowledge and democratic science, including 'the promotion of constructive dialogue between scientists and non-scientists. An important condition for a dialogue between equals is that the assessment of science funding applications be democratized.'[22] New information technologies are making these initiatives possible.

The IT revolution does not always lead to greater openness, however. The revolution has created a new image in our minds of how multiversity research and society are connected. In the IT model, governments fund basic research at multiversities, provide support for visionary applications, and purchase the early products. Basic research is done in many locations: at the major research universities, in specialized institutes such as Bell Labs or Xerox PARC, and in the industrial laboratories of companies like Fairchild Semiconductor, Intel, and Texas Instruments. Software is written at universities, consulting firms, and, of course, by giant companies like Microsoft. Professors move back and forth among the universities, institutes, and corporations. Academics spin off their findings into private companies. The IT revolution also requires highly specialized venture capital markets. Governments, corporations, research universities, entrepreneurial graduates and professors, and venture capital firms are the consortia of the information age. Many observers take this framework as the new paradigm for all national innovation, and the new paradigm for the interconnection between the multiversity and the economy. The iconic model is Silicon Valley. Clustered around Stanford University are research labs of major corporations, small start-up companies created by entrepreneurial professors and their students, and venture capital firms supplying risk capital for the new ventures. This new image invites the multiversity and its professors to be actively engaged in the commercialization of research and to espouse the privatization of knowledge against the long scientific tradition of public knowledge. These issues are taken up in chapter 9, where the commercial character of our age and its effects on multiversity research are examined.

The meaning of 'the library' is being transformed, too, as enormous quantities of information are made available to students and scholars over the Web – both new primary sources and published work. At first, most of the material on the Web was not in the library; the Web was an addition to traditionally published material. Then, gradually, academic journals, previously only available in the library, were digitized and made available electronically; then the new issues became immediately available online. Now, there are massive initiatives to put all published work – past and present – online. Google has embarked on a project with five partners (the New York Public Library, and the libraries of Oxford, Harvard, Stanford, and the University of Michigan) to digitize the contents of their libraries, including the material still under copyright. The digitized books will not be available online, only an elaborate searchable catalogue with a few pages from each book. Another major initiative, the Open Content Alliance, again a consortium of libraries, is putting hundreds of thousands of volumes whose copyrights have expired up on the Web. The dream is enticing. Lawrence Lessig, a professor at Stanford Law School and founder of the Stanford Center for Internet and Society, writes: 'Perhaps the single most important feature of the digital revolution is that for the first time since the library of Alexandria, it is feasible to imagine constructing archives that hold all culture produced or distributed publicly. Technology makes it possible to imagine an archive of all books published, and increasingly makes it possible to imagine an archive of all moving images and sound.'[23] And this would not just be a library for all universities, it would be a library for everyone. As a recent *New York Times* essay on these scanning projects noted, many of us have 'thousands of books at home, can walk to big-box bookstores and well-stocked libraries and can get Amazon.com to deliver the next day. The most dramatic effect of digital libraries will not be on us, but on the billions of people worldwide who are underserved by ordinary paper books. It is these underbooked – students in Mali, scientists in Kazakhstan, elderly people in Peru – whose lives will be transformed when even the simplest unadorned version of the universal library is placed in their hands.'[24] The multiversity and its libraries should join vigorously this democratization of information.

More and more multiversities are recognizing the potential of information technology to enhance the role of professors as public intellectuals. Many professors post digests of their research on special-topic websites; many contribute to the discussion groups on the Web, and some now write their own 'blogs' (in the lingo of this world, a blog, short for weblog, is a website where a person posts a log of his or her thoughts). Consortia of universities or scholarly associations have mounted huge amounts of material on special-topic websites. Each website offers links to related websites managed by others; often the sites do not collaborate or work together on any basis other than linking their sites. All of these are available to people outside the university via the new technology.

The multiversity has yet to demonstrate much commitment or imagination in enhancing its responsibility to be critic and conscience, however. The role is always difficult, but this cannot excuse inaction. The university as an institution cannot be the conscience or critic, because under the social contract the university enjoys autonomy from the government and, in return, must remain neutral on issues of the day. Nonetheless, the university as an institution has a responsibility to foster, protect, and value the contributions of professors and students as critics and conscience of society. The Web offers new means to connect, communicate, and publish, creating possibilities for increased democratic dialogue. The university could use the Web to create virtual Hyde Park Corners or town hall meetings; it could host open online seminars on controversial issues of the day, or it could present research findings to assist in developing policy alternatives. Social criticism is important to our democracy, and the multiversity is an essential, and specially protected, source of informed critique. The multiversity could do more to fulfil this responsibility to democracy in the information age.

The IT revolution raises profound dilemmas about copyright and intellectual property. When information becomes digital, it can be copied and given to someone else virtually for free. This offers wonderful opportunities for sharing knowledge, but tears away traditional protections for those who have created it. How in the information age can we share knowledge and yet protect the incentives and rights of those who create knowledge? Lawrence Lessig argues that how society answers this question will determine the nature and future of creativity.[25]

Most of the new possibilities brought by the information age are not threatening; they enhance the work of the multiversity. However, in some areas the potential changes in the information age are more uneven; there can be many gains but also many losses, and much of the investment may bring little improvement. This is particularly true for undergraduate education, the central task of the multiversity. Here is where we find the most extreme predictions – and the greatest worries. There are many Jeremiahs, but just as many prophets of a New Jerusalem.

Teaching and Learning (and Technology)

To think deeply about the implications of the information technology revolution for undergraduate education is to think deeply about the mission of the university. It requires that we think about the purposes of an undergraduate education, what will be taught, and how we will teach it. In the years ahead, if we want to think carefully about undergraduate teaching and learning, we will have to think carefully about the implications of the information age, especially the implications for how we teach the curriculum. History tells us that past industrial revolutions took decades before the implications were fully felt; the same will be true for the IT revolution. It will be reshaping undergraduate education for years to come.

A dystopian vision of university teaching in the information age has been offered by professorial gadfly David Noble, in his 1997 essays *Digital Diploma Mills: The Automation of Higher Education*. Noble regards information technology as an industrial technology of mass production. The technology allows education to be standardized: courses are provided over the Web, with little involvement of the professor ostensibly giving the course. Commercial interests provide 'educational products,' drawing 'the halls of academe into the age of automation.' Noble concludes by quoting an earlier study of distance education: 'In his classic 1959 study of diploma mills for the American Council on Education, Robert Reid described the typical diploma mill as having the following characteristics: "no classrooms," "faculties are often untrained or nonexistent," and "the officers are unethical self-seekers whose qualifications are no better than their offerings."' This Noble declares 'is an apt description of the digital diploma mills now in the making. Quality higher education will not disappear entirely, but it will soon become the exclusive preserve of the privileged, available only to the children of the rich and the powerful. For the rest of us a dismal new era of higher education has dawned. In ten years, we will look upon the wired remains of our once great democratic higher education system and wonder how we let it happen.'[26]

Noble foresees standardized, mass-produced university courses delivered online. Private corporations will dominate, both as new private virtual universities and as suppliers of the online courses to be delivered by existing universities. Implicit in his prognosis is a belief that online education will be of lower cost and lower quality and that the lower cost and greater convenience of online education will drive out the higher-cost, higher-quality traditional pedagogy.

Others see the future differently. Nicholas Negroponte foresees a dramatic change in the human-computer interface, bringing a utopia: 'The best metaphor I can conceive of for a human-computer interface is that of a well-trained English butler. The "agent" answers the phone, recognizes the callers, disturbs you when appropriate, and may even tell a white lie on your behalf. The same agent is well trained in timing, versed in finding the appropriate moments, and respectful of your idiosyncrasies. People who know the butler enjoy considerable advantage over a total stranger. That is just fine.'[27] Negroponte suggests that digital butlers can help plan your schedule, help buy and cook your food, and help plant and weed your garden. He doesn't talk about universities, but if there can be digital butlers, there will be digital professors. In such a world, undergraduate education is enormously improved. The education can be tailored to, and responsive to, the needs of each individual student. It can be delivered at a time, place, and pace suited to the individual. This is a world of student-centred and student-led learning, connected to the student's own professor and other students online, and assisted by digital professors and other online materials.

The vision of a New Jerusalem assumes that IT brings higher quality education and that the extra costs, if any, will be worth the extra benefits. Often, the implicit assumption is that this higher quality online education is also at a lower cost. Again, the new technology will supplant the old.

What will the future bring? Will there be digital diploma mills or digital professors? Will traditional pedagogy be replaced by online courses? Will undergraduate learning be enhanced or degraded?

For the computer and the World Wide Web to become a digital professor requires two major breakthroughs: first, in speech-recognition and voice-recognition software and, second, in artificial intelligence.

The Information Technology Revolution   199

The human voice, and the language it uses, is rich and complex. A talking computer must both speak and understand. No talking machine yet sounds like a human voice. Dertouzos, writing in 1997, concludes that 'speech-understanding systems with vocabularies of a few thousand words that stick to specific domains ... should be commercially available well within a decade.' [28] But they will be restricted to domains where the discussion is narrow and well-structured. 'Though you will be able to use them to book a flight, you won't be able to discuss politics with them, because of the incredible richness of concepts that such a broad topic would entail.'[29] Artificial intelligence is similarly limited. Digital professors are creatures of science fiction.

Likewise, the dystopian predictions have not come to pass. The development of online courses has been slow at multiversities. The new technologies are being used to complement traditional pedagogy, rather than replace it. Professors still control their courses. The process of using information technology, contrary to David Noble, is nothing like industrial mass production. Many consortia, both of multiversities and private firms, established in the 1990s to provide online university courses have failed, even ones involving elite research universities.[30] Online courses have not driven out traditional pedagogy. David Noble's prophesy of digital diploma mills has proven wildly off the mark.[31] Nonetheless, we should not doubt that university teaching is going through a great technological revolution. There are hundreds of experiments going on, in every discipline and every multiversity, using IT in teaching. Every multiversity has an office that encourages and supports these innovations. The tantalizing questions remain: what will university teaching look like in twenty years, and will it be any better?

A little-recognized effect of the controversy over online courses is that it has stimulated a debate about undergraduate teaching, a more probing and more vigorous debate than multiversities have seen in decades. This debate is forcing a new look at existing courses and existing practices, and much of what we see in existing practices is not very good. Undergraduate teaching has not been a priority of most multiversities or most professors. Many undergraduate classes are very large, and many undergraduates are disengaged from their studies. The new technologies have forced professors to ask again the age-old questions. What is the purpose of my course? What is the role of the lecture, the seminar/laboratory, the list of readings, and the assessment? How do students learn? Do learning styles differ? These questions must be posed and answered as part of answering how IT might improve learning.

Clark Kerr notes that 'this is the fourth revolution in the technology of education and the first in 500 years. The first came as specialized teachers or tutors supplemented the teaching of children by families and of apprentices by journeymen, as sedentary agriculture and cities replaced a nomadic existence. The second revolution, writing, occurred about the same time as the first, the third with the printing press, and now the fourth with electronic communications.'[32] In Kerr's typology, we have had three revolutions in the technology of education: the teacher, writing, and the book. To this we are now adding IT: computing, communications, and information technology.

Kerr's typology of revolutions in the technology of education is too limited. It can be enriched by adding two other great changes in the way university teaching is done; and when we recognize these changes, we are better able to forecast the implications for undergraduate education of the IT revolution. One revolutionary change in teaching was the introduction of the laboratory and the laboratory demonstration into the curriculum; this occurred when the 'new science' entered the university. The Scottish universities of the eighteenth century led in introducing science and medicine into the curriculum and pioneered the use of laboratories in teaching.

Another revolution in university education occurred when universities adopted the research ideal in the late nineteenth century, and it became essential to the character of university teaching that the professor be an active scholar. The university professor must not only have a deep literacy in his or her discipline, but must also be a scholar, doing research and contributing to that literature. Thus, research is both a task for the professor and a qualification to be a teacher. This became the fundamental distinction between teaching at the university and teaching at other educational institutions. Each professor designs her or his own course, within broad guidelines set by the particular department. The design and revision of a course are acts of creative scholarship for each professor. The professor is a model of the discipline: a practitioner in the field, exemplifying how literacy is obtained, how knowledge claims are assessed, and how new knowledge is created. It was also at this time that the lecture was introduced as a form of teaching. In their lectures, the professors, as active scholars in the field, would critique existing knowledge and present and analyse the most recent advances. Their lectures are specific to them and are always changing. Professors are not teachers anymore, they are teacher/researchers.

The ways of teaching at modern multiversities are many and varied, with differences across disciplines and differences across universities in the same discipline. And there are many ways to characterize and analyse the processes of teaching and learning. Nonetheless, below I construct a conceptual schema of an undergraduate university course, as it was before the introduction of the new information technologies. With this conceptual schema in hand, we can ask how the new information technologies might transform the university course, perhaps even supplanting the old approach.

A student's undergraduate degree program is made up of courses, usually fifteen to twenty full-year courses for a four-year degree. A student chooses a major program, within these courses. The student's program of study is modular, built up from discrete, relatively autonomous courses. In my schema, each course can be conceptualized as having six components: the lecture, office hours, the seminar/laboratory, the library, assessment, and serendipity.

The lecture is prepared and given by the professor. In today's budget squeeze, lower-year courses usually have a large number of students, with minimal opportunities for discussion or questions. Upper-year courses are much smaller, with more opportunity for discussion and questions. The professor sets aside a number of hours per week in which they will be available in his or her office to answer questions, have a discussion, or provide other sorts of assistance. Students come singly, but also often in groups.

The seminar/laboratory is a smaller group, designed by the professor but often supervised by a graduate student. Not all courses have a seminar/lab component, but many do, especially the large lower-level courses. The seminar (tutorial) provides opportunity for discussion, student presentations, questions-and-answers, and working through assigned problems. The laboratory (including the computer lab) provides hands-on experience with the methods and equipment used in a particular discipline. The laboratory is fundamental to teaching the experimental, empirical basis of scientific knowledge. (In smaller courses, usually in upper years, we can think of the lecture and seminar/lab combined as one.)

The library component is a symbol for the literature of a discipline. In most courses, this means books, chapters, and articles in academic journals; in fine arts courses, it also means images or music. It also means the primary source materials that students may use in doing their own research and analysis. The professor provides a reading list, but the students go much beyond it.

Each course has a system of assessment: examinations, usually written but sometimes oral, tests, essays, problem sets, and laboratory reports. The student's contribution to seminar discussions is sometimes evaluated and included in calculating a final grade. Assessment allows students to see how well they have mastered the material; but equally important, assessment is a structured exercise in the presentation of ideas or a sustained argument or critical thinking.

Serendipity is the learning that takes place outside the formal structure of a course or guidance of a professor; outside the listening in the lecture, outside the discussion in the seminar, outside the reading from the library. Serendipitous learning occurs in conversation among students, perhaps in the same course and the same discipline, perhaps not. It occurs in corridors, coffeeshops, pubs, and dorms, on and off campus. Serendip is the old name for Sri Lanka – the three princes of Serendip had the gift of making desirable discoveries by accident: serendipity.

This is the schema of an undergraduate course, of teaching and learning, prior to the IT revolution. Online courses are built upon exactly the same schema. The new technologies have been used to offer the same discrete course. The software to deliver a course, called courseware, has the same six components. Each course creates a website, containing the six components: lecture, office hours, seminar/laboratory, library, assessment, and serendipity.[33] If all the components are filled in, the courseware platform can deliver an entire course online, and through a sequence of courses, an entire degree. And, if all courses were online, there would be a virtual university.

The lecture component involves placing the professor's lecture notes and other textual material on the course website, often enhanced with pictures and sound. Interviews with the professor and other experts can be presented. Often, this online content is complemented by a text or other books that the student buys, just as in an 'old style' course. The office hours are handled through e-mail exchanges between student and professor. The seminar/laboratory component is provided by software that allows for text-based discussion among seminar participants and the seminar leader, again often a graduate student. Some software simulates the laboratory experience. The library is emulated by providing links to information on the Web. And there is an ever-increasing amount of material on the Web; the multiversity student today has sources that could only be dreamt of a few short years ago.[34] Much assessment can be done online. There is discussion software to permit serendipitous conversation among students, although online text-based conversation rather than face-to-face oral conversation.

How do the new online courses compare with the traditional pedagogy? Some components, at least superficially, seem very similar. The lecture online, the office hours, and assessment online look similar. Serendipitous learning can occur through online discussion, although with much diminished possibilities. The Web cannot entirely reproduce the library, at least not yet, because most published work has still not been digitized. The Web does offer easier access to information, and much of the Web's information goes beyond what is available in the library. But the Web does not yet offer access to everything currently in the library. In their awe and delight with the new technology, many people do not appreciate that most of the books in the library are still not available on the Web. You can look up the books in the library catalogue on the Web, but you cannot read the book itself on your computer screen. There remains an inescapable need for actual books and for libraries. A university that relied only on the Web would be utterly impoverished.

The component most difficult, indeed almost impossible, to replicate online is the seminar/laboratory. It is very difficult to recreate online the interactive discussion of a live seminar, and in most cases it is impossible to recreate the scientific laboratory. The laboratory experience of the science and engineering curriculum cannot be moved online. There is no online substitute for being in a real lab, just as in the fine arts, there is no substitute for being in a dance studio or life-drawing class.

The new courses do have some advantages, though. Old courses occur at a specific time and specific place on campus: students must come to the specific place and must learn at the pace of the lectures and seminars. New online courses can occur any time and any place there is a computer hooked to the Web. Students can learn from anywhere and at their own pace. And it must be acknowledged that traditional pedagogy has its problems – in today's budget pincers, many lectures are huge, allowing but little contact with professors, and many seminars/labs are led by inexperienced graduate students. Perhaps online courses can mitigate these shortcomings.

The great question for undergraduate education in the information age is whether we can develop online courses that replicate, or even improve upon, the learning in traditionally delivered courses. There has been a great deal written on this question, as the many experiments using IT in teaching are reported and assessed. While useful, I have not found this literature especially insightful, in part, because the authors so obviously have been optimists or sceptics; most often they are optimists. To my mind, more insight is provided in another literature.

Orality and Literacy

In the discussion thus far, like most writers, I have treated information technology as a type of industrial technology. But this is not helpful when examining the implications for teaching and learning. The central question for teaching and learning is whether we can replace oral, face-to-face communication between professor and student, and between student and student, with online communication. In their essence, the Internet and the Web are communication technologies. The technology may have an economic and social impact comparable to that of the industrial revolution, but in thinking about the impact on teaching, scholars like David Noble have been wrong to conceptualize IT as a mass production industrial technology. Information technology will not turn university courses into standardized products delivered by private corporations. Instead, information technology should be conceptualized as a communication technology. We gain perspective by analysing the impact of previous revolutions in communication technologies, like the invention of writing, or the printing press, or television. We will learn more about the impact of information technology on multiversity education by reading communications scholars such as Harold Innis, Marshall McLuhan, or Walter Ong, than by reading histories of the industrial revolution.

Beginning with the pioneering scholarship of Harold Innis,[35] communications scholars have argued that the media of communication shape the character of knowledge and how it is used, and that marked changes in the media of communication have profound implications for societies. The sweep of historical analysis by communications scholars begins with the oral tradition, moves to the literate tradition brought by the invention of writing and the creation of a scribal culture, through to the invention of the printing press and movable type by Johann Gutenberg in 1454. The next great shift was the 'industrialization' of book production in the early nineteenth century, when paper was produced by machinery and power was applied to the printing press. Finally, these scholars examine the electronic media of communication: radio, telephone, and television. In the famous aphorism of Marshall McLuhan, 'the medium is the message.' The medium of communication shapes the very character of knowledge.

In oral societies, the transmission of knowledge 'can be visualized as a long chain of interlocking conversations between members of the group. Thus all beliefs and values, all forms of knowledge are communicated between individuals in face-to-face contact ... Changes in [their] content are accompanied by the homeostatic process of forgetting or transforming those parts of the tradition that cease to be either necessary or relevant.'[36]

Literate societies, societies after the discovery of writing, 'cannot discard, absorb or transmit the past in the same way. Instead, their members are faced with permanently recorded versions of the past and its beliefs; and because the past is thus set apart from the present, historical inquiry becomes possible. This in turn encourages scepticism; and scepticism, not only about the legendary past, but about received ideas about the universe as a whole. From here the next step is to see how to build up and to test alternative explanations; and out of this there arose the kind of logical, specialized, and cumulative intellectual tradition of sixth-century Iona.'[37]

The change after the invention of writing was enormous, but gradual. The circulation of manuscripts was limited because manuscripts, handwritten by scribes, were few and expensive. Furthermore, the information in manuscripts was not standardized; supposedly identical copies produced by each scribe actually differed, sometimes greatly.[38]

With Gutenberg's movable type and the printing press, books replaced manuscripts as the means to transmit knowledge through time and over space, and wide dissemination became possible. Mechanically created copies are exact; after each revision or refinement, all subsequent copies are identical. All readers confront the same text. The standardization of notation was important not only for spelling and grammar, but also for mathematics, musical scores, and astronomical tables. The book as a communication medium supports linear, abstract knowledge, allowing long, complex, patterns of reasoning. Back-looping and forward-looping are facilitated, allowing readers to re-establish where they have been and to see where they are going. The book is suited to the accumulation and progress of knowledge. Existing ideas are captured and codified to be juxtaposed against new ideas; new, challenging ideas can be easily disseminated.

The invention of the book made private reading possible, and created popular literature. The book was vital to the Catholic Church, allowing distribution of the canonical texts, especially the Bible; but equally vital to the Reformation and resistance to Catholic views on canonical text. The book is both fixed and multiple, public and private, shifting knowledge in complex and contradictory ways. Universities enormously influenced the development of the book, by creating a demand for books, and by demonstrating that books could be used for non-religious purposes.[39]

The nineteenth-century industrialization of printing accelerated the influence of books, magazines, and newspapers. When combined with urbanization, improvements in transportation, and increasing primary education, truly mass circulation became possible. Broadsheets, dime novels, and penny dreadfuls flourished. These – not radio and television – were the first mass media. Industrialized publishing was needed to produce the books required by the rapid expansion and revised curricula of universities in the late nineteenth century. Some scholars argue that the expansion of universities was held up until the nineteenth century because not enough books could be printed before then.

The book and the university grew up together. The book so shaped the university and is so integral to its mission that we think of university culture as a book culture, and indeed it is. However, the university is equally an oral culture. Universities are best understood as a combination of oral culture and book culture.

With the industrialized book and the huge increase in demand for university education during the late nineteenth century, one might have thought that university education would be radically transformed. Books could be sent anywhere, making education possible any time and any place; the sage on the stage could be replaced by the guide on the side. But university education did not change. Rather, the number and size of universities expanded to meet the demand, using the traditional pedagogy. During the 1960s, a new mass medium, television, and another surge in demand for university education were similarly predicted to create a new technology of university education, but it did not happen. The universities expanded again, again using the traditional pedagogy. What each new communication medium primarily did was facilitate distance education, meeting the needs of those who could not come to the expanding campuses that still used the traditional pedagogy.

Walter J. Ong studied cultures of the spoken word and cultures of the written word, his work culminating in his famous book, *Orality and Literacy: The Technologizing of the Word*. The written word uses our sense of sight, whereas the spoken word uses our sense of sound. Ong writes: 'sight isolates, sound incorporates.' 'Because in its physical constitution in sound, the spoken word proceeds from the human interior and manifests human beings to one another as conscious interiors, as persons, the spoken word forms human beings into close-knit groups. When a speaker is addressing an audience the members of the audience normally become a unity, with themselves and with their speaker.'[40] In education, spoken words flow between teacher and student, student and teacher, and between student and student, forming them all into a close-knit group.

Ong notes that orality is redundant or capacious: 'Redundancy is also favoured by the physical conditions of oral expression before a large audience, where redundancy is in fact more marked than in most face-to-face conversation. Not everyone in a large audience understands every word a speaker utters, if only because of acoustical problems. It is advantageous for the speaker to say the same thing, or equivalently the same thing, two or three times.'[41] Teachers use this requirement of speech to offer students variants of the material, sometimes subtly different, sometimes explicitly different. Printed words cannot so easily offer this ingenious facility.

The teacher embodies knowledge and teachers at the multiversity, as researchers, embody the process of knowledge creation. Ong notes that speech is empathetic and participatory, rather than objectifying and distancing: 'For an oral culture, learning or knowing means achieving close, empathetic, communal identification with the known.'[42] At the multiversity, in each course, there is orality. Four of the six components of each course are oral: the lecture, office hours, the seminar/laboratory, and serendipity. In three, there are teachers. The lecture is given by the professor, the established scholar in a field, the professor holds office hours, and the seminar is led by the graduate student, an apprentice scholar in a field. The student is brought into empathetic identification with the known and also with the process of knowledge creation. The student also forms an empathetic identification with other students who are joined in the process of learning.

Oral communication is face-to-face. The spoken word comes to us from a person, with facial expression, gesture, and body language. Common sense has always known these to be subtle means of communication, and now confirmation is being provided by psychologists and neuroscientists. Conveying passion for your subject, demonstrating the potential of a life of erudition, and encouraging curiosity are amplified in a face-to-face medium, muffled in the printed word, and virtually silent through a computer screen.

The university lecture is wrongly conceived when it is viewed as a forum to convey content. On the contrary, no matter how large the lecture hall, students are enabled to make empathetic identification with the professor. We should remember also that the lecture as a form of instruction, originally adopted in the nineteenth century, was not a means to 'teach more students using the same professor.' Rather, the lecture was a means to allow the professor, specialist in the field and active researcher, to present the most up-to-date findings and to report the dialogue of the research community. The modern university lecture, however large, remains closer to its origins than its critics realize.

Communications scholars have shown the significance of writing and printing to the administrative and legal systems needed by nations. They also note that the oral medium is elastic and fresh and invites intellectual exchange. Harold Innis, in examining Greek democracy, saw 'in the relative balance of oral and literate modes a strengthening of democracy.'[43] The modern multiversity has this same balance of oral and literate modes, and this balance plays an analogous role in strengthening liberal learning. The written contains existing knowledge, whereas the oral is elastic and encourages intellectual exchange. Each university course combines the written and the spoken, reinforcing the dynamic between received knowledge and scepticism in a liberal education, and infusing a democratic ethos, preparing students for citizenship.

Making the Comparison: Quality and Cost

An online course cannot replace the orality of a traditional course. Oral communication, with its incorporating inclusion of speaker and listener, with its capacity for empathetic identification, with its redundancy, freshness, and flexibility, cannot be duplicated by online technologies. A university education uses the spoken word. The oral communication between teacher/researcher and student cannot be replicated when the professor disappears behind the computer screen. The lecture hall and seminar room will not disappear. Likewise, out-of-class, online communication between students cannot replace serendipitous face-to-face conversations. Theodore Schultz, a distinguished scholar of the economics of education, observes that one of the functions of education is to 'identify and encourage.'[44] This can be identification and encouragement of both the gifted and the troubled. Such a process is almost impossible without oral, face-to-face interaction.

A university education – whether traditional or online – also uses the printed word. An online course cannot provide that balance of literate and oral modes, that dynamic tension between received knowledge and a questioning intelligence, which are so much a part of the 'old pedagogy,' and so much the essence of university learning.

No matter what our route to exploring the implications of new information technologies for teaching in universities, the final destination is the same: traditional pedagogy is superior to online pedagogy. Common sense tells us this. Careful examination of the nature of the technology tells us this. The history of past communications revolutions confirms it. And experiments with actual online courses in the twenty-first century confirm it again.

Predictions of the demise of the residential university are wrong. The number of students coming to the campuses of multiversities will not decline. If offered a choice, students will choose on-campus, oral education over an education delivered entirely online. Rather than displacing traditional pedagogy, online education makes the value of oral education more evident.

All universities in Canada, the United States, and the United Kingdom are living in the pincers: one arm is the financial limit of the constrained welfare state and the other arm is the increasing demand for higher education generated by demography, increases in participation rates, and increases in lifelong learning. We do not know whether governments will provide funding for the increased demand at the same level as for existing programs, but it seems highly unlikely that they will. Many commentators, and not a few legislators, see the expansion of online education as a way to escape the pressure of the pincers.

If online education is really part of the answer, it must be less expensive than on-campus education. But is it less costly? The answer is proving to be no. When online teaching began, the analysis of costs was confusing and inconclusive. Many thought that online education offered great savings. The economies of online courses were thought to follow because once the course was created it could be offered over and over again at little extra cost. But the courses, once designed, cannot simply be repeated year after year because professors revise their online courses just as they revise traditional courses; this constant revision is part of the role of the professor as both a teacher and a researcher and is a defining characteristic of university teaching. It is expensive and time-consuming to change an online course. And, most important of all, the economics of small-group interaction have not been evaded: one graduate student can lead a face-to-face seminar of 15 to 20 students but one graduate student is still needed to handle the online discussion of fifteen to twenty students. Online courses with interactive discussion are expensive in just the same way as traditional seminars are. In fact, the very advantage of the online network – the ease in interactive communication – makes it expensive. It takes huge amounts of time for the professor and graduate students running the course to respond to individual online inquiries and to participate in discussions.

The clear conclusion is that good quality online education is no less expensive than good quality face-to-face education.[45] Delivering courses online is not a mass production industrial technology. Online courses are not a cost-saving, and they are not a means to escape the budget squeeze in meeting the increasing demand for university education. This conclusion helps to explain why online courses have not 'driven out' traditional courses, and why private companies have not emerged as suppliers of undergraduate education. However, the new information technology can produce higher quality undergraduate education, compared with existing practices, in two areas: distance education and part-time education.

Improving Accessibility: Online Courses

Distance education courses, sometimes called correspondence courses, are at the opposite pole to on-campus courses. The students do not come to the campus. 'Old style' distance education already uses communication technologies – the book, the written assignment, telephone, and videotape – to bridge the physical distance between professors and students. In the simplest model of distance education, books and other printed materials are mailed to students for them to read and study. Interaction with the professor occurs through exchange, by mail, of written assignments. Assessment is done in the usual way: examinations are held at supervised off-campus sites. More sophisticated models complement the simple model with instructional audio tapes, instructional television, video-conferencing, and telephone conferencing. Whatever the additions to the simple model, distance education predominantly utilizes book-based and written communication. But the Web offers an enormous advance over existing distance education by facilitating interactive communication between professor and student and between students. Not surprisingly, and quite appropriately, academic units whose mandate is distance education have moved swiftly into online education. Martin Trow has surveyed the use of IT in the University of California system especially in undergraduate education and he found the greatest adoption of e-learning by these units.[46] The United Kingdom's Open University and Athabasca University (Canada's open university) are world leaders in the provision of online education.

Most students in distance education are part-time; most are mature students; and most remain in full-time employment during their studies. They are unable to come to campus. The new technologies can greatly enhance their educational experience. A course fully online can compete very effectively with other forms of distance education in terms of the quality of education.

The new technologies are also transforming part-time education. Many part-time students come to campus for courses delivered in the traditional manner. Again, the majority are mature students and remain in full-time employment during their studies. The courses for part-time students are generally held on campus in the evening, meeting once a week (for three hours) rather than meeting several times per week, as do the regular daytime courses. But for many part-time students, coming to campus is a problem, and they have only an atrophied on-campus experience. Many on-campus part-time students will shift into fully online courses. In the ideal situation, these distance and part-time initiatives combine a short on-campus component with the online activities.

The growth in courses online and the emergence of virtual universities are better conceptualized as an expansion of distance education and part-time education, rather than as a replacement for on-campus, full-time education.

Many of the largest programs of distance and part-time education have been career-focused. The new private universities in the United States with an e-learning focus, such as the University of Phoenix,[47] are offering such career-oriented degree programs. The private software firms, which originally saw a market for all types of undergraduate education, are now concentrating on career-oriented courses. This is the market where we will see the most direct competition between public universities and the new private sector providers.

Distance and part-time education are part of the collective responsibility of universities in a democracy, part of their responsibility to make higher education accessible. In the United States, this has been particularly important in the mandates of land grant universities. Canada and the United Kingdom have open universities with this as their sole mandate. Many multiversities have a division responsible for distance and part-time education. The information age offers new ways to fulfil this old responsibility.

Distance education and part-time education are the most evident and most substantial commitments of the multiversity to lifelong learning. In 1996, the W.K. Kellogg Foundation, with the National Association of State Universities and Land-Grant Colleges, established the Kellogg Commission on the Future of State and Land-Grant Universities. One of its reports, *Returning to Our Roots: A Learning Society*, begins by stating: 'We write as twenty-four presidents and chancellors of public state universities and land-grant institutions to make the case that our institutions must play an essential role in making lifelong learning a reality in the United States. The concept of lifelong learning has been talked of before, but, for the first time, we now have the technological means to make it a reality. We are convinced that public research universities must be leaders in a new era of not simply increased demand for education, but rather of a change so fundamental and far-reaching that the establishment of a true 'learning society' lies within our grasp.'[48] The multiversities in the United Kingdom and Canada would surely endorse this statement, so central is it to their mission in a democratic society.

The vision of lifelong learning is widely shared, and the demand for such higher education is strong. People want to move up in their jobs or get new qualifications to increase their flexibility or be retrained for a new career altogether. Many seek refresher courses or to learn the latest ideas and techniques. Most professions now require annual continuing education for their members. Multiversities already have substantial enrolments in these areas, most importantly in the fields of business, information technology, and continuing education for the professions. The new information technologies are well suited to this career-oriented education. The students are mature, motivated, and seek a well-defined body of information. They cannot leave their jobs and want education that is tailored to their learning needs and accessible at a time and place convenient to them.

This articulation of a learning society, and the education needed, is familiar. However, it has subtly, and perhaps inadvertently, emphasized only one dimension of lifelong learning: learning that is applied in a profession or a career. This articulation sees lifelong learning as a complement to a job and a career. It sees very little, however, lifelong *liberal* learning, where knowledge is valued for its own sake and where lifelong learning cultivates informed and active citizens.

There is no gainsaying the importance of lifelong learning in a career and the responsibility of the multiversity to provide it. This is the area of greatest demand, in the sense of there being a market where people will pay a fee for the course of instruction. However, liberal learning continues through life, just as career learning does. For many people, lifelong liberal learning is more significant – if only it were recognized as such. Most of our lifelong liberal learning occurs outside a university or any educational institution. Reading magazines of ideas and watching television news documentaries or science programs are all forms of liberal learning. Reading books continues through life; a trip to any bookstore reveals the range of literature and non-fiction being read. The benefit of liberal learning does not stop with undergraduate study; liberal learning is needed through life for us to flourish as citizens, parents, friends, and individuals. Pick up any daily newspaper and see how every article illustrates how liberal learning can deepen our understanding of the world we live in, and help us make our way in it. Coming to grips with terrorism is helped by knowledge of the history of the Middle East; debates about drug policy are linked to psychological theories of addiction; decisions to renew your mortgage at a fixed or variable interest rate require knowledge of financial markets; appreciating the just-released movie is enriched by knowing, say, the traditions of film noir; novels can illuminate our own yearning for dignity and love; as churches struggle to accommodate new gender relations, philosophy can be of help. The strongest argument for liberal learning in undergraduate study is that it is the foundation for lifelong liberal learning.

Universities contribute to this lifelong liberal learning through part-time courses, non-credit continuing education, public lectures, alumni events, and so on. Indeed, the multiversity's responsibility to be public intellectual, critic, and conscience is a responsibility to contribute to the lifelong liberal learning of the entire society.

The new information technologies are so recent that few multiversities have explored how they might enhance lifelong liberal learning – most multiversities have focused only on career-oriented learning. But there are surely opportunities for creative contribution to lifelong liberal learning. Some universities now offer free online courses to their alumni. One can easily envision further possibilities. The English department could connect with local book clubs to provide context and theoretical perspective. The biology department could moderate a forum on new reproductive technologies. A city's downtown redevelopment could occasion a special website, maintained by the university, for local history and people's experiences. The new information technologies have expanded the multiversity's means to provide lifelong liberal education. The only limitations are our creativity and commitment.

Improving Quality: Hybrid Courses

Although online courses cannot provide higher-quality, lower-cost undergraduate education than traditional on-campus instruction, nonetheless undergraduate teaching in the multiversities is being profoundly transformed and no doubt still-unforeseen innovations lie ahead. The same mix of common sense, study of history, and pedagogical experiments demonstrates that new IT *can enhance* the existing courses. The technology will be used as an add-on to the traditional pedagogy. A combination of traditional pedagogy *plus* IT is superior to the traditional course. The great transformation in university teaching will come in finding the best hybrid, blending the new and the old. This is where we can find the greatest improvements to undergraduate education in the years ahead.

What parts of the new technologies will enhance learning? How can these be best combined with the lecture/seminar/library pedagogy? Should the new technology simply be an add-on, or could the number of lecture hours be reduced and opportunities for small-group interaction increased? These are questions being addressed today.

Although courseware developed by private firms is designed to allow a course to be delivered entirely online, far more often such courseware is used in conjunction with a course delivered in the traditional way. The courseware is used to create a hybrid course, and the online material becomes an additional source of information for students. The lecture is delivered orally, face-to-face, as always, but the lecture outline (or even a lecture video) is placed on the website. Students are able to review material easily, and work through it at their own pace, and at a time and location suited to them. Questions can be posed to the professor by e-mail. Seminars are held as before. The online component of a seminar affords an additional means of discussion – and the discussion can go on between residence rooms at 3 a.m., if desired. There is growing evidence that the online seminar draws the quiet, shy student to contribute in a way that the face-to-face seminar does not. The World Wide Web does offer new sources of information, and new ways to organize and search information. These are not substitutes for the library, but additions to it. Online assessments are added to the usual forms. Online assessment is very helpful for self-paced learning. All these additions to the traditional course are unquestionably of value.

Faculty members have always designed their own courses by deciding upon the content of lectures, gathering illustrations and simulations, preparing exercises and essay topics, and putting together a reading list. Now, course design can include creating online material oneself or utilizing components created by others. In the parlance of the IT world, these online materials are called 'learning objects.' A learning object might be a visual representation program used in an introductory physics course, or a video clip of a Churchill wartime speech used in a British history course, or a simulation of cell division for a biology course, or photographs of nineteenth-century factory workers used in a course on the Victorian novel. As these learning objects are developed and improved, they are being shared among professors and across universities. Finding the right learning object can be problematic and time-consuming, but several initiatives are speeding up the process of evaluation and sharing. In the United States, project MERLOT is a large consortium of higher education systems and institutions gathering an inventory of learning objects. MERLOT's mission is to improve the effectiveness of teaching and learning by expanding the quantity and quality of peer-reviewed online learning objects. A similar Canadian initiative is POOL (the Portal for Online Objects in Learning).[49]

Martin Trow concludes his survey of California universities by suggesting that 'mass higher education at the university seems to be emerging as some combination of traditional forms of lectures and seminars, enriched by IT both here and now and at the student's convenience in time and place.'[50] He notes how individual professors are creating 'handicraft' learning objects for use in their courses, not always employing standardized industrial products: 'So the development of courseware is already being demystified; it will increasingly be part of the bread and butter of college and university teaching, not the monopoly of experts and the equally expensive development and marketing firms.'[51]

Gradually, every university course will have a website with textual material, links to relevant sources on the Web, and provisions for discussion among students. More assessment will be done online. Already, most textbook publishers include a website related to their text, as well as lists of related websites. There is no question that IT will be more and more widely used. On balance, because IT will be in addition to traditional pedagogy, it will make each undergraduate course more expensive.

Regrettably, to date, many of the information technology initiatives have been rather simple add-ons to traditional pedagogy, and because the initiatives have mainly served to increase the ease and convenience of students, they have done little to alter the learning outcome. Students can access the course website at any time and from any place. If one misses a class (and one might become more likely to miss class), the disruption is reduced because the lecture notes are available on the Web. There is less need to arrange to go to the professor's office because e-mail is available 24/7. Many professors worry that these new technologies, while making a student's life more convenient, have reduced the quality of undergraduate learning. Fewer students come during office hours, and lectures are not as well attended. This is particularly true at multiversities in large metropolitan areas where most students commute to campus. Some students regard the point-form outlines of lectures available on the Web as a sufficient substitute for reading the assigned material. Many professors note that today's students – dubbed the 'Net generation' – turn very quickly to the bite-sized chunks of text on the Internet but are less willing to read books or lengthy articles. In wireless classrooms, many students appear to be diligently taking notes but, in truth, they are surfing the Web or e-mailing friends rather than listening to the lecture. And, unquestionably, the Web has made plagiarism much easier. Information technology holds many dangers as well as opportunities for undergraduate education.

True innovation, innovation that goes beyond convenience, will build upon the unique characteristics of this new communication technology, allowing activities that would have been impossible under the old technology of teaching. Most innovations in pedagogy have exploited the Web's special potential as an information source: the Web makes information more accessible and makes new information and new learning objects available. We can see time and space constraints overcome, and we can see many examples of multimedia. However, certain unique characteristics of IT have been less exploited: its network structure and hypertext as a means of organizing and searching information, for example. Exploiting these will yield true innovation in undergraduate education.

Unlike print or other electronic media, the Web supports 'immediate and intense interaction, so that communication is not point to point (like a telephone), not point to multipoint (like television) but multipoint to multipoint. There is a powerful network effect that can be used to create learning communities.'[52] This interconnectivity and network structure over geographical space is unique to this communication technology. The networked interconnection is of two distinct types. One is the interconnection of discussion; like a conversation in a room, anyone can post his or her comment, or message, for all others to read. The other type is an interconnection around documents. Everyone can post documents for others to read, or everyone can work together on the same document. In the network, each person can be both listener and speaker, both reader and author. We are only just beginning to understand and explore how this powerful networking potential can be integrated into university teaching and learning.

One often-heard complaint about undergraduate education is that students do not learn to work in teams. Traditional pedagogy has difficulty in arranging collaborative work. The Web is ideally suited to collaborative work through its ability to allow each member of the group to contribute as an author in a collective project. Very promising experiments are under way in collaborative learning assignments.

Thus far, most pedagogical initiatives have occurred within a single course. This is not surprising because one professor is responsible for each course, and that professor has implemented the initiative. However, if we pull back and examine an entire undergraduate degree program, we see that our current modular course-based pedagogies have difficulty linking across courses, and difficulty both drawing upon what has gone before and exploring themes across courses. The network structure of the Web could allow professors to establish these links, while also allowing student conversations across courses. The Web could create a learning community of students in different courses. It could facilitate creative new ways to conduct interdisciplinary study and broader liberal learning.

The network of the Web can also connect students in different universities. A seminar in literature (or any other subject) at a U.S. university could be joined with a seminar at a Canadian university, or a British university, or anywhere else in the world. The Web brings wonderful opportunities to enhance the international awareness of students and to deepen their cross-cultural understanding.

Another frontier of the new technology is the organization of information through hypertext. Few pedagogical experiments have yet been to this frontier to explore how professors and students in a course might create a hypertext organization of information. The few experiments have happened in literature courses, where the concept of intertextuality used in literary theory has a direct analogue in the technology of hypertext. Real experimentation will begin when students build their own hypertext collections of information for their own purposes.

One of the most successful explorations of IT led to the construction of the Rossetti Archive, using hypertext, and to the creation of the Institute for Advanced Technology in the Humanities, at the University of Virginia. The lessons of these experiences are several. First, the experiment used one of the unique features of the new technology, in this case hypertext. More important, however, it recognized that 'throwing IT resources at people who have no special interest in them or desire to exploit them doesn't work ... Educational change at the level of the university is driven by the active research work of the faculty. Changes in pedagogy and classroom dynamics follow from research.'[53] The hypertext Rossetti Archive is a research project that transformed the teaching of literature at the University of Virginia. Similar teaching transformations will follow in other disciplines, as scholarly research exploits the new opportunities bought by information technology.

The transformation of traditional undergraduate teaching and learning at the multiversity will be evolutionary, not revolutionary, but nonetheless inexorable. Those multiversities that truly innovate can wonderfully improve the education of their undergraduates, but the outcome is by no means certain. Some multiversities will improve the ease of life and convenience of their students – but do little for their education.

The Genius of the Place

The Web brings tremendous connectivity, with new opportunities for place-to-place and person-to-person connection. The same power over time and place is also a threat: subtle, cumulative, and endangering the genius of the place. The university has always been a *place*. University learning has always been among a community of people gathered at the same time and in the same place, a very special place.

Sheldon Rothblatt, in a reflection upon campus architecture and design notes that Cardinal Newman, like many of his generation, believed places to have special meaning; places set off associations and create predispositions in the observer. Rothblatt quotes Alexis de Tocqueville: 'One's first feeling in visiting Oxford is of unforced admiration for the men of old who founded such immense establishments to aid the development of the human spirit.'[54] Liberal education meant exposure to all the domains of knowledge and awareness of their history and progress. The architecture of the college, its precincts and passages, the 'genius of the place,' sets off associations and creates the predisposition towards liberal learning. The buildings are witnesses to past events, inhabited by past scholars, and lived in by past students: 'They had been inhabited by great personalities, perhaps only lesser ones, but that hardly mattered. What mattered was that history added length and breadth to a place and filled it with memory, with tradition, and with connections and responsibilities which the sojourner must not ignore.'[55]

Newer universities could not be Oxford, nor could urban universities. Mass higher education 'allows for but does not insist upon the personal experiences to be derived from an encounter with spaces that teach.'[56] The multiversity, although often based around a college of liberal arts, is a conglomerate of multiple missions and accommodations (architectural and conceptual) to new demands, making the genius of the place harder to identify and to maintain. Nonetheless, campus design and architecture on both sides of the Atlantic are still intended to set off associations and create sensibilities for learning, and most importantly to create places where professors and students can meet and converse.

The erosion of place-based undergraduate education has been slow and continuous, and now much accelerated by information technology. The acceleration began with the arrival of the personal computer in the mid-1980s. With the PC, it became less necessary for professors to come to campus. Professors did their own correspondence, typed their course materials, and wrote their research papers with the word processor, reserving their best computer system for their office at home, not at the university. When the library catalogue is online, fewer trips to the library are needed. The World Wide Web has reduced the need to go to the library still further. Collaboration with colleagues, even from one's own department, can now be done by e-mail. The primary loyalty of many faculty members was already to their discipline and research field, rather than to their home university; the connectivity of the Internet strengthens bonds with colleagues doing similar research at other universities still further.

Multiversities have many secrets: one of the best-kept is how little time professors spend on campus, in their offices, available to undergraduates. The PC may boost research productivity, but it diminishes campus community. In a sad irony, the atomization of faculty because of IT is greatest in the humanities, where one expects face-to-face discussion. Scientists still come to campus for their labs; humanists are at home with their PCs, books, and the World Wide Web.

The erosion of the student's sense of place also has accelerated with the coming of the Web in the mid-1990s. Before, the PC and the Internet were fairly esoteric instruments for most students, then browsers and search engines made the Internet easy to use. In another irony, many Web-based initiatives are well-meaning attempts to serve students. Students lead busy lives, juggling work and study (and play), often commuting long distances to campus. Why not make student services, library catalogues, course materials, lecture outlines, and all accounts, records, and information available on the Web? This would be more convenient for students; information would be available from any place; they could access it when needed. The multiversity has done this, but so well that students need to come to campus less often, and on each visit need to spend less time there, affording far less opportunity for serendipitous learning.

The campus is suffering a reverse Metcalfe's Law: the fewer conversations you have on campus, the less likely you are to go, and the fewer people come to campus. The value of joining the campus conversation network declines. Multiversities have been worried about the decline of their campus-based community, but they have not yet found a means to bring people back to campus. Perhaps there are none, and the best we can hope for from IT is to strengthen a virtual community. There can be little doubt that a great challenge of the information age will be to sustain the genius of the *place* that is the university.

8 Postmodern Thought

This third item on my list of characteristics of our age that will change the multiversity – postmodern thought – is not always found on other people's lists. The choice was influenced by my experience as dean of the Faculty of Arts, especially reading appointments files and tenure and promotion files of faculty members in the humanities and the social sciences. Postmodern thought appeared in more and more files, and in more and more disciplines. Moreover, in its orientation and epistemology, it is radically different from the other academic work. Also, I came to believe that many of the conflicts on campus, beneath the surface level of disagreement, were caused by differences in epistemology between the modernists and the postmodernists.

Postmodern thought is one of the dominant intellectual movements of our times and helps define the character of our age. It is a thoroughgoing critique of the western rationalistic tradition and is thus a thoroughgoing critique of the multiversity. There is a fierce clash between the modern and the postmodern within the multiversity, and one of the great challenges ahead for the multiversity is how it will deal with postmodern thought.

The modern world is a product of Renaissance humanism, the Scientific Revolution, and the Enlightenment. These same transformations were the necessary precursors of the modern university. The fundamental ideas and values of the multiversity and the fundamental ideas and values of modernity are so close as to be almost indistinguishable. The university helped create modernity, just as modernity helped create the university.

Modern societies are marked by the growth of science, improvements in medicine, and the development of technologies. Modern thought synthesizes reason and observation in an instrumental rationality and believes that problems can be solved. Modernity believes in progress: ends can be identified, the means discovered by reason, and the systematic focusing of resources will bring their realization. There is an emphasis on the individual, her powers of reason, her right to choose, and therefore her freedom. Modernity believes that over time individuals have been shedding the confines of tradition, superstition, and ignorance and that the process must continue. Modernity celebrates the advance of knowledge; it is energetic and forward-looking.

Modernity's story is the story of rationality and human progress. In this story, the university, after what must be acknowledged was a slow and reluctant transformation in the late nineteenth century, claims a place of pride. The pairing of modernity and the university was complete by the early twentieth century. Since then, the story of the research multiversity and the story of the modern world have been moving together.

There has emerged a critique of this story of the modern world, however, and therefore a challenge to the story of the multiversity. This critique rejects modernity's belief in reason and truth, arguing that there can be no objective understanding of reality. It contests modernity's narrative of individual emancipation; instead, it sees continuing oppression. The twentieth century's record – of war, genocide, and environmental destruction – is proof that modernity has not brought progress. This criticism of modernity is an intellectual movement that offers an epistemological challenge to the scientific method, an alternative characterization of history, and a penetrating criticism of our society. Like all intellectual movements, it is impossible to capture precisely; it is heterogeneous, containing many variations and contradictions within it. It is more than an intellectual movement; it is also an artistic movement, a cultural attitude, and a political orientation. I need to label this bundle of ideas, this movement, this political orientation – and the term I have selected is *postmodern thought*. Following the structure of previous chapters, I will first deal with the bundle of ideas that is part of the character of our age – I will look at the ideas of postmodern thought; then I will examine the implications of this intellectual ferment for the multiversity.

My first point, before looking at the ideas, is that the controversies provoked by postmodern thought are very real and very fundamental. My purpose is not to take sides in these controversies; rather, it is to understand the controversies. And, I would argue, the multiversity must recognize the controversy but cannot take sides. Rather, it must struggle to ensure that there is scholarly dialogue between the disputants, instead of misunderstanding and warfare.

Following a continuing theme, this chapter affords another opportunity to study the influence of ideas upon our society. Remarkably, in our world so dominated by science and technology, these postmodern ideas have emerged from research in the humanities, from the study of linguistics, philosophy, literature, and history. To explore the nature of postmodern thought is also to explore the power of the humanities to shape our world and how we understand and experience it. The seminars in the English and philosophy departments are as influential in creating our understanding of the world as are the seminars in the economics department in reshaping the welfare state, or as are the laboratories of the computer engineers in producing the information technology revolution.

Finally, the exploration of postmodern ideas affords another opportunity to examine the professor as public intellectual, engaged and critical of society. Much current social criticism, particularly leftist social criticism, is rooted in postmodern thought. Ironically, at the same time, the postmodern world brings a pervasive ambivalence about academic authority.

Postmodern Thought Defined

I choose the term *postmodern thought* with considerable trepidation. Such umbrella words imply a coherence and consistency that are not there. Anyone attempting to define postmodern thought always points out the many meanings of the word. However, such umbrella words are needed and useful; for example, such umbrella words as 'modernity,' or 'Enlightenment,' do identify a defining, if elusive, essence. For better or for worse, I am placing a diverse body of thought under the umbrella of postmodern.

Moreover, the word 'postmodernism' is surrounded by controversy. Some writers I will discuss in this chapter as postmodern would reject, often vehemently, that the term should describe their thought. Furthermore, many writers clearly associated with postmodern thought, such as Jacques Derrida or Michel Foucault, became intellectual celebrities and, like all celebrities, are judged by the whims of fashion. Many readers on seeing the word 'postmodern' will think of a movement that was once very 'in' but is now passé. But postmodernism is a body of thought of great importance and resilience. At the heart of postmodern thought is an epistemology: a theory of knowledge, a theory of how we come to know the world 'out there.' Postmodern thought is a profound reflection upon the questions: How can we know what is real? How can we know what is true? This epistemology is rooted in linguistics and the study of how words convey meaning. The epistemology of postmodern thought disputes the epistemology of science and of the modern world. Postmodern thought is also a profound reflection on values and whether we can discover any universal values.

The Routledge Companion to Postmodernism is an accessible and comprehensive reference guide. It begins by acknowledging the difficulties of definition: 'It is striking that few people can say with any sense of assurance what the term "postmodern" actually means or involves. Some theorists have suggested that it is as much a mood or attitude of mind as anything else, but one nevertheless wants to know what constitutes that mood or attitude. That is what *The Routledge Companion to Postmodernism* is designed to answer.'[1]

The *Companion* goes on: 'In a general sense, postmodernism is to be regarded as a rejection of many, if not most, of the cultural certainties on which life in the West has been structured over the last couple of centuries. It has called into question our commitment to cultural "progress" (that economies must continue to grow, the quality of life to keep improving indefinitely, etc.), as well as the political systems that have underpinned this belief. Postmodernists often refer to the "Enlightenment project," meaning the liberal humanist ideology that has come to dominate Western culture since the eighteenth century; an ideology that has striven to bring about the emancipation of mankind from economic want and political oppression. In the view of postmodernists this project, laudable though it may have been at one time, has in its turn come to oppress humankind, and to force it into certain set ways of thought and action. It is therefore to be resisted.'[2] Postmodern thought rejects the grand story of modernity.

The *Companion* contains a number of essays about postmodernism, beginning with one entitled, 'Postmodernism and Philosophy.' As a philosophical movement, postmodernism is best described as 'a form of scepticism – scepticism about authority, received wisdom, cultural and political norms, etc. – and that puts it into a long-running tradition of Western thought that stretches back to classical Greek philosophy.'[3] Postmodernism is antifoundational; it sets out to challenge and 'undermine other philosophical theories claiming to be in possession of ultimate truth, or of criteria for determining what counts as ultimate truth ... Postmodernism has drawn heavily on the example set by antifoundationalist philosophers, perhaps most notably the iconoclastic nineteenth-century German philosopher Friedrich Nietzsche, whose call for a "revaluation of all values" constitutes something of a battle cry for the movement.'[4] Postmodern thought is sceptical about the possibility of objective truth and sceptical about the possibility of universal values.

Postmodern thought is politically engaged critical thought. John McGowan, a professor of English at the University of Rochester, highlights this in his *Postmodernism and Its Critics*, as he attempts a definition: *postmodernism* is a term used 'to designate a specific form of cultural critique that has become increasing conspicuous in the academy since about 1975. This critique is resolutely antifoundationalist – eschewing all appeals to ontological or epistemological or ethical absolutes – while also proclaiming itself resolutely radical in its commitment to the transformation of the existing Western social order. The four most prominent variants of postmodern theory are poststructuralism, the new Marxism, neopragmatism, and feminism.'[5] Many would characterize postmodernism's critical orientation as leftist, although others would argue that the left-right dichotomy is no longer useful. Nonetheless, it is clear that postmodernism is a critique of both capitalism and liberal democracy.

Postmodern thought has been shaped fundamentally by developments in the humanities, especially in the interconnections of philosophy and linguistics. Postmodern thinking does not accept that language can describe an objective reality or that sentences and text convey an unambiguous meaning. In the face of such ambiguity, how is meaning conveyed in the world? How can we live our lives? How do we know what is real? Postmodernists argue that, in this indeterminacy, certain structures for the making of meaning come to dominate. These dominant structures are established by the powerful as a means to preserve their dominant position. The powerful are those who control the liberal capitalist society. The postmodern sensibility exposes the linguistic basis of power and exposes how language can exclude and marginalize.

Literary critics with a postmodern sensibility examine literature and find that things are not as they seem. The language and representations in novels, plays, and poetry are neither evident nor straightforward, they argue. Racism, sexism, and colonialism are concealed within the most innocent narrative. Authors always included in the best that has been thought and said, from William Shakespeare to Jane Austen, are reread with a new critical apparatus to reveal their racism, sexism, or colonialism, and their complicity in existing power relations.

Postmodern thought clashes with the university's fundamental values and clashes with the story that the university tells about its place in the world. The university has promoted and defended 'the cultural certainties on which life in the west has been structured.' The university is an institution of the 'Enlightenment project.' The university has been a place to study and revere the best that has been thought and said. The university is deeply committed to the belief that reason and observation yield objective knowledge, which brings personal emancipation and progress. Although the university is a place for sceptical thought, it has never been radically antifoundational; indeed, it is in constant search of foundations.

Part of the ambiguity of the word 'postmodern' arises because it suggests a temporal sequence: modernity is followed by postmodernity. Modernity was yesterday and now we have postmodernity. Yesterday we had modern thought, today we have postmodern thought. This temporal sequence interpretation should be acknowledged, but set aside. Modernity still exists and continues; many continue to have faith in rationality, science, and progress. Postmodernism is a critique of modernity; postmodern ideas coexist with modern ideas; modernity produces postmodernity. Nonetheless, we must retain historical context. Postmodern thought does emerge at a specific time: in the later twentieth and early twenty-first centuries. Furthermore, at this same historical moment, society is changing rapidly under pressures from technological change, the collapse of statism, and growing globalization. Things do seem contingent and chaotic; relativism does seem to have replaced our confidence in universal values. The optimistic story of modernity does seem inadequate. Perhaps we now live in a new society – a postmodern condition.

Postmodern social theorists try to describe and understand this postmodern condition and they see pluralism, contingency, and ambivalence. In our advanced capitalist democracies, they see consumerism triumphant. They see a weakening of social authority, fragmentation, and a plurality of lifestyles and ethics. Ours is a society of mass culture and spectacle.[6] The postmodern world is characterized by the unprecedented development of the mass media, particularly the visual media.

Postmodern thinkers are fascinated by these media and investigate how they shape our reality. Postmodern thinkers are particularly fascinated by the implications of the revolution in information technology.

In part because of this resolute desire to confront our actual society, in part because of its rejection of any esthetic absolutes, and in part because of its particular methodologies of textual analysis, postmodernism erases the distinction between high culture and popular culture. Text is text to be analysed. Also, popular culture is important because in it we can discover the hidden structures of power in our postmodern society. In all, postmodernism is highly confrontational to the humanities as traditionally conceived: 'traditionally, the humanities thought of themselves as conserving, transmitting, and interpreting the highest achievements of human civilization in general and Western civilization in particular.'[7] Although coming from the humanities, the postmodern sensibility rejects this project altogether.

This postmodern world is the world our undergraduate students inhabit. For such students – raised on television, movies, video games, and the World Wide Web – what is the appropriate undergraduate curriculum for a liberal education? The postmodern world is also the society that must support the multiversity. Will a consumer society, fragmented and disjoint, suffering a crisis of authority, support the multiversity?

Postmodern thought is controversial, given to excess, and some of its claims are preposterous. Many academics ignore anything that carries the word 'postmodern' in its title. Others hope it will go away. Some declare that postmodernism is a fad that has passed, but postmodernism is not a fad, and it will not go away. Its controversies rage in many disciplines, in literature, political science, sociology, law, social work, and education, in some cases so intensely as to debilitate whole departments. It has opened new divides on campus between scientists and humanists. It challenges our long traditions of liberal learning. Recall Cardinal Newman on the university as a place of liberal learning: 'an assemblage of learned men, zealous for their own sciences, and rivals of each other, are brought, by familiar intercourse and for the sake of intellectual peace, to adjust together the claims and relations of their respective subjects of investigation. They learn to respect, to consult, and to aid each other. Thus is created a pure and clear atmosphere of thought, which the student also breathes. [And so the student] apprehends the great outlines of knowledge, the principles on which it rests, the scale of its parts, its lights and its shades, its great points and its little, as he otherwise cannot apprehend them.'[8] If there are epistemological wars, can there be liberal learning? How the new ideas are addressed and how the controversies are resolved, and more specifically how curriculum, faculty hiring, and research priorities adapt, will be a measure of the multiversity in the years ahead.

The debate must also include the wider society. Postmodern ideas puzzle many outside observers and seem to contradict their deeply held conception of the role of universities. This puzzlement and misunderstanding weakens the social contract between the university and society, especially society's support for the humanities and social sciences. If universities are to sustain and renew this social contract, they must overcome the misunderstandings, addressing postmodern ideas together with society.

Much postmodern writing is an obscure stew, larded with jargon. Perhaps the squabbles should be ignored by the outside world, left in the academic journals, conferences, and department meetings. But the influence of postmodern thought has long since escaped beyond the university. Postmodern thought is reshaping the curriculum in primary and secondary schools; it alters how national histories are told; it influences the practice of politics and law. Postmodern thought is informing how we see and experience the world. We might rephrase John Maynard Keynes's famous declamation: the ideas of postmodernists, both when they are right and when they are wrong, are more powerful than is commonly understood ... Practical men, who believe themselves exempt from any intellectual influences, are usually the slaves of some defunct postmodernist.

Many writers have tried to characterize the variations of postmodern thought: some divide it into critical postmodernism and establishment postmodernism, others into hard postmodernism and soft postmodernism, still others into sceptical and affirmative postmodernism. Such attempts to delineate two broad orientations are not without their problems, but nonetheless they are helpful. I will use the categories of extreme postmodernism and moderate postmodernism.[9] The extremists differ from the moderates chiefly in 'the intensity of their opinion and their willingness to carry their post-modern conviction to its most extravagant, excessive conclusion.' They deny resolutely the possibility of objective truth or universal values. But with such radical uncertainty, academic work cannot be judged; one is left only with the play of words. No program of social reform can be justified, no regime criticized. Moderates accept the postmodern methodology and critique, but temper it. They seek an approach to truth and values that is non-dogmatic and tentative, always open to exploring one's own limitations and to acknowledging one's blindnesses. But they do not reject the possibility of ethical judgments or the possibility of social reform. In what follows, I will articulate the range of postmodern ideas and on occasion distinguish the extreme and moderate variants.

Past Critiques and Accommodation

We should not begin this debate between postmodern thought and the scientific and Enlightenment traditions, however, without recalling that the scientific and Enlightenment traditions almost immediately called forth counter-reactions and that the story of modernity has always been criticized. The essence of enlightenment is to ask: What do I know? What can I know? Reason always questions the received wisdom and scrutinizes the current way of doing things; reason interrogates the dominant story of society. Modernity criticizes itself. There are many who have noted the irony that postmodern thought is the outcome of resolutely modern thinking, it is the outcome of rational scepticism.

Romanticism rejected the central propositions of science and the Enlightenment.[10] Romanticism celebrates emotion over reason; the untutored and natural against the learned and the sophisticated. Romanticism recognizes that there may be no universal values and that virtues may be in conflict and tragedy may result. Progress and emancipation are not assured. In 'Dover Beach,' Arnold writes: '[The world] hath really neither joy, nor love, nor light, nor certitude, nor peace, nor help for pain.' The modern world brings confusion and tragedy, not progress. Postmodern thought has much in common with Romanticism.

Although a rejection of the modern story, Romanticism is itself an integral part of modernity. It is a reaction against the belief that reason can answer all questions and explain all things. Modernity carries, therefore, its own contradictions and critique. The university accommodated itself to this duality of Enlightenment and Romanticism. Literature and fine arts, as intuitive and emotive media of expression, are studied in the university alongside science and engineering.

Another critique of modernity came from the left of the ideological spectrum.[11] Marx and Engels wrote scathingly in 1848 of modernity's so-called progress: 'Constant revolutionizing of production, uninterrupted disturbance of social conditions, everlasting uncertainty and agitation distinguish the bourgeois epoch from all earlier ones ... All that is solid melts into air, all that is sacred is profaned, and man is at last compelled to face with sober senses his real condition of life and his relations with his kind.'[12] These sentences from *The Communist Manifesto* could easily describe the postmodern condition – and indeed many postmodern writers have used these exact words.

The twentieth century brought equally devastating characterizations of the true nature of liberal democratic capitalism. None of these was more penetrating than that of Max Weber, who saw the west as passing from a charismatic-traditional world to a rational-bureaucratic one.[13] Our experts are 'sensualists without heart and specialists without spirit' whose formal rationality produces the 'disenchantment of the world.' Reason, technology, and bureaucracy combine not to make us free, but to enslave us. In Weber's famous image, we are not free but live in an 'iron cage.'

Again, these critiques of the project of modernity, these critiques of rationality, science, and the Enlightenment, whether Marxist or Weberian, were accommodated within the university. In fact, they were more than accommodated. The works of these social critics became foundational texts in the social science disciplines of the twentieth century, most clearly in sociology and political science.

Postmodern thought has much in common with these earlier critiques and, indeed, some of the current variants of Romanticism and Marxism, I would place under the postmodern umbrella. Some postmodern works are on the way to being foundational texts. But postmodernism is more challenging to the fundamental ideals of the university and will be harder to accommodate. True, postmodernism, especially in its moderate variety, manifests the best traditions of rational scepticism, and the controversies it provokes are evidence of lively intellectual debate. The postmodern critique of our society is in the long tradition of social criticism. In all, moderate postmodern thought fits well into the traditions of the university. However, postmodernism attacks the epistemology of science, and in its extreme relativism denies the possibility of objective truth. In its most extreme form, postmodernism denies the possibility of emancipation, of political reform, and even of progress itself. It argues that much of university research is complicit in the structures of dominance and oppression. These criticisms confront the multiversity of our postindustrial democracies at its core.

Language, Reality, and Power

Philosopher John Searle, of the University of California, Berkeley, recognizes the potency of postmodern thought, how it differs from earlier critiques, and how it will be more difficult to accommodate in the university. He does not seek to resolve the disputes; rather he seeks to identify what exactly is in dispute. He identifies 'the elements of the Western conceptions of rationality and realism,' what he calls the 'Western Rationalistic Tradition,' as what is now under challenge in postmodern thought.[14] Although clearly Searle is a supporter of this western tradition, his clear-minded analysis offers a good starting point for understanding the epistemological differences between modern and postmodern thought.

As a prelude, he begins: 'A decisive step in the creation of the Western Rationalistic Tradition was the Greek creation of the idea of a *theory* ... [which] allowed the Western tradition to produce something quite unique, namely systematic intellectual constructions that were designed to describe and to explain large areas of reality in a way that was logically and mathematically accessible. Euclid's *Elements* provides a model for the kind of logical relationships that have been paradigmatic in the Western tradition.'[15] The Greeks did not complete our modern notion of theory; that did not come until the Scientific Revolution, when abstract theory was combined with the idea of systematic observation and experiments. The theory must be tested against observation, and observation could inform the creation of theory. Newton's mechanics, his laws of motion in *Principia*, complete the paradigm.

Searle explicates the Western Rationalistic Tradition as a set of propositions. The foundational principle, called realism, is that 'reality exists independently of human representations.'[16] We may speak about something, or write about it, or characterize it in a system of mathematical equations, but that something exists 'out there' independent of us, or our representations. 'The elliptical orbit of the planets relative to the sun, the structure of the hydrogen atom, and the amount of snowfall in the Himalayas, for example, are totally independent of both the system and the actual instances of human representation of these phenomena.'[17]

Searle highlights the role of language in the rationalistic tradition. His second proposition is: 'At least one of the functions of language is to communicate meanings from speakers to hearers, and sometimes those meanings enable the communication to refer to objects and states of affairs in the world that exist independently of language.'[18] The words we use convey meaning directly. If I have an idea in my mind, and I tell you about it, then you are enabled, in your mind, to know this same idea. Or, if I use a word to refer to some external reality, you are able to know exactly what external reality my word refers to. Language has both a communicative and referential character.

With realism and appropriate language, Searle's third proposition is that 'truth is a matter of the accuracy of representation. In general, statements attempt to describe how things are in the world that exists independently of the statement, and the statement will be true or false depending on whether things in the world really are the way that the statement says they are.'[19] This is called the correspondence theory of truth. Within this tradition, 'knowledge is objective. Because the content of what is known is always a true proposition, and because truth is a general matter of accurate representation of an independently existing reality, knowledge does not depend on nor derive from the subjective attitudes and feelings of particular investigators.'[20]

These propositions define the Western Rationalistic Tradition, a tradition deeply embedded in the multiversity. They underpin the scholarly ideal, summarized by Searle as 'the *disinterested* inquirer engaged in the quest for *objective* knowledge that will have *universal* validity.'[21] And, Searle asserts, this ideal is now under attack from postmodern ideas.

The Western Rationalistic Tradition is accepted without question in the pure and applied sciences; it is synonymous with the scientific method. Certainly, the rationalistic tradition is most easy to explain in the setting of science. However, the writers of the Enlightenment were explicit in their belief that this paradigm should be used in the analysis of human affairs. As the social sciences developed in the twentieth century, they became dominated, in the Anglo-American world, by scholars who, explicitly or implicitly, accepted this paradigm as a benchmark. Each social science discipline might not analyse its methodology or epistemology too explicitly, and there were always critics who argued that the rationalist empirical methodology of science should not be used in the social sciences, but nevertheless always setting the context was this rationalistic, empirical tradition as a conceptual benchmark.

For many people, the propositions of the rationalistic tradition are simply common sense; they are so self-evident that any critique is at best puzzling and at worst delusional. Of course, there is a reality 'out there' that exists independently of us. And the pursuit of knowledge is the struggle to understand and explain this reality. We develop theories and test our theories against the facts. Yet, there is today within the multiversity in many disciplines a fundamental critique of this tradition.

Not surprisingly, one line of criticism begins in the literary disciplines where notions of truth and objectivity were never as necessary as in the sciences, and mathematical representations of reality were unimportant. Ironically, the humanists' criticism begins as the rationalistic tradition is applied to the study of literature, words, language, and meaning. The criticism is the product of a rationalist undertaking. An essential element of postmodernism is the emphasis on language. Postmodern thought is modern thought that takes 'a linguistic turn.'

Terry Eagleton, of Oxford University, begins his wonderfully provocative *Literary Theory: An Introduction*, by asking: 'What is literature?' One way to answer the question is to examine how language is used in literature and contrast it with how language is used in writing that is not literature. 'On this theory, literature is a kind of writing which, in the words of the Russian critic Roman Jacobson, represents an "organized violence committed on ordinary speech." Literature transforms and intensifies ordinary language, deviates systematically from everyday speech.'[22] We read Mathew Arnold's 'Dover Beach':

> And we are here as on a darkling plain
> Swept with confused alarms of struggle and flight,
> Where ignorant armies clash by night.

And we know instinctively we are in the presence of the literary 'because the texture, rhythm and resonance of your words are in excess of their abstractable meaning.'[23] Any study of language that begins with the literary, or poetic, use of words will allow immediately that words are not always a direct representation of some external reality 'out there.' The representational character of language is not self-evident; a gap between literature and the rationalistic tradition appears at once in the study of literature and language.

As the study of literature is transformed into the study of language, we immediately begin to ask: How do words work? How is meaning conveyed?

An influential approach to the study of language, called structural linguistics, was developed by the Swiss linguist Ferdinand de Saussure in the early twentieth century. Structural linguistics studies each individual word, examining its meaning and the relation of each word to another. Language is an interwoven structure, and each word derives its meaning only through its relation to other items in the structure. Consider the statement: the man is in the room. This statement means something quite different from: the room is in the man. Saussure said language is like a chessboard: each piece has its relevance and meaning, not intrinsically, but through its relation to other pieces.

Each word is also a complex construction. A word, such as 'man,' is a string of graphical symbols on a page. Language is a system of signs: each sign is made up of a signifier (the graphical symbols on the page) and the signified (the concept or meaning). There is no intrinsic reason why the string of letters m-a-n should mean 'man,' except our culture and history. Other languages use different graphical symbols, a different signifier. (French, for example, uses the graphical symbols 'homme.') The signs are part of the structure of language. Saussure founded the field of semiotics, the study of signs. Structural linguistics is a subfield of the larger field of semiotics.

In language, one sign can be substituted for another. Consider a longer statement: 'The man was in the room, and then he walked quickly out of the room.' We might rewrite this as: 'The man was in the room, and then on winged feet he fled his walls.' We have substituted certain words for others, substituted certain signs for other signs, and yet the meaning has not been lost. The substitutions can be a metaphor, as 'winged feet' substitute for 'walked quickly,' or the substitution can be a metonym, as 'walls' substitute for 'room.' We know what is meant by 'on winged feet he fled his walls,' because of a general background of signs that are part of our history and culture.

In his structural and semiotic approach to the study of language and literature, Saussure sought to develop a scientific, rather than esthetic, analysis. In the tradition of Euclid and Newton, Saussure's analysis identified the objects of study – words – and sought to understand the laws that governed their interrelationships. The analysis would discern the relations between signifier and signified, and articulate the deep structural laws that lay within a language.

The further application of Sausurre's structural approach took many thinkers in quite another direction. They did not find the universal certainties of Euclid or Newton's laws of motion. Instead, structural analysis recognized that each signifier was culturally determined, and that the structure of a language, with its substitution of signs through metaphors or metonyms, was specific to a culture. The aspirations to sciencelike certainties of the structuralists were completely rejected by many who followed after: the poststructuralists. The poststructuralists see the connections between signifier and signified as problematic. There is no objective, universal connection between signifier and signified – the connection is culturally contingent. The communicative and referential character of language, which Searle notes is integral to the Western Rationalistic Tradition, is challenged. The linguistic analysis of poststructuralism is at the core of the postmodern epistemology.

The 'scientific' structural orientation evaporates inevitably into analysis of the cultural context. Also, inevitably, all texts are connected to other texts. When we use the metaphor 'winged feet,' the meaning is connected to Greek texts and winged Apollo and hundreds of other texts using the 'winged' metaphor. For postmodernists, meaning is intertextual, lodged in infinitely complex interwoven relationships, 'an endless conversation between the texts with no prospect of ever arriving at or being halted at an agreed point.'[24] The compatibility of this postmodern linguistic sensibility with new information technologies is evident.[25] Ted Nelson's hypertext, his dream of new ways of writing and connecting, is electronic intertextuality. The World Wide Web makes intertextuality explicit.

If we were to look up a word (a signifier) in the dictionary, we can find its meaning, but only in terms of other signifiers. The process is infinite and circular, we never get to ultimate meaning. As we look at language and try to understand how language functions, 'instead of being a well-defined, clearly demarcated structure containing symmetrical units of signifiers and signifieds, it now begins to look much more like a sprawling limitless web where there is a constant interchange and circulations of elements, where none of the elements is absolutely definable.'[26]

Postmodern analysis denies the possibility of sciencelike laws in language and meaning. The meaning of a text is not obvious; furthermore, the surface meaning is not the whole or true meaning. Jacques Derrida, an influential poststructuralist, developed a method of analysis and literary criticism that would deconstruct a text. The method is used to identify features in the text that betray and even subvert the surface meaning.

Language and structures inherently are unstable. Meaning is fleeting, not fixed. Meaning will be different between different readers. But somehow in each society we function. How is this intrinsic instability overcome? Amid this cultural contingency, out of this play of signifiers and the infinite web of interconnections, nonetheless certain meanings are elevated to a privileged position. These meanings become the centres around which other meanings are forced to turn. Now we come to the most controversial steps in postmodern thinking – certain meanings come to dominate, these meanings emerge out of power relations, and the crucial power relations for determining meaning are those of liberal democratic capitalism and of patriarchal social relations.

The most influential postmodern analysis comes from Michel Foucault, the French philosopher, in his historical studies of medical science, prisons, madness, and human sexuality. On examining the 'progress' of western thought, he did not find the accumulation of objective knowledge as the western rationalist tradition would suggest. Rather he found discourses. Linguistic analysis defines a discourse as 'a passage of [spoken or written] language that reflects the social, epistemological and political practices of a group.'[27] A discourse not only reflects these practices, the discourse constitutes and creates the social, epistemological, and political practices. Foucault demonstrates how the discourses are not a representation of an objective world 'out there,' but rather the discourses constitute the world and construct it. Discourses are 'practices that systematically form the objects of which they speak.'[28] He rebelled against the structuralist approach. Instead, he argued that the categories we use to describe the world are not unique; they are but choices among many, although so often we are unaware of this power. He sought to map the 'unconscious of science' and to discern its patterns of selection, exclusion, and deception.

Postmodern analysis finds similar powers to construct reality in economists, lawyers, physicians, educators, and indeed, all our 'experts.' Postmodern thought is intensely sceptical of all attempts to claim an objective reality and emphasizes that much reality is constructed and socially created. Furthermore, the power to construct reality is held by the dominant groups in society, and these groups construct reality to maintain their position of dominance. The old aphorism that knowledge is power is reaffirmed, but in a new, linguistic, way.

One of the most important contributions of postmodern analysis, Jean-François Lyotard's *The Postmodern Condition: A Report on Knowledge*, is directly concerned with the nature of knowledge and the place of the university. The book is a report to the Council of Universities of the Province of Quebec, addressing the question of how knowledge is legitimated in a postmodern world. At the time it was written, Lyotard was a professor of philosophy at the University of Paris at Vincennes. He begins: 'Our working hypothesis is that the status of knowledge is altered as societies enter what is known as the postindustrial age and cultures enter what is known as the postmodern age.'[29] He goes on, in the spirit of Foucault: 'I will take as my point of departure a single feature, one that immediately defines our object of study. Scientific knowledge is a kind of discourse.'[30] In the postmodern world, science is a discourse that constructs rather than objectively represents reality. The research at the multiversity is a discourse that constructs rather than represents reality. How then can knowledge be authenticated?

Lyotard introduces the concept of a 'grand narrative,' which is a 'story that underlies, gives legitimacy, and explains the particular choices a culture prescribes as courses of action. A grand narrative, also called a master narrative, provides coherence by covering up the various conflicts ... that arise in the history of a society. Examples of such narratives are Christianity, the Enlightenment, Capitalism and Marxism. A grand narrative operates as a meta-narrative providing a framework in which all other cultural narratives find their ground and acquire their meaning and legitimacy. Postmodernism is heralded when grand narratives lose their credibility and little narratives proliferate.'[31] Lyotard identifies two grand narratives in the legitimation of knowledge. The first is the narrative of emancipation, especially connected with the rise of the modern nation state, in which freedom is achieved through scientific knowledge. The second is the narrative of the questing speculative human spirit, especially associated with the modern university, and summarized in the phrase: knowledge for its own sake. One could read chapters 2 through 5 of this book as a telling of these grand narratives and of the university's crucial role in the story. Lyotard argues that these grand narratives are now rejected. Without them, we must ask how knowledge can be legitimated and what then becomes of the university?

Edward Said, who was a professor of comparative literature at Columbia University, applies the methodologies of discourse analysis and deconstruction in his *Orientalism* to examine how academic western scholarship has portrayed the Orient (the lands to the east of the west). He argues that western scholarship is a discourse; it has defined and created the Orient. The Orient only exists to us through the essentialist categories and conclusions of Orientalist scholarship. And crucially, 'Europe was always in a position of strength, not to say domination ... Knowledge of the Orient, because generated out of strength, in a sense *creates* the Orient, the Oriental, and his world.'[32] This cultural dominance not only stood alongside the more evident political and economic dominance of imperialism, but Said makes an additional and even more provocative assertion: western scholarship was a precursor to imperialism and 'colonial rule was justified in advance by Orientalism, rather than after the fact.'[33] Later, in *Culture and Imperialism*, Said examines how canonical writers such as Jane Austen and W.B. Yeats portray the relations of colonies to the imperial nation and finds that even imaginative literature is complicit in the power structures of imperialism. Said's writing has been hugely influential, helping to establish the field of postcolonial studies, a crucial component in postmodern thought.

Said does not dwell upon it, or draw it out, but his analysis is a severe indictment of universities and their works. He defines *Orientalism* in several ways, one of which focuses on scholars and their institutions: 'The most readily accepted designation of Orientalism is an academic one, and indeed the label still serves in a number of academic institutions. Anyone who teaches, writes about, or researches the Orient – and this applies whether the person is an anthropologist, sociologist, historian, or philologist – either in its specific or general aspects is an Orientalist, and what he or she does is Orientalism.'[34] Said's analysis implies that universities and their professors, despite their own belief in disinterested research, have been the handmaidens of cultural dominance and imperialism. The multiversity, far from being autonomous from the state, supports the state's imperial ventures. His analysis and many postmodern ideas force us to rethink the relationship between the multiversity and power.

Jean Baudrillard, a sociologist at the University of Paris Nanterre, is one of the most provocative, and outrageous, of postmodern thinkers. He pushes the split between signifier and signified to such a radical extreme as to declare that reality no longer exists. Few of us would follow Baudrillard to this conclusion. But, if we pull back somewhat, we might find some sympathy with this sensibility. Consider the modern practice of politics. What is the reality 'out there'? What is the reality of our prime ministers and presidents, their policies, and the alternative policies on offer? How do we come to 'know' the leaders and their policies? We know them through the mass media of newspapers, television, and the World Wide Web. There is no objective reality; rather, reality is created for us by the media, the commentators, and the 'spin doctors' of the prime minister's and the president's offices. They create an image for us that becomes the reality. Students of politics speak of the political agenda and the discourse of public policy. Consider the following quotation from a public policy textbook that is most decidedly not postmodern. The agenda and discourse define 'what is relevant in public life, how issues are defined, whose views should be taken seriously, and what sort of "solutions" are tenable ... These [political] issues and problems do not exist apart from the words and symbols used to describe them. They are constructed in the sense that political issues and problems are not inevitable and inherent.'[35] Politicians and their communications advisers seek to control the agenda and the discourse: they seek to create reality – often they do so very successfully.

These self-conscious manipulations of words and images are to be found everywhere in our postmodern world in advertising. Even multiversities, those bastions of the Western Rationalistic Tradition, are not above such practices. They have vast communications departments intended to create an image of the multiversity, to create the reality to be used when our children choose which multiversity to attend and when we decide where we will donate money. Advertisers now speak of 'branding.' Is this not a socially created reality? Multiversities are actively engaged in branding, the multiversity's communications departments are postmodern to the core.

Many scholars reach the same conclusions as Lyotard and Foucault, although arriving by a different route. They too reject most of modernity's story that reason and science have brought progress and emancipation. They too reject the rationalistic epistemology and are sceptical of authority and those who claim to have absolute truth (or that absolute truth is knowable). They too argue that much of what passes for truth masks a defence of privilege and power. They too find in literature and the social sciences much disguised sexism and racism. And, therefore, I will include them under the umbrella of postmodern thought.

The American philosophical tradition of pragmatism, in recent years with a strongly linguistic turn, has always had an intense epistemological scepticism, rejecting the representational character of language and the correspondence theory of truth. The most public of these philosophers, Richard Rorty of Stanford University and the University of Virginia, writes: 'Pragmatists think that the history of attempts to isolate the True or the Good, or to define the word "true" or "good," supports their suspicion that there is no interesting work to be done in this area. It might, of course, have turned out otherwise. People have, oddly enough, found out something interesting to say about the essence of Force and the definition of "number." They might have found something interesting to say about the essence of truth. But in fact they haven't.' Pragmatists do not say there is no such thing as truth, nor do they have relativistic or subjective theory; 'they would simply like to change the subject.'[36] They believe that the structure and vocabulary of the rationalistic tradition is just not very useful.

Feminism is another crucial part of postmodern thought. Modernity's grand narrative is that reason and science brought progress and emancipation; this, feminists reject. They argue that modernity systematically disadvantaged women (and other groups). Moreover, perhaps, the very ideas and ideals of modernity sustained the oppression because they were unable to reveal the patriarchy – the 'set of social relations between men ... which ... establish or create interdependence and solidarity among men that enable them to dominate women.'[37] Feminist literary critics offer interpretation much like Said's; he exposes Orientalism and they expose patriarchy. Feminist philosophers fundamentally critique the rationalist tradition. Philosopher Sandra Harding, of the University of Delaware and the University of California, Los Angeles, summarizes the variations in feminist epistemology under three approaches: 'Feminist empiricism, feminist standpoint theory and feminist postmodernism, each progressively more radical in their epistemological commitments. While feminist empiricists accepted positivist principles of value-neutral inquiry and criticized actual scientific practice for failing to live up to these ideals, feminist standpoint theorists suggested that knowledge must necessarily be "socially-situated" and perspectival, and they argued that some perspectives, such as the perspective of the feminist, were epistemologically privileged. Postmodernists, however, questioned whether any perspective could be said to be privileged over any other, leading them down the path of relativism.'[38] This continuum effectively reveals the difficulties in characterizing postmodern thought: Does feminism belong under the heading of the postmodern? Certainly some empiricist feminism does not, but most feminism, including standpoint theory, reflects the postmodern sensibility and, indeed, is hugely influential in postmodern thought.

Closely connected to postcolonialism and to feminism is a body of thought that can be loosely grouped under the heading of multiculturalism. The Anglo-American world is now multicultural – many of its people have recently come from outside that world. Anglo-American culture – the literature, language, food, music, television, and so on – is marked by the irruption of non-European influence. For many, this multiculturalism is to be celebrated, and they welcome this diversity, also believing that immigrants need not adopt the host's customs, values, and beliefs in order to sustain a stable and coherent society. But even among the multicultural liberals, there is an implicit recognition that multiculturalism might imply that there are no absolute values or absolute notions of truth or authority. Multicultural thought becomes postmodern as it takes a linguistic turn, emphasizing, like postcolonialism and feminism, how the language and discourse of the powerful can define and dominate cultural, racial, or ethnic groups and how language and image are crucial in the construction of personal identity. Like much postmodern thought, it is intensely critical of the current situation in our liberal democratic societies, arguing that the 'other' has been marginalized and excluded. Multicultural thought directly contests liberal notions of equality and citizenship. Gerard Delanty, in his analysis of the late modern or postmodern university, examines this thrust of multicultural thought. In a chapter entitled 'The New Politics of Knowledge: Culture Wars, Identity, and Citizenship, he writes: 'Social citizenship is today being challenged by cultural citizenship. The political impetus of modernity was the search for equality which eventually became the basis of social citizenship in the welfare state. Today the centrality of equality has been challenged by demands for difference. To be equal and to be different are the two main problems facing citizenship today. Education has become a major site of this double conflict.'[39]

To conclude, much of pragmatism, feminism, and multiculturalism can be included under the umbrella of postmodern thought. Although postmodern thought is diverse and varied, it nonetheless shares much: it shares a linguistic turn, a focus on language, reality, and power, and a radical critique of Anglo-American society. It is profoundly sceptical of received wisdom and of cultural and political norms. Postmodern reality is fragmented. There is no objective reality 'out there,' each of us experiences the world and derives meaning from the signifiers differently. There are no *laws* underlying the reality of society, and thus *theories* cannot be created to describe and explain large areas of reality, as had been hoped. Euclid's *Elements* and Newton's *Principia* cannot be the conceptual models for our thought. Language does not represent reality; the link between signifier and signified is loose and shifting. There can be no correspondence theory of truth. Reality, because it is socially constructed, becomes political. The meanings that come to prevail are created by the dominant in society, who seek to retain their position of dominance. Master narratives are constructed to organize life, but they exclude and marginalize.

The conclusion is profound: postmodern thought rejects the scholarly ideal of 'the *disinterested* inquirer engaged in the quest for *objective* knowledge that will have *universal* validity.' The great conflict is now between those who hold this idea of the university and those who reject it.

W(h)ither the Humanities and Liberal Education?

Much under the postmodern umbrella undermines the claims of the humanities to a central place in an undergraduate liberal education. The humanities seem adrift, or worse. There are wars – the culture wars – within the humanities, and perhaps with their legitimacy undermined, the humanities will wither and liberal education will be undermined.

The humanities have been, until quite recently, at the heart of a liberal undergraduate education. Up until the mid-nineteenth century, the classical and early Christian texts, in Greek and Latin, formed the core of humanities studies in a liberal education. Gradually, with the shift from the *artes liberales* ideal of liberal learning to the liberal-free ideal, and with the introduction of modern, vernacular literature into the curriculum, the classical and early Christian texts almost disappeared. These texts had been the source of values and standards of conduct in a liberal education intended to create virtuous and competent citizens. Nonetheless, the civic purposes of a liberal education were carried forward by the humanities. There were great dangers in the modern world, as it became more utilitarian, more industrial, and more democratic. Matthew Arnold's answer was the study of culture. In the reading of the great works of literature, philosophy, and history, students were to be exposed to the highest achievements of western civilization and gain insight into human nature and the human condition. These works gave access to the beautiful and the spiritual, which must have a place with the rational and the scientific. In reading the literature and history of their own country, students would become citizens of their nation and aware of its place in western tradition. The reading of literature would lead, in Lionel Trilling's phrase, 'to an improvement in the intelligence, and especially the intelligence as it touches the moral life.'[40]

Postmodern thought undermines these claims. It questions the importance of reading the western tradition in a liberal education. Most of the public still believe in its importance and are deeply troubled by the postmodern rejection of this tradition. They wonder – openly – whether the multiversity has lost its way. They also wonder – openly – whether they should support a multiversity that holds these views.

The position of the humanities within liberal learning had been weakening over the entire postwar period, and not all the current dilemma can be attributed to postmodern thought. Nonetheless, postmodernism makes inescapable certain troubling questions around the value of the humanities: Why read literature? What is the justification for studying literature? One answer has always been: for pleasure. But it is a difficult pleasure, and only close study gives us access to it. Postmodernism, with all its theoretical apparatus, drains away the pleasure. It leads to a disenchantment of literature, just as Max Weber said our expertise leads to a disenchantment of the world. Literary works become just physical facts, collections of graphical symbols on a page, links between signifier and signified to be examined. We soon recognize that the system of signs in a literary novel is analytically similar to the system of signs in a movie, a political speech, or in a comic book. In a science of signs, a comic book is just as complex in the relations between signifier and signified as a novel, and just as worthy of study because we have no ethical or esthetic standards to justify choosing one over the other. The distinction between high and low culture blurs and disappears. Small wonder that controversy rages when Mickey Mouse and King Lear are read side-by-side.

The disenchantment of literature goes further. The idea of literature, especially *English literature* as we now use the term, is a rather recent invention and only in the nineteenth century did it enter the university curriculum. Matthew Arnold and those who followed him created a grand narrative about the emergence and importance of English literature. A postmodern analysis questions and rejects this grand narrative. The definition of what is literature, of what is the best that has been thought and said, is socially created by value judgments, and these change over time: 'These value-judgments themselves have a close relation to social ideologies. They refer in the end not simply to private taste, but to the assumptions by which certain social groups exercise and maintain power over others.'[41] The imaginative, romantic notion of English literature and the rise of English as a subject of study, postmodern scholars have argued, should be recognized as an ideology suited to the politically dominant classes of nineteenth-century England. In such analyses, the reading and study of literature is but a project of ideological domination under a master narrative. The master narrative must be challenged and the texts deconstructed to discover their inadvertent meaning and reveal their power to include and exclude. Postmodern Marxist, feminist, and postcolonial scholars argue that the best that has been thought and said – the western canon – has disguised within it values and views that sustain patriarchal relations between men and women, and a Eurocentric dominance of the rest of the world. Collectively, this postmodern critique has fought to change what is to be included in the curriculum.

Gerald Graff delightfully captures the controversy in *Beyond the Culture Wars*, as he recreates a faculty debate about 'Dover Beach.' The protagonists are the younger female professor (called YFP) and the older male professor (called OMP). The debate begins in the faculty lounge as OMP returns from his lecture about Matthew Arnold's 'Dover Beach,' appalled that most of his students found the poem incomprehensible.

YFP says she can appreciate the student's reaction and recalls 'that being forced to study 'Dover Beach' in high school caused her to form a dislike for poetry that it had taken her years to overcome.'

OMP: In *my* humble opinion – reactionary though I suppose it now is – 'Dover Beach' is one of the great masterpieces of the Western tradition, a work that, until recently at least, every seriously educated person took for granted as part of the cultural heritage.

YFP: Perhaps, but is that altogether to the credit of the cultural heritage? Take those lines addressed to the woman: 'Ah, love, let us be true to one another ...' and so forth. In other words, protect and console me, my dear – as it's the function of your naturally more spiritual sex to do – from the 'struggle and flight' of politics and history that we men have been assigned the regrettable duty of dealing with. It's a good example of how women have been defined by our culture as naturally private and domestic and therefore justly disqualified from sharing male power.

OMP: That's the trouble with you people; you seem to treat 'Dover

Beach' as if it were a piece of political propaganda rather than a work of art ... To read poems as if they were statements about gender politics replaces universal concerns of art with the gripes of a special-interest group.

YFP: It's not that 'Dover Beach' and *Macbeth* are 'statements about gender politics' but that these texts assume definitions of men's and women's 'natures' that still shape our behavior and that we blind ourselves if we read them as accounts of universal experience.[42]

Do we continue to include 'Dover Beach' in the curriculum, even after we have discerned its assumptions about men's and women's natures? Perhaps we should open up the curriculum, previously dominated by dead white European male writers, and include more works by women and people of colour. But what criteria should we use for inclusion? Postmodernism has rejected the possibility of esthetic criteria. *Is* there a body of work that every seriously educated person should read as part of the cultural heritage?

All these tensions have become full-scale cultural wars, fought not only on campus but also in the press, the granting councils, and the legislatures when considering the funding of universities. The wars are especially intense in the United States because a strong tradition of liberal education has meant that courses in humanities or 'Western Civilization' were required of all students and because these courses were justified as means to create a common democratic culture. For a melting-pot nation, the recipe defining the shared culture is vital. Canada has adopted a more heterogeneous vision of what it means to be a 'Canadian,' and the United Kingdom is only beginning to address the implications of difference in a university curriculum. But everywhere, the postmodern attitude exists as a powerful critique of the humanities, and it must be addressed.

The debate is partly about what books should be studied. It is also, and more fundamentally, about why we study the humanities. Originally, the humanities provided the values and standards for citizenship. Later, they were a buttress against philistine, industrial society, and they cultivated the intelligence as it touches the moral life. The Harvard Redbook placed great emphasis on how the humanities can inculcate common beliefs and shared values and a sense of heritage. But after postmodernism, can the humanities have any such roles? Do the humanities still have a central role in a liberal education for citizenship?

Most multiversities have ducked the debate. They have relaxed any requirements for specific courses in a liberal education and allowed students to choose. The multiversity has offered a liberal pluralist – or cafeteria – solution. Fundamental critique is handled by adding new courses. The confrontation is avoided in general avoidance of universitywide discussion of the undergraduate curriculum. The culture wars continue, usually as guerilla wars, but periodically breaking out into hot wars. Both the public and the university deserve better. The cafeteria approach will be destructive, ultimately, not simply because the guerilla wars will not cease, but because there is such a gap between the multiversity's public statements on behalf of the humanities and the reality of the undergraduate curriculum. This can only erode public understanding and support for the humanities and weaken the social contract on which the university depends. The debate must occur, and it must occur within a larger debate about the undergraduate curriculum. It is a debate that only the university can lead. The public must be part of it, but the multiversity must promote and lead the debate.

Culture Wars, Political Correctness, and Academic Freedom

Postmodern thought is changing the multiversity. Not only is it stimulating a vigorous, often rancorous, debate within individual disciplines, it has also brought new degree programs and departments, for example, in women's studies, postcolonial studies, queer studies, cultural studies, and science studies. It has challenged the conception of a canon of western literature, exposing it to devastating criticism. The postmodern attitude of mind has argued that many practices of the university – in particular, following the linguistic turn of postmodern thought, many uses of language at the multiversity – were unwelcoming to women, visible minorities, gays and lesbians, and fought vigorously to change these practices, the use of language, and the climate within the university. (The postmodernists are by no means the only proponents of such changes; reform liberals have been strong proponents.) But its influence goes beyond the curriculum change spurred by the conflict between different academic theories. Postmodern thought has politicized the debates.

Extreme postmodernists argue that support for the traditional canon is not disinterested; rather the canon and its supporters act on behalf of the powerful against the marginalized. Searle asserts, correctly, that 'part of what happened is that in the late 1960s and 1970s a number of young people went into academic life because they thought that social and political transformation could be achieved through educational and cultural transformation, and that the political ideals of the 1960s could be achieved through education.'[43] Of course, this is nothing new: education and political change have always been connected, and people have entered academic life because of their desire to affect change. For example, many were drawn to economics because of the Keynesian possibility of reducing the scourge of unemployment. 'Many of the multiculturalist proposals for curricular reform involve a subtle redefinition of an academic subject from a *domain to be studied* to that of a *cause to be advanced*.'[44] This politicization of the humanities is new and enormously controversial.

The politicization of the humanities becomes still more controversial when it is coupled with demands to change how we use language through antiracist and antisexist speech codes. Debate, even conversation, is stifled because of hypersensitivity to slights in the use of words. Demands for the 'policing of language' can become acutely provocative under pressure from student and professorial activists.

All this attracted great attention outside the university, especially in the United States, where it is often lumped under the heading of 'political correctness' or PC. The term *politically correct* was first used by those on the far left as a self-mocking description of 'comrades whose holier-than-thou espousal of party dogma made other comrades want to spit.'[45] But it has now become a derogatory term used to describe 'holier-than-thou espousal of postcolonial, feminist, and multicultural dogma.' The term PC is now used to encompass a host of academic reforms and attitudes advocated by postmodernists. There are no doubt causes of political correctness beyond postmodern thought, but PC derives its intellectual strength from the postmodern analysis of language, identity, and representation. The postmodern mood or attitude – now labelled PC by its critics – has ignited an enormous blowback.

The polemics are outrageous indeed. The critics claim that PC is destroying higher education. PC, it is alleged, has thrown out the classical works of western culture, forsaken standards of truth and objectivity, abandoned merit through preferential admissions policies and faculty hiring policies, and has bullied any dissenting voices into silence. In response, the defenders claim they are valiantly fighting to open up space for those repressed and marginalized by the patriarchal capitalist power structure.

The most troubling theme of the controversy is the allegation that political correctness has compromised academic freedom: people are afraid to speak their minds for fear of being hounded and branded as sexist or racist. The multiversity should be a place where ideas can be expressed and explored freely; the university should be 'an intellectual experiment station' in which ideas, sometimes even ones distasteful to the larger community, might be explored.[46] The allegation that people are not free to speak their thoughts – if true – is devastating to the multiversity. Academic freedom is essential if the multiversity is to fulfil its mission; the multiversity is deeply threatened if the wider community becomes convinced that the university is not a place of free speech. I am constantly surprised, and troubled, by how often those I speak to from outside the university are convinced that PC has suppressed open thought within the university. Authors of university novels, those mine-canary social observers, have filled their recent works with examples of PC gone wild.

The worry in the United States that academic freedom may be threatened (a risk no less present in Canada and the United Kingdom[47]) led the American Association of University Professors (AAUP), which had drafted the famous 'Declaration of Principles' in 1915, to sponsor a group of distinguished academics to re-examine the principles of academic freedom. 'Could the principles be defended in the context of poststructuralist philosophy? Was the traditional practice possible in a charged political climate?'[48] Their essays are published as *The Future of Academic Freedom*. The essays are erudite, reflective, and troubled. Academic freedom can be compromised, and on many occasions has been compromised. We must not deny or shrink from this. But we also must think carefully about the issues, more carefully than most of the PC controversy has allowed.

Louis Menand, in the introductory essay in the above-mentioned volume, notes that there does not exist, and cannot exist, an 'unproblematic conception of academic freedom that is philosophically coherent and that will conduce to outcomes in particular cases which all parties will feel to be just and equitable.'[49] He recalls Isaiah Berlin's famous essay 'Two Concepts of Liberty' which distinguishes between *negative* liberty and *positive* liberty. *Negative* liberty is freedom from restraint, freedom from interference in one's pursuits; *positive* liberty is freedom to act, freedom to realize one's potential without restraint. Those who see political correctness as suppressing academic freedom are using the concept of negative liberty; those who see the multiversity as a place with still lingering sexism and racism that must be addressed are using the concept of positive liberty.

Academic freedom must include both negative and positive liberty. We cannot deny that some people's freedoms are curtailed in the postmodern pursuit of positive liberty. The question we must struggle with is whether we have struck the correct balance between positive and negative liberty. Unquestionably, in many instances at many multiversities, political correctness has cowed dissenting voices and cast an unacceptable limit on academic freedom. Also unquestionably, however, postmodern thought has demonstrated that many traditional ways of thinking create unacceptable limits on positive liberty. We must ask ourselves, despite examples of PC-induced censorship, whether the multiversity is any less a place of free expression than it was before. Some wise observers have noted that today's university is far more exploratory, tolerant, and open than the university of the conformist 1950s.

Edward Said, author of the concluding essay in *The Future of Academic Freedom*, reflecting on identity, authority, and freedom writes: 'There *is* something hallowed and consecrated about the academy; there *is* a sense of violated sanctity experienced by us when the university or school is subjected to crude political pressures.' But this does not free the academy from the intellectual and political reality of their society. 'Each community of academics, intellectuals, and students must wrestle with the problem of what academic freedom in that society at that time actually is and should be.'[50]

The Social Sciences and the Natural Sciences

Postmodern thought originated in the humanities, but its influence is far more wide-ranging. The postmodern sensibility is influential across all disciplines – in the professions, even in some aspects of science, but most particularly in the social sciences.

The Enlightenment writers believed that the study of social phenomena should proceed, broadly, in the same way as the study of natural phenomena. The method of science should be applied to the study of society; we should strive for a science of society. In this spirit emerged the social sciences. On the face of it, such an approach confronts great difficulties. It requires that the world of human beings be analysed in the same way as the world of planets and plants, engines and atoms. The human world is so different from the physical world: the human world brings questions of consciousness and free will, of the relation between the individual and the group, of rationality versus emotion, and of moral values. None of these are present in the natural sciences; how could a scientific methodology possibly be useful in the study of social life?

Nonetheless, the dominant approach in social science accepted that the human world, like the physical world, conformed to laws and could be analysed using the methodology developed in the natural sciences. The Western Rationalistic Tradition, discussed by Searle, applied in the social sciences, just as in the sciences. There could be theory: theories of individual behaviour, theories of society, and theories of social change. Reality exists independently of human representations and there is a correspondence theory of truth. Close empirical observation is crucial; taxonomies of social facts are important. Social science shared the same Enlightenment faith in progress as analysis in the natural sciences: ignorance was the cause of much human misery and bondage; knowledge could improve the human condition and bring freedom.

In the social sciences, these aspirations to sciencelike knowledge motivated the positivists. The first self-conscious articulation of the positivist position came from Auguste Comte in the nineteenth century; he even used the term *social physics* to describe the science of society. Laws govern the social world, just as they govern the natural world, and the purpose of social science is to discover these laws. Following the analogy from the natural sciences, the positivist tradition in social science asserts that good social science is value-free, maintaining a separation between facts and values. Also, it asserts that only explanations based on observable factors are scientifically valid. Positivists make extensive use of statistics to describe reality, to identify interrelationships, and to test hypotheses. Many positivists are methodological individualists, seeking explanation for all social phenomena in the behaviour of individuals.

Although the positivist tradition has dominated among practising social scientists, every one of its propositions has been vigorously criticized by other social scientists. Many social scientists argue that the natural sciences cannot offer a methodology for the social sciences; that facts and values can never be separated; that many explanations must be based on non-observable phenomena; and finally, many social scientists have rejected methodological individualism in favour of a holist approach. Each of these lines of criticism has much in common with the postmodern sensibility; this both helps to explain the extensive postmodern orientation in current social science and also makes it difficult to separate these older critical traditions from more recent postmodern thought.

Nonetheless, postmodern thought has made a decisive intervention and widened the divides within social science. Pauline Marie Rosenau, professor of political science at the University of Quebec at Montreal, begins her *Post-Modernism and the Social Sciences: Insights, Inroads, and Intrusions* with: 'Post-modernism haunts social science today. In a number of respects, some plausible and some preposterous, post-modern approaches dispute the underlying assumptions of mainstream social science and its research product over the last three decades. It rejects epistemological assumptions, refutes methodological conventions, resists knowledge claims, obscures all versions of truth, and dismisses policy recommendations.'[51]

Much in the postmodern critique is not new to social scientists. Certainly, most social scientists are familiar, if not always comfortable, with value relativism, because social scientists have always recognized the diversity of values and that science could not arbitrate among conflicting values. Similarly, most social scientists are familiar, if not comfortable, with the idea that there remains inequality, marginalization, and oppression in the world, even after all our so-called progress. Likewise, they realize that it is problematic to claim social reality can be objectively described; they realize that in social science the observer often influences that which he or she is observing and, furthermore, that social scientific research can contain hidden bias, reflecting the perspective of the researcher and the wider power relations. These controversies have always been part of doing social science. But postmodernism, in all its variants from neopragmatism and poststructuralism, to the new Marxism and feminism, has reprovoked these methodological controversies, brought them to the fore, and forced a reappraisal of basic assumptions, theories, and methods. The most penetrating thrust of postmodern thought is its linguistic analysis. There has been a linguistic turn in social science, and there are culture wars in the social science departments.[52] There is a similar linguistic turn and culture war in many of the professions.

It is impossible in this space to elaborate the powerful influence of postmodern thought across the social sciences and professions, especially given what is here included under the expansive umbrella of postmodernism. Nonetheless, certain themes stand out and can be illustrated with examples. The postmodernism in the social sciences rejects the metanarrative of Enlightenment and progress. Rather than a story of improvement in material well-being and increasing freedom, many social scientists see decadence, continuing poverty and oppression, and increasing regimentation and control. They are intensely critical of society today, and explicitly, or by implication, intensely critical of liberal democratic capitalism. This critical stance towards society today – towards liberal democratic capitalism – leads some of postmodernism's opponents to characterize the postmodern attitude as the 'academic left.'

Characterizing postmodern thought as the academic left creates all sorts of ironies and strange bedfellows. Many on the left despise postmodern thought because it rejects all metanarratives, including the metanarrative of emancipation, and because its value relativism undermines the basis of social criticism and the arguments for reform. (Of course, Marxism is one of the metanarratives of emancipation that extreme postmodernism rejects.) But, certainly, postmodern thought shares with the left a critical stance towards liberal democratic capitalism. Furthermore, postmodern thought emerged and gained influence as the alternative of socialism collapsed. Many writers have noted that postmodernism ideas, particularly feminist, postcolonial, and multiculturalist ideas have been a locus of resistance to the neoliberal regimes of the past decade and a half. Postmodernism is not 'left' in the classical ideological sense; but, nonetheless, postmodernism's controversies have been whipped up further by this political identification and by postmodern thought's resolutely critical stance.

Deconstruction and discourse theory have been applied throughout the social sciences and many professions. Social science analysis, it is argued, is not a theory representing a reality that exists independently of human representation; rather, social science analysis is a discourse – 'practices that systematically form the objects of which they speak.' To social scientists in a positivist tradition this is anathema, not surprisingly, because if pushed to its extreme, this proposition destroys social science. In fields like anthropology, sociology, and political science, and in professions like law, social work, and education, many professors are exploring the implications of discourse analysis. While not accepting the extreme conclusion, they are pushing against established knowledge and practices following the moderate strand of postmodernism. Their analysis finds that much supposedly objective knowledge can be seen as a historically specific social construction and exposes much previously unrecognized sexism and racism within social science.

Many social science professors are finding their discipline to be 'Orientalist,' in its own way – the language and discourse of their social science has created reality and from a position of dominance. This postmodern work confronts how women, people of colour, gays and lesbians have been analysed, and these professors struggle to conduct work that is more open and less Orientalist. This perspective – that much of past social science and history can be condemned as Orientalist – is very influential. It underpins much multiculturalism. It is very influential, for example, in faculties of education and is now shaping our future teachers and the future curriculum of our schools. It is also influential in faculties of social work and faculties of law – in any field where the issue of inequalities of power is a central concern.

Paradoxically, this postmodern sensibility in social science, in its extreme form, is undermining the welfare state. We tend to associate criticism of the welfare state with neoliberals, who have argued that many well-intended programs of the welfare state have actually made things worse. However, extreme postmodern analysis argues that the well-intended programs of the welfare state are actually instruments of social control and mask continuing sexism, racism, and homophobia. Furthermore, extreme postmodernism's rejection of ethical and moral absolutes undermines the rationale for progressive reform.[53]

On the other hand, some moderate postmodernism is supportive of the welfare state. This strand, while denying the metanarrative of emancipation, points out continuing marginalization and exclusion, and argues for a reformed recommitment to the ideal of social citizenship. A crucial dilemma for Anglo-American democracies is whether they have adequately addressed, under their commitment to universal individual rights, the very real differences among their citizens. Postmodern thought argues that they have not, and in its moderate strand provides a basis for beginning to address how marginalization and exclusion might be reduced. In its linguistic analysis, it identifies both how we have failed and, therefore, what must be done to realize our aspirations for democratic citizenship.

The practices and advances of natural science have provided the paradigm for the Western Rationalistic Tradition. But even the sciences are not immune from postmodern criticisms. Postmodern professors – from discourse theorists to feminists and pragmatists – claim that things are not as they seem even in science. At the radical extreme, the philosopher of science Paul Feyerabend declares that there are no objective truths, scientific, political or moral 'out there' in the world.[54] Others point out that science and technology have not brought progress and emancipation, but war, environmental degradation, and alienation. Furthermore, the radical feminists argue, the relation of knowledge to power is clear: 'Despite the deeply ingrained Western cultural belief in science's intrinsic progressiveness, science today serves primarily regressive social tendencies; and [that] the social structure of science, many of its applications and technologies, its modes of defining research problems and designing experiments, its ways of constructing and conferring meanings are not only sexist but also racist, classist, and culturally coercive.'[55]

Somewhere between Feyerabend and traditional science are professors working in science studies, developing the history, philosophy, and sociology of science. Many have offered a constructivist interpretation of science, what I would label a 'moderate postmodern approach.' A recent survey of this literature by Jan Golinski, in *Making Natural Knowledge: Constructivism and the History of Science*, concludes that the literature offers 'a new understanding of science itself. In the last few years, scientific knowledge has come to be seen as a product of human culture, an approach that has challenged the tradition of the history of science as a story of steady and autonomous progress.'[56] A constructivist outlook 'regards scientific knowledge primarily as a human product, made with locally situated cultural and material resources, rather than as simply the revelation of a pregiven order of nature.'[57]

The scientific community, when it hears of the extreme postmodern conclusions, is puzzled, but goes about its business. Occasionally, when it pays more attention, it is angry and outraged. Indicative of such reaction, at once both thoughtful and polemical, is the book *Higher Superstition: The Academic Left and Its Quarrels with Science*, written by two scientists, Paul Gross and Norman Levitt, and published in 1994. Gross and Levitt identify a large and diverse body of writing, not internally consistent, but united by at best a scepticism towards science and its practices, and at worst by open hostility 'toward the *actual content* of scientific knowledge and toward the assumption, which one might have supposed universal among educated people, that scientific knowledge is reasonably reliable and rests on a sound methodology.'[58] The literature, that so troubles them shares 'a commitment to the idea that fundamental political change is urgently needed and can be achieved only through revolutionary processes rooted in a wholesale revision of cultural categories.'[59]

Gross and Levitt claim that most of this postmodern study of science is muddle-headed and that its writers are scandalously unfamiliar with actual science as practised. They see 'books that pontificate about the intellectual crisis of contemporary physics, whose authors have never troubled themselves with a simple problem in statics; [and] essays that make knowing reference to chaos theory, from writers who could not recognize, much less solve, a first-order difference equation.'[60] Nonetheless, they recognize that the postmodern critique is deep and its influence pervasive. They agree that scientists are not threatened: scientists are not about to change their view of themselves and how they do their work. Gross and Levitt do, however, believe that we must take the postmodern critique seriously. 'What *is* threatened is the capability of the larger culture, which embraces the mass media as well as the more serious processes of education, to interact fruitfully with the sciences, to draw insight from scientific advances, and, above all, to evaluate science intelligently.' This postmodern literature 'has to be read as the manifestation of a certain intellectual debility afflicting the contemporary university: one that will ultimately threaten it.'[61] These words are polemical, indeed, and indicative of the wide gulf now opened up between scientists and postmodernists.

A Postmodern Multiversity: A House Divided against Itself

In 1959, C.P. Snow delivered the Rede Lecture at Cambridge University entitled 'Two Cultures and the Scientific Revolution.' He argued that the university, indeed western intellectual life, was splitting into two cultures: the literary intellectuals and the scientists. The two cultures are separated by a 'gulf of mutual incomprehension – sometimes (particularly among the young) hostility and dislike, but most of all lack of understanding. They have a curious distorted image of each other. Their attitudes are so different that, even on the level of emotion, they cannot find much common ground.'[62] Snow argued that such a gulf was severely limiting to human development and he placed the greatest responsibility on the educational system to bridge the gulf between the cultures. His lecture resonated across the world and provoked enormous discussion.

In a later essay, Snow acknowledged that he was 'speaking as an Englishman, from experience drawn mainly from English society.'[63]

(Rereading the lecture, its Englishness is evident.) Snow saw that the gulf was not so wide or as unbridgeable in the United States. He also saw the emergence of a third culture in fields such as social history, economics, political science, psychology, medicine, and architecture, fields that are concerned with how human beings are living and have lived and that require a passing knowledge of both the literary and the scientific. This third culture might help to bridge the gulf.

The gulf between C.P. Snow's cultures has not proven to be as unbridgeable as he had worried. Certainly, the gulf did not become debilitating; the two cultures never went to war. However, the multiversity now has another two cultures: the modern and the postmodern. There is the same lack of understanding, but now there is hostility and often debilitating conflict.

Not surprisingly, many postmodernists have written and reflected upon whether 'the university' is possible after postmodern thought.[64] The university has always been closely connected to the project of modernity; the multiversity is deeply disrupted by the antifoundationalism and value relativism of postmodern thought. The most provocative analysis and image has come from Bill Readings in his book whose title reveals the conclusion: *The University in Ruins.* Slightly less apocalyptic analysis by other authors nonetheless concludes that there can no longer be an 'idea of the university,' all that remains is fragmentation and difference: 'the postmodern university is characterized above all by "contested knowledge" and the emergence of local knowledges.'[65] But the postmodernists overstate their case. The beliefs and practices of much of the multiversity, especially in the pure and applied sciences, have been unaffected by the postmodern challenge, and even where postmodern thought is powerful, in the humanities and social sciences, there are many who reject it outright. The multiversity is more a battleground than a ruin.

Such a keen observer of the multiversity as Clark Kerr identifies how we deal with postmodern ideas as a crucial issue for the future of the multiversity. In the final 2001 edition of his book *The Uses of the University*, Kerr, looking ahead, identifies 'the fractionalization of the academic guild' as a great danger. Of course, we know that fractions within the academic guild are already well established because the university is organized into faculties and departments, and because of the continuing specialization of knowledge into more and more arcane fractions within disciplines. Furthermore, the tensions between fractions will be exacerbated, as universities become more differentiated hierarchically among themselves, as the differences in faculty salaries widen according to their academic discipline. However, Kerr asserts: 'The ultimate conflict may occur over models of the university itself, whether to support the traditional or the "postmodern" model.' Kerr concludes his book with three wishes, one of which is 'that an open, in-depth debate would take place between proponents of the traditional and the postmodern university instead of the sniper shots of guerilla warfare.'[66]

Most professors are wary of postmodernism, but willing to focus upon the moderate strand, to see postmodernism as part of dynamic, restless, critical rationality. Some are optimistic and conclude that whatever the outcome, their discipline will emerge stronger as a result of the criticism and debate. Together, these professors are the majority, which suggests that the critique of postmodern thought will be accommodated within the university just as were the critiques of Romanticism, Marx, and Weber. However, the accommodation will be more difficult, and never really complete, because the postmodern sensibility so attacks the legitimacy of much of what the multiversity does.

Some professors will fiercely push the conclusions of extreme postmodernism, and still others will, with equal ferocity, condemn those conclusions. The wars will continue. Each multiversity will have to recognize that these wars are inevitably part of their future and manage as best they can. The postmodern sensibility and its conflict with modernism will be a flashpoint for years to come. It is vitally important that the leadership of the multiversity have a deep and nuanced understanding of postmodern thought. Beneath the surface of many academic controversies lies the difference between modernists and postmodernists in their epistemology and political stance and in their sense of the relation between language and power. Eruptions can occur in unexpected and debilitating ways. Recently, the president of Harvard University announced he was stepping down following continuing controversy about his remarks to a conference about women in science. This sad story can be read in many ways, but one reading is that, whatever the surface conflict, beneath is the incomprehension between good people on different sides, incomprehension between modernists and postmodernists.

Edward Said ends his essay in the volume *The Future of Academic Freedom* with quotations from Cardinal Newman, offering a remarkable glimpse of how the multiversity might proceed after postmodernism. Said writes that we need not deny 'what Newman said so beautifully and so memorably' – '[A university] has this object and this mission; it contemplates neither moral impression nor mechanical production; it professes to exercise the mind neither in art nor in duty; its function is intellectual culture; here it may leave its scholars, and it has done its work when it has done as much as this. It educates the intellect to reason well in all matters, to reach out towards truth, and to grasp it.' Said then goes on: 'Note the care with which Newman, perhaps with Swift the greatest of the English prose stylists, selects his words for what actions take place in the pursuit of knowledge: words like *exercise, educates, reach out,* and *grasp.* In none of these words is there anything to suggest coercion, or direct utility, or immediate advantage or dominance.'[67] Although Newman may have been arguing for English and Christian values in knowledge, he 'delivers a different and less assertive idea than on the surface [he] might have intended.' In Newman, Said the postmodernist points out, we can still read 'what education and freedom are all about.'[68]

9 Commercialization

We live in a commercial age. The ethos of the market economy creeps into more and more areas. Mass marketing and mass media drive out local craft and reflective thought. Everything is commercialized. Even areas always regarded as outside the market, such as education or museums, health care or symphony orchestras, are discussed as market phenomena. Each has products to be bought and sold; suppliers must be entrepreneurial to meet the demands of savvy consumers in an intensely competitive market. In the past, such language would never have been used to talk about universities. Where once universities talked about learning, professors and students, and the curriculum, today, multiversity officials talk about their market, their customers, their entrepreneurial initiatives, and even about their brand. The most widely heard lament about multiversities today is about creeping commercialization. How the multiversity will deal with this commercialization is one of its major challenges for the years ahead.

Much can be placed under the heading of the 'commercialization' of multiversities. Many writers use different terminology to describe the phenomenon. Some write of the privatization of universities; Derek Bok, former president of Harvard University, writes of *Universities in the Marketplace*; the starkest metaphor is 'academic capitalism,' used by Sheila Slaughter and Larry L. Leslie in their book, *Academic Capitalism: Politics, Policies, and the Entrepreneurial University.* Under such headings we can place many current trends at universities: the increasingly utilitarian, job-oriented attitudes of students, rising tuition fees, the pressures on professors to seek external grants and contracts, the use of business terminology and business methods in academic administration, the increasing emphasis on marketing as the university represents itself to society, the sale of on-campus advertising rights, and the ever more vigorous pursuit of external funds.

Each of these trends is powerful and contributes to the commercialization of multiversities, but there is not space to address all of them. In this chapter, I will focus upon two interrelated trends in connection with the research mission of the multiversity. The first is the shift in government policy towards treating support for multiversity research as part of economic policy. The second is the demand that the commercialization of research become an explicit responsibility of the multiversity. These trends indicate a fundamental change in the social contract between the multiversity and society.

The emerging social contract presumes that the transfer of ideas from the university to the economy can be facilitated and managed. Most fundamentally, the new social contract makes this transfer process part of the mission of the multiversity and one of the responsibilities of professors. This is a radical change. Henry Etzkowitz and Andrew Webster, in *Capitalizing Knowledge: New Intersections of Industry and Academia*, believe it is so radical as to constitute an academic revolution: 'The academic revolution of the late nineteenth and early twentieth centuries introduced the research mission into an institution hitherto devoted to the conservation and transmission of knowledge ... Building upon the first revolution, the second academic revolution is the translation of research findings into intellectual property, a marketable commodity, and economic development.'[1]

The responsibilities of the multiversity and its professors have always been summarized as teaching, research, and service. Service included service to one's own university, one's scholarly discipline, and the wider society. Now, this service responsibility to society is being explicitly specified to include the commercialization of research. However, this shift brings great dangers and it may compromise the integrity of both research and teaching. The close connection of research and the economy may distort the choice of research topics and move people away from basic research. Critical thought may be repressed. Commitments to private firms may curtail the open communication of research results upon which the scientific enterprise has always been based and may undermine the ideal of academic freedom.

As in previous chapters, I will approach commercialization – this characteristic of our age – as a bundle of ideas. This ferment of ideas helps define our age. In the first part of the chapter I explore the ideas, and in the second I explore their implications for multiversities. Once again, the analysis provides a case study of how ideas emanating from multiversity research are reshaping society.

Since the Second World War, as part of implementing the welfare state, national governments accepted the responsibility to pursue full employment and to encourage economic growth. Government policy recognized that universities are important for economic growth, particularly that mass university education and university research contribute to economic growth. This connection between the universities and economic growth was not subject to much scrutiny. Furthermore, scrutiny seemed unnecessary because unemployment was relatively low, and economic growth proceeded robustly through the 1950s and 1960s, and into the 1970s.

The high unemployment after the mid-1970s and the slowdown in productivity, however, rudely and painfully exposed this hubris. Long-term employment and robust economic growth were not assured. The troubles in the United Kingdom and Canada were especially severe, but the United States was not immune. The question of how governments could encourage economic growth and ensure employment for their citizens became urgent. The Keynesian remedies were not working. The deep recessions of the 1980s and early 1990s, and the wrenching economic restructuring of those decades, were a profound trauma, and the burst of productivity improvement of the late 1990s in the Anglo-American world has not removed the insecurity. The question remains: Is our future prosperity secure? Will there be jobs for us and our children?

Many analysts believe we have entered a 'new economy' and assert that future economic growth in the postindustrial economies will be overwhelmingly determined by technological innovation. The most evident and dynamic technological change is in communications and information technology (IT). But other new, and perhaps equally transforming, technologies are on the horizon, most especially biotechnology and nanotechnology. The economic prosperity of a nation in this new economy will depend upon how it generates and adopts new technologies – ideas will explain the wealth of nations. John Evans, former president of the University of Toronto, declared: 'We now live in a world in which the organized ability to create and commercialize new ideas is the critical determinant of economic success.'[2] It is little wonder that democratic governments now ask multiversities to take on this task.

We have returned to Adam Smith's theme, *An Inquiry into the Nature and Causes of the Wealth of Nations*. We ask: What determines economic growth and the wealth of a nation? More and more, the answer is – ideas. Then we ask, what should be the role of government in encouraging economic growth, in encouraging new ideas? And finally we ask what Adam Smith did not ask: What should be the role of multiversities in creating and commercializing ideas?

These questions about the role of government and the role of multiversities are asked now in a new context – the constrained welfare state. The growth of government spending has been reduced; there is intense competition for public funds and new demands for accountability upon those who receive them. Multiversities receive substantial public funds, both for operating costs and to support research. The governments that provide funds to universities are asking whether this money is used in the most effective way to encourage economic growth. The contribution of the university to the economy must be examined and justified, particularly the contribution of multiversity research. Finally, and perhaps most telling, the multiversity is squeezed for funds and hopes desperately that the commercialization of research will bring it new money by sharing in the patent revenues from new discoveries.

The intellectual rationale for government support for university research comes from the field of economics. Recent developments in economics, sometimes labelled 'the new growth theory,' provide the intellectual rationale for recent changes in government research policy and the demand to commercialize university research. Before looking at the new growth theory, however, it is important first to examine the economic ideas that it builds upon and incorporates.

Human Capital Theory

In the late nineteenth century and throughout the twentieth, economics developed formal mathematical models of the behaviour of households, of firms, and of the entire economy, and these have now become the standard methodology. In the standard economic model, the output of a nation's economy depends upon the inputs used and the available technology. The standard model assumes there is an unchanging available technology. The inputs are natural resources, labour, and physical capital (buildings and machines). Most economists believed that the increase in national output per worker was mainly the result of increases in the amount of physical capital per worker. This was confirmed by casual empirical observation: poor countries had low capital-to-labour ratios, and wealthy ones had high capital-to-labour ratios. This analysis suggested that the key to national economic growth was investment in physical capital, and for much of the twentieth century government policies to encourage growth focused upon encouraging physical investment.

During the 1950s, the economist Robert Solow of MIT, who would later be awarded the Nobel Prize in Economics for his contributions to the theory of economic growth, statistically tested the proposition that increases in capital per worker explained increases in output per worker and found that only 19 per cent of long-run change could be attributed to increased capital intensity.[3] The remaining productivity growth, the residual after improvements to the capital-to-labour ratio, Solow said, must be attributable to improvements in the 'quality' of labour and to technological progress. The analysis of national economic growth, thus, had to be expanded to analyse the quality of labour and to analyse how new technologies are discovered in an economy.

Economic analysis proceeded in two directions: it developed human capital theory, and it began to analyse ideas as an economic commodity. Both have had enormous implications for thinking about multiversities in society.

Human capital theory is an approach to understanding labour markets and education. Labour can be analysed as human capital. Workers of different quality possess different amounts of human capital; investments can be made to increase an individual's human capital. The most important way to invest in human capital is through education (on-the-job experience also is a means to acquire additional human capital). Human capital theory provides the framework for the economic analysis of the decisions that people make about how much education to acquire. People acquire an education – invest in human capital – if the rate of return is sufficiently high. The cost of the investment is tuition, books, and the income foregone by going to school rather than joining the workforce. The return on the investment is the increase in income over a lifetime of the educated person relative to a similar person who did not obtain the education. The rate of return to a university education is high and has been rising.[4]

This framework helps to explain a puzzle: tuition fees have risen sharply in recent years, yet the demand for university education continues to grow, and participation rates from all income groups continue to increase. Normally in economic analysis if the price goes up, the quantity demanded falls – but this has not happened in the case of university education. The explanation lies partly in that the price of a university education is not just tuition but also the foregone income, and so the true price of a university education has not gone up nearly as rapidly as tuition alone – the price has not gone up as much as we think. But the key to the explanation is that the incomes of university graduates have been rising relative to non-graduates, so that although tuition has risen, the rate of return on an investment in human capital is still high. Human capital theory has been used in designing student assistance programs, most obviously the widely recommended income-contingent repayment programs (discussed in chapter 6). But, more significantly, human capital theory has become the dominant methodology for understanding and explaining the demand for university education. The model structures our thoughts and the thoughts of government policymakers, and in such a model the benefit of a university education to an individual is measured solely as the increase in the resulting income. There is no place for curiosity, social idealism, or the satisfaction of intellectual accomplishment. Also, in this model, our language has changed: the relationship in the classroom is no longer between professor and student, engaged in teaching and learning; rather, it is an economic exchange between a provider of education and a customer who wants to invest in human capital.

The increase in human capital through education is important in explaining national economic growth. Economies grow, not just by investing in physical capital, but also by investing in human capital. Economists augmented Solow's analysis to include improvements in the quality of labour – increases in human capital – as part of the explanation of economic growth. But even after human capital was factored in, the increase in physical capital and the increase in human capital could not fully explain economic growth; there still remained a large residual that had to be attributed to technological change.

The Economics of Ideas

The second body of analysis incorporated into new growth theory is that ideas can be analysed as an economic phenomenon. Research generates ideas; ideas are a new way of doing things, a new technology, a new way of combining the inputs of capital and labour to produce output. In the standard theory of the firm, firms are profit maximizers, making decisions about how much physical capital and how much labour to employ given the available production technology. To analyse ideas, this theory is widened to recognize that firms can allocate their resources to try to find a new production technology. Firms make decisions about how much to invest in research and, therefore, in how many new ideas to produce. Firms consider several things – the costs of research, the likelihood of finding a new way of doing things (a new technology), and the increased profits they will receive from their ideas – and then they make the decision about investing in research as part of their overall plan to maximize profits. Firms make all their decisions in the same way, whether deciding about how much labour to hire, how much physical capital to acquire, or how much to invest in research: all are determined by profit maximization. Firms will invest in research if the expected future revenues exceed their costs. Thus, ideas can be analysed as an economic commodity and fitted into the models of firms and markets. The theory can provide an explanation of why firms invest in research and an explanation of how much research will be undertaken by the private market economy.

Significantly, however, an idea is a specific type of commodity. In economic analysis, commodities are divided into two types: public goods and private goods. A public good is a commodity whose use by one person does not preclude its use by another person, even at the same time. A classic example is a lighthouse: if I use the lighthouse to guide my boat, it does not diminish your use of the lighthouse to guide your boat. Consumption of such commodities is said to be non-rivalrous. In contrast, most commodities are private goods: my consumption means the good is not available for anyone else to consume. Consumption is rivalrous. Apples, machines, and clothes are examples of private goods. If I eat the apple, you cannot; if one firm uses a machine, another firm cannot; if I wear these clothes, you cannot. An idea is a public good, not a private good. This was elegantly articulated by the United States' first patent examiner, Thomas Jefferson, who wrote: 'He who receives an idea from me, receives instruction himself without lessening mine; as he who lights his taper at mine, receives light without darkening mine.'[5]

Economics has recognized since Adam Smith that the capitalist economy does very well at producing private goods without any guidance from government. The market economy will allocate resources efficiently to produce apples, machines, or clothing – to produce goods that are rivalrous in use. The market works well because a price can be charged for a rivalrous commodity. If there are only private goods in the economy, a competitive private market allocates resources efficiently – this result is a benchmark in economics. Then, the question is posed: In what situations will the private market fail to ensure an efficient allocation of resources? If the private market fails, there is a possible role for government to improve things. For example, economic analysis demonstrates that a non-competitive private market, a monopoly, does not allocate resources efficiently, and thus, there may be a role for government to regulate monopolies to ensure an efficient resource allocation. Several economists, notably, Sir John Hicks at Oxford, Kenneth Arrow at Harvard, and Gerard Debreu at Berkeley, were awarded Nobel Prizes in Economics for the rigorous mathematical proof of these theorems about the efficiency of private markets and the possible sources of the market's failure to achieve an efficient allocation of resources. Economics also recognizes that the market economy is very poor at producing an efficient amount of public goods. Private firms will not produce enough public goods because the public goods cannot be sold to one buyer as the consumption is non-rivalrous. They may not even produce public goods at all. We do not rely on the private market to build a lighthouse but rely on government to do so. Following this same logic, there is a strong presumption that private firms will underinvest in research because the ideas that come from the research are a public good. The firm cannot reap all the benefits from the research, and so it will not invest enough in it.

When an idea is analysed as an economic commodity, it is referred to as 'intellectual property.' The creator of the idea wants to retain the 'intellectual property rights,' that is, the right to determine the idea's use and realize the economic gains from its use, just as the owner of a piece of physical property wants to determine its use and realize the gains from its use. A functioning market economy requires clear and enforceable property rights. But physical and intellectual property differ fundamentally: physical property is a private good, whereas intellectual property is a public good.

This analysis of ideas as an economic commodity provides a reason for governments to subsidize research. Private markets fail to provide the efficient level of research, and therefore, public subsidy is needed for the optimal allocation of resources. This argument is most compelling for basic research. Private firms will not undertake basic research because they cannot capture the benefits of that research. Therefore, governments should support basic research. This logic provides a rationale for government support to basic research in multiversities.

The New Growth Theory

Solow had found that technological progress explains much of economic growth. Therefore the task for economics was to develop a rigorous analysis of technological change, to incorporate it into the model, that is, to include technological change as part of the decision-making of economic agents within the operation of markets and, thus, make technological change endogenous to the analysis. The task was to develop a new theory, of endogenous growth. This has been done and now is the framework used by economists to analyse economic growth. Although very sophisticated mathematics was necessary to develop the theory, there is not so much that is new – the key concepts are human capital theory and the economics of ideas – as there is a fundamental shift in emphasis. The emphasis is shifted from physical capital to human capital, research, and technological innovation.

This sparked a renaissance of interest in the work of Joseph Schumpeter, an Austrian economist of the first half of the twentieth century. Schumpeter's seminal book, *The Theory of Economic Development*, was published in German in 1911, although not in English until 1934. Schumpeter offered a radically different conceptualization of a capitalist economy. For him, the central dynamic of capitalism was not in decisions about how much labour and capital to utilize, as in the standard economic model, rather Schumpeter emphasized that 'innovation – including the introduction of new products and production methods, the opening of new markets, the development of new supply sources, and the creation of new industrial organization forms – lay at the heart of economic development, facilitating the growth of material prosperity.'[6] The dynamic of the capitalist economy in Schumpeter's analysis arises because successful innovations displace old ways of doing things, what he later called 'the process of creative destruction.'

In the new growth theory, new knowledge is important. Ideas about how to do things are crucial. A leading theorist, Paul Romer of Stanford University, asserts: 'The key step in understanding economic growth is to think carefully about ideas,'[7] about how ideas are generated and how they are applied. The great contribution of endogenous growth theory has been to demand that economic analysis recognizes ideas as a fundamental input into production. In the traditional model, a nation's output depends upon the inputs of natural resources, labour, and capital. In the new growth theory, a nation's output depends upon the inputs of natural resources, labour, capital, and *ideas*. Ideas are not exogenous, an afterthought, but a focal point. Economic analysis is deployed to understand how economies produce new ideas and how these ideas are used in production.

In thinking about the role of ideas in an economy, the concept of a public good needs to be further refined. A *pure* public good is not only non-rivalrous in consumption, but it also non-excludable; that is, it is very, very difficult to prevent others from consuming the commodity. However, exclusion may be possible, even though consumption is non-rivalrous. If exclusion can be achieved, then the public good becomes more like a private good, and private markets can function better.

New ideas from research are non-rivalrous, but there are means to enforce exclusion. For example, the use of the new idea can be restricted through patent or copyright protection. The creator of the idea can secure the intellectual property rights to it. A new idea protected by patent or copyright becomes more like a private good. These protections increase the ex ante incentive for private firms to invest in research. Perhaps the market economy would invest the proper amount in research. However, ex post, patent protection restricts the benefits to society of a new discovery. The new discovery is a public good, and another person's use of it does not diminish the original usage. It would always be to society's benefit to extend the use of this public good. Finding the correct balance between giving firms an incentive to invest in research via patent law and allowing the new discoveries to be freely used by all is a critical part of a nation's innovation policy. There is always a tension between private knowledge (which gives people incentives to do research) and public knowledge (which maximizes the societal benefits of each new discovery).

A prominent version of the new growth theory has been developed by Paul Romer. He begins by recognizing that technological progress in industry requires concerted, profit-oriented activity. His analysis then posits that research 'yields two distinct components: specific designs embodied in products that can be patented and produced, excluding rival firms from the same activity; and knowledge of those designs that is essentially a public good.'[8] The public-good portion of the research in a private firm 'spills over' into the general pool of knowledge. Romer then posits that to create still further new designs, specialized human capital must be devoted to the task. 'The human capital is made more productive by interacting with the stock of knowledge, which includes knowledge of all designs previously achieved along with the scientific knowledge published by academic researchers.' As the pool of public knowledge grows, further research is more productive and this facilitates the creation of more new designs. 'The more human capital an economy possesses, the more productivity-enhancing new products it can develop and the more the design knowledge stock is enhanced, permitting sustained economic growth in a virtuous spiral.'[9] In this way of thinking, ideas are a factor of production, but of a very special sort: ideas exhibit increasing returns to scale. The more ideas we have, the more new ideas we can discover, which helps to explain why the developed world can enjoy sustained high rates of economic growth.

The implications of endogenous growth theory for multiversities are reinforced by another development in economics: new economic geography. The new economic geography analyses why certain industries tend to cluster in one region of a country or to be primarily in one country rather than another (although the countries are similarly advanced economically and technically). Standard economic analysis would predict that industries should be spread across a country, rather than clustered, and that similar countries should tend to have similar industries. Part of the answer is that new ideas spill over between firms faster in geographical concentrations. If you have an initial cluster and another location does not, the original cluster will tend to have an advantage and perpetuate itself. The quirks of history matter, and we get what economists call 'path dependence': where you start is important to your future trajectory. This raises the possibility that governments might intervene, strategically, to help a cluster get established, capturing the initial advantage, and setting the region off on an improved trajectory.[10]

Multiversities can be assets in regional economic development. The old conflict between town and gown is gone, replaced by cooperation or at least synergy. This also implies that targeted research, focused on a specific industry, might be part of a strategy to set off a new trajectory of economic growth in a region. Rather than curiosity driving research, economic strategy drives research.

University research has always been linked to the national government, but new growth theory and the idea of path dependence identify linkages that are important to city governments. The new growth theory emphasizes how ideas spill over from one firm to another, from one activity to another, in the dynamic of economic growth. Spatial proximity and a well-functioning city enhance this process of cross-fertilization. City-based multiversities are crucial parts of this process. Here the new growth theory is catching up with the insights developed by Jane Jacobs in her book *The Economy of Cities*, published in 1969. She argues that cities were the crucial locus of innovation and that ideas spill over easily from one activity to another in a city. Today, multiversity presidents and local business and political leaders meet regularly to coordinate a regional economic strategy, and national governments realize that cities and their multiversities are a vital part of national economic policy.

Stanford University and Silicon Valley

There are many examples of the close connection between multiversity research and the economy, but the iconic model emerged around the Stanford Industrial Park, in the town of Palo Alto, California, after the Second World War. Today around the world, this model is called Silicon Valley. Its story provided much stimulus to the new growth theory and new economic geography. Silicon Valley is the great case study on the interaction of human capital, location, the commercialization of ideas, and the multiversity. This experience has inspired much of the change in government thinking about support for university research. All governments and all multiversities dream of creating their own Silicon Valley.

A Stanford historian writes: 'Silicon Valley, located on the San Francisco, California, peninsula, radiates outward from Stanford University ... At the turn of the century, when fruit orchards predominated, the area was known as the Valley of Heart's Delight. Today, semi-conductor chips made of silicon are the principal product of the local high-tech industries. It has been said that an institution is but the lengthened shadow of one great man. Inasmuch as Silicon Valley is an institution, Fred Terman was such a man.'[11]

Terman was a professor of electrical engineering at Stanford and had studied under Vannevar Bush at MIT. During the 1930s, Terman was concerned with the lack of employment opportunities for Stanford graduates and that the best students had to go east for the truly challenging jobs. His response was twofold. He encouraged high-tech industry to locate in what became Silicon Valley, and he encouraged his students to become involved with local industries, to visit industrial labs, to offer consulting services, to invest in companies, and even to start their own companies. In the late 1930s, Terman suggested to two of his graduate students, William Hewlett and David Packard, that they start a company to produce their new electrical components. The Hewlett-Packard Company became one of the earliest occupants of the Stanford Industrial Park.

After the war, Professor Terman became dean of engineering at Stanford, and later provost and vice-president. Stanford had enormous lands given by Leland Stanford, but under the terms of the bequest, these could not be sold. The university needed money. Long-term leases to companies locating in the research park offered a major new source of income. The Stanford Industrial Park was created – bringing an elite research multiversity and high-tech companies into close proximity. Terman called the park Stanford's secret weapon and arranged that leases be limited to high technology companies that were complementary to the research done by Stanford faculty members. After Hewlett-Packard, Eastman Kodak opened a research centre in the park, as did General Electric. William Shockley, co-inventor of the transistor, moved there from Bell Labs in the east to set up his new firm to produce transistors. Eight young scientists, including Robert Noyce and Gordon Moore, left Shockley's company to found Fairchild Semiconductor, and later they started Intel Corporation. The pace of change was phenomenal, captured famously in Moore's Law. The breakthroughs were in both basic and applied science. New ways of doing drove out the old: here were the dynamics of Schumpeterian capitalism.

Silicon Valley 'radiates outward from Stanford University.' This description is both geographical and conceptual. Stanford Industrial Park is the physical location, and the interaction of Stanford scientists and local industries is the conceptual framework. In the 1950s, Fred Terman established the Honors Cooperative Program, under which local industries sent a select group of employees for part-time graduate work, and the industries paid fees, in addition to tuition, to cover the full cost of the program. He also established the Industrial Affiliates Program, whereby affiliates pay membership fees to enjoy a special relationship with the university's scientists. The program facilitates professor-industry liaison, provides special research reports to the affiliate, provides it with special assistance with regard to recruiting students, and provides for Industrial Visiting Scholars at the university. All of these are part of the Silicon Valley model.[12]

Many new firms were spun off from the research by Stanford students and professors. In 2001, a survey identified the 150 largest Silicon Valley firms. Stanford proudly reports that thirty-seven of these 150 companies, representing 42 per cent of total revenue, were founded or co-founded by people with a current or former affiliation with Stanford University.[13]

In return, Stanford gained new resources to support all of its activities, including, it must be acknowledged, new resources for curiosity-driven basic research. It would be hard to argue that the arrangements have diverted Stanford from the pursuit of basic knowledge – Stanford remains a place where the most fundamental laws of nature are sought. Its students found better jobs. New money came from extra tuition, industrial affiliate fees, and also from patent revenues. In 1998, Stanford realized almost U.S. $47 million from licensing income. Other income gains were indirect, but even more substantial. Successful industrialists became strong financial supporters – William Hewlett and David Packard together contributed more than U.S. $300 million to Stanford University.

The power of the Silicon Valley story is overwhelming. Its success is obvious to the world. Sometimes other initiatives have had similar results, the most famous being Route 128, outside Boston. This model of government-multiversity-industry relations now defines the way people think about research, about productivity increase, and about the economy, almost to the exclusion of other ways of thinking.

There have been many attempts to understand what makes Silicon Valley so successful. One of the most analytical is a collection of essays edited by Martin Kenney, entitled *Understanding Silicon Valley: The Anatomy of an Entrepreneurial Region*. Identification of 'the crucial ingredients of Silicon Valley – a strong research university with close links to industry, entrepreneurial corporate and academic cultures, aggressive venture capital markets, supportive government institutions, a pleasant climate, a technology park' – is relatively easy, although using the recipe elsewhere is rather more difficult.[14] Other crucial ingredients are identified. Labour flexibility – moving from job to job, moving around among university, government, and the private sector – is a means for ideas to circulate in an ecology of innovation. Venture capitalists and lawyers are key actors and also act to speed the spread of new ideas. It is a very different picture of a university from what is usually seen: 'They do more than teach students. They actively encourage their faculty to take what they know and start companies. They also encourage faculty to contribute their talents to established companies in the area as consultants ... [But], the flow of knowledge doesn't just go from inside to out. Knowledge also moves in from the rest of the region. Indeed, some of the most highly attended classes at Stanford are those taught by, or include lectures by, key figures in the Valley, carrying what they know back to the school.'[15] This is an entrepreneurial university; this is academic capitalism.

The IT story has been repeated in the life sciences and biotechnology. The same dynamic of basic science and applied science is at play, just as the same dynamic of university-industry-venture capital-government relations is at work. A survey of research in the life sciences, by Walter Powell and Jason Owen-Smith, concludes: 'the traditional view of the university researcher as a dedicated and disinterested, though passionate, searcher for truth is being replaced in the life sciences by a new model of scientist-entrepreneur who balances university responsibilities and corporate activities in the development of new compounds and devices to both improve human health and generate revenues for the investigator, the university, and the investor.'[16] Intriguingly, Silicon Valley is also a major centre for biotechnology.

It is not surprising – given the similar experience in information technology and biotechnology – that governments across the Anglo-American world are changing the social contract for university research in the same way and that multiversities are undertaking the commercialization of research in the same way.[17] This evolution provokes enormous controversy. Clearly something quite fundamental is changing. But we should not overstate the change and should remember that universities have been closely connected to industry since the industrial revolution.

The University and Industry

In the early nineteenth century, Oxford and Cambridge stood gloriously apart from commerce and industry, and many cite this as the golden age of knowledge for its own sake. (In reality, things were not so pristine because the Oxbridge curriculum was the gateway for careers in the civil service and clergy.) Unfortunately, Oxford and Cambridge also stood gloriously apart from scientific thought and from all but the children of privilege and wealth. The Scottish universities, in contrast, were connected to commerce and industry, and they were accessible to far more people. This is a lesson we must not ignore today: the applied orientation of multiversities is inseparably connected to accessibility. Therefore, the democratic role of the multiversity is inseparably connected to applied research.

Michael Sanderson analyses English universities in his book, *The Universities in the Nineteenth Century*. He notes that the English universities founded in the nineteenth century were, from the outset, closely involved in secular areas of national life: 'One of the most important of these areas was industry and commerce.'[18] Many of the universities were created and supported by the philanthropy of industrialists, sometimes out of pride in family or city, but more often to promote and complement local industry.

This same transformation occurred in nineteenth-century American universities. Nathan Rosenberg and Richard Nelson, two of the most perceptive American scholars on economic growth, make this point clearly. American scientific research in the nineteenth century was very practical and problem-oriented. American universities were especially responsive to local needs and aspirations. Rosenberg and Nelson assert that 'the passage of the Morrill Act in 1862 reflected and supported American views about the appropriate roles of university research and teaching. The purpose of the act was eminently practical; it was dedicated to the support of agriculture and the mechanical arts. Moreover, control of universities was left to the states ... Thus the leadership of state universities was heavily beholden to the needs of local industries and to the priorities established by state legislators.'[19] The new industries needed trained manpower and research on their particular problems. The state universities were quick to introduce new fields as their practical value became clear. Rosenberg and Nelson conclude that 'one of the major accomplishments of the American universities during the first half of the twentieth century was to effect the institutionalization of the new engineering and applied science disciplines.'[20]

After the Second World War, when the multiversity emerged and the U.S. government provided substantial support for its research, the connection of university research to the economy became more explicit, but it took a new form. The nature of the connection was similar across the Anglo-American world, following the paradigm of Vannevar Bush in *Science – The Endless Frontier*. Perhaps the greatest influence of Bush's paper was to institutionalize one particular paradigm for thinking about the university-economy connection, incorporating what has come to be called the linear model.

The linear model makes a sharp distinction between basic (or pure) research and applied research. For Bush, 'basic research is performed without thought of practical ends.' Its defining characteristic is its contribution to 'general knowledge and an understanding of nature and its laws.' Furthermore, Bush sees an inescapable tension between basic and applied research: 'Applied research invariably drives out pure.' Bush also maintains that the dynamism of technological change comes from basic research: 'Basic research is the pacemaker of technological progress.'[21] There is a linear sequence originating from basic research, which then stimulates applied research, which leads to development research, and finally, to new products or processes. The paradigm is completed by a second proposition. Bush believes the university is the place for basic research, while the industrial lab is the place for applied research – and the two must not be confused.

The linear model, with its sharp distinction between basic and applied research, with its belief that basic research is the engine of technical progress, together with the presumption that universities should engage in basic research, helped to define the American research multiversity, especially during its golden age to the mid-1970s. This paradigm meant that the university-industry connection did not require much scrutiny or management. This paradigm shaped government policies in Canada and the United Kingdom, just as it did in the United States. Most academics both accept this paradigm as an accurate description of scientific and technological progress and believe the paradigm should govern all scientific research, and indeed, all university research – the multiversity should focus upon basic research, not applied research: it should steer well clear of commercial interests.

Such acceptance by academics is understandable. This paradigm is consistent with core ideals of the university. This paradigm resonates with the ancient ideals of critical, independent thought. The university is a place of liberal learning, without regard for application. The ideals of liberal learning and of basic research are one and the same: human beings are innately curious, and knowledge is valued for its own sake. The university is an autonomous institution, and therefore maintaining distance from business is appropriate. Academic freedom is justified by a theory that knowledge is best advanced when disinterested researchers are free to follow where their curiosity might lead. Again, the maintenance of distance from the economy is vital. Thus, critical thinking, liberal learning, institutional autonomy, and academic freedom are all consistent with and complemented by this paradigm.

No matter how strongly espoused and how consonant with multiversity ideals, however, this paradigm was not the complete picture. Such is the nature of the conglomerate of ideas which is the multiversity. The traditions of the Scottish universities, the English universities of the later nineteenth and twentieth centuries, and of the land grant universities continue through the postwar period, even to today. A great deal of multiversity research is, and has always been, very much applied and responsive to the needs of industry and this mission has coexisted with the multiversity's commitment to the search for knowledge for its own sake. Professors act as consultants to companies, just as they do to governments and civil society organizations. Professors have usually owned the intellectual property rights to their written work, for example, when they write textbooks. Students are trained in applied professional programs both because they seek an education that will prepare them for a career and because the economy needs skilled professionals. These close connections between industry and the multiversity have not threatened the latter's core ideals; indeed, they are a necessary part of the multiversity's service to society. But, even with greater historical awareness of university-industry connections, it is clear that the postwar paradigm is being changed. The multiversity and industry are in much closer partnership and in a new form.

Commercialization of Multiversity Research

A survey of government policies towards higher education across the Anglo-American world highlights the profound change in paradigm and that this change is remarkably similar across all countries. The support for research and development (R&D) 'was probably the area in which the most dramatic policy changes occurred ... National policy shifted from promoting basic or fundamental research to privileging science and technology policy aimed at national wealth creation ... The very words used to describe R&D changed. R&D was no longer focused on basic or fundamental research, which came to be referred to rather derisively as "professors' curiosity-driven research," but on pre-competitive, strategic, or targeted research.'[22]

The U.K. patterns of government-university-industry relationships are typical in the Anglo-American world and can be used to illustrate the new framework. The key components of the new framework are: a new government policy, new non-government organizations, and a new mission for the multiversity. First, the U.K. government circulated a White Paper in 1987, whose ideas were incorporated into the Education Act of 1988. The White Paper argued that universities 'should serve the economy more effectively' and 'have closer links with industry and commerce, and promote enterprise.' Research should be targeted 'to prospects for commercial exploitation.' Second, business supported this policy shift and new non-government organizations were created to promote the change. In the United Kingdom, corporate leaders formed the Council for Industry and Higher Education. Finally, and most crucial and controversial: another White Paper was published in 1993, entitled 'Realizing our Potential: Strategy for Science, Engineering, and Technology,' which explicitly called for universities as institutions, most particularly their research, to become institutions of an economic strategy for national competitiveness in the global economy.[23]

The same shifts occurred in the United States: new government policies, new non-government organizations, and an additional mission for the multiversity. Two key initiatives shaped U.S. developments. The Bayh-Dole Act of 1980 allowed universities (and other non-profit institutions, such as hospitals) to claim the intellectual property rights for inventions supported by federal research dollars, and follow-up legislation allowed universities to assign or sell their property rights to other parties. Previously, the government had retained the intellectual property rights to discoveries supported by federal research grants; the universities could obtain the ownership rights, but only through a complex and cumbersome bureaucratic process. These acts gave American universities a tremendous incentive, especially during a time of financial stringency, to commercialize their research. It also gave professors an incentive to participate in the commercialization of their ideas. Multiversities established offices for technology transfer and worked to facilitate collaborations with industry. These trends were reinforced by the second crucial initiative. The National Science Foundation (NSF), the national granting agency most supportive of basic research, established programs to facilitate industry-university collaboration, specifically programs to support engineering research centres, industry-university cooperative research centres, and science and technology centres. Most state governments developed similar programs.[24]

Research policy in Canada has been evolving in the same way. Canada's national economic strategy has sought to increase domestic research and development and to make university research more responsive to the demands of the economy. In the 1980s, the Corporate-Higher Education Forum was established by university presidents and industry leaders. Research parks were created on university campuses to facilitate technology transfer. Networks of researchers and industries across the country were created, similar in structure and intent to the collaborations being developed by the NSF in the United States. The Canadian federal government made major new financial commitments to university research. This new support for university research was welcome on the campuses, but there were strings attached: the support was targeted and contingent. For example, the Canada Foundation for Innovation provides major capital grants to universities for research infrastructure; however, the infrastructure mainly supports research in science, health, and engineering, and the federal capital grants cover only one-third of the cost, requiring institutional and private sector matching funds. The federal Ministry of Industry, Science and Technology in 1999 convened an Expert Panel on the Commercialization of University Research, which inter alia recommended that 'commercialization' become the fourth fundamental responsibility of universities, joining teaching, research, and service.[25]

The changes in the paradigm for thinking about research are evident, but we must be measured in our characterization. Governments through the national granting councils still support much basic research; applied research motivated by the needs of the economy has by no means driven out curiosity-driven research. The change is not uniform. It has been especially great in some areas like information technology and biotechnology, but very small in many other areas. For example, in many departments of political science or sociology, one would be hard-pressed to find any change at all. Nonetheless, the changes are inescapable and fundamental.

There are many dimensions and forms, within the multiversity, of the transfer of research into industrial practice. Martin Kenney, in *Biotechnology: The University-Industrial Complex*, provides a comprehensive overview of university-industry relationships, devoting particular attention to the biotechnology industry. Nevertheless, his overview has general application. He identifies two major categories of relationship: those between individual professors and companies and those between the multiversity as an institution and companies. Both deserve our scrutiny.

Consider, first, the many forms of relationship between individual professors and companies. Professors can act as consultants under contract to companies. The work to be done is specified in the contract and not driven by the curiosity of the researcher. Nonetheless, there is considerable room for, even expectation of, original research under many contracts – the professor is given a problem for which there is no easy solution and asked to apply her or his professional expertise in search of an answer. Such work can lead to new knowledge and publication in scholarly journals. Also, there can exist a symbiotic relationship between company and professor: the company 'leaves room' in the contract for additional original basic research in order to attract the best professors to work on the company's particular problem. Often, the professor's relationships with outside companies become more frequent and extensive and the professor sets up a consulting firm to manage external arrangements, a practice common in the professions and social sciences. Scientists sometimes patent their results and license the patent to companies. More recently, particularly in IT and biotechnology, the professor 'spins off' a start-up firm to commercialize the results of his or her research – the professor becomes part-owner of the new company.

The forms of multiversity-industry relationship are many. Companies can make unrestricted or restricted donations; they can contract for research work or buy patent rights from the university. The multiversity and corporations can operate joint labs, and companies can fund laboratories to conduct research in certain areas. Multiversities often share ownership of the patents on a professor's discovery or share ownership of the spin-off company – and hope to make money from their ownership. Virtually every multiversity has established an office of technology transfer to facilitate these relationships.

Prompted by the new government policy, multiversities have made a strategic commitment to commercialization. Many multiversities have signalled this new priority by creating a new vice-president, responsible for technology transfer. In the United States in the 1980s, only a few multiversities had technology transfer offices. By 1998, all but two had organizational units for managing intellectual property, securing patents, selling licences, and facilitating faculty spin-off companies. A professional association, the Association of University Technology Managers, has been formed in the United States; among other things it reports on technology transfer activities at universities. Its report for 1998 documented the top twenty universities in terms of gross licensing income. Columbia led with U.S. $61.6 million in gross licensing income, and the twentieth university had a reported U.S. $5.4

million.[26] The measures of the multiversity's research successes are now not just the numbers of articles published in international scholarly journals, but also the numbers of patents and spin-off companies that result from the research.

There seem to be advantages to all parties in technology transfer and in the commercialization of research. The government encourages economic growth. Industry improves its products and processes, and recruits good students, already familiar with the firm's technological problems. Students get good jobs, moving easily from classroom to employment. The multiversity receives more financial support from society, in return for taking on the new tasks. Extra money is available to support all the multiversity's other tasks. Yet, there are many risks and dangers. Moreover, some of the advantages are more hope than reality.

Risks and Dangers

There are financial risks. Realizing a return from commercializing a new invention is a very uncertain undertaking. The history of research and patenting shows that much research has no pay-off, and most patents do not generate much revenue. To demonstrate the point, in the market economy, banks will not lend money to finance the commercialization of basic research – the outcome is too uncertain. Instead, financing comes from venture capital firms, which are specialized institutions willing to take the underlying risk. The technology transfer offices of multiversities have entered the world of venture capital; however, universities and university people are not by nature or experience venture capitalists. We have taken some the insights of Joseph Schumpeter, but neglected others. Schumpeter believed that research and its application in the economy are separate tasks, requiring different people, and different institutions. Multiversities now are drifting far away from where they have any expertise – some have drifted so far that they are putting up their own funds into venture capital investments. Few at the university appreciate how uncertain are the returns from these activities and how highly skewed the distribution of returns. The returns to all university-held patents are heavily concentrated on a few patents, and these are mainly in biotechnology. Many university technology transfer offices cannot cover their costs; the technology transfer initiative will drain money away from other tasks, not contribute. Even in the most successful offices, the contribution to general operating revenue will be minor. Commercialized research will not be a significant source of revenue for most multiversities.

Although the new model works well for information technology and biotechnology and, therefore, close proximity of multiversities and these industries is appropriate, the new model does not work particularly well for many other fields of science and engineering. In most industries in our economy, the connection between breakthroughs in basic science and new products is tenuous. In these industries, technological change of immediate commercial benefit is driven by industrial research, at the engineer's bench in the company lab. Close proximity will not be very helpful. Richard Nelson, in *The Sources of Economic Growth*, reports the outcome of a broad survey of industry. There is 'considerable industry scepticism over the ability of academics to contribute directly to industry innovation ... the industry views expressed at the Roundtable were that the academics should stick with the basic research they are doing and heed their training functions, and stop thinking of themselves as the source of the technology.'[27] Technology transfer is not needed and will not work for many industries. We are too enamored of the Silicon Valley story: it cannot be the basis for thinking about all multiversity-industry connections and economic growth across the entire economy.

The contractual relations between industry and the multiversity carry huge dangers that the directions of research will be dictated solely by economic concerns and the dissemination of the results will be severely limited. Examples of these new contractual relations are everywhere, but one will suffice here; one that has been particularly controversial: the Novartis contract with the University of California, Berkeley. 'The $25 million project is under the guidance of an "oversight" committee composed of two members from the Novartis company, a biotechnology firm, and three from UC Berkeley. The committee in charge of distribution of research funds has two of its five members from Novartis. Novartis has "first rights" to license new discoveries made in the university's Department of Plant and Microbial Biology, which its funds help to support. These "first rights" apply to discoveries based on funding by state and federal agencies as well as by Novartis. Novartis can "delay" publication of research findings, and Novartis staff can work in university laboratories.'[28] The dangers are real and the controversy understandable.

The new entrepreneurial tasks for professors bring new dangers for conflict of interest and conflict of commitment. The possibilities of conflict of interest are obvious and have troubled observers for many years. Multiversities have worked strenuously to develop and enforce new policies and procedures for their faculty. Powell and Owen-Smith report: 'The faculty with whom we spoke downplayed the salience of these ethical issues, noting that a variety of procedures are now in place to mitigate these conflicts, and stressing that more than a decade of experience with such conflicts has produced routines for resolving them.'[29] But fresh abuses continue to emerge with discouraging regularity. Conflict of commitment problems are harder to recognize and address. How are we to determine the commitment to the university of a professor who moves seamlessly from university lab to company lab, and whose students move back and forth with the professor? Are these professors 'just getting by,' like the deadwood professor of popular lore, or are these professors fully engaged in their duties to their multiversity? Multiversities have done far less than they should have to clarify conflict of commitment, articulate what are full-time responsibilities to the university, and to hold professors accountable to these standards.

As departments at specific multiversities become associated with specific companies, multiversities risk being drawn into the fray of commercial competition. This is already occurring in the life sciences. Powell and Owen-Smith note: 'Commercial scientists in other companies tell us they feel less willing to collaborate with academic researchers in such departments because they worry that information will pass to their commercial rivals. Universities are becoming venues through which commercial competition takes place.'[30]

The new responsibility to commercialize research shifts the priorities of the multiversity and alters the balance of power within the multiversity. The paradigm favours applied research over basic research; it favours biology, medicine, engineering, and computer science over all other areas – the social sciences, humanities, fine arts, and professions. It complicates governance: multiversity-industry partnerships are hybrid arrangements, most common between research centres of the multiversity and a company, with the result that research centres gain power and influence at the expense of departments, which traditionally have provided the structure for governance within the multiversity.

The greatest danger of this new responsibility to commercialize research is neither financial nor ethical. The danger is to the ideals of the university, the ideals upon which it has been founded and built. The danger is especially acute because if the multiversity is to resist giving priority to research that promotes economic growth and to resist the task of commercializing research, it must resist its two greatest patrons – government and industry.

This new social contract for commercialization of research requires that ideas should be private. When an idea becomes privately owned, it becomes intellectual property, to be bought and sold in the market. The firms in the multiversity-industry alliances want the research results to be private, in order to make a return on their investment. The multiversity wants the research results private so that it can make money from licensing the patent. The professors want the results private because they own a share of the spin-off company. Intellectual property rights are at the centre of university research policy in the new social contract – ideas should be private. This is a radical change. In the past, the university has always been defined by a commitment to public ideas.

Robert K. Merton, a sociologist of science at the University of Chicago, wrote a famous paper in 1942 entitled, 'The Normative Structure of Science.' Here he set out 'the ethos of science,' but the framework went beyond science. His paper defines the ethos of all research in the multiversity. Merton begins: 'Science is a deceptively inclusive word which refers to a variety of distinct though interrelated items. It is commonly used to denote (1) a set of characteristic methods by means of which knowledge is certified; (2) a stock of accumulated knowledge stemming from the application of these methods; (3) a set of cultural values and mores governing the activities termed scientific; or (4) any combination of the foregoing.'[31] Merton's focus is (3), the culture and mores of science, the moral rules governing scientists. 'The ethos of science is that affectively toned complex of values which is held to be binding on the man of science.' The goal of science is the extension of certified knowledge. For Merton, 'four sets of institutional imperatives – universalism, communism, disinterestedness, organized scepticism – comprise the ethos of modern science.'[32]

A moral imperative for all scientists is that ideas be public. In Merton's words, 'communism, in the non-technical and extended sense of common ownership of goods,' is an integral element of the scientific ethos. 'The substantive findings of science are a product of social collaboration and are assigned to the community.' No one can or should lay a claim of ownership to a new finding, so reliant are they on those who have gone before and those who are part of the community of science. 'Newton's remark – "if I have seen further it is by standing on the shoulders of giants" – expresses at once the sense of indebtedness to the common heritage and a recognition of the essentially cooperative and cumulative quality of scientific achievement.'[33]

The thrust to private knowledge in the new social contract is in radical contradiction to the ethos of science, to the ethos of research in the multiversity of democratic societies.

The commercialization of research is also a radical contradiction of the traditions of academic freedom. Walter Metzger, in his analysis of the origins of academic freedom, suggests that the 'rationale for academic freedom has been endowed with certain fundamental values, values not original to science, but implicit in scientific assumptions and inherent in scientific activity.'[34] Among these values are cooperativeness, the commitment to public knowledge, and disinterestedness.

To be disinterested is to be free from bias and to be free from concerns for your personal interests, especially your financial interests. The ethos of science requires disinterestedness, and this has always been regarded as crucial for insuring integrity in scientific research. The privatization of knowledge, most especially the corporate support for research and the financial involvement of professors in the commercialization of their research, is a radical contradiction of the norm of disinterestedness. As the multiversity itself seeks to earn money, the institution is no longer disinterested. The disinterestedness of professors and of the multiversity has always been a crucial supporting structure to the ideal of academic freedom.

The worries about the integrity of scientific research are not idle speculation. Much medical research is tainted by worry that the research has been sponsored by a corporation. Some academic journals now require that the authors disclose the source of their research funding. Presumably, professors should also disclose any equity interest in firms that might profit from the research results. If such connections might bias the research, might they also not bias what is taught in the classroom? There should be similar disclosures made to students by their professors.

It is no wonder that the new social contract, which asks that multiversities commercialize research findings, provokes such anguish. Equally, it is deeply troubling that so many in the government *and* the multiversity are making the shift with so little reflection or consternation. There is a prodigal adaptation to the spirit of our time. The multiversity is drifting away from its historical commitments to public ideas, to the principle of disinterestedness, and to academic freedom.

The Battle: Public Ideas or Private Ideas?

The drift towards private knowledge is not without opposition, however. Even within the new technologies themselves, there are currents flowing in the opposite direction. The discourse around research, innovation, and technology transfer emerges principally from information technology and the life sciences, and so it is there that we can best explore the thrust to privatize knowledge and the countervailing currents to keep knowledge public.

Alvin Kernan, in his reflections on the history of printing, speaks of 'print logic' and of the 'logic' of a technology. The logic of a technology 'is its tendency consistently to shape whatever it affects in a limited number of definite forms or directions.'[35] Every technology has a logic. What is the logic of information technology and biotechnology? Do they favour public ideas or private ideas?

The story of Silicon Valley, and the phenomenal wealth of IT entrepreneurs, would seem to make the answer obvious – information technology favours private ideas. The information technology revolution is driven by new ideas commercialized at breakneck speed, by venture capital, by stock options, and by start-up companies. It generates private wealth on a breathtaking scale. Never before have research dynamism, private ideas, and capitalism been so complementary. But on even a moment's reflection, the answer is not so obvious. Information technology digitizes information, and digitized information is a classic example of a public good. Digitized information – whether text, image, or sound – can be transferred from one person to another at almost no additional cost. One person can use the digitized information without diminishing another's use if it. The IT revolution makes ideas a public good as never before, as the recording industry has discovered. One reason that intellectual property rights have become so important in the information age is that they are so hard to maintain once the intellectual property is digital.

The information technology revolution has released many other forces favouring the publicness of ideas. The creators of the Internet and of the World Wide Web, like Vincent Cerf and Timothy Berners-Lee, are deeply committed to the open democratic logic of the technology. Their computer code is an Esperanto that allows everyone to converse. Michael Dertouzos has remarked that companies have always been asking: 'How can I make the Web mine?' whereas Tim Berners-Lee has always been asking 'How can I make the Web yours?'[36] The

Web has flourished because Berners-Lee's democratic ideals are built into the technology itself. The technology of data transfer and the protocols of the Internet and Web are constructed to allow openness and inclusion, without any central guidance or control. Access and inclusion – publicness – are inherent in the technology.

Information technology also contains a bias for cooperative, collective learning and innovation because the writing of computer code is ideally suited to cooperative, collective activity. The open source software movement derives from this logic in the technology.

The remarkable story of Linux software is a story of cooperative, collaborative innovation. All computers require an operating system, a complex bundle of software to execute and coordinate all the tasks. During the 1950s and 1960s, operating systems were written to run only the computers of one manufacturer. This created problems for large institutions who purchased computers from several manufacturers, or when people moved their work from one institution to another, or when institutions tried to collaborate. The huge American Telephone and Telegraph Company (AT&T) developed a cross-platform operating system called UNIX. AT&T, by government regulation, was not allowed in the business of selling operating systems and therefore gave UNIX computer code, free, to anyone who wanted it. Among the takers were multiversities and their computer science departments. 'Computer science departments could use the source code to teach their students about how operating systems were written. The system could be critiqued ... And as the system became understood, fixes to bugs in the system were contributed back to AT&T.'[37] However, after the breakup of AT&T, portions of the company were allowed to enter the computing business. UNIX was privatized, and users have to obtain a licence to use the current version.

To Richard Stallman, an MIT researcher, this was a moral affront. It broke with the spirit of openness in science and privatized the collective creation of a generation of professors and students. In response, Stallman created the Free Software Foundation and set about to write a free, UNIX-like operating system. Stallman and all his open source contributors made progress over the 1980s, but still lacked one component of the operating system, called a 'kernel.' Enter Linus Thorvalds, a Finnish undergraduate student. He wrote the code for the kernel and released it free on the Internet. Before writing the code, he asked people over the Internet what they would like to see in a kernel, and after releasing his code, invited others to use it and offer improvements. The process started by Stallman and Thorvalds became Linux (this is not UNIX), a new operating system that is open source software and the collective, collaborative creation of thousands of computer scientists.

Linux is now the fastest-growing operating system in the world. IBM has embraced Linux, as have many companies and governments. Moreover, this is not the only story of dynamic innovation based upon public ideas and collective, collaborative creation. IBM used to have its own private software to run servers, but an open source creation, Apache, has proven superior. IBM now commits its own resources – in excess of U.S. $1 billion – to supporting the development of Linux and Apache, even though the software is free. IBM, of course, still makes money. The improving, free software increases the value of the equipment that IBM sells, and IBM also sells services in conjunction with the free software. But the innovative process driving the improvements is open and collaborative. No one owns the software. This public innovation process is a bias in the nature of computer software code; it is a logic of information technology.

The logic of information technology, thus, involves a struggle between the public ethic and the private ethic. Which triumphs will determine how the ideals of the multiversity are changed by the information age. The information technology revolution has two visions of the best way to create new knowledge. One vision says new knowledge is best generated by private ideas, the other vision says new knowledge is best generated by public ideas. These visions are at war for the soul of the information age and for the soul of the multiversity.

The multiversity is not a passive bystander is this struggle. It can do much to determine the outcome. Unfortunately, the multiversity as an institution has done little to resist the forces of privatization or to ally with the forces of openness. Some individual professors work on open source projects, but just as many have started their own software companies. The multiversity has done much more to accommodate the start-up companies than to support open source. Multiversities have been concerned to establish intellectual property rights with an eye to the licensing revenues. Most professors, despite their public commitment to public information, have found themselves defending private information. Corynne McSherry, in *Who Owns Academic Work?* has identified an awful irony in the present dynamic: many professors are using the language of academic freedom to claim ownership of the things they produce. They want to own and control the digitized lectures that they create. Once, academic freedom was built upon public information; now, academic freedom is invoked to create private information.[38]

The multiversity has hardly recognized these opposing currents in the new information technology, much less been an articulate and steadfast champion of public scientific knowledge. The open source ethic does have a whiff of the hippie, and many of its leaders, like Richard Stallman, are eccentric utopians. Multiversities have been afraid to inhale, unable to separate the ethos from the hippie personages. Despite their responsibility to be critic, conscience, and public intellectual, multiversities have been, sadly, silent. They have rather too easily and too swiftly accommodated to their new role as engines of economic growth. The IT revolution also has the whiff of the heroic entrepreneur, of innovation-driven capitalism bringing waves of creative destruction. Of this, the multiversity has been less afraid to inhale.

The same battle between public information and private information is also raging in the life sciences – leaders in the move to commercialize research. The life sciences are the greatest contributors to multiversity revenues from patent licenses. 'On all but one campus, life science innovations drive revenue earnings, often accounting for nearly 100 percent of overall royalty income. Even at universities known for their strength in engineering and physical science (for example, Stanford, MIT, and Cal Tech), life science revenues account for the lion's share of licensing returns to intellectual property.'[39] The interpenetration of the academy and business in the life sciences is extraordinary. 'By the mid 1980s, most full professors of molecular biology held equity positions (they were given stock in return for their expertise) in spin-off companies (small corporations based on products developed in university or government laboratories) that sold products to large corporations and were on national advisory boards of corporations with biotechnology products. Corporations supplied 45 percent of the funding of academic biotechnology.'[40] The life sciences seem to flourish and advance with private ideas.

Once again, there are countervailing forces. On the side of public knowledge, there is the established principle that the raw products of nature are not patentable by their discoverers: one cannot patent the oxygen molecule. Biotechnology deals with nature at the most fundamental level. The DNA sequence is at the core of all living nature, and the logic surely points to this being public information. Ever since the discovery of DNA by Watson and Crick, people have dreamed of understanding its structure and so understanding more fundamentally than ever before the laws of nature within the human body, the processes of disease and recovery, and the process of human evolution. This logic for public knowledge is powerfully reinforced because the DNA sequence holds such possibilities for the good of humanity, and such terrifying possibilities of abuse.

On the other hand, the logic of biotechnology also favours private knowledge and patents. The task of the sequencing the DNA, and then eventually understanding and using the knowledge, is unimaginably large. But it can be broken down into discrete investigations, yielding specific advances. The investment of resources into scientific research is encouraged by allowing the patenting of these discrete investigations. The eventual medical use of genetic knowledge will require enormous and risky further development and long clinical trials. People are discouraged from undertaking this without ownership of the original ideas.[41]

In their essence, the struggles over open source software and over the patenting of genetic materials are a debate about how to advance knowledge. On one side are those who believe that science will advance faster when researchers enjoy free access to new ideas. On the other are those who believe that without ownership of intellectual property rights no one will have an incentive to invest in research and development. The multiversity, contrary to its history and contrary to most of its long-held values, is shifting towards favouring the belief that private ideas rather than public ideas are the best way to advance knowledge.

A New Idea of the University: The Dominant Discourse

With this focus on economic development, on the translation of research findings into intellectual property, and this explicit responsibility to commercialize research being added to the multiversity's traditional responsibilities of teaching and research, are we experiencing, as Etzkowitz and Webster argue, an academic revolution as important as when the multiversity added research to its mission?

Certainly, there are many critics who believe we are, but reflection is called for. Universities have been closely tied to industry for more than 150 years, and they have been commercializing research for more than eighty years. Most of this commercialization, for example, the application of research findings in agriculture or the awarding of copyright to professors for the textbooks they write, is seen as beneficial on balance.

The recent dramatic change is confined to a small number of disciplines in the life sciences, information technology, engineering, and agriculture. The multiversity has many components: the humanities, social sciences, the pure sciences, and many other applied sciences and professional schools. Most professors in these areas go about their teaching, research, and service in much the same way as they did twenty years ago. Steven Brint reflects on what he calls 'the rise of the practical arts' at the expense of the liberal arts. He concludes that 'one of the more surprising outcomes of the rise of the practical arts is not *how much*, but *how little* has changed, at least at the major research universities.'[42] The most prestigious academic bodies are still connected to the traditional arts and sciences. 'These are the institutions that tend to speak for the values of higher education at the most elite level.' Furthermore, 'while public figures rely on technical experts drawn from a variety of fields to help develop and assess policies, they rely almost exclusively on liberal arts faculty and writers influenced by them to define broader themes and to suggest proper contexts for understanding.'[43]

These balanced reflections are important. Yet, to dismiss the worries about the imperative to commercialize research would be complacent. There are, indeed, real threats to the core ideals of the multiversity. The multiversity is being comprehended in a new way, it is being talked about in a new way – there is a new idea of the university. Chapter 3 told the story of the emergence of the multiversity and chose to comprehend the multiversity as a conglomerate combining four ideas of the university: the university as a place of undergraduate liberal education; the university as a place of graduate education and advanced research; the university as a place of professional education; and the university in service to society, accessible, pragmatic, and conducting applied research. To these four ideas or archetypes, our age is adding a fifth – the university as an institution of the economy, and this new idea threatens to overwhelm the others.

What does it mean to say that the multiversity is being conceived 'as an institution of the economy'? The meaning has two parts; one relates to how we think about the multiversity and the other to how we think about the economy. In our age there have been major changes in both. We now think about the multiversity differently. The multiversity's contribution to economic life is becoming the organizing principle around which we conceive of all of the multiversity's activities. With this new idea, for example, our categories of description and analysis change: education becomes, instead, increases in human capital; research becomes, instead, the creation of intellectual property, which can be commercialized; the university becomes a provider of educational services, and students become clients or customers. We also think about the economy differently. When we consider a nation's economy and the list of all the institutions of economic life and what institutions are necessary for economic growth, the multiversity has been added to the list. This is very new. Even recent studies by economic historians of the sources of economic growth and the institutions that have supported it through history give little or no prominence to or even much mention of the role of universities.[44]

Whenever we analyse an economy, key concepts in the analysis are natural resources, labour, capital, and technology; and economic growth comes from increases in human capital, from investment in physical capital, and from innovation and technological change. Economies are made up of many institutions: there are property rights, the laws of contract, and the rule of law; there are labour markets, capital markets, and output markets; there is the banking system and other financial institutions; there are the sectors of the economy: the agricultural sector, the mining and forestry sector, the industrial sector, and the service sector. There are many intangible institutions: economies require trust among the participants, each has a regulatory environment, and they require risk-taking and entrepreneurship. Countries and their governments, when they seek to strengthen their economies and to promote economic growth, examine these institutions and try to strengthen them and improve their functioning. They examine property rights and the enforcement of contract; they examine labour markets and financial markets and the system of regulation; they look at the manufacturing sector and the service sector. They look at the level of trust and of entrepreneurship. (Also companies, when they think of locating in a country, examine these institutions.) Today, when governments in the Anglo-American world craft their economic policies, they also examine their multiversities. This is a fundamental shift. Now, recalling Romer's words, 'the key step in understanding economic growth is to think carefully about ideas.' Multiversities are seen as fundamentally important institutions for economic prosperity, just as important as banks or a well-functioning labour market. Sound economic policy requires not just sound monetary policy or sound trade policy, but also sound policy for supporting multiversities and their research. It is these two parts combined – these new ways of analysing both the university and the economy – that create the new idea of the university: the university as an institution of the economy.

When we talk about this new idea, and especially about the multiversity's responsibility to commercialize research, we are talking in certain ways, we use certain language. How might this new idea and this new way of speaking about the multiversity affect the multiversity? The linguistic methodologies of postmodernism – of Derrida, Foucault, and Lyotard – can be helpful.

We have begun to speak of the multiversity in a new way, we have a new discourse. The language of innovation – of human capital, technology transfer, the entrepreneur, intellectual property, and the spin-off company – is a discourse. Like any discourse, the discourse defines the proper objects of our gaze. This language is not a mirror of objective reality; rather, the language constructs our reality. Foucault sought to uncover the 'unconscious of science' through his discourse analysis. We can discover the 'unconscious of the multiversity' in its various discourses.

The multiversity is a complex entity. To help us comprehend it, let us return to James Duderstadt, former president of the University of Michigan, and how he characterized it, unselfconsciously and without irony, as 'a very complex, international conglomerate of highly diverse businesses. To illustrate, imagine how one might characterize the business lines of the "University of Michigan, Inc." With an annual income of $3 billion and an additional $3 billion of investment assets under active management, the U of M Inc., would rank roughly 470th on the Fortune 500 list.'[45] This is the new discourse of the new idea of the university. How far from the language of Cardinal Newman we have travelled! What a different university we have constructed by our choice of words. Moreover, James Duderstadt is not the exception. The website of the University of Oxford prominently and proudly proclaims Oxford to be the 'most innovative university in Britain.' In telling us about its research, Oxford does not speak of its contribution to our understanding of nature and its laws. But, Oxford does report that Isis Innovation, its wholly owned technology transfer company, founded in 1988, 'files on average one new patent application a week and spins out a new company from university research every two months.' Furthermore, 'among U.K. universities, Oxford is at the forefront of encouraging enterprise among students, teachers and researchers.'[46] This is not how

Cardinal Newman would have described the purposes of Oxford. This discourse of innovation creates the reality of the university for us.

The discourse of this new idea of a university is telling a story. It provides, in the methodology of Lyotard (considered in chapter 8), a grand narrative, 'the kind of story that underlies, gives legitimacy, and explains the particular choices a particular culture prescribes as possible courses of action. A grand narrative, also called a "master narrative," provides coherence by covering up the various conflicts.'[47]

The discourse, the grand narrative – of the entrepreneurial multiversity responsible for commercializing its research – is new. It conflicts with other parts of the multiversity's mission, with other discourses, and other narratives – narratives of liberal learning, disinterested scholarship, and social citizenship. A great challenge to the multiversity of our age is how this conflict of discourses will be resolved or at least managed. The multiversity has always lived with conflicting ideas – indeed this defines the multiversity – but the outcome is not assured by past history.

The new discourse threatens to become dominant. Presidents and vice-chancellors adopt it in their public speeches. It fills the websites and brochures of universities as they present themselves to the world. Many professors embrace it, as do many students. No doubt, this is partially explained because the discourse allows the multiversity to justify itself to the society that supports it. Contribution to economic growth is a government priority, and multiversities are eager to show how they can help achieve this priority. Also, the discourse dominates because commercialized research promises increased revenues, so badly needed in the constrained welfare state. But the new discourse threatens to overwhelm other discourses and the other ideas of the university.

We are not well served by this dominance.

The dominant discourse offers a truncated vision of innovation and of the sorts of innovation needed by society. Its focus is strictly economic, but stunted even within that domain. Consider an example. We know that cities are important incubators of economic innovation, and so we ask: How we can better design our cities? The answer to this question is as important to economic well-being as the next breakthrough in information technology, but the answer will not come through technology transfer and the commercialization of research. The list of such examples could be extended easily. Also, the new discourse does not recognize how important innovation from social science and the humanities is to our well-being. Take another example. Biotechnology will certainly bring improvements to our health, but many people suffer ill-health because they do not take their medicines as prescribed or do not have access to medical care. To improve health, we need to understand why people do not follow through with their prescribed medications and how to ensure wider access to health care. These answers will not come from biotechnology.

The new discourse, by speaking of research as public-private partnerships, patenting, and licensing, shapes the intellectual contributions we see as worthy. Research that does not fit is eased to the background and ceases to be. The language cannot encompass the philosopher returning to the question of justice, the English professor analysing images of empire in British literature of the nineteenth century, or the mathematician puzzling over Fermat's last theorem. It does not refer to social scientists working to offer a redesign of the medical care system or a redesign of cities. All such work is inherently public and the ideas cannot be privatized, commercialized, and placed directly in the service of the market. Such research is marginalized in the new discourse.

The discourse shapes how we see the work of a professor. The new discourse subtly conjoins the heroic scientist and the heroic entrepreneur. Both are bold, independent, and courageous in overcoming static routines. They join the heroic individualist of popular culture. What a contrast to a library-based scholar, reading and reflecting, and then writing a reinterpretation of a literary work or a reinterpretation of the meaning of justice.

The discourse also shapes the way we understand education. If attendance at university is described as the acquisition of human capital, this implies that the motivation for attending university is to increase future income. No one denies this motivation is important, but in this discourse other motivations do not fit the model – they do not exist. There is no place for knowledge for its own sake, no intrinsic reason to read the humanities, no place for education for citizenship, and no place for educating professionals to be sensitive to the public interest.

This discourse is a grand narrative. It provides coherence, but covers up the conflicts. It covers up the other, the different. It ignores other ideas of the multiversity. We must not allow the discourse of commercialization to dominate. Each time we hear a politician or president speak of the multiversity, we should pause to ask ourselves: What sort of university is he or she describing? We should examine our multiversity websites, the promotional material we send to students and to donors, and the press releases we issue to ensure that they are not limited to the discourse of innovation and commercialization. Most importantly, however, when we conceptualize and talk about the multiversity, we must ensure that our words allow all the ideas of the multiversity – including the idea of the multiversity as an institution of democracy.

10 Globalization

The final item on my list of characteristics of our age is on virtually everyone's list. Some of the courses that I teach at the university analyse the role of government in society, and at the beginning of term, as a prelude to our discussions, I often ask my students: What is the nature of our society, and what are the defining characteristics of our age? One characteristic is always identified: globalization. Globalization defines our age and every institution is disrupted by it.

The impact of globalization is a prominent theme of recent writing about universities. Peter Scott, vice-chancellor of Kingston University in the United Kingdom and editor for sixteen years of the *Times Higher Education Supplement*, has written: 'Globalisation is perhaps the most fundamental challenge faced by the University in its long history. The forces of globalisation are refashioning not only economic structures and life-styles; they are also challenging the authority of the nation state (in which so many of our notions of civic and democratic rights are embedded); they are penetrating deeply into the private world of informal associations, communities, families, and even, deeper still, into the intimate world of personal identity. If globalisation is having such a radical impact on the great institutions (and ideas) of the modern world – the Market, the State, and the Individual – surely it is likely to have an equally radical impact on that other great institution-idea – the University.'[1]

The university has always belonged to the borderless world of ideas. In the modern era, however, the university has also been intimately connected with the nation state, as well as with colonialism and imperialism. And now it is connected to globalization. The university is both a force of globalization and being reshaped by it.

Globalization is neither a single condition nor a single process. It has political, economic, cultural, and environmental aspects. Many of the processes of globalization have been going on for decades, even centuries. Some sceptics argue that current levels of global interdependence are no greater than in previous epochs, particularly the nineteenth century and the beginning of the twentieth.[2] Yet, certain things make our current era fundamentally different, and two stand out. First is the communication made possible by the information technology revolution, especially the Internet and the World Wide Web. Second is the demise of authoritarian socialist governments, their planned economies, and the end of the Cold War. Both the Internet and the end of the Cold War date from the late 1980s. We can date our present age of globalization as beginning in 1989, symbolically with the fall of the Berlin Wall. This is the globalization reshaping the multiversity of the twenty-first century. (A third, fundamentally different, aspect of globalization in our age is resource depletion and environmental interdependence; but this is beyond the scope of this chapter.[3])

The world economy is becoming one, no longer divided into planned economies and market economies. This world economy is no longer organized into nationally based production-line firms, but rather into transnational enterprises coordinating flexible, modular, and dispersed production. The political systems of nation states are becoming more alike with political liberalization, democratization, and increased international attention to human rights. Organizations of all types – governments, companies, and civil society institutions – form international connections and join international organizations. Barriers decline. Interaction speeds up. Money, products, people, and ideas are more mobile. The local and the global commingle: what happens on the other side of the world affects our local community and what we do at home influences the other side of the world. Globalization brings much promise, but also many discontents. The nation state seems to lose its salience and power. The processes of globalization are unpredictable, creating many winners and many losers: globalization brings expanding prosperity and emancipation, yet, it also creates inequities and destroys local cultures.

The multiversity is the most global of institutions. Its students, especially its graduate students, come from all over the world. The research of its professors is communicated, studied, and applied all over the world. Few institutions have the global interrelationships of a multiversity. The scholarly community is a world community. However, our multiversities at the same time still remain the most national of institutions. Oxford is ineffably English, just as the University of Michigan is ineffably American, and the University of Toronto is Canadian.

There is now a very large, and rapidly growing, literature on globalization and the university, much of it highly critical of the changes being wrought upon the multiversity. Sheila Slaughter and Larry L. Leslie, in *Academic Capitalism: Politics, Policies, and the Entrepreneurial University*, argue that 'the globalization of the political economy at the end of the twentieth century is destabilizing patterns of university professional work developed over the past hundred years';[4] the university, once protected and apart from market values and forces, is being transformed by globalization into academic capitalism. Similar analysis runs through the essays collected in *Universities and Globalization: Critical Perspectives*, 1998, and *Globalization and Higher Education*, published in 2004.[5] This literature emphasizes how globalization reduces the sovereignty of the nation state, forces reductions in government spending, and insinuates a market ethos into academic life.

I will use this literature about globalization and the multiversity, but following the approach of previous chapters, I want first to explore the bundles of ideas that help us understand the new international order and globalization, and only subsequently analyse the implications for the multiversity. This approach leads to the political science literature about globalization, a literature written by scholars not concerned with the implications of globalization for universities and with a longer time perspective than most of the current writing about globalization and universities. This approach highlights, as the current literature does not, the university's long connection to the nation state, and to imperialism, and that the university itself is a force for globalization. Furthermore, it reveals how current globalization brings a deep tension within the multiversity between nationalism and cosmopolitanism.

To study globalization is to study how ideas – especially in the social sciences – construct and give meaning to the world. It is to see, again, the power of ideas originating from research at the multiversity. The world is infinitely complex, turbulent, infinitely detailed. As professors publish their research about globalization, the world is shaped, categories are defined, causation is argued, and the world's story is told. Ideally, this research would allow us to anticipate future developments and show us the means to achieve our goals.[6] However, postmodern thought alerts us that our concepts, theories, and models of globalization do not correspond easily to some objective reality 'out there.' Rather, this research helps to create our reality. Furthermore, it is impossible to separate an objective analysis of globalization from our values about what we believe international relations should be. These are inescapable dilemmas in social science research. To study globalization is also to offer a case study of these constant dilemmas in understanding social reality.

The focus of this book is the multiversity of the Anglo-American world. Compared with universities in almost all other countries, these multiversities will be less affected by the globalization of the twenty-first century. The Anglo-American multiversities are already well established and very successful, and they have operated with extensive international connections. Globalization encourages a convergence of education systems, often reshaping and even erasing indigenous models. The Anglo-American model, however, is not being reshaped; rather, it is the standard, and other systems are adopting its models of degree structures, curriculum, organization, and governance. In much of the developing world, there is an explosion of demand for higher education but few resources to provide it. This often leads to a major role for foreign institutions, either as direct providers or partners with local institutions, in meeting the demand. The Anglo-American countries face little of this. Finally, of course, the Anglo-American world faces none of the threat and turbulence as English becomes the lingua franca of international academic communication.[7] Nonetheless, the implications of globalization on Anglo-American multiversities are profound.

Much of the current writing about universities and globalization lacks historical context, but without such context it is difficult to appreciate the nuanced complexity of the multiversity's engagement with the nation state and the relations between states. Before turning to current globalization and the multiversity of the Anglo-American world, it is important to explore international structures of the past and the place of the university within them.

Universities in the World of Nation States

The origins of our current global political order are found in Europe – in the movement from the overlapping allegiances of the medieval world to the nation states of the modern world.[8]

Medieval Europe was a fluid, fragmented, and divided political terrain. The nation state, as we know it, did not exist. (Intriguingly, with diminished national sovereignty today, some scholars characterize our globalizing era as 'the new medievalism.'[9]) The medieval universities were part of this fragmented fluid structure, a structure nonetheless united by Christianity and Latin as the lingua franca, and thus, medieval students and scholars moved easily across Europe. From its very beginnings, the university was 'international' and had established some autonomy from state power.

The transformation of the European geopolitical order began in the middle of the seventeenth century. Following the peace treaties of Westphalia of 1648, Europe was gradually configured into states, each with a defined territory. The state is sovereign within that territory; within its boundaries, the state makes the laws and enforces the laws – there are no private courts or private armies, as in the medieval world. All citizens within the territory owe allegiance to the state. There exists no higher authority than the state. Each state recognizes the sovereignty of other states. States pursue their self-interests in international relations. Over the next three hundred years, the entire world would be configured into this 'Westphalian model' of sovereign states.

The state is a political organization with sovereignty over territory. It is useful to distinguish the concept of a 'state' from the concept of a 'nation.' A nation is a people, a community, bound together by common history and culture. Nations are actual communities, but equally communities of the imagination, that fulfil our primordial needs for connection and belonging. A nation can be united by land, history, and the shared experience and ways of living that is their culture. Often nations are united by language, religion, and race.

When the nation and the state share the same territory, the 'nation state' is created. The nation state becomes the political organization that allows a nation to preserve and enhance its language and culture and that also allows the nation, with its own particularities, to control its own destiny. Nations seek to be sovereign over their territory and so to allow their people to flourish. When a nation is governed by someone else, the nation often wants to break free; it wants national self-determination, and to form its own state. The idea of nation is powerful, perhaps the most powerful idea of the modern era. In his book *Nationalism*, Peter Alter writes that nationalism is 'a political force which has been more important in shaping the history of Europe and the world over the last two centuries than the ideas of freedom or parliamentary democracy or of communism.'[10]

Sometimes the 'nation' exists before the nation state is created, and we speak of ethnic nationalism. Equally often, the state comes first, and then the state works to create the nation – the sense of community and belonging – and we speak of civic nationalism. Every state has its nationalism in one form or the other, usually a mixture of both. And their universities have been closely connected with nationalism and nation-building.

The nation-builders of the nineteenth century saw universities as crucial instruments in their project. Universities fit easily into the Westphalian order – supplying civil servants for governments, science and technology for industrialization, and transmitting the cultural heritage of the nation. The University of Berlin was founded to serve the new German nation. The Scottish universities, the University of London, the English civic universities, the American land grant universities, and the Canadian universities all made commitments to serving the nation state. The famous motto of Princeton University used to be: 'Princeton in the Nation's Service.' The university, through its liberal education, prepared students for citizenship – national citizenship. The study and scholarship of the nation's history, politics, and literature helped to create the imagined community of the nation.[11] The nineteenth-century university was an institution of the nation state and nationalism, sometimes ethnic nationalism, sometimes civic nationalism, but always working to bind the community together as a nation.

The interconnection of the globe increased dramatically during the nineteenth century, as the European states pressed outward across the world in a competitive struggle of exploration, colonization, and empire-building. Some scholars see this era as a time of globalization more intense than our own. World trade and foreign investment surged. There were huge migrations of people from Europe to the New World. The world was bound together by ship, rail, and telegraph. There can be no doubt that from 1800 to 1914 the world experienced the rush of globalization as it never had before.

Globalization, then as now, was comprised of multiple processes, propelled by many forces. It was propelled by imperial dreams and by the expansive demands of capitalism for new markets and new sources of raw materials. These we recognize – and in our postcolonial world condemn – as defining the nineteenth century. But globalization was propelled by much else, as well. It was propelled by religion and missionaries, eccentric and romantic adventurers, human curiosity, the desire to discover and understand, and the pursuit of knowledge for its own sake. Globalization was propelled by the spirits and values of the university.

In 1831, Charles Darwin sailed with HMS *Beagle* around Tierra del Fuego and up to the Galapagos Islands and then on around the world. In 1859, he published *On the Origin of Species by Means of Natural Selection*. Earlier, Alexander von Humboldt (brother of Wilhelm von Humboldt, who had established the University of Berlin), celebrated as one of the great figures of modern science and described by Darwin as 'the greatest scientific traveller who ever lived,' had documented the flora, fauna, and topography of South America under the sponsorship of the King of Spain. In 1803, while on the west coast of South America, Humboldt charted and measured the Peruvian current – a vast movement of cool Pacific water from the Antarctic to the equator that we now recognize as crucially influential in global weather patterns and that is now known as the Humboldt Current. On returning to Europe, Humboldt became one of its most revered and famous citizens, as a man of science – a science that slipped beneath nationalism to bind together peoples of many nations. Born in Berlin, most at home in Paris, he lived for many years in Prussia, where he served the court as a diplomat; yet, between 1811 and 1818, he made numerous scientific explorations across Russia. His renown allowed him to link the recently established scientific societies of European nations. The republic of science was born as an international republic, not a national republic.

Curiosity and an adventurous spirit were found not only among the scientists but also among the humanists. None is more extraordinary than Gertrude Bell.[12] Born in 1868 in northern England of a wealthy industrialist's family, unlike most of her sex and class, Bell went on to university, studying history at Lady Margaret Hall in Oxford. At the age of twenty-six, she began to study Persian and translated the works of the Persian poet Hafiz. Her translation is still celebrated: 'though some twenty hands have put Hafiz into English, her rendering remains the best!'[13] In 1900, Bell moved to Jerusalem to study Arabic and began a life that immersed her in the Arab world. She travelled and mapped the deserts of the Middle East and came to know and love the Arabic language, people, and culture as few Europeans have ever done. She published academic studies of Middle Eastern archaeology, languages, and literatures. Always connected to the British government, and at a level comparable to Lawrence of Arabia, she was influential in the British imperial enterprise. She was, in Edward Said's term, an Orientalist;

yet, at the same time, she knew and loved the Orient as few of the Occident could. Gertrude Bell participated in the Paris Peace Conference of 1919, helped to draw the boundaries of Iraq, and established the Baghdad Museum of the Iraqi Department of Antiquities. (This is the same museum damaged in the 2003 invasion of Iraq, and pillaged in the chaotic aftermath.) A plaque was hung[14] in the museum, bearing the inscription:

> Gertrude Bell
> Whose memory the Arabs will ever hold in reverence and affection
> Created this Museum in 1923
> Being then Honorary Director of Antiquities for the Iraq
> With wonderful knowledge and devotion
> She assembled the precious objects in it
> And through the heat of the Summer
> Worked on them until the day of her death
> On 12th July 1926

Nothing better captures the dilemma of humanistic scholarship in a globalizing world than the life of Gertrude Bell, translator and scholar, servant of the British Empire, and Orientalist, with this plaque as her epitaph.

There can be little doubt that the university was an active collaborator in colonial and imperial expansion. Many graduates of Oxford and Cambridge were destined for the civil service, particularly the Foreign Office and the Colonial Office. Edward Said has argued that Orientalism, as an institutionalized academic study of the Orient, was a necessary complement to British imperialism. Colonial expansion was inevitably accompanied – often preceded – by scientific exploration, particularly by geologists and natural historians, like Charles Darwin and Alexander von Humboldt, and by humanists like Gertrude Bell.

Globalization also spreads the idea of the university itself, with its belief in knowledge for its own sake, institutional autonomy, and academic freedom. We should not be so blind as to believe that the ideals of higher learning originated in Europe and moved out into the world – other cultures have equally old ideals of higher learning – but nineteenth-century globalization spread a particularly European institutional structure and a particularly democratic ideal of sceptical thought. Philip Altbach, a distinguished American scholar of higher education, notes: 'All of the universities in the world today, with the exception of Al-Azhar in Cairo, stem from the same historical roots – the medieval European university and especially the faculty-dominated University of Paris. Much of the non-western world had European university models imposed on them by colonial masters. Even those few countries not colonized by western powers – such as Japan, Thailand, Ethiopia and a few others – adopted the western academic model. This is the case even where, as in China, well-established indigenous academic traditions already existed.'[15] Also, globalization stimulated a desire for university education in the newly connected nations. Their students travelled to the established universities, and new universities were created back home. The University of Berlin, with its commitment to the research ideal, was especially influential around the world.

The 1800–1914 period of globalization collapsed with the First World War – the world's first truly global war. The Paris Peace Conference of 1919 began the process of creating a new world order, in which empires were partially dismantled and in which the principle of national self-determination was paramount. New nation states were born. However, in the period after 1919, the relations between states were not stable. Their economies were being integrated, but this brought new instabilities. The international gold standard collapsed. International capital flows and exchange rate fluctuations spread turbulence from one economy to another. Tit-for-tat devaluations and tariff wars compounded things. International trade atrophied, the stock market crashed in 1929, and economies were plunged into depression – the Great Depression – one tugging down the other. The dreams of nations for territorial expansion and of empires for dominance were not over, and for the second time in twenty-five years a terrible war engulfed the world. After the Second World War, the task was to ensure these horrors never happened again. The task was to build upon a postcolonial system of nation states and introduce international governance systems to prevent another world war and to stabilize international economic relations.

The years from 1945 to 1989 were another period of intense globalization. The new international politico-economic order was complex, but it had a number of basic characteristics. The fundamental unit was the sovereign nation state – the Westphalian system encompassed the globe. The remaining colonies in the empires of European states became nation states, heralding the postcolonial era. Within this world system, the nation states of the world were divided into three camps: the communist camp, the liberal-democratic-capitalist camp, and non-aligned nations. All were struggling in the Cold War. The grand battle was between communism and democracy, between a planned economy and a capitalist economy (although, it should be remembered, many countries were military or civilian dictatorships). Overlaying this pattern, there was a fundamental cleavage between the rich countries and the poor countries. Finally, even as the world of sovereign nation states was reaching towards this full extension, the United Nations had been created, formally in 1945, to implement systems of international regulation and governance – both political and economic. The postwar nation states remained sovereign, but they were ceding authority in order to stabilize the international order. International political governance worked through international law, the United Nations, and the promotion of human rights; international economic governance worked through the regulation of international trade and international finance.

During the mid- and late 1940s, four international economic structures were formed to stabilize and regulate global economic and financial relations. Never again should unstable capital flows and tit-for-tat trade wars be allowed to bring chaos to international trade and the devastation of unemployment to domestic economies. In 1944, at the U.N. Monetary and Financial Conference, the Bretton Woods Agreement was reached, officially replacing the gold standard and establishing the international exchange rate regime for the next thirty years. Also created were the International Monetary Fund (IMF), the International Bank for Reconstruction and Development (IBRD, now known as the World Bank), and the procedures that led to the General Agreement on Tariffs and Trade (GATT).

The multiversities of the Anglo-American world, through their research, their professors, and graduates, were extraordinarily influential in creating the postwar systems of international economic and political relations, just as they had been extraordinarily influential in creating the welfare state. John Maynard Keynes was a towering figure in both of these projects. Keynesian ideas for stabilization of the world's economy shaped the new international economic order, just as Keynesian ideas for stabilization of one country's economy shaped the welfare state.

Not all of the states joined this economic order. The Soviet Union was party to the early discussions, but did not join. Established upon the Communist victory in China in 1949, the People's Republic of China did not join. In 1949, the Council for Mutual Economic Assistance (CMEA, also known as COMECON) was formed for managing the trade and financial arrangements of the planned economies of Eastern Europe and the Soviet Union. Thus, the world economy was organized into two great blocs, those of the planned economies whose international connections were structured by COMECON and like agencies and those of the market economies whose international connections were structured by Bretton Woods, the IMF, the World Bank, and GATT. Many of the non-aligned nations straddled the blocs, having heavily planned economies while participating in the IMF and the World Bank. The world's economy was far from being one integrated whole during the 1945–89 period.

It is an overstatement to say that the international connections of universities, and the movements of students and professors, were dictated by these economic trading structures, but indisputably university connections were stronger within blocs than between blocs. For example, the Anglo-American universities had much stronger ties with European universities than with Russian or Chinese universities. Many universities of the developing world, especially in Africa and Asia, had stronger ties with Russian universities than with Anglo-American universities. For all its inherent internationalism, the university's international connections were framed by the geopolitical order.

Postwar globalization on the political front deserves our attention, too, although within the antiglobalization movement economic globalization is the sole focus. New forms of international political regulation were created through the United Nations, most particularly through the U.N. Charter and the Universal Declaration of Human Rights.[16] It would be incorrect to conclude that the Westphalian system of sovereign states had been superseded by a system of world government, because the separate states remained jealously sovereign, even as the United Nations was created. Nonetheless, the states did agree to abide by tight restrictions on the use of force to solve international disputes and made commitments to grant their citizens basic rights.

On 10 December 1948, the General Assembly of the United Nations adopted and proclaimed the Universal Declaration of Human Rights. It is a stirring document and remains a bulwark and triumph of globalization. Article 1 reads: 'All human beings are born free and equal in dignity and rights. They are endowed with reason and conscience and should act towards one another in a spirit of brotherhood.'[17] The ideals of the Enlightenment, ideals so closely associated with the university, were now proclaimed for the whole world.

Most of us, when we think about human rights, think about basic civil and political rights. For example, when we consider the human rights record of a country, we ask: Do the citizens of that country have freedom from arbitrary imprisonment? Or, do they have the right to vote in free elections? The Universal Declaration of Human Rights does, indeed, articulate these human rights, but it also articulates the rights of social citizenship. The declaration describes the same rights around which Thomas H. Marshall organized his famous 1949 essay, 'Citizenship and Social Class': civil rights, political rights, and social rights.

The Universal Declaration of Human Rights describes the rights of civil citizenship: the right to life, liberty, and security of person (Article 3); the right to equality before the law and to a fair trial (Articles 6 to 12); the right to own property and not to be arbitrarily deprived of property (Article 17); and the right to freedom of thought, conscience, and religion, and to freedom of opinion and expression (Articles 18 and 19). The declaration describes the rights of political citizenship. Article 21 reads: '(1) Everyone has the right to take part in the government of his country, directly or through freely chosen representatives. (2) Everyone has the right of equal access to public service in his country. (3) The will of the people shall be the basis of the authority of the government; this shall be expressed in periodic and genuine elections which shall be by universal and equal suffrage and shall be held by secret vote or by equivalent free voting procedures.' Although communist countries and many dictatorships signed on to these rights, to read them aloud today is to hear a description of liberal democracy.

The Universal Declaration of Human Rights also describes the rights of social citizenship: the right to work and the right 'to a standard of living adequate for the health and well-being of himself and of his family, including food, clothing, housing and medical care and necessary social services, and the right to security in the event of unemployment, sickness, disability, widowhood or old age or other lack of livelihood in circumstances beyond his control' (Article 25) and the right to education (Article 26). The document declares that education shall be directed to the full development of the human personality, and includes 'higher education [which] shall be equally accessible to all on the basis of merit.'[18] The university both as an ideal and as an institution is embedded in the Universal Declaration of Human Rights. Globalization has made these ideals, world ideals.

We might even say that the Universal Declaration of Human Rights embodies the vision of the liberal democratic welfare state – and extends it to the world. This political process of globalization is just as important and just as powerful as the economic process, although it receives far less attention from the critics of globalization. These human rights have not yet been realized everywhere: they are monitored, but remain non-justiciable and unenforceable. However, the power of the ideas is undiminished. Globalization continues to spread and demand attention to the U.N. declaration's ideas about human rights.

Postwar globalization was also a bundle of cultural processes, spreading ideas, values, and cultural practices. Certainly, the university is a crucial cultural institution and practice in the west, and in any nation. Every new country has created its universities and connected them to the world of universities. The interconnections of the world's universities are most obviously routes for the flow of science, engineering, medicine, and technology. But they are also routes for cultural flows, routes where national cultures meet, clash, interact, and understand each other. They are routes for the flow of secular ideologies, not just of the Enlightenment and science, but also of individualism, Marxism, feminism, postmodernism, and environmentalism.

The multiversities of the Anglo-American world emerged and flourished during the period of globalization after the Second World War. As globalization proceeded, the international connections of the multiversity multiplied. It was in this era that Princeton changed its motto from 'Princeton in the Nation's Service' to 'Princeton in the Nation's Service and in the Service of All Nations.'

The scholarly community has always been international; contributions to knowledge are recognized and welcomed regardless of nation or race or creed of the author. The multiversities – the research universities – are the major institutions of this scholarly community. In the postwar period, international scholarly associations and international academic journals grew and prospered. International conferences proliferated; a cliché of university novels became the professor jetting around the world (and therefore seldom on campus and available for undergraduates).

During the later postwar period, an emerging theme in university strategic planning was the call to internationalize the university – its curriculum, its student body, and its research. The call was to revise the curriculum to include an international perspective, encourage international students to come to the Anglo-American universities, and our students to study foreign languages and to take some of their study in another country. This theme in academic planning continues and will become even more important within the multiversity in the years ahead.

The multiversity's approach in the postwar period might be called 'liberal internationalism.' It was not subject to much reflection or critical analysis; after all, who could criticize programs to facilitate scholarly exchange and international collaboration, or programs to allow students to better understand the world and initiatives to allow nations to share knowledge? Within the senior administration, it was not asked how often the multiversity was actually an agent of its country's foreign policy rather than an autonomous institution pursuing international academic contacts. Had people looked more closely, they would have acknowledged that many of their international initiatives were supported by government and by foundations with the explicit purpose of advancing national foreign policy. The international activities of many U.S. multiversities were a product of the Cold War, when the government sought to build relations with other countries of strategic interest and to develop graduates with knowledge useful in foreign policymaking and national defence. This was the genesis in the United States of many international research centres and of many 'area studies' programs in the curriculum.

Within the research activities of the multiversity, the possibility that western scholarship could be part of imperialism was the subject of much study in what became the flourishing field of postcolonial studies. However, the possibility that the multiversity itself was part of imperialism did not much influence the strategy of liberal internationalism. Likewise, the multiversity was not asked to analyse very carefully the cleavages of postwar globalization. How did its activities influence the split between the capitalist and the communist worlds or between the rich and poor countries? It was simply presumed that it would be better if these splits were overcome and that liberal internationalism could help to mend the splits. The multiversity could maintain relations with both sides. Thus, for all these international connections during the postwar era, the multiversity remained fundamentally a national institution, rooted in the Westphalian system of nation states, while nonetheless participating in the changing international order. In the turbulence of today's globalization, however, this comfortable liberal internationalism of a still-national institution is being shaken.

Globalization in Our Age

The political, economic, cultural, and environmental processes of globalization – many of which have been going on for centuries – rush with a new intensity because of the information technology revolution and the end of the Cold War. In our age, the most intense of all the forces of globalization are economic, and these economic forces are the source of the greatest discontents.

During the 1980s, the great debate about how to organize an economy was coming to an end. The world economy would no longer be divided into separate camps but would be integrated into one. Changes in mainland China led the way. After the economic mismanagement during the Cultural Revolution, China embarked on a process of economic modernization and reform and spoke openly of an outward-looking strategy. In 1980, China joined the IMF and the World Bank. Gradually, the Chinese economy was reformed, giving the state less and less influence on prices and resource allocation, and was becoming open to foreign investment and foreign trade. In 2001, China joined the WTO (the successor to the GATT), an organization devoted to freer international trade. What happens in the Chinese economy now affects us all.

Influenced strongly by the Chinese experience, the non-aligned nations of the developing world also began to adopt another economic model. From heavily managed economies, relying upon planned investment and public ownership, and government-regulated prices, and with high tariffs to protect domestic industry, the developing nations, too, shifted to a more market-oriented and outward-looking system. And, of course, the most dramatic example of economic change was in Eastern Europe and the former Soviet Union after the fall of the Berlin Wall in 1989. With the collapse of state socialism, new countries were established (some were re-established), and these countries moved at often precipitous speed to introduce a market economy. For the first time in history, the world economy could become one economy, organized around the private markets of capitalism. By the mid-1990s, most states had joined the WTO and were committed to freer trade and less-regulated economies. There were sharp disputes about culture, agriculture, and services, but they had joined the world economy.

The IMF and World Bank were especially influential in this process, both in the developing world and the former communist economies. They provided much of the advice, foreign exchange loans, and direct loans to manage the transition. By the 1980s, many developing nations were deeply in debt. As a condition for further loans or the restructuring of repayments schedules, the IMF and the World Bank demanded economic reforms called 'structural adjustment programs.' The economic model became known as the 'Washington consensus.' The model required fiscal austerity, privatization of state enterprises, and market liberalization – especially the removal of government interference in financial markets and investment and the removal of barriers to international trade.

Just as the world economies were adopting a common set of principles, just as the developing world and the planned economies were making the transition, the level of economic interdependence was radically increased by the revolution in information technology. World capital markets could become completely integrated. The processes of production could be split up and distributed across the world, often (though by no means always) seeking the lowest-wage and least-regulated economy. Finance and production are now coordinated across the globe using the Internet.

In the judgment of many critics, economic forces in our age of globalization have broken free of all restraint. In their view, the world is now governed by the dictates of the market alone, unconstrained by any authority. National governments are weakened, as are international agencies such as the United Nations. The IMF and the World Bank now act to make the world easier for transnational corporations, rather than to stabilize the international financial system and to assist nations in their economic development.

A vast coalition of antiglobalization groups has formed across the world, and their influence has enormously increased by communication and coordination over the Internet. The coalition includes social activists of all kinds: environmental groups, women's groups, labour groups, churches, and indigenous peoples. Loosely connected, and without any grand blueprint for an alternative, they are united in the belief that globalization is driven by unrestrained capitalism, particularly American capitalism, and that such globalization benefits the rich countries at the expense of the poor, destroys indigenous cultures, and is environmentally unsustainable. They protest the great inequities created by globalization, most particularly between the developed world and the developing world, but also within the developed world. The movement does not really want to close down globalization or return to planned economies, rather the cry is: slow down, celebrate diversity, protect the vulnerable, protect the environment, and give democracy a chance.

What are we to make of our age of globalization? Where does the multiversity stand? Globalization has benefits along with its perils. It spreads economic prosperity to many regions, freeing people from the tyranny of subsistence; it also destroys much indigenous economic activity. It distributes the knowledge of science and technology, while it threatens local religions. It spreads the advances of scientific health care, but also brings new diseases to unprepared peoples. It is the vehicle for cross-cultural understanding and the vehicle of Orientalism. It brings notions of freedom, democracy, and universal human rights, and yet it destroys traditional values and cultures. The multiversity of the Anglo-American world has been active on both sides of the ledger.

Our troubled confusion is captured in the titles of many books and articles about 'globalization and its discontents.' Usually an author wants a unique title, but my own library contains four books bearing this phrase in its title. The title is obviously apropos; this is the twenty-first century's play on the title of Sigmund Freud's book: *Civilization and Its Discontents*. Freud asked whether civilization freed us or enslaved us. Is civilization a benefit or a harm to humanity? We are asking the same questions of globalization in our age. Is globalization a benefit or a harm to humanity?

There are many aspects and processes of globalization, many possible implications of globalization for the Anglo-American multiversity, and many possible ways to gather the interconnection of globalization and the multiversity into themes. No doubt there will prove to be many unforeseen implications. Peter Scott, who has written extensively on these issues, argues that 'universities may be surprised by the impact of globalization – not because it will be greater than expected and, therefore, stretch to the breaking-point the university's capacity for adaptation; nor because it will be smaller than expected and, therefore, globalization will be a more limited catalyst for change; but because universities may look in the wrong direction and, therefore, be caught off their guard.'[19] The processes of globalization are fast-moving and volatile: the analysis of this chapter may become dated in the time between my writing and your reading. But whatever the frame of analysis, we should also recognize a paradox of the multiversity in the age of globalization: the multiversity is buffeted by powerful external forces, while at the same time it is a powerful institution in its own right, contributing through the mobility of its students, professors, and ideas to globalization. The Anglo-American multiversity causes globalization, just as it is reshaped by it.

In this chapter, I have selected four themes to focus upon in considering the implications of globalization for the multiversity. The first is the pressure from globalization to further 'internationalize' the multiversity. The second is the implication of diminished national sovereignty and market fundamentalism for the multiversity. These first two themes dominate most writing about globalization and the Anglo-American university. The third is scarcely addressed at all: the implications for the multiversity of new cleavages, and the potential for armed conflict in the new global order. The fourth, which deserves more attention than it has received, is the implication for the multiversity of the deep tension, created by globalization, between national culture and cosmopolitanism.

Internationalizing the Multiversity

The most evident implication of globalization for the multiversity, certainly most evident in the lives of students and professors, is the high priority now given to internationalization. This is no less significant for being so well-recognized. To ensure that the priority for internationalization is addressed in all its activities – in student and faculty recruitment, curriculum design, and research – most multiversities now have a senior vice-president or other senior administrator with explicit responsibility for internationalization and international relations.

Many initiatives fall under the heading of 'internationalization.' The most important objective of internationalization is to ensure that undergraduate education 'prepare graduates who are internationally knowledgeable and interculturally competent.'[20] This requires more emphasis on the study of foreign languages, a revision of the curriculum to ensure an international perspective throughout, and the development of opportunities to study abroad during the degree program. Also, multiversities seek to recruit more international students in order to make undergraduate education at home more international. Many multiversities, especially in England, have been very successful in these recruiting initiatives, with the result that the high tuition fees charged to foreign students are now a crucial portion of their total revenue. Across most of the Anglo-American world, particularly in the large metropolitan areas, globalization has meant that the undergraduate student body of the multiversity is now incredibly diverse – in terms of race, religion, ethnicity, country of birth and even language spoken at home. Some of the drive to 'internationalize' the undergraduate curriculum results from the need and desire to respond to this polyglot reality. Some multiversities have entered into joint degree programs with foreign universities, and many deliver some of their degree programs abroad, often in concert with a foreign institution. Most of the initiatives to internationalize undergraduate education at the multiversity are in the long tradition of liberal internationalism: internationalization is seen as an unalloyed 'good' for the multiversity, and a successful multiversity is one that leads in these internationalization activities. The writings and speeches of 'vice-presidents international' are filled with admonitions that we must do more and with analyses of how we can narrow the gap between rhetoric and reality.

Similar in its liberal international spirit is the desire to internationalize research activities. As knowledge becomes more specialized and communication easier, especially through the Internet, international research collaborations become more important. International networks of researchers are replacing national and local groupings. Globalization further strengthens the role of international standards in the assessment of academic work. 'Particularly in Europe, but increasingly in other parts of the world, international recognition has become the ultimate standard for assessing the research and scholarly quality of individual faculty and academic departments. National assessment systems such as those developed in England link international recognition of scholarly activity directly to research funding of institutions.'[21]

Just as globalization produces a global market for students, it also creates a global market for professors. For much of the postwar period, language barriers, local traditions, and, very often, explicit government policies restricted the hiring of foreign academics. These barriers are falling, however, and the best multiversities will be those that can attract the best faculty from around the world.

Multiversities are also being 'internationalized' by perceptions beyond their precincts – by the development of world rankings of universities. Rankings of business schools by the international business press have existed for many years and now are the subject of annual news stories as the new rankings are released. But now all disciplines – even the humanities – are being ranked, as well as universities individually. The *Times Higher Education Supplement* now publishes a world university ranking, and in a revealing example of the power and nature of globalization, one of the most influential international rankings of universities is done by the Institute of Higher Education of Shanghai Jiao Tong University in China. Globalization is producing worldwide competition among multiversities and creating a more evident hierarchy. These pressures no doubt encourage convergence across diverse systems of higher education. At present, the Anglo-American model is clearly dominant: in the Chinese rankings of 2005, forty-three of the top fifty universities were located in the Anglo-American world.

All of these implications of globalization are important. How well each multiversity responds to the need to internationalize will do much to explain its future success, although most of these pressures of globalization simply continue, albeit with much greater force, pressures that have been operating throughout the post-1945 period. But many aspects of current globalization, the globalization since 1989, are new and much more troubling in their implications.

National Sovereignty, the Welfare State, and Market Fundamentalism

A recurrent theme in the analysis of globalization is the diminished sovereignty of the nation state. Governments are less able to influence the economy and culture within their borders. In part, this is because our increasing interconnectedness – political, economic, cultural, and environmental – has made all societies more open to forces beyond their borders and so inevitably less able to control what happens inside their borders. At another level, however, economic globalization impels governments to give up the instruments of control that they still could use. Free trade agreements require that governments renounce the use of tariffs. National business elites, supported by major international agencies like the WTO, the IMF, and the World Bank, have concluded that the best government for economic prosperity is constrained government: there should be lower taxes, balanced budgets, freer trade, privatization of government assets, and deregulation of markets. Nations that do not conform will be punished; transnational corporations will move their activities to more conforming states and the knowledge-worker elite will depart for more flexible, dynamic locales.

Nowhere is this diminished national sovereignty more threatening than to the welfare state, the historic bargain between capitalism and democracy. In the welfare state, the market could not operate independently of political influence. Its fluctuations would be modified by macroeconomic policies, and its rewards would be altered by redistributive tax policy and expenditure programs. Its citizens would be provided with social insurance and social services. But globalization seems to require that markets be freed from democratic control.

Elected governments cannot stabilize the fluctuations of the world economy, or alter its rewards; in addition, competitive tax cuts among nations seem to require that the welfare state be rolled back. Thus, globalization, its critics contend, explains the constraints on the welfare state. Thus, globalization also explains the reduced government commitment to multiversities, which in turn has forced them to increase tuition fees, seek external donations, and rely more heavily on external research contracts. Globalization will keep the welfare state small and keep multiversities in the pincers.

There is much merit in this argument: globalization does constrain the welfare state. However, the constraints on the welfare state do not come only from globalization, or in countries like Canada, England, and the United States, even primarily from globalization. The critique of these welfare states began long before the current age of globalization, and we misunderstand the challenge to the Anglo-American multiversity of the constrained welfare state if we attribute it to globalization. The limits to the growth of government come primarily from forces within, rather than from without. As discussed in chapter 6, the constrained welfare state has many causes. Today, we can add globalization as a contributing cause, but not the determining one.

Furthermore, the dictates of globalization for the Anglo-American world in respect to multiversities are to *increase* public spending on education and research rather than reduce it. As global capitalism distributes production across the world, taking advantage of low-wage countries, the developed world must rely on securing high-skill components of the production process. In addition, advanced research and the commercialization of new ideas drive the productivity growth of developed nations. Both require more investment in multiversities, not less. The public sector may not supply all of the funds, but the multiversity is rising in importance with globalization.

Critics of globalization often argue that it is an American-led process, that it will force other countries to adopt an American-style welfare state, and that it will shrink the welfare state because the American welfare state is smaller than that of most other developed countries. The American public sector, however, spends more on universities than other countries. Paradoxically, to match the American model would mean that governments, including those of Canada and England, would have to spend *much more* on their multiversities.

There is another paradox. Globalization pits nation against nation to reduce tax rates, but it also pits nation against nation to attract high technology firms, advanced services firms, and highly skilled knowledge workers. Nations with a well-developed welfare state – with stable inclusive societies, good schools, hospitals, universities, public amenities, and infrastructure – are better able to attract firms and people.[22] Low taxes per se do not attract firms, because low taxes mean low levels of public services. Rather, firms and people are attracted by the right balance and mix of taxes and services.

Many critics of globalization argue that it is infusing the ideology of market fundamentalism into society and into the university. Charles W. Smith begins his essay, 'Globalization, Higher Education, and Markets,' by stating that 'globalization is understood by most people to entail an ever increasing dominance of markets and market ideology worldwide. In the case of higher education, this dominance is formulated in numerous ways, including commodification of education, greater reliance upon corporate management styles, greater sensitivity to "customer" interests, and "bottom-line" decision making.'[23]

Again, there is much merit in the criticism: globalization does spread market fundamentalism, and market fundamentalism corrupts the ideals of the university. But globalization is not the only explanation for the spread of market fundamentalism, nor is it the primary explanation. Worries about market values corrupting higher education go back at least to Thorstein Veblen in the early twentieth century. Market values are also being spread by the critique of the welfare state, by demands to use efficiently the limited resources of the university, and by the pressures to commercialize university research. The late 1990s were certainly filled with market triumphalism, but the mood has been tempered. The benefits of government action are part of the discussion, again, both in national affairs and international affairs.[24]

One aspect of market fundamentalism is new, however. Current globalization has, indeed, speeded up 'the commodification of education.' In 1995, the General Agreement on Trade in Services (GATS), a treaty of the WTO, came into force. GATS establishes a multilateral regime for trade in services, including educational services, just as the General Agreement on Tariffs and Trade established the multilateral regime for trade in goods. All members of the WTO (149 countries in December 2005) are bound by GATS and have committed themselves to undertake negotiations on specific issues and to enter successive rounds of negotiations to progressively liberalize trade in services. The first round of negotiations was to begin by 2000 and be completed by 2005, but the latter deadline has not been met. The final implications of placing higher education under GATS are still unclear, in part because under GATS each country must make explicit commitments for free trade in each type of service and can place limitations and conditions on market access. Many nations have been reluctant to consider education a 'commodity' and to consider 'trade' in education as the same thing as trade in commodities like manufactured goods, and so they have been reluctant to make specific commitments under GATS regarding education. Although the final results remain to be seen, it is clear that fundamental change is afoot. 'GATS seeks to establish "open markets" for knowledge products of all kinds – including higher education. The idea behind GATS and, for that matter, behind globalization is that knowledge is a commodity like any other and should be freely traded around the world. The proponents argue that free trade will benefit everyone by permitting competition in the market of ideas and knowledge products.'[25] The controversy over international trade in education has been further provoked by the spectre of for-profit educational institutions delivering education over the World Wide Web and disrupting the domestic university system of a country. Under GATS, foreign providers must be treated in the same manner as domestic providers. A coalition of university associations from the United States, Canada, and Europe has signed a declaration asserting that 'higher education exists to serve the public interest and is not a "commodity," ... Given this public mandate, authority to regulate higher education must remain in the hands of competent bodies as designated by any given country. Nothing in international trade agreements should restrict or limit this authority in any way.'[26]

We should not, however, overstate the implications for the multiversity of the Anglo-American world as a result of these thrusts of globalization.[27] It is true that globalization has reduced national sovereignty, helped to constrain the welfare state, reinforced the ideology of market fundamentalism, and supports the logic of analysing education as a commodity to be traded. But globalization makes other calls upon the multiversity. Globalization requires higher spending on universities and calls upon the scholars of the multiversity to better understand other nations and cultures and also to explain the turbulent dynamics of globalization. Education and research become more valuable with globalization. The challenge is to realize the opportunities without sacrificing the ideals.

Cleavages between Nations after the Cold War

To characterize any world order, we must not only describe its political systems and its economic systems, as we have done so far. We must also identify the crucial cleavages, particularly the cleavages that create the possibilities of war. Perhaps because of its comfortable liberal internationalism, the writing about the multiversity and globalization has not taken up this question (although, in contrast, this is the focus of a major strand of the political science literature about globalization). But we cannot properly comprehend contemporary globalization unless we recognize that it involves the political-military world order that has replaced the Cold War as the basic cleavage between countries. The open questions today are: What is this political-military world order that has replaced the Cold War? What are the crucial cleavages in the new world order that might lead to war? Only as we analyse these issues can we begin to understand the full implications of globalization for the multiversities of the Anglo-American world.

Many writers have attempted to capture the essence of the world order in place since the Cold War. Each attempt, though deeply flawed, does distil something of the disorienting essence of globalization. Our age of globalization is complex and turbulent, driven by a multitude of conflicting forces. How are we to understand it? Here we can see how multiversity research – especially ideas from professors in the social sciences – constructs the world. There is no objective reality. The research of the social scientists seeks to characterize crucial aspects of the infinite complexity of social life. Through their terminology and analysis, social scientists construct our world and make meaning for us.

The first, and still most controversial writer in this context, is Francis Fukuyama, who argued in 1989 that 'a remarkable consensus concerning the legitimacy of liberal democracy as a system of government had emerged throughout the world over the past few years, as it conquered rival ideologies like hereditary monarchy, fascism, and most recently communism. More than that, [he] argued that liberal democracy may constitute the "end point of mankind's ideological evolution" and the "final form of human government," and as such constituted the "end of history."'[28] Fukuyama did not mean that all history would end, in the sense that there would be no more important events, no more change. Rather, he meant that history could be read as a coherent evolutionary process that would end 'when mankind had achieved a form of society that satisfied its deepest and most fundamental longings.' Fukuyama maintains that modernization inevitably involves acceptance of the logic of science and the logic of free markets as the means to satisfy mankind's economic needs and longings. But we are not simply economic beings. We also, he argues, struggle 'to be recognized as a human being, that is, as a being with a certain worth and dignity.' Previous political orders divided man into a relationship of lordship and bondage, but Fukuyama argues that we have reached the end stage of history where liberal democracy solves 'the question of recognition by replacing the relationship of lordship and bondage with universal and equal recognition.'[29] Fukuyama believes that war is fundamentally driven by the desire for recognition, anger at lack of recognition, and the desire to be recognized as greater than others. If liberal democracy solves the problem of recognition, 'a world made up of liberal democracies, then, should have much less incentive for war, since all nations would reciprocally recognize the other's legitimacy.'[30]

Fukuyama's analysis omits too much. It has little to say about the power of clan and religion, military superiority, inequality across the globe, or environmental insecurity, and how these might lead to war. Nevertheless, his analysis should not be cavalierly dismissed. His work does highlight something about the recent evolution of political and economic systems, whether or not it is yet a consensus, never seen before in history. His description of the end point of ideological evolution and the final form of government may not be so controversial – for they are laid out in the U.N.'s Universal Declaration of Human Rights.

When stated as boldly as by Fukuyama, the end-of-history view is condemned as naive and hopelessly western in bias. However, although we might refuse to admit it, the end-of-history view is implicit in much of the liberal internationalist spirit within the multiversity. This is the spirit of the international republic of science, international student exchange, international research collaboration, and cross-cultural understanding. To the extent that Fukuyama's view is correct, the multiversity will flourish with the end of history.

Thomas L. Friedman, a foreign affairs columnist for the *New York Times*, and author of the widely read book, *The Lexus and the Olive Tree: Understanding Globalization*, shares much with Fukuyama. But where Fukuyama sees consensus and stability, Friedman sees cleavage and turbulence. Friedman says the Cold War order was the economy of Karl Marx and John Maynard Keynes, whereas now we have globalization and the economy of Joseph Schumpeter. This globalization brings Schumpeter's waves of creative destruction and Silicon Valley's 'next killer app.' It is a world where 'innovation replaces tradition. The present – or perhaps the future – replaces the past. Nothing matters so much as what will come next, and what will come next can only arrive if what is here now gets overturned.'[31] And so globalization creates a cleavage, between the Lexus and the olive tree. The Lexus is a luxury car, the fruit of global capitalism. It represents an age-old human drive – 'for sustenance, improvement, prosperity and modernization – as it is played out in today's globalization system. The Lexus represents all the burgeoning global markets, financial institutions and computer technologies with which we pursue higher living standards today.'[32] But globalization uproots the olive trees of our lives. 'Olive trees are important. They represent everything that roots us, anchors us, identifies us and locates us in this world – whether it be belonging to a family, a community, a tribe, a nation, a religion, or most of all a place called home. Olive trees are what give us the warmth of family, the joy of individuality, the intimacy of personal rituals, the depth of private relationships, as well as, the confidence and security to reach out and encounter others ... One reason the nation-state will never disappear, even if it does weaken, is because it is the ultimate olive tree – the ultimate expression of whom we belong to – linguistically, geographically and historically.'[33]

Where is the multiversity in Friedman's globalization? Does it support the Lexus or the olive tree? The multiversity would rather not be asked, and it has not reflected critically upon itself. There are, of course, ways in which it supports both. It is obvious how it helps to build the Lexus, and we hope it does not plough up the olive trees. Humanist scholars in the Anglo-American multiversities study the languages, literatures, histories, and cultures of other nations – often in celebration and respect, and in solidarity with those who resist their denigration or destruction. But these scholars have not always escaped a perhaps-inadvertent Orientalism. Also, multiversity professors author some of the most insightful and strident criticism of globalization's effects on the olive tree. Nonetheless, the multiversity is an agent of globalization; it leads to the triumph of reason, science, and technology over tradition. The international republic of science connects people across nations, but the conversation uses a lingua franca. Mathematics and the scientific method provide the lingua franca, but English accompanies them. The development of the modern university has meant the marginalization of religion within its precincts. The multiversity should recognize that it is part of globalization, and in doing so it must recognize that it is part author of the discontents. On balance, the multiversity does less to support the olive tree.

Benjamin R. Barber, of Rutgers University, diagnoses a cleavage similar to what Friedman sees – between tradition and modernity – but he sees an aberration in each. Barber's cleavage is between Jihad and McWorld, and both threaten democracy. Both thrive in a global order untempered by the democratic sovereignty of people, as exercised in the nation state and in international institutions. Barber published his eerily prescient book, *Jihad vs McWorld*, in 1995. It begins by asserting: 'History is not over ... The collapse of state communism has not delivered people to a safe democratic haven.' He envisions tumult and chaos, quoting Yeats: 'the centre will not hold, mere anarchy is loosed upon the world.' Barber sees our very human pursuit of material comfort degenerating under a rush of unregulated capitalist forces that produce a mediocre uniformity and 'that mesmerize peoples everywhere with fast music, fast computers, and fast food – MTV, Macintosh, and McDonald's – pressing nations into one homogeneous global theme park, one McWorld.'[34] Simultaneously, our very human struggle to preserve our particularities of language, religion, tribe, and nation degenerates and 'holds out the grim prospect of a retribalization of large swaths of humankind by war and bloodshed: a threatened balkanization of nation-states in which culture is pitted against culture, people against people, tribe against tribe, a Jihad in the name of a hundred narrowly conceived faiths.'[35]

It is easy to claim that the multiversity stands against both McWorld and Jihad, but it is hard to believe it will flourish in their chaotic clashing world. Barber argues that McWorld and Jihad can be found often in the same country at the same time, for example, there is both Jihad and McWorld in the United States (as they are both in Iraq), locked in a powerful and paradoxical dialectic. 'Yet, Jihad and McWorld have this in common: they both make war on the sovereign nation-state's democratic institutions. Each eschews civil society and belittles democratic citizenship, neither seeks alternative democratic institutions ... Jihad forges communities of blood rooted in exclusion and hatred, communities that slight democracy in favour of tyrannical paternalism or consensual tribalism. McWorld forges global markets rooted in consumption and profit, leaving to an untrustworthy, if not altogether fictitious, invisible hand issues of public interest and common good that once might have been nurtured by democratic citizenries and their watchful governments.'[36] The multiversity is an institution of democracy; if democracy is degraded by these cleavages of globalization, so is the multiversity.

Barber's book was published before 11 September 2001, before Islamic Jihadists terrorized the United States by converting passenger airliners into missiles and striking the twin towers of the World Trade Center in New York City. Thus, it predates the American-defined war on terrorism and the American-led invasions of Afghanistan and of Iraq.

It is too soon to know whether the essential character of the world order after the Cold War has now become a war between the United States (and certain allies) and Islamic terrorism. It is too soon to understand the long-run implications of the invasions of Afghanistan in 2001 and Iraq in 2003. Nonetheless, the true nature of the new order may now be revealing itself. Some writers attempting to capture the essence of globalization after the invasion of Iraq have identified a new theme: American empire. What will be the place of the multiversity if the world order after the Cold War is, indeed, organized as the American Empire?

In this view, the current period becomes understood as an extension of the world order after 1945, a period in which the United States, by both design and inadvertence, was building an empire. The nations within the empire were not bound together by proconsuls from the imperial centre; rather they were bound together by free markets, liberal democratic governance, and mass culture under the umbrella of U.S. military power. With the collapse of authoritarian state socialism and many military dictatorships, the American empire has become supreme across the world. The twenty-first century may well be the American century, the century of the American Empire, binding nations together and policed by the American military.

Given its enormous power, the United States can shed any constraints on its sovereignty – it can withdraw its support from multilateral organizations and pursue its interests unilaterally. It could renew its military to ensure that its military superiority can never be challenged. Military supremacy would be based upon technological superiority, especially in information technology, and allow projection of power across the world with minimal use of military manpower. This line of strategic thinking entered the White House with the appointment of many of its proponents to senior positions in the administration of President George W. Bush. Then on 11 September 2001, the

American empire was attacked at its very heart. Swiftly, the new strategic thinking was integrated into American policy, as revealed in the presidential document of September 2002 entitled, *The National Security Strategy of the United States of America*, and in what has become known as the Bush doctrine.

With the end of the Cold War, the document reads, 'the United States possesses unprecedented – and unequalled – strength and influence in the world,' but there is a new threat, the threat of terrorism. And it is no longer a threat, it is a war. 'The United States of America is fighting a war against terrorists of global reach ... The struggle against terrorism is different from any other war in our history. It will be fought on many fronts against a particularly elusive enemy over an extended period of time.' 'The U.S. national security strategy will be based on a distinctly American internationalism that reflects the union of our values and our interests.'[37] The Bush doctrine declares that the United States will never allow its military superiority to be challenged as it was in the Cold War, it will rely on pre-emption rather than deterrence and containment to deal with rogue states that might provide terrorists with weapons of mass destruction, and although it will seek the help of allies, it will not hesitate to act unilaterally. This strategy was implemented in the 2003 invasion of Iraq.

The United States sees itself not just in a struggle, but at war. It is a war that will last a long time. President Bush declared to the world: 'You are with us or you are with the terrorists.' Those who do not support the United States must suffer the consequences.

It is far too early to foretell the outcome as the U.S. national security strategy works itself out and the world reacts. No doubt American 'actions' will be met by 'equal-and-opposite reactions' by countries such as Russia or China, or Iran and Syria, and their initiatives to counter American influence. Also, the threat of terrorism continues – there have now been terrorist bombings in England and plans discovered for such attacks in Canada – and another terrorist attack within the United States could set off a violent and unpredictable dynamic. This cleavage of globalization ruthlessly exposes the too-comfortable liberal internationalism of multiversities.

The Anglo-American multiversities face a dilemma both because they are parts of individual nations and because they are within the American empire. Many of their international activities are financed by their national governments. Multiversities are always 'representatives' of their nation states in international connections, and therefore their institutional autonomy is constrained in international affairs. It is easier for the multiversity to be autonomous from the nation state in national affairs than in international affairs. Located in the heart of the empire, Anglo-American multiversities become 'representatives' of the empire – whether they wish to be or not.

The dilemmas of being a university within the empire multiply when the empire is at war, because war demands obedience and loyalty, not autonomy and criticism. Academic freedom is curtailed. How will the multiversity react when a security agency asks about the travels and publications of a faculty member or about the finances and e-mail of, say, an Arab foreign student? It can demur, but what if the request carries the force of wartime law? The threat of terrorism has made us afraid, and it threatens academic freedom. We should recall an earlier threat to academic freedom, the threat in Darwin's day and the plaintive reflection: 'we are literally afraid of the world in which we live.' Fear can restrict academic freedom in ways both subtle and overt. Michael Ignatieff, then of Harvard University, a human rights liberal, yet a supporter of the invasion of Iraq, and author of *The Lesser Evil: Political Ethics in an Age of Terror*, has argued that the chief impact of terrorism on liberal democracy has been to strengthen executive power – the power of presidents and prime ministers – at the expense of courts, the legislature, and a free press. Democracy is not just majority rule, balanced by minority rights. It is also checks and balances, system of 'adversarial justification' of executive measures by legislatures, courts, and a free press.[38] Ignatieff might easily have added, as part of the system of adversarial justification, the research of university professors. Have the multiversity's professors fallen back from their roles in adversarial justification? The crucial role of multiversities in democracy is being threatened by the cleavages on the war of terrorism.

The war on terrorism, the war in Iraq, and the related Israel-Palestine conflict, have brought explicit threats to academic freedom not seen for a long time. Students and professors shout each other down at campus events. The world of e-mail and websites brings new threats. A most controversial American example is Campus Watch, a pro-Israel website. It declares it will 'monitor and gather information on professors who fan the flames of disinformation, incitement and ignorance.' This website encourages students to monitor and report on their professors – all allegedly in the name of accuracy and good scholarship,[39] words that could have come from Orwell's *1984*. In another controversial example, in Britain, a pro-Palestinian coalition of professors led the

Association of University Teachers to support a boycott of two Israeli universities (now overturned by a counter-coalition).

Another provocative and controversial characterization of the political-military order after the Cold War has recaptured much attention. In 1996, Samuel P. Huntington of Harvard University published *The Clash of Civilizations and the Remaking of World Order*. In that book he advances a provocative thesis: 'spurred by modernization, global politics is being reconfigured along cultural lines ... Alignments defined by ideology and superpower relations are giving way to alignments defined by culture and civilization.'[40] 'In the emerging era, clashes of civilizations are the greatest threat to world peace, and an international order based on civilizations is the surest safeguard against world war ... The avoidance of major intercivilizational wars requires core states to refrain from intervening in conflicts of other civilizations. This is a truth which some states, particularly the United States, will undoubtedly find difficult to accept.'[41] Clearly, President Bush has not heeded Huntington's warning. Influential, widely read, and widely condemned, nonetheless, the book reminds us of certain realities that we might just as soon forget. These realities can be accepted without accepting Huntington's larger thesis. Several are germane to multiversities.

Multiversities are most comfortable in the world of liberal internationalism and rather too easily have supported the ideal of globalization creating shared values and institutions across the world. Huntington astutely skewers this way of thinking with the title of 'the Davos Culture': 'Each year about a thousand businessmen, bankers, governments officials, intellectuals, and journalists from scores of countries meet in the World Economic Forum in Davos, Switzerland. Almost all these people hold university degrees in the physical sciences, social sciences, business, or law, work with words and/or numbers, are reasonably fluent in English, are employed by governments, corporations, and academic institutions with extensive international involvement, and travel frequently outside their own country. They generally share beliefs in individualism, market economies, and political democracy.'[42] The multiversity is part of the Davos Culture. Huntington's first point is that the Davos Culture is not nearly as widespread or influential as supposed. 'It is far from a universal culture, and the leaders who share in the Davos Culture do not necessarily have a secure grip on power in their own societies.'[43]

Huntington's next two points are interrelated. One is the rise of religious belief, especially religious fundamentalism. 'The Westphalian separation of religion and international politics, an idiosyncratic product of Western civilization, is coming to an end,'[44] and religion will increasingly intrude into international affairs. The other is that political ideology as a basis of identity and commitment is being replaced by culturally based forms of identity and commitment. Cultures continue to differ even as modernization and democratization proceed. A world divided by religion and cultural identity is a world less hospitable to the multiversity and its values.

Another point made by Huntington is one that the secular internationalism of the multiversity has refused to recognize. The accepted liberal analysis is that religious fundamentalism and Jihadism are the product of ignorance, poverty, and despair. Huntington argues that fundamentalists more often belong to the more modern sectors of the middle class. Islamic activists 'probably include a disproportionately large number of the best-educated and most intelligent young people of their respective populations, including doctors, lawyers, engineers, scientists, teachers, and civil servants.'[45] The spread of universities does not necessarily secularize, bring homogeneity, or even cultural understanding.

Finally, Huntington's, analysis offers a salutary rebuke to those who see globalization as a move to western universalism. (Paradoxically, the antiglobalization movement accepts that western values and institutions are being spread universally – but they protest and resist it.) Huntington argues that globalization does not impose western values and institutions. He sees the west not as ascendant, but as in decline compared with resurgent civilizations. He demands that we recognize, for example, the power of China and India. Together they represent one-third of the world's population. Their economies are growing at 8 to 10 per cent per year, more than double the rate of the American and European economies. Any characterization of the new world order that does not incorporate this reality is myopic, indeed. Both China and India are investing huge amounts of money in their elite universities, and these universities will become major forces of globalization in ways that we cannot yet anticipate.

Multiversities have within themselves both a tendency to accept western universalism and a desire to respect global cultural diversity. These have coexisted in dialectical tension though out the history of universities. Globalization after 1989 has severely disrupted and complicated the dialectic. In the world order after the Cold War, the multiversity has drifted more towards western universalism. Managing these dialectics in an era of terrorism and religious fundamentalism is one of the greatest challenges to the multiversity brought by globalization.

Citizenship, National Culture, and Cosmopolitan Democracy

Globalization affects not only the world order in which the multiversity participates, but also the nation state in which each multiversity lives.

Our modern ideas of citizenship and the modern nation state were established at the same time and evolved together in the Westphalian system. A citizen could find both identity and community in the nation state. To be a citizen has meant to belong to the community of the nation state, a community defined over a specific geographical territory. Citizenship brought both rights and obligations. The rights of citizenship included (following Marshall's typography) civil rights, political rights, and social rights. The nation state has been the basis of political participation and obligation; it provided the structure for democracy. The citizen owed loyalty to the nation state and obedience to its laws. The good citizen, even in minimalist conceptions, is politically engaged, votes, and serves on juries. In more expansive conceptions, the good citizen gives priority to the public good over private interest, is civil and tolerant, and engages in active deliberation within the community. After the Second World War, a new bond between the citizen and the nation state was formed in the welfare state. Throughout all its history, the nation state has fostered a sense of national identity and worked to sustain and create a national culture. The national culture – the nation's language, history, stories, and myths – provides identity to members of the territorial community. The national culture is a source of the bonds of solidarity and the willingness to consider the common good over the private good. Some would argue that without these bonds of solidarity, democracy cannot function.

To all of this, universities have always been intimately connected. The university has always been an institution of the nation state, a contributor to nation-building, and an important institution in the democratic life of a country. It has preserved, enhanced, and transmitted the national culture, particularly through the undergraduate curriculum of a liberal education. Also through undergraduate liberal education, it has prepared students for democratic citizenship.

Globalization disintegrates this territorially bounded national community. People move in and out with ease. Social solidarity is harder to maintain. Partially because it is less able to do so, and partially in deference to the requirements of transnational capitalism, the nation state no longer so vigorously seeks to sustain a 'national' culture. Forces from outside the territory disrupt and disturb. The welfare state is constrained, less able to provide economic security, social insurance, and social services, and so the bond between citizen and government becomes weakened. Citizens begin to see their rights as grounded less in the nation state and more as grounded in universal human rights. Globalization opens means for political participation outside the nation state. Citizens can find their identity and community in groups beyond the territory; the World Wide Web makes possible even 'virtual communities' that have no territory whatsoever.

As globalization disintegrates the territorially bounded nation state, disrupting conceptions of citizenship, culture, and national community, so it disrupts the multiversity. This disruption is what Bill Readings addresses in his book, *The University in Ruins*, when he writes that the raison d'être of the university was the national cultural mission but 'the University is becoming a different kind of institution, one that is no longer linked to the nation-state by virtue of its role as producer, protector, and inculcator of the idea of national culture.'[46] The question is then: What sort of institution will it become under the pressures of globalization. Readings sees the university becoming 'a bureaucratically organized and relatively autonomous consumer-oriented corporation.'[47]

This can be rejected as too pessimistic. It is unlikely that globalization will transform the multiversity into an autonomous consumer-oriented corporation. But Readings does raise a fundamental point: the multiversity may no longer have a national cultural mission. The multiversity must confront the question of whether it will remain a national institution, or through globalization be decoupled from the nation state and transformed into a transnational institution. Although their leaders will deny it, many of the elite multiversities of the Anglo-American world are disengaging from their national culture and their nation state.

In many dimensions, the disengagement is understandable and innocent enough. Multiversities recruit students from all over the world, especially at the graduate level. A high percentage of foreign graduate students is taken as a measure of the institution's eminence. Multiversities are forming joint degree programs, where students and faculty move between campuses. Multiversities now aggressively pursue their fundraising outside the country. Foreign trips to meet alumni (and to raise money) are a regular part of the president's or vice-chancellor's agenda. Research grants regularly come from agencies outside the country, and research contracts are with international corporations as well as with national corporations. The world of research has always been international, but globalization – with its ease of communication and relatively unrestricted movement of people – is transforming the organization of international scholarship. Research teams work as networks, with nodes at multiversities around the world. All these attenuate the national connection of the multiversity, although merely continuing long-standing trends.

In other dimensions, the disengagement is more disruptive. Multiversities are part of the university system in their countries and historically have situated themselves within that system, formed consortia within the system, and judged themselves against other universities within the national system. However, elite multiversities are pulling away from the national system of higher education. They are situating themselves among the multiversities of other countries, competing against them, and judging themselves against them, although often engaging in joint initiatives with them: their benchmarks are the world's best multiversities.

This global competition brings new resentments and complexity into the national system of higher education. Although this top tier is breaking away from the national system, at the same time these multiversities lobby for special funding from their national governments, arguing that they need more resources to compete internationally, to be the equal of the world's leaders. These arguments have been part of the rhetoric of the Russell Group of multiversities in the United Kingdom. The claims for special treatment strain national resources, particularly in countries outside the United States. Because American multiversities have more resources, international competition forces other countries to try to match these resources, but such support can only go to a few strategically chosen multiversities in each country. Globalization reinforces the hierarchy of multiversities within national systems of higher education and fosters divisive competition.

Most fundamentally, the decline of the national cultural mission and the disengagement from the nation state threatens the traditional place of the humanities and, indeed, perhaps the place of a liberal education itself. Globalization may have profound ramifications for the curriculum of liberal education at the multiversity. What sort of citizenship is involved – are we to make students national citizens or citizens of the world? Is it meaningful or desirable to think of a national culture? Does the traditional argument for the role of the humanities in developing the national culture and citizenship still hold? Will liberally educated students be engaged in national democratic life? These questions will be part of the debates about liberal education in an era of globalization and are taken up in chapter 12.

The multiversity is becoming less and less a national institution and more and more a transnational institution. Of course, the multiversity will not completely divorce itself from the nation state, but the shift is significant. Ambivalence and turbulence will characterize the years ahead. The leadership of the multiversity will need to be sensitive to this shift in the ongoing renegotiation of the social contract, particularly because the fundamental support for the multiversity still comes from within the nation state.

The concepts of citizenship and democracy are disrupted in our era of globalization. Globalization weakens the bond between citizen and nation state and offers diminished opportunities for democratic participation because the nation state is unable to control the processes of globalization. How then can the multiversity make its contributions to citizenship and democracy in a globalized world? To answer this question, we must move beyond the multiversity's traditional association with the nation state. Even as globalization weakens national citizenship and diminishes national democracy, globalization opens up new conceptions of democracy. Among the most important of these is the idea of cosmopolitan democracy, and it is here that the multiversity will find its new role in an era of globalization.

We think of a cosmopolitan as someone who has lived and travelled in many countries, is sophisticated in the appreciation of each, and most especially, is someone who is free of national prejudices.[48] The adjective 'cosmopolitan' can apply to values that transcend the boundaries of local community or nation. For example, the international human rights movement declares that there are cosmopolitan values, and these are articulated in the U.N.'s Universal Declaration of Human Rights. A cosmopolitan citizen is a citizen, not of a city or nation, but of the world. A cosmopolitan democracy is based upon cosmopolitan values and calls upon citizens to respond in ways that respect the inherent dignity of all human beings.

The growing interest in cosmopolitan democracy arises precisely because of globalization. It becomes possible because of the collapse of the communist alternative and because of the global spread of human rights ideals. It becomes urgent because the democracy of the nation state is curtailed by globalization. Economic globalization compels nations to deregulate economic activity and limit the welfare state, while global problems transcend the territory of the nation state. David Held, of the London School of Economics and a leading theorist of cosmopolitan democracy, writes: 'In the liberal democracies, consent to government and legitimacy for government action are dependent upon electoral politics and the ballot.' But this notion becomes problematic as soon as the 'relevant community' is questioned. 'What is the proper constituency, and proper realm of jurisdiction, for developing and implementing policy with respect to health issues such as AIDS or BSE, the use of nuclear energy, the management of nuclear wastes, or the harvesting of rainforests?'[49] As problems go beyond national borders and the outcomes of decisions stretch beyond national borders, serious questions arise for democratic theory and practice. 'At issue is the nature of a constituency (how should the boundaries of a constituency be drawn?), the meaning of representation (who should represent whom and on what basis?), and the proper form ... of political participation (who should participate and in what way?).'[50] This is the world in which the multiversity must rethink its democratic role.

Held and other like theorists argue that globalization necessitates the development of cosmopolitan democracy. But, he also argues that a world government analogous to a nation state, or a world federation of nation states, is not the solution. A cosmopolitan democracy does not replace the nation state, rather it complements it. Cosmopolitan democracy builds upon the existing principles of liberal democracy within nation states and upon the existing political principles of the international order (international law and human rights). 'Advocating a "double democratization" of political life, the advocates of cosmopolitan democracy seek to reinvigorate democracy within states by extending it to the public realm between and across states. Supranational democracy and territorial democracy are conceived as mutually reinforcing, rather than conflicting, principles of political rule. Cosmopolitan democracy seeks "a political order of democratic associations, cities, and nations as well as regions and global networks." ... The aim is not to establish a world system of government, but rather "a global and divided authority system – a system of diverse law and overlapping power centers shaped and delimited by democratic law."'[51] The precise shape of a cosmopolitan democracy is not yet known, and is not knowable, given how many separate institutions are involved and each responding in its own specific way.

The multiversity and the international scholarly community should be deeply involved in achieving a cosmopolitan democracy. The multiversity must find a place in this 'double democratization,' invigorating both national and international life, with loyalties to both. This will not be easy because cosmopolitanism is not always popular at home. Nationalists, populists, and ordinary folks are always suspicious of the cosmopolitan. But the multiversity is well suited to this dual role.

Cosmopolitan democracy involves a major role for civil society, that is, for organizations that are part of neither the political order nor the economic order. The multiversity is such an organization. Democracy is not just about voting and political representation. Democracy is also about public discussion, particularly public discussion using generally accepted rules of debate and evidence. Professors can contribute enormously to the transnational deliberation required for a cosmopolitan democracy. Civil society institutions can contribute to solving problems that cross state boundaries, and it is precisely these problems that increase dramatically with globalization.[52] In the Westphalian system, these cross-state issues are handled by diplomacy between nation states. In cosmopolitan democracy, civil society crosses boundaries and helps to address such problems. Global organizations such as human rights and environmental organizations, or Médecins sans frontières, can raise and discuss issues that cross over the borders of the nation states. The multiversity, a major institution of civil society, can be a forum to involve such organizations, and the research community itself can be the vehicle for transboundary discussion.

Cosmopolitan democracy is not without its critics.[53] Some argue that it remains too committed to the liberal conception of the individual and that it has not provided the moral basis for collective action; others argue that its multilayered system offers no means for democratically adjudicating disputes among the actors. Some point out that the institutions of civil society have not solved their own problems of democratic representation and participation; others claim that the concept of cosmopolitan democracy diverts attention from the democratic nation state, which is and will remain the basis for identity, community, and political participation. Finally, some critics point out that cosmopolitan democracy is a western construct, a construct that ignores the reality of U.S. dominance in the world order, and merely legitimates a new form of imperialism. If the multiversity is to recognize and accept a role in cosmopolitan democracy, it must understand and confront these criticisms. It cannot simply see cosmopolitanism as a continuation of liberal internationalism.

Globalization profoundly disrupts the Westphalian system of territorially bounded nation states and with it the conceptions of citizenship, national culture, and democracy. Because the multiversity is a creature of the Westphalian system and the nation state, and because it has always had special responsibilities regarding citizenship, culture, and democratic life within the nation, it too, is profoundly disrupted. The multiversity cannot escape the disruption. The multiversity's evolution will be shaped by how it navigates the turbulence and by how it manages the tensions between its national identity and its cosmopolitan identity.

Looking Ahead to Part Three

The university is a medieval creation that has evolved through history and is still evolving. In the second half of the twentieth century, a new and distinctive form of university emerged across the Anglo-American world – the multiversity. James Duderstadt described the multiversity as the top of the evolutionary ladder of the higher education ecosystem. But what lies ahead for the multiversity? Part Two has been an exploration of the character of our age, most particularly the crucial ideas of our age: the constrained welfare state, the information technology revolution, postmodern thought, commercialization, and globalization. These will drive the evolution of the multiversity in the years ahead. The question, and indeed the worry, is what will the multiversity look like in twenty years, as it adapts to these ideas of our age? Virtually everyone who writes about the university regards the past with pride and the future with apprehension and sees the challenge for the multiversity as adapting to the character of our age while remaining true to its core ideals. This apprehension is surely warranted.

The multiversity is a great unwieldy bundle. Our age brings centrifugal forces as never before, and the bonds that hold together the multiversity are weakening, especially under the relentless pressures of constrained finances. The applied sciences, engineering, and medicine are positioned to flourish because they contribute most obviously to economic prosperity and can better survive the increased reliance on tuition fees and private donations. The multiversities with leadership in these fields may further differentiate themselves and become the top of the evolutionary ladder. Many of the professions are equally well positioned to flourish, and professional education related to career is well suited to using the new information technologies. Some professional schools may split away. In contrast, the humanities and social sciences are struggling, their contributions to economic prosperity becoming less clear. Tensions within the multiversity may become severe if teaching loads and salary levels differ greatly across its waxing and waning parts. A great challenge for the senior administration and for the entire collegium will be to mitigate these tensions. It will require that the multiversity support with its own resources some areas – most especially the humanities – threatened by external forces. But the bundle is unlikely to break apart.

A more likely outcome will be an increasingly obvious hierarchy within the multiversities – a greater division between the well-off and the less well-off. Fundraising will significantly help only a few institutions, likewise the revenues from patents and licences. Governments, given limited resources, will concentrate those resources on a few selected institutions. Some multiversities will make wise strategic choices and flourish, while others, through poor choices or inaction, will decline. Globalization brings the pressures of international competition that will reinforce this new hierarchy. There will be fewer institutions atop the ecosystem in each country, and an international elite will emerge; indeed, it is already quite visible.

Perhaps this hierarchy is desirable. It need not mean that our society and our students are ill-served. The real apprehension is that as all multiversities evolve, theirs will be a prodigal adaptation, adapting only too well to the ideas of our age and sacrificing the ideals that define the university. Lost will be the pursuit of knowledge for its own sake, the commitment to liberal learning, and to disinterested research. Institutional autonomy and academic freedom will be more apparent than real. The multiversity will shed many of its historic functions to become primarily an institution of the economy. We must not allow this prodigal adaptation. Within the renewed social contract, it is our place to choose.

PART THREE

Renewing the Social Contract

11 The Multiversity and Liberal Democracy

There are many ways to understand the Anglo-American multiversity, its history, and its ideals. I chose to identify four ideas or archetypes of a university and to comprehend the multiversity as a combination of these four ideas of a university in one institution. The first idea is the university as a place of elite undergraduate liberal education – Cardinal Newman's university. The second idea is the university as a place of professional schools, as in the medieval university with its three 'higher' faculties of law, medicine, and theology. The third is the university as a place of graduate education and research – basic research, disinterested, and motivated by pure curiosity, exemplified by the University of Berlin. Finally, there is the university connected to society, like the Scottish universities and the American land grant universities: responsive to government, accessible to all who are qualified and conducting applied research. Chapter 5 added governance as another defining characteristic: a multiversity is an autonomous institution whose professors have academic freedom and which has collegial self-governance on academic matters.

The multiversity, combining these four sometimes conflicting ideas into one conglomerate, emerged to meet the needs of Anglo-American societies in the second half of the twentieth century, a time of great transformation. One transformation was in the economy: ours became postindustrial economies, where advanced learning, theoretical knowledge, and research are crucial. Another transformation was in the polity: our liberal democracies became welfare states, with governments taking on new responsibilities for the well-being of their citizens. Because of these two transformations, the multiversity emerged supported by government financing for mass undergraduate education and for research at multiversities.

The multiversity – this distinctive adaptation of the university to the later twentieth century – has become an institution of centrality and enormous power in society. Not only does it educate many of our undergraduates and most of our professionals and graduates with advanced degrees, it is the centre of society's research enterprise: the multiversity's research is the source of ideas, ideas that matter to our economy, to our democracy, and to our culture. The chapters of Part Two offered case studies of the power of multiversity research, from the laboratories of physicists and computer engineers that power the revolution in information technology, from the seminar rooms of the linguists and humanities professors that reshape our understanding of language, reality, and power, to the writings of economists and political scientists that provide the structure and directions of causation in our understanding of globalization.

The multiversity takes on many tasks for society and receives much financial support from government – they are bound together in a social contract. Yet, today, despite its power and many privileges, the multiversity feels beset and fears that the social contract has been dangerously devalued and attenuated. In our age, it is vital that we re-articulate and re-explore the social contract. In particular, we should recognize that the university in each era is also the trustee of the ideals that it has inherited: the ideals of liberal learning and knowledge for its own sake, of disinterested, curiosity-driven inquiry, and also of academic freedom, accessible education, civic engagement, and contribution to economic and cultural flourishing. The university is trustee for the value of a life of the mind. Will this inheritance be preserved under the pressures of our age?

Here we might recall Eric Ashby's reflections on the history of the university: 'An institution is the embodiment of an ideal. In order to survive, an institution must fulfill two conditions: it must be sufficiently stable to sustain the ideal which gave it birth and sufficiently responsive to remain relevant to the society which supports it. The university is a medieval institution which fulfills both these conditions.'[1] Can the multiversity be sufficiently responsive to our age and yet be sufficiently stable to sustain the ideals which gave it birth? In each age, the social contract must be examined and renewed. The task is especially urgent today.

The five chapters in Part Two of this book examined crucial characteristics of our age and their implications for the multiversity. The future of the multiversity will be determined by how it adapts to the character of our age. Each chapter raised many specific issues that must be addressed in the renewal of the social contract. These specific issues deserve attention in their own right, but will not be reiterated or discussed further here.

Mission Drift

Looking across all the characteristics of our age – across the constrained welfare state, the information technology revolution, postmodern thought, commercialization, and globalization – and their implications for the multiversity, it is clear that something quite fundamental is changing. The character of our age threatens to transform the multiversity and its role in society. The multiversity is drifting, uncertain about the balance among its various tasks and ideals. The multiversity is suffering from mission drift, and our inheritance is at risk.

The greatest change in our age both symbolically and substantively is that there has emerged a new 'idea' of a university, a fifth idea added to this unwieldy conglomerate – the idea of the multiversity as an institution of the economy, bringing together a new way of thinking about the university and a new way of thinking about the economy. This idea of the university as an institution of the economy is becoming dominant, threatening to overwhelm the other ideas.

The mission drift is evident in many other ways. There is less attention to the multiversity's central task of undergraduate education, and in particular, there is less commitment to the idea of a liberal education. Also, the humanities, which once had a special place in liberal learning, are being marginalized both because they do not obviously contribute to economic prosperity and because of the self-criticism of postmodern thought. There is little emphasis on the ideal of citizenship in undergraduate education; instead, we shift towards education that develops skills in an academic discipline. The government's emphasis on economic growth in our globalizing world has moved the multiversity away from basic research and towards applied research. Research has become less disinterested and more motivated by commercial gain. The multiversity is becoming less autonomous and more under the influence of government and business.

This struggle between the ideals of the university and the demands of society is not new. Cardinal Newman sought, in his idea of a university, 'to elevate the university to the moral centre of modern culture and to do so by freeing the university from the grip of utilitarian and hedonistic schools of thought.'[2] Matthew Arnold struggled against the philistinism of the liberal, commercial society of nineteenth-century England. Our age presents these old struggles in a new way.

There is no doubt that the financial pressures of the constrained welfare state contribute to mission drift. As real government support per student declines, the pincers of declining support and increasing needs are squeezing and squeezing. Tuition keeps rising. Multiversities are becoming increasingly reliant on private philanthropy and on contracts with industry to finance their activities, sacrificing their commitment to the disinterested pursuit of knowledge. The need to find new resources preoccupies presidents and vice-chancellors.

Virtually everyone who is deeply committed to the multiversity, when talking about renewal of the social contract, looks first at financial issues: at the financial constraints on multiversities, the need for greater support for research, and the enormous difficulties for students brought by rising tuition. This financial perspective dominates discussion about multiversities today. Every government commission, and every submission by the multiversities to government, every submission by students to the policymakers is dominated by discussion about the constrained finances of the multiversity and how more money is needed to ensure accessibility and to improve quality. Unquestionably, the financial issues are important and *do* belong on the agenda in the renewal of the social contract, even at the top of the agenda. Government must give greater financial support to multiversities; just as tuition must also increase, accompanied by improved financial assistance for students.[3]

Lack of money is not the whole agenda for the renewal of the social contract, however. Such an agenda omits and marginalizes much of what the multiversity does and stands for. Without other items on the agenda, the multiversity is diminished and it atrophies. The emphasis on financial issues does not resist the mission drift; indeed, the reverse is true. Faced with lack of funds, the multiversities, in their appeals for increased support, have used the logic of economic growth as justification: multiversities are crucial to economic prosperity in the twenty-first century, they argue, so please give us more money. The single-minded emphasis on the need for more resources, justified by the multiversity's contributions to economic well-being, only contributes to the drift.

Each of us could create an agenda of what deserves special attention in rethinking the social contract. Here in Part Three, I offer my agenda.

Each of these last two chapters offers an item for special priority. Neither requires additional money. Each emphasizes a mission of the multiversity beyond the economic mission. And together an emphasis on these two missions will help anchor the multiversity against the drift of our age.

The top priority on my agenda is to identify another 'idea' of the university, to establish an additional explicit mission for the multiversity: the multiversity should be identified as an institution of democracy and have a responsibility to contribute to democratic life. This is the subject of this chapter. The second priority on my agenda is renewed attention to undergraduate liberal education. This is the subject of the final chapter. The two are closely connected because much of what I argue should be done regarding undergraduate education flows from the conviction that the multiversity is an institution of democracy.

The Multiversity as an Institution of Democracy

In Part One of this book, I began to explore the role of the multiversity as an institution of our democracy, a role that emerged to significance in the post-1945 transformation of the polity and the creation of the welfare state. Articulating and understanding this democratic role of multiversities should, I believe, be the focus in the social contract for our age. The purpose of this chapter is to draw together and deepen the analysis of multiversities as institutions of democracy and to consider certain implications of this democratic mission, in particular, the implications for research, for professors as public intellectuals, and for the development of deliberative democracy.

Universities have always served society and, after a long period of reluctance, eventually in the twentieth century they became attentive to its increasingly democratic character. Today, however, in the liberal democracy of our knowledge-based society, there has been a qualitative shift, a shift that we have not yet properly recognized or digested. Multiversities should now be regarded as integral institutions of liberal democracy. This requires two changes: a change in how we think about the multiversity and a change in how we think about democracy. It requires a new idea of a university.

When I say that multiversities should be considered institutions of democracy, I do not mean that their internal governance should become more democratic.[4] Nor do I mean that multiversities should give up elite academic standards in pursuit of egalitarianism. Academic work by its nature requires rigorous judgment – the separation of the excellent from the ordinary – and so by its nature is elitist. It must remain so, for indeed the need for high standards within a democracy has never been greater. Nor do I mean that multiversities should do more to support 'progressive' causes. Some professors argue that our democracy has atrophied, that powerful interests have overwhelmed the popular will, and that universities should join in 'progressive' democratic resistance. This is not my argument. To be an institution of democracy does not mean to align with progressive causes. What I do mean, in saying that the multiversity is an institution of democracy, is that to be a democracy a country requires many institutions, and the list of required institutions goes beyond the familiar political institutions of a constitution, universal suffrage, and regular elections. One example of an additional institution is a free press – democracy requires it. Now the multiversity should be regarded as such an additional institution – democracy requires multiversities that have an explicit mission to contribute to democratic life.

We have been slow to highlight the democratic purposes of multiversities. A major colloquium of American university presidents has observed that 'few leaders in research universities today would make [the] claim that their fundamental mission is to serve democracy.'[5] We have been slow for a number of reasons, most obviously because we are acutely aware that the multiversity must remain autonomous from even democratically elected governments.

Perhaps, too, we have not recognized this new idea because political philosophers when they talk about liberal democratic theory do not talk about universities very much. Liberal democracy and the modern university developed during the nineteenth and the first half of the twentieth centuries, sharing many philosophical foundations and complementarities. With the emergence of the multiversity and the welfare state, the many democratic responsibilities of universities in society, albeit implicit rather than explicit, became clearer. Yet, even the most recent presentations of liberal democratic thought do not give any special attention to universities. Remarkably, for example, John Rawls, the most influential liberal theorist of the late twentieth century, makes scant mention of universities, even while developing the concept of public reason.

A notable exception among contemporary political philosophers is Alan Ryan, master of Oxford's New College and author of *Liberal Anxieties and Liberal Education*. Ryan submits that liberalism does not want to preserve, like conservatism, but neither does it want to tear down and build again, like communism. Liberals 'see they are inheritors of traditions they do not themselves want to overthrow, but they want everyone to explore these traditions for themselves.'[6] Liberal democracies realize, Ryan argues, that this liberal freedom brings great dangers. Liberals suffer three great anxieties. The first is that liberalism will lead to cultural disaster, to mediocrity, to what Matthew Arnold called 'the brutalization of the masses.' The second is that liberalism will undermine loyalty to community, and so we shall become unanchored in the world. The third is that liberalism will lead to political violence. 'Liberals have always been on the side of economic, political, and intellectual change; they have hoped that change would culminate in freedom rather than chaos or estrangement, but they have always known that they might unleash forces they could not control.'[7]

Ryan suggests that these anxieties explain the commitment of liberals to a liberal education. Education, in the broad sense, is vital. Liberal education is the buttress against the dangers of mediocrity, of being unanchored in the world, and of political chaos. Liberals seek not just cultivated and tolerant citizens, they want to create an 'educat*ing* society, rather than an educat*ed* society.' They seek 'the transformation of the entire society into a community that was reflective and broadly cultivated, as well as liberally educated in the usual sense.'[8] Ryan says that this emphasis on the entire society also explains why the political philosophy of liberalism deals with liberal learning, but not with the institutions of education, like universities. Nonetheless, a special role for universities, most especially for a liberal undergraduate education, in liberal democratic societies is evident.

Perhaps we should not expect special mention of universities in the writing of political philosophers, because political philosophy proceeds at an abstract, theoretical level. Rather, we should simply accept the fundamental complementarities in outlook of liberal democratic thought and the multiversity. However, now at the beginning of the twenty-first century, the relationship of the multiversity and liberal democracy in postindustrial societies of the Anglo-American world has moved beyond complementarities. The multiversity and democracy are central components of each other. We cannot fully understand a postindustrial democracy without understanding its multiversities; and we cannot fully understand the multiversity without recognizing its crucial role in postindustrial democracy. This must inform our renegotiated social contract.

The argument that multiversities should be considered institutions of democracy interweaves several strands of thought. Much of the argument is positive analysis: the multiversity 'should' be considered as an institution of democracy, as 'a full understanding and interpretation of its emergence and current role' supports the conclusion that the multiversity is an institution of democracy. Other parts of the argument are normative analysis: the multiversity 'should' be considered to be an institution of democracy because this will help anchor the multiversity against mission drift and because this will help to vitalize democratic life.

Most of the positive analysis was developed in Part One. All the tasks of the multiversity – undergraduate education, professional education, graduate education, and research – have a crucial role in the liberal democracy of postindustrial society. Accessible university education is a fundamental commitment of our democracy and essential to ensure equality of opportunity and the rights of social citizenship in the welfare state. A liberal undergraduate education is, in part, an education for democratic citizenship. The multiversities educate our professionals, not just in the old learned professions of theology, law, and medicine, but in all the myriad professions established over the past fifty years. The practice of all professions involves an imbalance between the professional and the client, and virtually all professions have been granted self-regulation rather than being regulated by government. Therefore, in a democratic society, it is important that all professionals be attentive to issues of their clients' interests and the public interest. The multiversity shares the responsibility to educate professionals for this attentiveness, on behalf of our democracy.[9] In our knowledge-based, postindustrial society, the multiversity's professors as public intellectuals contribute scientific, social scientific, and humanistic knowledge to political deliberation and to lifelong learning. Also, the multiversity contributes as critic and conscience in a democratic society. Finally, the multiversity as a research institution, financed by our democratic governments, is crucial in the dynamic of generating the new ideas that so influence our society. The multiversities have a democratic obligation to ask what questions are being studied and to assess the impact of the new knowledge.

In the past, these democratic roles were seen as implicit, but I believe that these democratic roles should now be drawn forward and made explicit. They should be made explicit, first, because the multiversity is publicly supported. But more significantly still, they should be made explicit because the multiversity has become an institution with enormous power in postindustrial welfare states. The education that it provides and the research that it conducts fundamentally shape our society; who gets access to this education, what research questions are studied, and how the results are used are of fundamental importance. In 1967, Daniel Bell provocatively characterized this profound shift when he stated: 'If the business firm was the key institution of the past one hundred years, because of its role in organizing production for the mass creation of products, the university will become the central institution of the next one hundred years because of its role as the new source of innovation and knowledge.'[10] It is not enough to say that under the social contract the multiversity takes on tasks for society, while at the same time it should be autonomous and its professors should have academic freedom, and that any service to democratic life will flow implicitly from the system of governance. These responsibilities to democracy must be articulated and the institution held accountable for how well it fulfils these tasks.

Another strand of the argument is that I believe we need a new idea of a university to combat mission drift and to counteract the power of the idea of a university as an institution of the economy. I do not believe that the idea of the multiversity as an institution of the economy will, or should, go away. Given the nature of our age, given the pace of technological change and the dynamism of globalization, the multiversity must be considered an institution of the economy. As Clark Kerr notes so perceptively, the multiversity is not a reasoned choice among elegant alternatives; it is an imperative rooted in the logic of history.[11] We must face the reality that this new economic idea is legitimate and here to stay: the multiversity is a place to create human capital and to undertake research and then commercialize it. But this is not the only idea of the multiversity. It has been added to the other four ideas in this great conglomerate. I believe that we should add yet another idea – the multiversity as an institution of democracy and that this idea of a university provides needed counterweight to the economic idea.

The final strands the argument come, not as above out of an analysis of the multiversity, but out of an analysis of the meaning of democracy. We begin by asking the general question: What is democracy? And from that follows the practical question: What institutions in a country are necessary for a well-functioning democracy?

What Is Democracy?

All of us have some notion of what democracy is. We know it is 'government by the people and for the people.' We know that the original ideas of democracy came from ancient Greece and the first democratic 'states' were Greek city-states, most famously Athens. We know that a democracy should have universal suffrage and regular elections. Moreover, this seems to be democracy's day. Across the world over the past twenty years, especially since the end of the Cold War, many countries have become democratic and still others are struggling towards democracy.

Let us move beyond these familiar notions to think more carefully about the meaning of democracy and what institutions make a country democratic. Here we turn to the writings of political scientists, a literature that we do not usually read when studying about multiversities but that ought to be included if we are to comprehend fully the multiversity of today. In this brief exploration, I draw upon three recent books by distinguished scholars of democracy: *On Democracy*, by Robert A. Dahl, Sterling Professor of Political Science Emeritus at Yale University; *Democracy: A Very Short Introduction*, by Sir Bernard Crick, emeritus professor of Birkbeck College, University of London; and *Democracy: A Beginner's Guide*, by David Beetham, professor emeritus of politics at the University of Leeds. All these books are quite recent and are written for the general reader, as well as the student of democratic theory and practice. It is revealing that in the past few years there has been an outpouring of writing about democracy. This may be democracy's day, but the ideal has not been realized everywhere and at all times. We have not reached the end of history.

All three of these writers emphasize the distinction between the ideal of democracy and its actual practice, that democracy is always a work in progress, and that democracy has many opponents. We cannot be complacent, and we must always struggle toward the ideal. Whatever our accomplishments, our age is no exception; we must struggle to maintain a vibrant democracy. To identify multiversities as institutions of democracy is part of the struggle to realize the democratic ideal in a knowledge-based society of the twenty-first century.

One chapter in Dahl's book is titled 'What Is Democracy?' He begins with an imagined discussion among a group of people who know they have common goals that they cannot achieve on their own. They hope to attain these goals by working together and so agree to form an asso-

The Multiversity and Liberal Democracy 349

ciation, governed by a constitution, and to make decisions democratically. Dahl writes, such a constitution 'must be in conformity with one elementary principle: that all members are to be treated (under the constitution) as though they were equally qualified to participate in the process of making decisions about the policies the association will pursue.'[12] Thus, a democracy involves a group of people agreeing to make decisions together, although the people are different and will hold different views about what should be done. In democratic decision-making, all members must be *politically equal*.

Dahl sets out five standards that a process governing the association must meet in order to qualify as democratic:

> *Effective participation.* Before a policy is adopted by the association, all members must have equal and effective opportunities for making their views known to other members about what the policy should be.
>
> *Voting equality.* When the moment arrives at which the decision about policy will finally be made, every member must have an equal and effective opportunity to vote, and all votes must be counted as equal.
>
> *Enlightened understanding.* Within reasonable limits as to time, each member must have equal and effective opportunities for learning about the relevant alternative policies and their likely consequences.
>
> *Control of the agenda.* The members must have the exclusive opportunity to decide how and, if they choose, what matters are to be placed on the agenda. Thus the democratic process required by the three preceding criteria is never closed. The policies of the association are always open to change by members, if they so choose.
>
> *Inclusion of adults.* All, or at any rate most, adult permanent residents should have the full rights of citizens that are implied by the first four criteria.'[13]

Dahl then proceeds to discuss the governing processes of democracy when one moves from a small association to a country. In a country, because everyone cannot be part of the policy-making body, democracy requires certain institutions: elected representatives; free, fair, and frequent elections; freedom of expression; access to alternative, independent sources of information; autonomous associations; and inclusive citizenship.

Curiously, Dahl, and likewise Crick and Beetham, say almost nothing about education, about how good citizens are created, or about universities in their discussion of democracy. But, if you read their work in the context of thinking about the mission of the multiversity in society, the importance of the multiversity seems very evident, living as we do in a research-driven, postindustrial world. *Effective participation* surely requires accessible education through to the university level, and *enlightened understanding* surely requires an educated citizenry and professors who speak publicly about their research. The role of the multiversity in ensuring freedom of expression and alternative sources of information is equally clear. Dahl concludes his book with reflections upon current threats to democracy. He worries that traditional institutions of civic education – primary and secondary education, widespread information available through the media, political parties, and interest groups – are proving deficient. Globalization, the increased complexity of issues, and the communications revolution are overwhelming citizens' capacity to engage intelligently in political life. He believes 'these older institutions will need to be enhanced by new means for civic education, political participation, information and deliberation.'[14] Again, the role for the multiversity is clear: it can enhance the older institutions and provide new means for civic education, political participation, information, and deliberation.

It can be argued that all educational theory is at the same time political theory, that any educational philosophy also embodies a political philosophy. Educational theory asks: What kind of person do we seek to create through education? Embedded in this question is another question: What sort of citizen do we want? Most writing on education and democracy has dealt with education of the young, with primary and secondary education.[15] However, we must keep primary and secondary education distinct from university education, because the democratic functions of each are separate.

This distinction is clear in Amy Gutmann's reflections: *Democratic Education*. Intriguingly, she began intending to write a book about liberal education but found her thoughts about liberal education better presented under the title of 'democratic education.' Her work demonstrates that ideas about liberal education are inseparable from ideas about democracy. The book begins: 'When citizens rule in a democracy, they determine among other things, how future citizens will be educated.'[16] There is a process, a conscious process, of social reproduction. One must ask what sort of moral character is to be cultivated, and who should share the authority for how future citizens are to be educated. Following the philosophical precepts of liberalism, she argues that the democratic purpose of primary and secondary education is the development of 'deliberative,' or what she calls interchangeably, 'democratic' character. Such character involves moral reasoning as well as 'the development of capacities for criticism, rational argument, by being taught how to think logically, to argue coherently and fairly, and to consider relevant alternatives before coming to conclusions.' Basic democratic virtues such as toleration, truthfulness, and a predisposition to nonviolence should be inculcated. Also, 'children must learn not just to *behave* in accordance with authority but to *think* critically about authority if they are to live up to the democratic ideal of sharing political sovereignty as citizens.'[17] The responsibility and power to determine the goals and content of primary and secondary education, to determine this conscious process of social reproduction, Gutmann argues, should be shared between parents, the state, and professional educators, but the state has the central role in primary and secondary education in a liberal democracy.

University education has related but different democratic purposes. In contrast to primary and secondary education, university education is not compulsory and involves only a portion of the eligible population. University education relies on the success of primary and secondary education, and should not undertake remediation if lower levels of education have failed to inculcate democratic character. A university education is less explicitly about character formation; 'although learning how to think carefully and critically about political problems, to articulate one's views and defend them before people with whom one disagrees is a form of moral education to which young adults are more receptive and for which universities are well suited.'[18] The university does continue the process of building democratic character, but the fundamental democratic purpose of a university is protection against the tyranny of ideas. Control of the creation of ideas – whether by a majority or a minority – subverts democracy. 'As institutional sanctuaries for free scholarly inquiry, universities can help prevent such subversion. They can provide a realm where new and unorthodox ideas are judged on their intellectual merits; where the men and women who defend such ideas are not strangers but valuable members of the community. Universities thereby serve democracy as sanctuaries of nonrepression.'[19]

Multiversities serve democracy, but paradoxically the authority of elected governments over the multiversity must be highly attenuated. The multiversity's democratic purposes are best served with institutional autonomy and academic freedom. This new idea of a university is well suited to existing principles of governance.

In Gutmann's work we can begin to see a characterization of the educational system as an institution of democracy. The characterization becomes sharper still when we move from a discussion of the general principles that define a democracy and on to examine what institutions are necessary in a country to achieve the democratic ideal in practice. The political science literature identifies three groups of institutions that are necessary for democracy to be realized: citizen rights, the institutions of representative and accountable government, and certain institutions of civil society.[20]

When thinking about the practical reality of democracy in a country, we tend to focus upon the second group of institutions: the institutions of representative and accountable government. A country is judged to be democratic if it has such institutions. The list of institutions in this group includes: a constitution, universal suffrage, regular elections, political parties, the rule of law, an independent judiciary, and so on. In Anglo-American democracies today, we require more than simply the existence and operation of these institutions. We also require that our governments consult the public as policies are being developed, that governments be transparent in how their decisions are reached, and that they be accountable for their decisions. The government's decision-making must be free from corruption or intimidation. The ultimate accountability of government is to the electorate through the ballot box (and this balloting must also be free from corruption, intimidation, or political violence), but accountability also means 'to give an account,' as in 'to explain and justify decisions' – governments must be open, must explain, and must justify their decisions. Both sorts of accountability require that citizens have access to information about what their elected officials are doing and have information sufficient to assess their government's decisions.

These institutions of democracy are obvious and familiar. But to realize a democracy, other institutions are needed. The most fundamental institutions are citizen rights. Beetham begins his discussion of the institutions needed to achieve the democratic ideal in practice: 'The starting point of democratic government is with the citizen – that is with you and me. It is from us that members of a government acquire their jobs and the tax revenues to perform their work on our behalf. It is to us that that they are continually looking for endorsement of their actions and policies, and to us that they are at the end of the day accountable. But this only happens because as citizens we have certain rights which do not depend on the government of the day, and which cannot be taken away from them. These rights should be seen as the foundation of democracy.'[21]

Although in Anglo-American democracies we may take these rights for granted, we do well to remember that 'they are not realised or respected everywhere in the world today, and they did not exist in previous centuries even in Western democracies. They are the result of struggles of the common people, often at considerable cost to themselves, to limit the power of oligarchic and oppressive regimes, and to make government more publicly accountable and responsive to the whole community.'[22]

These citizen rights were discussed earlier in chapter 4, The Multiversity and the Welfare State, where citizen rights were characterized using the framework of Thomas H. Marshall in his famous paper 'Citizenship and Social Class.' They were discussed again in chapter 10 in the context of the globalization of ideas. Marshall identified three types of citizen rights: civil, political, and social. These same three types are set out in the U.N. Universal Declaration of Human Rights.

The public education system is an institution required for social citizenship, because social citizenship – the right to share to the full in the social heritage – requires equality of opportunity, which education can help to provide. Also, education is a necessary prerequisite to civil and political citizenship. Education is so necessary for participation and inclusion in our society that primary and secondary education should be free – and compulsory. Accessible university education is a necessary component of social citizenship in postindustrial society. These educational rights are specified in the Universal Declaration of Human Rights. Article 26 (1) reads: 'Everyone has the right to education. Education shall be free, at least in the elementary and fundamental stages. Elementary education shall be compulsory. Technical and professional education shall be made generally available and higher education shall be equally accessible to all on the basis of merit.'[23] The university becomes an institution of democracy because the university is necessary for the full realization of social, civil, and political citizenship in a knowledge-based society.

Thus far, the institutions in a country necessary for democratic government include two groups: the institutions of representative and accountable government and the institution of citizen rights, but the institutions necessary for democratic life still have not been fully specified. It remains to add the third group: certain institutions of civil society.

Students of democracy since the time of de Tocqueville have noted that democracy is strengthened where citizens experience democratic decision-making – collective decisions within a group of people holding different opinions, on the basis of equality – within the institutions of civil society. Civil society is where people learn the practice of democratic decision-making. But the institutions of civil society have other equally significant roles in securing democracy. In order to ensure the accountability of democratic government and to assist the citizen in acquiring the information necessary for enlightened understanding, democracies need a free press. Democracies require interest groups and non-government organizations to facilitate the consultation as governments develop public policy, and again to assist in holding governments accountable and to assist with citizens' enlightened understanding. Citizen participation in these bodies is protected by their rights to freedom of association, freedom of assembly, and freedom of speech. And to the list of institutions of civil society necessary for democracy, which includes a free press, interest groups, and non-government organizations, we should add multiversities. Multiversities are equally needed to ensure the accountability of democratic government and to assist citizens in acquiring the knowledge necessary for enlightened understanding.

A crucial characteristic of liberal democracies is that authority and power should be dispersed; there should be organizations with authority and power that are independent, particularly of the state but also from the corporate institutions of the market economy. These independent organizations are often gathered together under the heading of civil society. Such organizations, sometimes voluntary organizations like religious groups, ethnic associations, or cooperatives, and, more obviously, organizations like labour unions and the media, provide countervailing authority to concentrations of power in government and business. They help create the checks and balances, what Michael Ignatieff called the system of adversarial justification, necessary for the democratic ideal to be realized in practice. The multiversity helps this dispersion of authority. This, most emphatically, does not mean that the multiversity becomes a place of opposition to the elected government. Rather, it means that the multiversity is a place for information, opinion, and deliberation, outside the formal structures of government. Today, in our age, in our world where knowledge is the most important factor in social and economic growth, the multiversity has become a crucial institution of civil society, crucial in counteracting the concentration of power in government and business. It becomes especially vital in our age to recognize *explicitly* this democratic mission of multiversities, because multiversities are drifting away from their traditional countervailing role and falling more under the influence of government and business.

It is noteworthy and puzzling that none of these books about democracy gives any attention to universities as institutions vital to democratic life. However, it seems obvious that in a knowledge-based society, a society in which, to recall Clark Kerr's words, 'new knowledge is the most important factor in economic and social growth' and in which new knowledge 'may be the most powerful single element in our culture, affecting the rise and fall of professions and even of social classes, of regions and even of nations,'[24] multiversities should have a vital democratic responsibility. We need to think about democracy in a new way[25] and include the multiversity as an institution of democracy: the multiversity is an institution crucial to the citizen rights of a democracy and the multiversity is an institution crucial to the civil society of a democracy.

Now let us explore in greater depth some of the implications of this new idea of the multiversity. The most fundamental implication relates to undergraduate education: to the importance of accessibility and to the purposes of a liberal education. These are taken up in chapter 12. The sections below explore the implications for society's support for research, for the idea of a professor as public intellectual, critic and conscience, and finally for the ideal of a deliberative democracy.

The Social Contract for Research

To analyse the relationship between society and research at the multiversity, it is useful to use the concept of a social contract developed in chapter 5. There, the social contract governed all the activities of the multiversity; here, the social contract between the multiversity and society governs research: society provides the support and the multiversity conducts the research. Society supports this research both directly and indirectly. The direct support comes from research grants, usually allocated through a publicly supported granting council that operates at some distance from government. Direct support also comes through research contracts with government departments or agencies that underwrite work on a specific task. The indirect support for research comes as the government, through its capital and operating grants, and the public, through tuition fees and donations, support the multiversity. In turn, the multiversity supports the research mission with modest teaching loads for faculty and substantial investments in libraries, databases and archives, laboratories, studios, and computer systems. How would this social contract change as we come to recognize the multiversity as an institution of democracy?

As we explore the implications for research of the idea of the multiversity as an institution of democracy, we should not lose sight of other ideas of the multiversity – as a place of basic, curiosity-driven research and as an institution of the economy producing human capital and commercializing research. These ideas remain part of the complex conglomerate that is the multiversity and they too have implications for conceiving the social contract for research.

Research is conducted all across the multiversity: in the sciences (in this chapter, the 'sciences' are defined to include both the pure sciences such as physics and chemistry and the applied sciences such as engineering and medicine), the humanities, the social sciences, and in the professional schools. The concept of a social contract for research has been widely used in discussions of science and science policy during the postwar period; and there have been many discussions of science and democracy, and science and politics. So as we think about democracy and research at the multiversity, let us start with the social contract for scientific research at multiversities and then turn to the social sciences and humanities.

The original postwar social contract for science was crucial in the emergence of the multiversity; it is outlined by David Guston and Kenneth Keniston in *The Fragile Contract: University Science and the Federal Government* as: 'Government promises to fund the basic science that peer reviewers find most worthy of support, and scientists promise that the research will be performed well and honestly and will provide a steady stream of discoveries that can be translated into new products, medicines, or weapons.'[26] Each word and phrase is important. The social contract funds *basic* research at multiversities rather than applied research. The research follows the curiosity of the professor, and the *peer review* of research proposals determines which projects should be funded. The research *can be translated* eventually into results desired by society; the connection between basic research and utility is indirect, but the presumption is strong. This was the social contract set out by Vannevar Bush in *Science – The Endless Frontier*. In the original social contract, the government was not very involved; any monitoring of the research was not done by government but rather through the processes of academic peer review; overall the system functioned on the basis of trust between society and the researchers.[27]

The postwar social contract for scientific research worked well, but things have changed. The old social contract is no longer valid. The government and the public want research to be more applied and the process of transforming new knowledge into useful products to be overt and explicitly managed. Recently, there have been breaches of research integrity, and as a result the government and the public want more explicit oversight. They want more say in the selection of projects and they want there to be more direct evaluation of the productivity of the research process. The constrained welfare state, in a globally competitive world, asks: Are we using our scarce funds most effectively; how do we compare one multiversity to another, and how do we compare our nation's research enterprise with that of other nations? In short, the sponsors of science research – the public and their democratically elected governments – want to be more involved at every stage. There is no going back to an age of unfettered research operating on trust. It is no longer acceptable for scientists at the multiversity to say: give us the money and let us follow our curiosity where it may. The legitimate demands of democracy on science research must be faced.

The old social contract disguised tensions between science and democracy that can no longer be avoided. Guston and Keniston note there are populist tensions and exclusionist tensions within a democracy when it supports scientific research. The goal of scientific research is the discovery of new knowledge. A populist orientation given voice through the political process 'may not lead most directly, or at all, to the truth sought by scientists.'[28] The populist voice will not make decisions according to what is most likely to discover the truth; the populist voice, for example, might argue for a 'fair' distribution of research funds across all regions of the country or for applied research at the expense of any basic research. The exclusionary tension arises because scientific expertise is required to assess the desirably of funding a proposed research program. Only other scientists can properly assess which proposals hold promise of yielding scientifically interesting results. Voters would be excluded from the deliberation.

As we recognize the multiversity as an institution of democracy, the demands of government and the public to be more involved in what research projects to undertake take a new legitimacy. But this legitimacy is also troubling because these demands of democracy threaten another commitment in the social contract, the commitment to university autonomy and academic freedom. Autonomy requires that university professors select the research projects, and part of academic freedom is the right to be judged by your peers. There is a balance to be struck, but when the multiversity is an institution of democracy it requires a tilt toward public involvement.

Donald Stokes in *Pasteur's Quadrant: Basic Science and Technological Innovation* sees a collapse of the postwar social contract based on the Vannevar Bush model, and recognizes the tensions between science and democracy. He does, however, offer a way forward. He argues we have been trapped by an over-simplified dichotomy between basic research and applied research that was at the centre of the postwar social contract. This dichotomy has been called 'the linear model': there is a fundamental separation between basic and applied research and a linear flow from basic research through to applied research and finally into the development of new products. True innovation comes from basic research. Universities do basic research where scientists are motivated by pure curiosity; industry does applied research where researchers are motivated by how basic findings can be applied. Stokes argues that the linear model is not an accurate representation of how scientific knowledge has advanced through history. In fact much scientific work is motivated by the *simultaneous* desire to improve our basic understanding *and* to find usable knowledge. He cites the example of Pasteur who was intensely interested *both* in discovering the basic laws of nature *and* in the application of this basic knowledge. Stokes also notes that in science policy there has often been 'mission-oriented basic research.' Stokes replaces the linear model with a quadrant model. In his quadrant model, scientific research can be characterized by how it is inspired: by whether it is inspired by the quest for fundamental understanding, or inspired by considerations of use. In one quadrant is research motivated solely by the quest for fundamental understanding, which he calls Bohr's quadrant, 'in view of how clearly Niels Bohr's quest for a model of atomic structure was a pure voyage of discovery, however much his ideas later remade the world. This category represents the research ideal of the natural philosophers, institutionalized in the pure science of the Germans in the nineteenth century and of the Americans in the twentieth, and includes Bush's concept of "basic research."'[29] Another category of research is inspired only by concerns with application, which he calls Edison's quadrant, 'in view of how strictly this brilliant inventor kept his co-workers at Menlo

Park, in the first industrial research laboratory in America, from pursuing the deeper scientific implications of what they were discovering in their headlong rush toward commercially profitable electric lighting.'[30] A third category of research is motivated both by the desire to discover nature's laws and by the desire to apply this knowledge in a specific task: Pasteur's quadrant. Most scientific research of the information technology and biotechnology revolutions takes place in Pasteur's quadrant. (Research in the fourth quadrant is motivated neither by a desire for basic understanding nor by a desire for use, rather it seeks only to describe the phenomenon – it is pure taxonomy.)

The original social contract for science emphasized research in Bohr's quadrant; the renegotiated social contract, Stokes argues, will have to focus on Pasteur's quadrant. A democratic society's support for research is founded, ultimately, on its interest in socially valuable applications of the findings. There is a place for pure research – Bohr's quadrant – and the findings of pure research will always be a vital force driving new applied work. Bohr's quadrant remains part of the multiversity's responsibility and the national granting councils still provide much of their support for basic, curiosity-driven research. But as we recognize the multiversity as an institution of democracy, the social contract must expand and be more focused upon use-inspired, basic research – Pasteur's quadrant.

As an institution of democracy, the multiversity must accept society's greater interest in applied science research and in technology transfer. These are perfectly legitimate requests of a democratic sponsor. The intense competition for public funds in the constrained welfare state requires that any claimant be able to justify the support they receive. The task is how to resolve the tensions between the *mores* of democracy and the *mores* of basic science within the expanded social contract. This must be the focus in renegotiation.

Stokes offers a useful framework from which to begin discussion, looking at a process to allocate available research funds. It is evident that the allocation of research money must involve a judgment of both scientific promise and social value. In designing processes to make these judgments, we must acknowledge and confront a basic asymmetry: 'judgments of social value will typically involve one or more goals that do not require deep technical background to comprehend, while judgments of scientific promise will typically require professional expertise that is held only by scientists.'[31] Nonetheless, the two judgments should not be separated, and there is much gain to be had by the creative involvement of scientists in exploring social need, especially since Pasteur's quadrant scientists are motivated by issues of social need, as well as by interest in basic knowledge. 'We can make a start toward understanding how a system of allocation can take account both of scientific promise and of social value by focusing on the fundamental distinction between funding basic research at the project level and the funding of basic research at a more aggregative level.'[32] At the microallocative level, Stokes argues for a dominance of scientists and questions of scientific promise in the decision, whereas at the macroallocative level the political process and questions of social value should dominate. He offers the current decision-making processes in health research as a model and suggests its lessons be applied across all scientific research.

Stokes's framework is helpful as we think about scientific research in a democracy and the renewal of the social contract. The new contract will require what Guston has called 'boundary organizations – institutions that sit astride the boundary between politics and science and involve nonscientists as well as scientists in the creation of mutually beneficial outputs.' The new system will be less based on peer review and trust (although these remain crucial) and involve more explicit project selection, and use of incentives and monitoring to insure the integrity and productivity of research. Guston calls this new framework 'collaborative assurance.'[33] Successful multiversities will be those which can contribute creatively to the establishment of this new framework.

In addition, the social contract must address explicitly the ethical and moral dilemmas confronting scientists that arise because of the commercialization of research – the peer-review, trust-based system will no longer suffice. Most particularly, the social contract must put in place means to deal with potential conflicts of interest and conflict of commitment that arise when scientists receive corporate support for their research and when scientists have equity positions in companies applying their research. A necessary first step is higher standards of disclosure, both when the research is published and, more controversially but just as necessary, in the classroom. Scientists, and all researchers, must disclose the sources of research funding and also any financial interest in the application of the results. Furthermore, the multiversity and its scientists need to engage more explicitly with society concerning the privatization of knowledge. Society supports the science research of the multiversity under the long tradition that such research is disinterested. The public supports institutional autonomy and academic freedom in the belief that academic research will be a disinterested pursuit of truth, but this support is at risk. As people become more aware that government research money is helping to fund the research that leads to a spin-off company owned by the professors, public support may wane. Public funding is not intended to help professors get wealthy. It is imperative that these controversies be addressed early and explicitly in our civic conversation about the social contract.

This structure for the social contract in a democracy is still incomplete, however. Missing is the responsibility of the scientific community to provide public intellectuals. Likewise missing is the responsibility to make the processes of conducting research and dissemination of the results more accessible. (As discussed in chapter 7, information technology provides new opportunities to make research more open and more democratic.) Also, scientists must ask the question: Research for whom? They must join other scholars to explore the effects of new scientific research on society and, with others, be critics of their own activities. The renegotiated social contract must place greater emphasis on these responsibilities of scientists to democratic life.

Also, the specification of the social contract should be extended to recognize that research in science is also supported by society because the professors who are actively engaged in research are at the same time teaching the graduate students who will become the advanced knowledge workers in the economy. (Most holders of master's and doctoral degrees go on to work in the private sector, not in universities.) Support for university-based research is partly based on this model of how best to train advanced knowledge workers. In the social contract, society's support for research in science is inextricably linked to graduate education and the need for highly educated workers in the economy.

Having analysed the new social contract for research in pure and applied science, let us turn to analyse society's support for research in the humanities, the social sciences, and the professions. Is there a social contract supporting this research and how should we view it as we recognize the multiversity as an institution of democracy? Although during the postwar period there were explicit discussions of a social contract for science research and discussions about science and democracy, there were few such discussions about multiversity research in the social sciences, the professions, or the humanities. This reveals much about the different roles of research in each of these domains: clearly society has a much better understanding of the need for and value of research in pure and applied science. Because of this history, articulating today's social contract for research in the social sciences and in the humanities will be much more difficult.

How then are we to proceed in thinking about the relationship between society and multiversity research in the social sciences, the professions, and the humanities? Here, I propose to take the framework developed for science and used in the discussion above, and see how it can be applied in other domains. This methodology is not without its drawbacks, for the obvious reason that the purposes, methods, and outcomes of research in other domains are so different. Nonetheless, it is powerful heuristic device; there are lessons from the experience of the social contract for science, and its application as a framework in other domains helps to deepen our understanding of the relationship between society and multiversity research in all domains. However, the huge challenge of articulating and specifying a social contract for research in the social sciences and the humanities cannot be denied and should not be underestimated.

Research in the social sciences has the closest analogies to research in the sciences, so let us begin there. The social sciences did promise a 'science of society' and that as social science advanced through research, society's affairs would be better managed, people would be better off, and social problems would be ameliorated. (Research in the professions may be regarded as part of this science of society; in this chapter the social sciences and the professions will be pooled into one category.) Early in the second half of the twentieth century, a surge of optimism about the social sciences in Canada, the United States, and England gave a great boost to social science research in the multiversities. Social scientists were routinely called upon for advice and to conduct studies for government departments and commissions. In the later decades of the twentieth century, as discussed in chapter 6, the optimism dimmed; many social problems did not seem so amenable to solution. Nonetheless, social science research remains in demand. There has, however, never been the same long-term commitment to social science research as there has been for science, and there has never been an explicit social contract for social science research.

Nor was there a 'linear model' in the analysis of social science research in universities. Had there been a linear model it would have read: the multiversities would do basic, curiosity-driven research in social science and the world-out-there would apply the basic research. Social scientists well understand the distinction between basic research and applied research, although in social science, it is much harder to distinguish basic from applied work. However, this distinction is not often made in social science. Rather, a different distinction is made: social scientists distinguish between positive research and normative research. Positive research seeks to explain a social phenomenon (much like basic science research seeks to explain); positive research is a quest for fundamental understanding, without any concern for how the knowledge might be used (or indeed whether the knowledge is useful at all). Normative research, like applied scientific research, seeks understanding in order that it might be applied. However, in social science, the research is applied in order that it might affect change in social conditions, and inevitably such work requires norms, or values, that we can use to determine what sort of change in social conditions is an improvement. Here a crucial difference between science and social science is revealed: science research, when it is applied, is not deemed to require assessment; whereas social science research, when it is applied, *is* deemed to require assessment and therefore to require norms for this assessment.

Despite their difference from scientists, social scientists at the multiversity have sought a social contract like that enjoyed by scientists – a contract with sustained long-term funding supporting curiosity-driven research selected on the basis of peer review – but have been unsuccessful. The national granting councils have supported curiosity-driven research, but society's support has not been formulated and expressed as a social contract. In part this is because social science has been less successful in producing an accumulating body of theoretical knowledge confirmed by testing against the facts of experience. Therefore, it is much less clear why society should support an ongoing commitment to basic research in the social sciences. The absence of a contract for basic social science research is also explained by the fact that social scientists themselves are less focused on basic research than are scientists. Much social science research combines the desire for fundamental understanding and the consideration of use, rather like Pasteur's quadrant; we might call this Keynes's quadrant. Almost all the rest of the research is dominated by concerns of use, by a desire to affect change social change, rather like Edison's quadrant; we might call this Beveridge's quadrant.

In negotiating a social contract for social science research in a democracy, the social scientists, like their colleagues in science, must give up their hope for a contract focused solely upon curiosity-driven pure research. The focus of the social contract for social science must be on research motivated by both the desire for fundamental understanding and the desire for application – on research in Keynes's quadrant. As in science, we must develop processes of decision-making that combine assessment of intellectual promise and assessments of social value. Stokes's distinction between microallocation and macroallocation may be helpful, but there are differences in social science. Many of the microallocative decisions can involve significant involvement of the external community; indeed some social scientists engage with the community to let them actually formulate the research questions. There will be different sorts of boundary organizations in social science than in science.[34] But, there will be similar shift to greater use of incentives and monitoring rather than reliance upon trust. And again as in science, the social contract for social science research must include the commitment to graduate education: preparing social scientists for productive lives in postindustrial society. Social scientists have no difficulty accepting their role as critic and conscience, but like scientists, can do much more as public intellectuals in democratic life.

Social scientists also must offer a more thoughtful position on possible conflicts of interest than they have in the past. Like scientists, they can have financial conflicts. But social scientists can also have ideological predispositions. Social science recognizes that an ideological position is acceptable, and may even be inescapable, but has not done enough to explore how this can shape the research undertaken and to discuss this with society. A long-term commitment from society to support social science research will require greater clarity and greater candor.

The concept of a social contract for research in the humanities is still more problematic. Research in the humanities has never been supported through government granting agencies with the same consistency, or at the same level, as research in the sciences or even the social sciences. In the United States, the National Endowment for the Humanities was not established until 1965. In the United Kingdom, the Arts and Humanities Research Board has only just been established. In Canada, humanities research has been more prominent because of its close connection to nation-building, particularly research in Canadian history and Canadian literature. The humanities have had long-standing grant support from the Canada Council and the Social

Sciences and Humanities Research Council. In considering how society supports research in the humanities, it should be acknowledged that much humanities research does not require the massive specialized infrastructure of science; rather it requires time and a good library. These have been already provided in the multiversity, and so the need for support from an external granting agency is less. Society's support for humanities research is perhaps better measured by the number of professors in the humanities, their time available for research, and the quality of the library. Here again, society's greater support for science is evident, as humanities professors generally have higher teaching loads and less time for research than their colleagues in the sciences.

Whatever its relative position, support for humanities research in the postwar era in all three countries has been amorphous and could not be called a social contract. It is a high priority within today's social contract for research to remedy this gap: to articulate and secure a social contract for humanities research at the multiversity, and in the context of the multiversity as an institution of democracy. As we do this, we are forced to confront the question: Why should democratic society support research in the humanities? There is not space in this book, nor is there capability in this author, to answer this question properly. Perhaps the best I can offer as a social scientist are the reflections of an 'outsider,' reflections that perhaps are stronger because they carry no worry about conflict of interest. My first and fundamental point is that at present there is no social contract for humanities research and we must work to establish one. This task must be high on the agenda. The humanities have never been as well supported as science and the social sciences; they are being marginalized by the character of our age; and thus the establishment of a social contract will be extraordinarily difficult. But it is extraordinarily important because uncertainty about the place of the humanities is part of the mission drift of the multiversity; if a social contract for research in the humanities can be articulated, it will help to reduce the drift.

In addressing the issues, we should be careful to distinguish between the value of *research* in the humanities, as distinct from the value of *study* in the humanities, and from the valueof *new works* in the humanities. Much of the current concern about the state of the humanities has more to do with whether students are studying them, and whether society is adequately supporting the creation of new works by writers, performers, and other artists, than with whether we have enough research at multiversities in the humanities. In this chapter, the focus is research.

Robert Proctor, in *Education's Great Amnesia: Reconsidering the Humanities from Petrarch to Freud*, defines the humanities as they emerged in the Renaissance as 'a program as education with three distinguishing characteristics: a) the concept of a unique, autonomous personal self, to be shaped through b) the study of language and literature of ancient Greece and Rome, c) according to the perspectives of a group of primarily literary academic disciplines.'[35]

The humanities have always been personal, connected to the development of the self. They have been 'a program of education,' with the result that the distinction between study in the humanities and research in the humanities is less meaningful than elsewhere. In science, there is a clear distinction between study in science and research in science. Researchers in the humanities are always engaged in the study of texts and so in their own process of personal development. Also, their research is justified because it will help others in their reading of the texts. Humanities research is much more closely linked to personal programs of education than research in science or social science. This perspective in humanities scholarship is made eloquently clear in the work of Harold Bloom, the great literary scholar of Yale University. The Prologue to one of his recent books begins by asking: Why read? The beginning of his answer is worth quoting at length:

> My ideal reader (and lifelong hero) is Dr. Samuel Johnson, who knew and expressed both the power and the limitation of incessant reading. Like every other activity of the mind, it must satisfy Johnson's prime concern, which is with 'what comes near to ourself, what we can put to use.' Sir Francis Bacon, who provided some of the ideas that Johnson put to use, famously gave the advice: 'Read not to contradict and confute, nor to believe and take for granted, nor to find talk or discourse, but to weigh and consider.' I add to Bacon and Johnson a third sage of reading, Emerson, fierce enemy of history and of all historicisms, who remarked that the best books 'impress us with the conviction, that one nature wrote and the same reads.' Let me fuse Bacon, Johnson, and Emerson into a formula of how to read: find what comes near to you that can be put to the use of weighing and considering, and that addresses you as though you share the one nature, free of time's tyranny. Pragmatically that means, first find Shakespeare, and let him find you.' 'Ultimately, we read – as Bacon,

Johnson, and Emerson agree – in order to strengthen the self, and to learn its authentic interests.[36]

Bloom's book is a work of humanities research, supported by Yale University and the larger democratic society, but the book is deeply connected to his own personal development and the encouragement of development in others.

Neither the linear model, with its distinction between basic and applied research, nor the quadrant model has been applied to humanities research, for reasons that are obvious. Nonetheless by attempting to apply the models, however contorted the attempt, we gain understanding of the nature of humanities research and the dilemma of trying to establish a social contract for humanities research in a democratic society.

Humanists, like scientists and social scientists, usually begin by arguing the value of knowledge for its own sake and seek society's support for pure curiosity-driven research in the humanities. There is an atavistic pride among humanities researchers that their work is unconcerned, or uncontaminated, with its application. The analogy with other university researchers is obvious enough. Just as in other fields, however, a social contract in a democratic society cannot be based solely on curiosity-driven research. The humanities must also address the question of social value, just as the scientists and the social scientists must.

Many leaders in the humanities, in seeking greater public support for humanities research, have begun to articulate its value to society. In an extreme example of this approach, the Humanities and Social Sciences Federation of Canada combines the social sciences and humanities under the term 'human sciences' and asserts 'these human sciences are an essential part of the full spectrum of science in Canada. They are our instrument for understanding human problems and possibilities.' 'The work of the human sciences is essential, for it allows individuals, communities, organizations, and societies to better understand the major social and cultural transformations affecting them in this age of high technology, the new economy, and changing international relations.'[37] In this approach, the humanities are converted into social sciences and become an instrument for social understanding, an understanding that will allow us to solve problems and achieve progress. A less extreme form of articulating the value of humanities research is revealed by the mission of the newly established Arts and

Humanities Research Board in England: to 'improve the breadth and depth of our knowledge of human culture, past and present, and thereby to enhance the quality of life and creative output of the nation.'[38]

Research in the humanities has always had certain instrumental purposes, particularly related to the development of national culture, but this strong emphasis on a social-science-like instrumentality is recent. As a strategy of building support for humanities research, the emphasis on instrumentality may be astute. If we can make the humanities seem like the social sciences (and even the sciences), then there will be more government grants for the humanities. The humanities do indeed meet such purposes. But the emphasis on social-science-like value reveals an atrophied conception of the humanities and of humanities research. This conception cannot be the foundation for justifying research in the humanities. One of the great difficulties in creating a social contract for humanities research is that we have almost lost the ability to articulate the value of humanities research beyond 'the better understanding of social and cultural transformations.'

Surely the starting point in building a rationale for humanities research must be to articulate what is unique about the humanities. Science and social science give us an incomplete knowledge of the world and of ourselves. They give us an incomplete basis on which to live our lives. The humanities offer an alternative, valuable in its own right.

Robert Proctor's definition highlights that the humanities are literary: they involve reading of texts, they involve language. In science, and much of social science, there is a presumption that there is an objective reality, that 'reality exists independently of human representation,' and that the words we use convey meaning directly. The signifier is fixed to the signified. However, for much of 'reality,' for much of the way we live our lives, this is not true. For example, when we use words like greed, or jealousy, or honour and declare that these motivate human behaviour, we do not think that there is an objective conception of greed, or jealousy, or honour. The signifier is not so fixed to the signified. We use images, metaphors, and myths to understand the world and in living our lives. The myth and the metaphor are just as important as the molecule and the model. Language, the imagination, the myth, and the metaphor are the domain of the humanities and the domain of humanities research.

Martha Nussbaum, in a wonderful work of humanities research,

Poetic Justice: The Literary Imagination and Public Life, offers a vision of the humanities unique in their sources and methods, and able to contribute to social life in a democracy. A classics scholar, she developed her ideas while presenting a course, Law and Literature, at the University of Chicago Law School, in which she and the students read Plato and Seneca, Dickens and Austen, Whitman and Richard Wright. Nussbaum begins:

> Speaking of political argument in America, Walt Whitman wrote that the literary artist is a much needed participant. The poet is 'the arbiter of the diverse,' 'the equalizer of his age and his land.' His capacious imagination 'sees eternity in men and women' and 'does not see men and women as dreams or dots.' Whitman's call for public poetry is, I believe, as pertinent to our time as it was to his. Very often in today's political life we lack the capacity to see one another as fully human, as more than 'dreams or dots.' Often, too, those refusals of sympathy are aided and abetted by an excessive reliance on technical ways of modeling human behavior, especially those which derive from economic utilitarianism.' The book 'grows out of the conviction, which I share with Whitman, that storytelling and literary imagining are not opposed to rational argument, but can provide essential ingredients in a rational argument.[39]

For Nussbaum, reading and humanities scholarship belong in law school and in the public square.

We should, however, acknowledge that there is no consensus among humanities professors on this front, and recognize that such public contributions of the humanities cannot be the ultimate foundation for a social contract. Bloom in his defense of reading declares that in reading we experience 'pleasure, which may explain why aesthetic values have always been deprecated by social moralists, from Plato through to our current campus Puritans. The pleasures of reading indeed are selfish rather than social. You cannot directly improve anyone's life by reading better or more deeply. I remain skeptical of the traditional social hope that care for others may be stimulated by the growth of the individual imagination, and I am wary of any arguments whatsoever that connect the pleasures of solitary reading to the public good.'[40]

Research in all fields tries to answer questions. In science, the answers accumulate and new questions are asked. Such is the power and accomplishment of science that we all understand this way of talking about knowledge and new knowledge; but the discourse of the advance of scientific knowledge has become the discourse for all forms of knowledge. In the humanities, answers accumulate and new questions are asked, just as in science; but sometimes the same text is examined again, indeed the text is valued precisely because it rewards our return to look for new meaning, and sometimes the same questions are asked again and again. Humanities research wants to explore the nature of beauty, to understand the meaning of justice, to experience and analyse the shared stories of people. Each era must research these old questions anew, drawing on the thinkers recent and ancient, but addressing the old questions anew. Thus, we can read Socrates on justice and John Rawls on justice as we puzzle the meaning of justice for us today; in contrast, we would never read ancient Greek authors alongside today's geneticists as we tried to understand the determinants of heart disease. A social contract for humanities research is a commitment to pursue new knowledge and new understanding, but is also a commitment to look at old texts again and to ask old questions again, questions for which there will never be an answer. We must find a way to articulate and accommodate the special qualities of the humanities in a new social contract. The route to long-term support for humanities research cannot be to make them seem like the social sciences or the sciences. Again, daunting though it is, we need to hear more from our humanities professors. The multiversity has a special responsibility to take up this task.

To close, let me emphasize what is common across all areas of research as the social contract is renewed, rather than what differentiates them. In our democratic society, in research across all of the sciences, social sciences, humanities, and professions, peer review and the curiosity of professors are the basic criteria, and criteria that we must not lose, but they cannot be the sole criteria for selecting which questions to address. There must be a simultaneous consideration of intellectual promise and social value, and a dialogue between professors and the public. The world of research remains mysterious to most outside the university, and even with improved dialogue much of the mystery will remain. Universities will continue to enjoy considerable deference but this brings a special reciprocal obligation. In a democratic society, the social contract must be tended. Like academic freedom, the social contract for research ultimately depends upon a public opinion that understands what universities are for and values what universities do. The multiversity and its professors must engage with the public about the nature of their research. This is the ultimate foun-

dation of the social contract for research in a liberal democracy.
Public Intellectuals in a Democracy

In Part One, chapter 5, I argued that under the social contract, multiversities – and therefore their professors – must accept the roles of public intellectual, critic, and conscience. These are not roles that the multiversity understands well, or that the public understands well. Also, they are roles that carry considerable risks to the multiversity; they risk betraying the commitment to disinterested, free inquiry. Sustained reflection upon, and understanding of, the dilemmas of a public intellectual in a democracy become a necessary part of implementing the new democratic mission of the multiversity. There will be no permanent solutions to these dilemmas; rather the dilemmas are inevitable and inescapable in the multiversity where professors pursue knowledge both for its own sake and for its contribution to public life. Some of the themes that will run through the reflections are expanded below; many of them have been with the multiversity for years but become more significant with its new democratic role.

Recalling chapter 5, we can start in the same way by asking: Who are the intellectuals in our society? Following a dictionary definition, intellectuals are people who enjoy mental activity and who work with their intellect. Our intellect is 'the capacity for understanding, thinking and reasoning, as distinct from feeling or instinct.'[41] Intellectuals operate by reasoning, thinking, and acquiring knowledge, rather than by emotion, tradition, prejudice, or common sense. They are curious and sceptical, rather than accepting and deferential. They like to explore, read, challenge, discuss, and know. In some usages, to be an intellectual is to have a highly developed taste, especially in literature, art, and music; in other usages, the intellectual is an outsider, a social critic speaking truth to power. I use the dictionary definition – intellectuals are those who work with their intellect. In this view, all professors are intellectuals and have always been intellectuals. Scientists, engineers, doctors, and lawyers are all intellectuals, and so are social scientists and literary scholars who do not offer social criticism.

Further, in my usage, the role of professors as public intellectuals arises because they conduct research, in an autonomous institution under the protection of academic freedom, not because they have the freedom of thought and speech that we all enjoy. Recalling Metzger's analysis of the origins of academic freedom, 'the evolutionists' formula did not level every opinion to equal value. It held that every claim to a discovery of truth must submit to open verification; that the process of verification must follow certain rules; that this procedure is best understood by those who qualify as experts. Hence, academic freedom does not theoretically justify all kinds of intellectual nonconformity, but only that kind of nonconformity that proceeds according to rules; not any private belief, but that kind of private belief that allows itself to be publicly tested.'[42] The professor as public intellectual is grounded in peer review of the research enterprise.

If all professors are intellectuals, what is the new role in the multiversity as an institution of democracy? The first role is to be a *public* intellectual. Of course, multiversity professors are 'public' intellectuals first in their classrooms, in their seminars, in their laboratories. The act of teaching in a research university is the act of public intellectuals. So is the publication of research. But their public role must extend beyond the campus and academic community. It must extend to speaking and writing for an educated general public about their fields and their research. This is an obligation to the public that supports the multiversity and a contribution to knowledge for its own sake – to lifelong liberal learning in a knowledge-based society.

The role of a public intellectual can also mean involvement in political and cultural life outside the university. The role of professors in public discussion has never been more important than today. Under the pressures of mass culture and mass media, serious and nuanced public discussion has atrophied. The liberal anxiety, identified by Alan Ryan, is well warranted. Jeffrey C. Goldfarb, in *Civility and Subversion: The Intellectual in Democratic Society,* calls the poor quality of public discussion in contemporary democracies a 'deliberation deficit.' Intellectuals, he argues are crucial democratic actors who are particularly able to help us deliberate together. The ability to use information has become a primary basis of power and wealth in postindustrial society. 'It is not that there is no exchange of information. Obviously the opposite is the case. Ours is a world of the electronic superhighway, with huge data banks on matters public and private. But information does not automatically lead to informed discussions ... We know very well how to process information, and we are getting better and better at it, but we have an exceptionally difficult time thinking about the information we process, especially with each other ... If intellectuals do not provoke serious talk about the problems we face, no one will. Without such talk democratic polities function undeliberately. Everyday political practices become strategic campaigns of mass manipulation.'[43]

Confusion and cynicism become the general rule. Public intellectuals can support democratic society by helping to go beyond the prevailing cynicism and manipulation.

Public intellectuals and democracies have always had an uneasy relationship, however. Democracy needs an informed critical citizenry and wants the contributions of intellectuals to public deliberations. Nonetheless, democracy is suspicious of the hierarchy of judgments by intellectuals. Richard Hofstadter, in his *Anti-Intellectualism in American Life*, characterized the common view of an intellectual as 'a person of spurious intellectual pretensions, often a professor or the protégé of a professor ... fundamentally superficial ... surfeited with conceit and contempt for the experience of more sound and able men.'[44] Populist democrats on both the left and right fear the intellectual. Goldfarb notes that on the populist left, intellectuals are seen as a force to reinforce privilege; whereas on the populist right, intellectuals are 'viewed as a cosmopolitan force which denigrates the common beliefs and folkways of ordinary people.'[45] For their part, intellectuals value cultural excellence and are suspicious of democracy's love of the commonplace. A democracy is not an easy place to be a public intellectual.

The mass media in democratic society present a dilemma for intellectuals. On the one hand, the mass media provide an extraordinary opportunity to communicate with a wide audience, and public intellectuals must perforce use the mass media. But, the mass media are unfriendly to complexity, to nuance, and to lengthy analysis. They set the agenda on their terms and can 'make it impossible for certain ideas to reach an audience or even be imagined. The logic of media communication often dominates the logic of intellectual criticism.'[46] This dilemma becomes acute in a media-saturated postmodern condition. Nonetheless, the information technology revolution offers possibilities to enhance public intellectual life if university intellectuals can understand and seize them.

Even when they want to participate in democratic public life, the role of professors as public intellectuals is fraught: the professor must negotiate the difference between ideological commitment and political engagement.

The more traditional view of how to negotiate this engagement, advanced by Goldfarb, holds that professors should be politically engaged but not ideologists. Ideologists have already decided upon the 'truth,' and are uninterested in deliberation. For them 'political action simply involves bringing their discovered truth to the people' and becomes a 'politics of coercion.' Professors should eschew ideology, but can find cause for action with political ideas and principles. Goldfarb writes: 'fascist and communist intellectuals are the archetypes of ideological intellectuals. But intellectuals of the contemporary left and right of less apparent totalitarian ambitions also have made the ideological move.'[47] This can be seen often in presumptive views, for example, of feminists about the evils of patriarchy or of neoclassical economists about the benefits of free markets.

Others, like the sociologist Bernard Barber, want to recognize that an objective social scientist and an ideologue have separate and distinct social roles; and to acknowledge that ideologues perform a clear function in society: the writings of ideologues justify or criticize some value or norm.[48] And still others, of a postmodern stance, argue that the separation is meaningless and that all politically engaged people are ideologues.[49]

With all of its dilemmas, it is not surprising that most professors withdraw from public intellectual life. They may not see a professional responsibility; it may simply be easier and more convenient to withdraw; or they may be confused about their role. But, in our postindustrial democracies, we must ask that professors be public intellectuals. Not every professor must engage in these activities – the current responsibilities for teaching, research, and service are already arduous – but collectively, the professoriate must accept the role.

Universities, however, have not emphasized this responsibility to be a public intellectual. Professors enjoying a profile as public intellectuals invariably say that most of their colleagues are wary (they say that it takes you away from real research, or that addressing the public requires too much dumbing-down); other colleagues are hostile (you have given up the pursuit of truth for the pursuit of celebrity); and some are simply envious (you are successful and I wish could be like you). The systems of evaluation in academic life are not equipped to evaluate the contributions of public intellectuals to public dialogue; promotion and tenure committees seldom give these contributions much attention. This needs to change. Similarly tenure and promotion must change to accommodate the social responsibility to be critic and conscience. The first step would be to recognize explicitly this mission of the multiversity, and next to develop means to evaluate public contributions – it will be difficult but no more difficult than evaluating teaching. Then they can be given weight in tenure, promotion, and merit decisions. Course releases could be made available for special projects related to the democratic mission. Granting councils could give more weight to activities as public intellectuals as part of research dissemination. Connections between academic departments and specialized journalists could be enhanced. The time spent by a professor as a public intellectual is time spent on the mission of the multiversity in a democratic society. When we evaluate departments – conducting an undergraduate program review or a graduate program review – we should evaluate the department's contribution not just in teaching and research, but also to democratic life. With a new mission comes a new accountability framework.

There seem to be fewer public intellectuals than in the past.[50] Also, it seems that among the few public intellectuals more are university professors than in the past. Indeed, the emergence of the term 'public' intellectual rather than simply 'intellectual' may reflect the concentration of intellectuals in universities. In the main, professors' activities are directed to a specialized audience: to undergraduate students, graduate students, and other professors. When they become involved outside academe, professors become public intellectuals.

Paradoxically, many social commentators like Russell Jacoby, author of *The Last Intellectuals: American Culture in the Age of Academe*, attribute the decline in the number of public intellectuals to the emergence of the modern research university and the increasing specialization of knowledge. The multiversity, as an autonomous institution whose professors have academic freedom, would seem a compatible home for public intellectuals. But it has both strengthens and weaknesses as a base for them. Jacoby argues the university is only superficially hospitable; he believes the rising importance of universities explains the decline in public intellectuals. Edward Said may argue that true intellectuals side with the weak, and that their work 'will neither make them friends in high places nor win them official honours. It is a lonely condition.'[51] But Jacoby sees the university life of intellectuals as very different. University-based intellectuals hold prestigious professorships at famous institutions: 'they are regularly wined and dined as well as handsomely compensated. Many leading intellectuals ... operate with agents who arrange fees and schedules for their many speaking engagements.'[52] The critical public intellectuals in the multiversity are not Edward Said's outsiders. Their very security and success in such an eminent institution of society means that they now write more for specialists than for the public. 'We face the rise of a new intellectual class using a new scholasticism accessible only to the mandarins, who have turned their back on public life and letters.'[53]

The turn of professors away from the public is not simply the result of security and success; it is reinforced by the very character of the multiversity, by the specialization of knowledge, the commitment to the research ideal, and the professionalization of academic life. Universities are organized by department. Professors give their primary loyalty to their department and their discipline and win accolades by publishing in the specialized journals of their field. Experts speak to other experts in their own special language, and the daily conversation of academic life is inaccessible to the public. The research community gives little reward to those who become skilled in public conversation.

It is obviously in the selfish interests of professors and the multiversity to speak publicly about the research enterprise, to engage the public imagination with the process and to explain the findings in language accessible to the curious educated public. When the public is engaged, it will be more likely to financially support universities. But the role of public intellectual cannot be motivated by this instrumental purpose alone; rather, it must be recognized as an obligation to democratic society. In postindustrial society, theoretical knowledge and new knowledge are increasingly important. Society finances the research at multiversities and multiversites are extremely influential. The multiversity, with its privileges of autonomy and academic freedom, has an obligation to make this knowledge as accessible as possible, to disseminate it as a public intellectual.

Deliberative Democracy

An alternate route to exploring the relationship between multiversities and democracy, and to deepening our understanding of this new relationship, is to turn away from the recent writing about multiversities and instead look at the recent writing on democracy. What have philosophers and political scientists been saying about democracy? Does the recent literature about democracy hold any implications for thinking about multiversities?

Recent writing about democracy[54] often begins, for obvious but justifiable reasons, by talking about the fall of the Berlin Wall and the collapse of authoritarian state socialism. The end of the twentieth century was democracy's moment across the world. The writing then moves to recall Francis Fukuyama's proclamation in *The End of History* that we have reached 'the end point of mankind's ideological evolution' and the universalization of western liberal democracy as the final form of human government. But this is immediately followed by a demonstration of the hubris of Fukuyama's prophesy. We have not reached the end of history. The form of human government is still contested across the world, and far from stable. Democracy remains fragile and must be nurtured continuously, even in the Anglo-American world.

One recurring worry in the literature concerns the disillusionment about electoral politics in our Anglo-American democracies, evident in declining voter turnout and declining participation in all aspects of organized party politics. The mood is captured well in the title of a recent book: *Disaffected Democracies*.[55] At best a bemused disinterest, at worst a hardened cynicism, is a common stance, especially among the young. The civility and public-spiritedness that should mark the liberal citizen seem to be disappearing. The quality of public discussion declines. When public discussion does occur, it is fractious and polarized.

These criticisms and worries have sparked a renewal of interest in liberal democratic theory among philosophers and political scientists, reflecting a deep concern about the legitimacy of liberal democracies. The recent literature about democracy is marked by two closely related themes: an emphasis on the idea of deliberative democracy and an emphasis on the idea of citizenship. Both themes have signal implications for the place of multiversities in democratic society. The question of citizenship will be taken up in the next chapter in discussion about undergraduate liberal education. Here we turn to the idea of deliberative democracy.

The literature on deliberative democracy considers how democracy can retain legitimacy given the inevitability of disagreement in our pluralist, complex societies. To political philosophy's usual emphasis on equality, liberty, power, and representation has been added a focus on disagreement. In politics today, whether on economic policy, foreign policy, or social policy, disagreement is fundamental. In the late twentieth century, in the phrase of John Dryzek, the theory of democracy has taken 'a strong deliberative turn.' Prior to that turn, democratic legitimacy was seen mainly in terms of aggregation of preferences or interests into collective decisions, through devices such as voting or representation. After the deliberative turn, 'democratic legitimacy came to be seen in terms of the ability or opportunity to participate in effective deliberation on the part of those subjects subject to collective decisions.' 'The essence of democracy itself is now widely taken to be deliberation, rather than voting, interest aggregation, constitutional rights, or even self-government.'[56] The deliberative democracy literature emphasizes that deliberation should occur not just in the explicit political process, but in many dispersed forums of civil society.

An influential contribution to the literature on deliberative democracy is a 1996 book by Amy Gutmann, then of Princeton University, and Dennis Thompson of Harvard University, titled *Democracy and Disagreement*. Their focus is moral disagreement in democracies. The book begins: 'of the challenges that American democracy faces today, none is more formidable than the problem of moral disagreement. Neither the theory nor the practice of democratic politics has so far found an adequate way to cope with conflicts about fundamental values. We address the challenge of moral disagreement by developing a conception of democracy that secures a central place for moral discussion in political life.'[57]

Gutmann and Thompson assert that 'when citizens or their representatives disagree morally, they should continue to reason together to reach mutually acceptable decisions.' 'Deliberative democracy asks citizens and officials to justify public policy by giving reasons which can be accepted by those who are bound by it. This disposition to seek mutually justifiable reasons expresses the core of the process of deliberation.'[58]

For Gutmann and Thompson, the disposition to seek mutually justifiable reasons in a democracy rests on three principles: 'reciprocity, publicity, and accountability.' Reciprocity deals with the *kind* of reasons that should be given in deliberation; publicity with the *forum* in which the reasons should be given; and accountability deals with the *agents* to whom and by whom the reasons should be given. The reciprocity principle governs both the moral and empirical arguments that will be part of deliberation. Within moral reasoning, reciprocity requires that citizens appeal to principles that can be shared by fellow citizens. The nature of such principles is often discovered only in the process of deliberation itself. If moral deliberation does not reach agreement, it requires accommodation based on mutual respect. In empirical reasoning, reciprocity requires that it utilize 'relatively reliable methods of inquiry. Such methods are our best hope for carrying on discussion on mutually acceptable terms.'[59]

This literature on deliberative democracy proceeds at a very abstract level, with little discussion of institutions through which it might be supported or accomplished. Nonetheless, on reflection, the crucial role of the multiversity in achieving a deliberative democracy becomes apparent. The development of positions based on careful thought is the essence of the examined life of liberal learning. The deliberative process, arguing one's position to others on the basis of 'relatively reliable methods of inquiry,' is wonderfully analogous to the process of research and scholarly deliberation. The deliberation of democracy will surely draw upon existing knowledge and call for new knowledge; it will require the adjudication of competing knowledge claims. It will require the involvement of public intellectuals and engaged, informed citizens. All these are the stuff and substance of the multiversity. The deliberation of democracy is not just in the political process, it must be throughout society, and wherever it occurs, the deliberation must be public. The multiversity is an ideal forum – in the classroom and through its graduates and its professors as public intellectuals – for such public deliberation in civil society. The multiversity's values are consonant with those required by deliberative democracy. It is a sanctuary of nonrepression where men and women who hold contrary ideas are full members of the community. The multiversity is an institution necessary for achieving a deliberative democracy.

Interestingly, some political scientists have made a strong connection between deliberative democracy and cosmopolitan democracy.[60] Both are grounded in the conviction that the essence of democratic legitimacy rests not simply in voting and representation but also in deliberation. Cosmopolitan democracy, therefore, does not emphasize the representative institutions of international affairs, but rather the shared deliberation across nations. Global democracy requires global deliberation. The multiversity is ideally suited to contribute to both deliberative and cosmopolitan democracy.

Much of the literature on deliberative democracy remains within the traditions of liberal political thought. But there is a portion that is harder-edged, more critical, part of the postmodern stance against liberal and Enlightenment values. John Dryzek, in his *Deliberative Democracy and Beyond: Liberals, Critics, Contestations*, calls this critical stance a concern with 'discursive democracy.' Discursive democracy is 'critical in its orientation to established power structures, including those that operate beneath the constitutional surface of the liberal state, and so insurgent in relation to established institutions.'[61] These postmodern writings represent 'a renewed concern within the authenticity of democracy: the degree to which democratic control is substantive rather than symbolic, and engaged by competent citizens.'[62] Followers of Michel Foucault argue that much discourse in politics is 'like a prison, it conditions the way people think.' These discourses must be exposed before democracy can be authentic. The postmodern literature also rejects the notion that traditional discussions of 'the citizen' are adequate; they too are a discourse that hides rather than acknowledges difference. Any reflection on liberal democratic theory, and the possible place of multiversities in deliberative democracies, must address this postmodern critique of current political discourse. Is the democratic deliberation of the multiversity merely part of a discourse that conditions the way people think? In part it is, but the diverse voices of multiversity professors are also the means to expose the subconscious of these discourses.

To conclude, this recent political science literature on democracy is extraordinarily helpful in reflecting upon the democratic role of the multiversities. We want our democracy to be not just representative, but also deliberative. The multiversity's role as an institution of democracy is to help create a deliberative democracy.

12 A Liberal Education for Our Age

The multiversity has many tasks. There is no one idea of the multiversity, but many, and the ideas live, however inconsistently, in the same institution. But we should recall Frank Rhodes's reminder: 'it is undergraduate teaching, and learning, that is the central task ... Almost everything else universities do depends on it ... It is through undergraduate education that the public encounters the university most directly, and it is on undergraduate education that the health of the research university will stand or fall.'[1]

The Central Task

On my agenda for renewal of the social contract, the top priority is to recognize that the multiversity, among its several ideas, is an institution of democracy. The second priority, which follows closely from the multiversity's democratic role, is to give increased attention to undergraduate education – there is nothing more deserving. The ideas of our age are more threatening to undergraduate education than to professional education, graduate education, or research. In the pincers of the constrained welfare state, multiversities have compromised quality in undergraduate education more than in other areas; undergraduate class sizes increase, and interaction between students and professors declines. The multiversity is often called the 'research' university – a signal of its top priority – and the character of our age further reinforces this priority. The prestige of a multiversity depends upon the quality of its research. Governments demand that research be increased and commercialized. Our age has many forces that are creating a competitive hierarchy among multiversities, both within countries and across countries. Presidents and deans do not want their multiversity to slide in the rankings, and therefore every president and dean emphasizes the need for new research grants and new publications.

The wider community, however, will not accept this low priority given to undergraduate study. Frank Rhodes went on: 'if research universities are to continue as major forces in American life, they need to give undergraduate education the sustained campus-wide attention it deserves. Approaches will vary from campus to campus, but the questions to be addressed are universal.'[2] The same is true for all Anglo-American multiversities.

The problems of undergraduate education have been simmering within the multiversity since its emergence. Clark Kerr, in his Godkin lectures, reflecting in 1963 on the future of this new form of university, noted: 'Recent changes in the American university have done them [undergraduate students] little good – lower teaching loads for faculty, larger classes, the use of substitute teachers for the regular faculty, the choice of faculty members based on research accomplishment rather than instructional capacity, the fragmentation of knowledge into endless subdivisions.'[3] Disappointment at the continuing failure to pay more attention to undergraduate education runs as a lament through Clark Kerr's forty years of observations of the American multiversity.

Similar distress is evident in other countries. For example, Tom Pocklington and Allan Tupper make it the focus of their critique of Canadian universities. 'Modern Canadian universities wrongly and seriously devalue the education of undergraduates.' Pocklington and Tupper advocate that 'universities must establish undergraduate teaching as their first priority. Undergraduate teaching must be recognized and valued for what it is: a complex and important activity that demands broad reading, disciplined thought, and great effort.'[4]

Undergraduate education has received more commitment in the multiversities of England, perhaps because mass university education has only recently arrived and perhaps because English undergraduate education is more specialized and therefore undergraduate education is more closely connected to the research specialization of faculty members. Peter Scott in a recent review of British universities concluded: 'since the mid-1980s, Britain has acquired a system of mass higher education – partly by crooked design and partly in a fit of absentmindedness – but a system that still retains many of the admirable qualities of an elite system. For instance, there continues to be a close and creative embrace between teaching on the one hand and research and scholarship on the other, a strong and continuing commitment to undergraduate education, and a still vital tradition of academic "intimacy" reflected in teaching styles, patterns of pastoral care and personal relationships between staff and students.'[5] Scott acknowledges that the future is obscure but remains optimistic that these features can be retained. His optimism may be misplaced, given the poor funding of British universities and the inexorable pressures of our age operating on all multiversities.

Undergraduate education was not always a low priority. In the nineteenth century, no one needed reminding that undergraduate education was the central task. It was unquestionably the pre-eminent task. Nineteenth century undergraduate education, exemplified by Cardinal Newman's Oxford, lives on in the Anglo-American imagination, elusively telling us what an undergraduate education *ought* to be. Students live in college; classes are small; students and professors are in regular discussion. College is a place of study and learning, but also a place of debates, and athletics; it is a place of living, a community, where knowledge is acquired and character formed. This pedagogy remains much admired, if impossible to sustain, and stands as a benchmark in Anglo-American discussions of undergraduate learning.

Viewed from one perspective, the decline of the residential college with its small classes is evidence of the declining priority of undergraduate education, and so a cause for lament. From another perspective, the decline is a necessary result of our democratic commitment to mass university education. Both living in residence and small classes are too expensive for mass university education. We have, however, achieved mass university education in our democracies, and that is an accomplishment to celebrate.

As we renew the social contract, there are numerous questions to address regarding undergraduate education at the multiversity, and they are made pressing by the character of our age. For example, the constrained welfare state brings rising tuition and concerns about access. The increasing use of part-time untenured faculty is deeply worrying. However, the focus of this chapter will be on only one of the many issues, the one I believe is most critical: the need to re-envision a liberal education. This, too, follows from the multiversity being an institution of democracy. If the multiversity is to fulfill its responsibilities to democratic life, it must offer its undergraduates the opportunity for a liberal education.

A powerful contributing cause to the declining importance of undergraduate education in our age is the ever-increasing importance attached to research. This tension is longstanding and inherent in the multiversity: ever since undergraduate teaching and advanced research were combined into one institution, a fierce debate has raged as to whether undergraduate teaching is complementary to, or competitive with, research.

In fact, the multiversity has proven to be a relatively hospitable home for undergraduate education. Within the multiversity, most professors teach both undergraduate and graduate students, as well as doing their research. This ensures that undergraduates are taught by people able to discuss the most current findings and controversies of the discipline and that undergraduates are introduced to the research enterprise. The multiversity allows, especially in the upper-level courses, professors to teach courses closely related to their own research. This close connection between the curriculum and the intellectual passions of the professor promotes good teaching. Within a multiversity, the student is better able to glimpse what lies ahead in study at an advanced level. The professor's research, the graduate school, and the many professional schools are there to observe, and so the student sees choices not visible in undergraduate-focused universities. At a multiversity, the student has access to better libraries, laboratories, and computer facilities.

Nonetheless, it must be candidly admitted that the research mission of the multiversity is potentially the greatest disadvantage to undergraduate education. The claims that teaching and research are competitors contain much truth. It must be acknowledged that the criterion given most weight in hiring professors at multiversities is their promise in research; that the process of tenure and promotion gives most weight to research accomplishments, although teaching and service are also evaluated; and that the highest accolades in the academic community go to its most distinguished scholars. Professorial time is limited: time spent reading and thinking about pedagogy is time not spent reading and thinking about a research problem. The tensions between undergraduate teaching and advanced research are obvious and widely recognized, but the means to redress the growing imbalance are less obvious, and initiatives to give teaching greater priority are honoured more in word than deed.

Frank Rhodes is a determined and eloquent champion of teaching within the research multiversity. He takes the title of his recent book, *The Creation of the Future: The Role of the American University*, from the writing of Alfred North Whitehead: 'The task of the university is the creation of the future, so far as rational thought, and civilized modes of appreciation, can affect the issue.'[6] This responsibility for tomorrow leads Rhodes to argue that university teaching must be approached as a moral vocation. He realizes that it is not now seen as a moral vocation in the multiversity, and offers suggestions for how to realize the goal. But his overall assessment is optimistic: 'not every professor is a star [teacher], of course. But most are responsible, passionately committed to their profession, and deeply concerned for their students.'[7]

Inadvertently, in supporting undergraduate teaching, Rhodes has revealed a problem for liberal learning. Professors are 'passionately committed to their profession,' to their discipline, to the advancement of knowledge in their field. From this flows that they are 'deeply concerned for their students,' as their students seek to learn their field. The degree program of the undergraduate is made up, typically, of sixteen to twenty full-year courses, taken over four years. Within these, students choose a major – for example, English, economics, or biology – and this becomes the focus of their study. The multiversity organizes itself in a similar way: into the English department, the economics department, the biology department, and so on. Professors in each department are responsible for the content of each course and for the regulations governing which courses are necessary to receive a degree. Professors care deeply about 'their' students and care deeply about the process of introducing students to 'their' discipline.

Within individual departments, undergraduate study does have some priority. We should recognize this and celebrate it. But what is missing in the multiversity is a priority for liberal education rather than disciplinary education, a priority for general education rather than specialized education. This priority, the multiversity has difficulty addressing, both structurally, because the multiversity is organized by department, and intellectually, because of the overwhelming power of the research ideal. Also, the spirit of our age is inhospitable to the ideal of liberal learning. In the constrained welfare state, legislators frequently ask whether government grants to multiversities have been spent effectively and then go on to measure the 'success' of undergraduate education by the success of the graduates in the labour market. Students have been told since they were very young how a university education is necessary for a career in the knowledge-based economy; and they arrive at university with a most instrumental attitude – how will this degree help me to get a job? The declining commitment to liberal learning, the declining commitment to knowledge for its own sake, contributes to mission drift in the multiversity. The urgent task for the multiversity is to renew its commitment to liberal education.

We must ask the two fundamental questions: What is the purpose of an undergraduate education and what should be in the curriculum? In so doing, we must go on to ask: What is the correct balance between a disciplinary education and a liberal education? These questions are perennial ones, but we must ask them again in the context of the ideas of our age. What does it mean to be liberally educated in our age – this information age, this postmodern time, this era of globalization? These questions have not received as much attention as they deserve at most multiversities in recent years, but they can be evaded no longer. By struggling with these questions, we will restore attention to many of the ideals on which the university is based.

First Democracy and Undergraduate Education

Before exploring the specifics of a liberal education for our age, I want to pause and consider again the multiversity as an institution of democracy, emphasizing the connections between education and democratic life. These connections are drawn out marvelously in a recent book, *First Democracy: The Challenge of an Ancient Idea*, by Paul Woodruff, the Darrel K. Royal Professor in Ethics and American Society and Distinguished Teaching Professor in the Department of Philosophy of the University of Texas at Austin. Woodruff analyses the 'first democracy,' in Athens, and finds that in it the place of education was fundamental and explicit. Woodruff asserts that the originators of democracy believed a government is a democracy insofar as it tries to express seven ideas: 'freedom from tyranny, harmony, the rule of law, natural equality, citizen wisdom, reasoning without knowledge, and general education.'[8] Especially interesting about Woodruff's analysis of first democracy are the last three ideas: citizen wisdom, reasoning without knowledge, and general education.

In a democracy, ordinary people are asked to make decisions rather than experts and ordinary people are asked to pass judgment on their leaders. Woodruff writes: 'the heart of democracy is the idea that ordinary people have the wisdom they need to govern themselves.'[9] The challenging question is: Do ordinary people have such wisdom? Many ancient philosophers were skeptical, arguing that experts would always be better qualified and that ordinary people would be too easily swayed by 'clever' speakers. These philosophers argued against democracy but the first democrats disagreed, arguing that citizens had sufficient wisdom. Citizen wisdom came, they believed, from three sources: human nature, experience, and general education.

In Greek mythology, human nature was formed as people received two gifts from the gods, Prometheus gave humans expert knowledge – *techne* – and Zeus gave humans reverence and justice 'so that reverence and justice would bring order to cities and be communal bonds of friendship' and thus allow humans to govern themselves. But there was a crucial difference between these gifts. Not everyone had the ability to acquire expert knowledge, but everyone had the ability to acquire reverence and justice. Reverence and justice were part of human nature. 'This is the most important and controversial idea behind democracy: it is a natural part of being human to know enough to govern your community.'[10]

Citizen wisdom was not just part of human nature as a gift from the gods; it was also acquired by experience, by tradition, by living as an Athenian. Each Athenian citizen had a role in educating other Athenians in the practices of good judgment and good government.

Finally, citizen wisdom comes from general education. Government, the Athenians appreciated, required 'reasoning without knowledge.' That is, the future cannot be known and the outcome of our decisions cannot be known with certainty. Even the expert cannot know the future, and the reasoning without knowledge needed in democracy must draw not only upon expert knowledge, but also upon the wisdom of citizens and open, often adversarial, debate. The proper preparation for such democratic deliberation is not technical education, but rather general education, what the Greeks called *paideia*. This general education 'should give a citizen the wisdom to judge what he is told by people who do claim to be experts.' '*Paideia* is the kind of education which makes for better citizens or (as we would now say) for better human beings. To the Athenians, "better" meant "having more *arête*," and *arête* meant "excellence" or "virtue."'[11]

In first democracy, general or liberal education was of the essence. Surely this is also true of today's democracy. Undergraduate education is the central task of the multiversity and ensuring that undergraduate education fulfills its commitment to democracy is crucial. In our democracy today, just as in the first democracy, citizen wisdom requires less emphasis on disciplinary education – *techne* – and more emphasis on general education, on *paideia* – on a liberal education.

A Liberal Education and its Curriculum

There is no single conception of what it means to be liberally educated. Our ideas go back to rich diversity of ancient Greek and Roman thought, and through history, the ideals of liberal learning have evolved and intertwined, in often contradictory ways. Some of this history was discussed in chapters 2 and 3.

Bruce Kimball is his *Orators and Philosophers: A History of the Idea of Liberal Education* characterized one theme of classical thought as the tradition of the orator. It was given coherent shape by the Romans, especially Cicero. Orators are engaged in public life. The first goal of a liberal education is the training of good citizens, virtuous and capable. This training requires values and standards of conduct, and respect for these values and standards. In the medieval synthesis of the oratorical tradition, the values are to be found in Greek and Roman literature and early Christian texts. In the nineteenth century, the values and standards could be found in the 'best that has been thought and said.' This tradition of the orator Kimball calls the *artes liberales* ideal of liberal education.

Kimball characterizes a second theme as the tradition of the philosopher. It also traces lineage to ancient thinkers, in this case to those such as Socrates and Aristotle who rejected the pre-eminence of rhetoric. In its stead, they gave pre-eminence to mathematics and philosophy, to the disciplined pursuit of knowledge. Like all classical thinkers, they are concerned with the human personality but argue that wholeness and virtue come from knowledge. The human personality must be freed from the constraints of tradition and orthodoxy; all must be subject to the scrutiny of philosophy, for the unexamined life is not worth living. During the seventeenth and eighteenth centuries, through the Enlightenment and the Scientific Revolution, the philosophical tradition was revived, and Kimball identifies it as a second ideal of liberal education: the liberal-free tradition. Its primary goal was freedom, especially from a priori strictures and standards. It emphasizes intellect and rationality, its method is critical scepticism, and it is tolerant and egalitarian. It also concerns citizenship, but citizenship based on volition rather than obligation.

The curriculum to achieve the *artes liberales* ideal is founded in the study of language and letters, the reading of texts, and the public expression of ideas. The humanities have a high priority. The curriculum to achieve the liberal-free ideal is more open, more methodologically oriented than subject-based. Priority in the curriculum is given to logic, mathematics, and philosophy, because these discipline the mind. Both traditions value breadth of knowledge, although the commitment to breadth is stronger in the *artes liberales* tradition. The difference is one of the relative priority given to the literary and oratorical versus the scientific and philosophical. Both traditions agree with Cardinal Newman: at a university, although students 'cannot pursue every subject that is open to them, they will be the gainers by living among those and under those who represent the whole circle.' And so they apprehend 'the great outlines of knowledge, the principles on which it rests, the scale of its parts, its shades and its lights, its great points and its little.'[12]

When students arrive at the multiversity today, we tell them that they can embark on a liberal education. In fact, I would argue, they cannot. Students will not find a degree program designed to provide a liberal education. They will not find a degree program based on either the *artes liberales* ideal or the liberal-free ideal. What they will find are degree programs based in individual academic disciplines.[13]

The curriculum in each department is designed to introduce the student to that discipline, and move the student to an increasing level of familiarity and sophistication within that discipline. It is regarded as important to make students aware of the current research in the discipline and to prepare them to read the academic literature. Professors often say that the purpose of the instruction is, for example, to learn 'to think like an economist,' or 'to think like a biologist.' Careful attention is paid, in designing courses and course sequences, to offer a track that will prepare the student for graduate school in that discipline. The department-based curriculum is intended to provide a liberal education only in the most indirect sense.

The argument that disciplinary education cannot be liberal education should not be accepted before acknowledging two countervailing views. Since the mid-nineteenth century, there has been an argument that a specialized education is the true liberal education. It is a modern view formed by the reality of rapidly expanding knowledge, the division of labour in life, and the conviction that mastery of one field is necessary for individual fulfilment. In 1870, Mark Pattison, rector of Lincoln College, Oxford, stated the view clearly: 'the system of general information, knowing a little of the surface of a half dozen things, has its value, but ... on the whole, the result of such an education is an inferior result to the result of a deep and thorough investigation of some one great branch of knowledge ... I think that true thoroughness in a scientific man, and true thoroughness in a philosophical [i.e., a literary] man would not tend to isolate him from other branches ... If you have got past a certain stratum in investigation, your sympathies begin to widen, and the more you know of your subject, the more you begin to see that it has ramifications into every other subject.'[14]

Although there is wisdom in this position, few would go so far as Mark Pattison and claim that disciplinary specialization is the *best* route to a liberal education. True, broad study can be shallow, and depth of investigation can, on occasion, lead to understanding of the breadth and interconnectedness of knowledge. Therefore, disciplinary education *can* help advance the goals of a liberal education. But specialization, on most occasions, leads to narrowness and the ignoring of other branches of knowledge. Specialists seldom get past that certain stratum in investigation and allow their sympathies to widen. Most would agree that study across several branches of knowledge, rather than deep investigation of one branch, is more likely to lead to an understanding of the breadth and interconnectedness of knowledge.

A second qualification to this claim is that a liberal education is not so much about the subjects studied, as it is about the spirit in which the study is conducted. Paul Axelrod's recent reflection on Canadian universities, *Values in Conflict: The University, the Marketplace, and The Trials of Liberal Education* takes this view. For him, the fundamental conflict is between the values of the marketplace and the values of liberal learning. Axelrod offers as a definition of liberal education: 'liberal education in the university refers to activities that are designed to cultivate intellectual creativity, autonomy, and resilience; critical thinking; a combination of intellectual breadth and specialized knowledge; the comprehension and tolerance of diverse ideas and experiences; informed participation in community life; and effective communication skills.'[15] Such a definition requires no specific curriculum or study of certain subjects. Axelrod believes these objectives 'can and should be integrated into scientific, technical, and professional education.' Any curriculum can be a liberal education, provided the study is done in the proper spirit.

This view highlights how liberal education requires a certain spirit in the teaching and learning. The multiversity can and should do much more to ensure that study in each discipline is governed more by the spirit of liberal learning, and less by the spirit of that discipline. However, attempts to reduce liberal learning to the spirit of the study rob the concept of its root meanings. I would strongly argue that an undergraduate education will not be liberal education if it is only disciplinary education. When Cardinal Newman said that undergraduate education should not be preparation for a job, he was recognizing that such an education could become deformed by this purpose. He also recognized, however, that undergraduate education could be deformed if it pursued knowledge in a single discipline. He wrote that a liberal education is the 'process of training, by which the intellect, instead of being formed or sacrificed to some particular or accidental purpose, some specific trade or profession, or study or science, is disciplined for its own sake.'[16] Study in one discipline can be just as deforming as study in preparation for a job.

Nevertheless, we know that students must specialize for part of their degrees. The undergraduate degree in a system of mass university education cannot be entirely general education. The postindustrial society demands specialization. One implication of specialization is that not all students will study the same thing – they may choose to concentrate their studies from the vast range of specializations available at the multiversity. In mass university education in a democratic society, students come from such a diversity of backgrounds, with such a diversity of interests, and go on to such a diversity of destinations, that such choice is essential. Whatever our conception of a liberal education, we must acknowledge that specialization will be one of the purposes of an undergraduate education; indeed it will be the primary purpose. Some small colleges or small universities might decide to offer their undergraduate degrees without any specialization and base them on a coherent conception of a liberal education, but this cannot be the model for the multiversity. The core of an undergraduate degree will remain the major in a discipline, and this specialization is an essential part of a liberal education.[17]

The purposes of a liberal undergraduate education have been variously articulated and with different emphases. Paul Axelrod's conception is cited above. Frank Rhodes outlined his idea of the purposes of an undergraduate education. It should develop: 'the ability to listen, read, and analyse with comprehension and to write and speak with precision and clarity in the expression of disciplined thought; the ability to reason effectively in quantitative and formal terms; the ability to engage people of different cultural perspectives; the appreciation of the modes of thought and expression of the natural sciences, the social sciences, the humanities and the arts; some sensitivity toward the ideas, values, and goals that have shaped society and some sense of the moral implications of actions and ideas; skill in one chosen area of knowledge, with an understanding of its assumptions, foundations, relationships and implications; [and should include] some active participation in the life of the campus community.'[18]

Many in the Anglo-American world today would place more emphasis on the need to develop a multicultural and global perspective, because of the nature of our world. Nonetheless, virtually all would recognize that the primary purpose of a liberal education is not to prepare for a job – although this most certainly is an indirect outcome. The liberal undergraduate education recognizes the value of knowledge for its own sake and, to recall Cardinal Newman, 'its end is fitness for the world.'

The first step to ensuring that an undergraduate degree provides a liberal education is to scrutinize each disciplinary degree program. We should assert that the purpose of each disciplinary degree is to provide both disciplinary and liberal education. Then we can examine the curriculum and the courses in each department to ensure that both purposes are served. The departmental curriculum should point not just toward graduate school, but also towards the breadth and interconnectedness of knowledge. As part of the curriculum in each discipline there should be an exploration of how that branch of knowledge relates to others. The curriculum should try to overcome the fragmentation of knowledge and demonstrate how various branches of knowledge are interrelated. And within its curriculum, each discipline should examine how it relates to democratic life and how its graduates might function as citizens. For example, the curriculum of the biology department would consider the future role of their graduates as citizen/biologist, and the history curriculum would consider the citizen/historian and so on. These tasks of curriculum reform will not be easy, because each department's curriculum has been designed to introduce students to that discipline, and the usual worry is that there is not enough time to really get to know that discipline. Much can be done, however, with modest changes in individual courses. Even a modest reorientation could make a great difference in making a disciplinary education more of a liberal education.

After the scrutiny of each discipline, we are left with the far more important issue of how to ensure that the *entire* degree provides a liberal education. This should be the priority in the renewal of the social contract in democratic society, the priority of the multiversity as an institution of democracy. To this end, I would offer a more specific proposal.

A Liberal Education Minor

My proposal is that each multiversity develop a structured program of liberal education – a liberal education minor – which students could take, *if they so chose*, in conjunction with their major. Thus, students would be able to complete a major in a discipline, *plus* a liberal education minor. The liberal education minor would be *specifically designed* as a liberal education. The degree regulations of most multiversities already allow students to take a major program in one discipline and a minor program in another discipline. For example, a student could take a major in political science and a minor in economics, or a major in biology and a minor in mathematics. Students often choose a major and minor that are related to each other, but there is no need for such close complementarity; a student could do a major in political science and a minor in biology. Under my proposal, a student could do a major in any discipline and a liberal education minor.

Many multiversities make some attempt to ensure that their undergraduates acquire a general education beyond the student's major. The most common approach is a compulsory breadth requirement: all students as part of their degree must take at least one course in each of the three great branches of knowledge: a course in science, in social science, and in humanities (including fine arts). The objective is that students learn, or at least become aware of, the methodologies of the fundamental branches of knowledge, the fundamental ways that we know and interpret the world. This breadth requirement is simple to implement: the existing courses in all departments in the multiversity remain the same, and the student chooses from a designated list. It requires no debate or consensus about the content of the courses, and the university remains organized in the same way. However, this requirement does not offer a program of study designed specifically around the principles of a liberal education. Nonetheless, its simplicity should not be allowed to diminish appreciation for how it meets a fundamental requirement for liberal learning: exposure to and some understanding of the fundamental branches of knowledge.

Another approach is a compulsory general education program. This too usually requires a course in each of the fundamental branches of knowledge – science, social science, and humanities – but does not use the existing departmental courses; rather, specially designed courses are created. However, a compulsory general education program is difficult to implement because it requires consensus among professors on the content of these courses, because it must confront the great heterogeneity of the student body, and because a compulsory program becomes a very large program, which fits uneasily upon the departmental structure of the university. Perhaps the most famous example is Harvard's general education program set out in *General Education in a Free Society* (the Redbook), discussed in chapter 3. Published in 1945, it sought to come to terms with mass university education and therefore with the diversity of student backgrounds and the new democratic purposes of undergraduate education. Although differing in specifics, and responsive to the particularities of their locale and their faculty members, many other multiversities implemented similar compulsory programs of general education. (Ironically, the Redbook curriculum was not fully implemented at Harvard, although its prescriptions were highly influential elsewhere.)

In 1995, reflecting on this tradition of general education, Sidney Katz, president of the American Council of Learned Societies, concluded: 'the tradition has by now weakened at most institutions and disappeared at some. There are no doubt many reasons for this phenomenon, ranging from a lack of a sense of novelty to rejection of liberal education in favor of vocationalism. Over the past decade, however, even the postwar version of liberal education has increasingly been rejected by significant numbers of faculty and students as being anti-democratic in its pro-Western, intellectually elitist assumptions.'[19] Much of the critique comes from postmodern thought. Canadian general education programs have suffered the same fate.

In postwar England, the undergraduate degree was, and remains, very specialized. It is a puzzle that England, the place of vigorous debates about liberal education during the nineteenth century, has not continued these debates during the later twentieth century. England's debates about undergraduate education do not include much debate about the place and meaning of liberal learning. Perhaps this is because of England's late move to mass university education. A debate about liberal learning will likely emerge as England becomes more racially and ethnically diverse, and as it becomes more concerned with social cohesion and assimilation, and as it struggles in the same way as Canada and the United States about the meaning of citizenship.[20]

I believe that it is no longer possible to generate a university-wide consensus for the content of a general or liberal education program which would be required for all students. My proposal for a liberal education minor is offered in the conviction that the project of liberal undergraduate education is today better served by allowing students to choose whether to emphasize liberal learning, rather than having it compulsory. Freed of the necessity of designing the program for all students, the liberal education minor will be more creatively imagined and constructed than compulsory general education programs. Only those professors committed to the ideal of liberal learning need be involved.

The liberal education minor would have more courses than a typical breadth requirement or a typical general education program, and the courses in the minor would not be existing departmental courses but specifically created for this program. My proposal would be five courses within a twenty-course degree. Students choosing to take the liberal education minor would be exempted from any breadth or general education requirements. It is noteworthy that in the past many of the courses specifically designed for a general education program were taught by professors who saw themselves as public intellectuals.[21] The connection of a liberal education with public intellectuals is no mere coincidence.

The content of the liberal education minor —what would be covered in the five specially designed courses – would differ across multiversities. Its content would respond to the interests of students and professors in each multiversity. There is no one design for a program of liberal learning. I believe the courses should ensure that all students study and engage with the humanities, social sciences, sciences and technology, and fine arts, although there is no need that this be accomplished by having one course devoted specifically to each. I can imagine that some multiversities might require a foreign language; others might have a more demanding mathematics and statistics component; or others that include a component of study abroad. On reading drafts of this manuscript, several colleagues urged me to include my own recommendation for the content of the liberal education minor. I have resisted, because the thrust of my recommendation is not about the specific content but rather that each multiversity should take up the question of what it means to be liberally educated and how should this be implemented in a curriculum. There are already many proposals for the curriculum of a liberal education to consider, for example, those in Robert Proctor's *Education's Great Amnesia: Reconsidering the Humanities from Petrarch to Freud* or in Charles Anderson's *Prescribing the Life of the Mind*. Harvard University, always a leader in such reflections, has over the past several years has been re-examining its core curriculum and has proposed changes.[22] Clark Kerr, following Ortega y Gasset's idea that a liberal education should create individuals possessed of 'general culture,' suggests that courses should deal with 'the expected "great ideas" and "great issues" prospectively facing the next generation so that students might better be able to cope with the challenges of the new age – to understand these challenges and to analyse competitive responses to them.'[23] Confronting and deliberating on the questions about the content of the liberal education minor at each multiversity are as important as the answers, and most certainly different multiversities will answer the questions in different ways. In the ideal, these deliberations at each multiversity would be public and would engage their community in reflection upon the purposes and curriculum of undergraduate education. These deliberations should be part of the ongoing renegotiation of the social contract and the multiversity has a special obligation to initiate and lead the discussion.

The true substance of my recommendation is not the specific content but that students should be offered an *opportunity*, an opportunity they are now denied: students at every multiversity should be offered the opportunity to take up a program of study *intentionally designed* to offer a liberal education. An ecology of experimentation would be encouraged across the system. In this spirit, however, I do offer some questions to consider in these deliberations about how to design the curriculum of the liberal education minor and two recommendations as to content. In no sense are these suggestions a blueprint.

Three Questions in Our Age

The literature on liberal education is filled with questions that must be addressed in designing the curriculum. They have been asked in every age. However, I believe that three questions are especially important to designing a liberal education specific to our age. As we design the liberal education minor, we should reflect intensely upon them: What are the barriers within our students to their thinking for themselves? Why should students study the humanities? Should we use the *artes liberales* and liberal-free traditions in designing a liberal education, or should we create a new approach?

There will not be one answer to these questions, or necessarily even any answer, but the struggle to understand them is of great value and should be part of curriculum design. The continuing struggle with these questions helps preserve the inheritance of the university and helps to anchor the multiversity against mission drift.

Liberal education has sought to create autonomous individuals, individuals who could think for themselves. However, the barriers to thinking for oneself have not always been the same. In classical times, the barriers were tradition, habit, and custom. At the time of the Enlightenment, the barriers were religion and the aristocratic political order. But what are the barriers today? Students are certainly not bound by tradition, habit, or custom. Indeed, most students in the United States, England, and Canada would need a liberal education to see how tradition, habit, or custom might have authority in someone's life. Neither religion (with some notable exceptions) nor an aristocratic order is a barrier to independent thought in today's students. Students arrive at the university well tutored in the notion that they should make up their own minds and that they should be sceptical of received wisdom. Yet, university students are not, nor are most of us, the autonomous individuals who are the objective of a liberal education.

The barriers to thinking for oneself are elusive, but real, in the modern era. Sociology has revealed how modern individuals are both free and yet fundamentally constrained by the social order. Max Weber argued that reason itself, bureaucracy, and technology, are barriers to freedom. In his famous image, we are not free but live in an 'iron cage.' Running through virtually every critique of modernity is the theme that we appear free but are enslaved. What is our iron cage today? We must puzzle out this question in designing a liberal education.

If students in previous eras came to the university from a culture based on tradition, what culture have today's student's come from? Today, they come from a media-saturated consumer culture; they live in a postmodern condition. Television, the Internet, advertising, mass consumption, fashion, and lifestyle have surrounded them since birth. David Lyon, in *Postmodernity*, writes: 'the postmodern is rightly associated with a society where consumer lifestyles and mass consumption dominate the waking lives of its members.' 'Consumerism knows no boundaries. It neither respects domains once immune from its effects, nor supports markers of cultural territory. As Philip Sampson notes, "Once established, such a culture of consumption is quite undiscriminating and everything becomes a consumer item, including meaning, truth, and knowledge." Product image, style, and design take over from modern metanarratives the task of conferring meaning ... All is fragmented, heterogeneous, dispersed, plural, – and subject to consumer choices.'[24] We do not understand fully this condition of postmodernity, but surely a culture that makes meaning through consumerism, image, and lifestyle will be as big a barrier to independent critical thought as a culture bound by tradition or religion.

The condition of postmodernity, moreover, carries a more profound barrier then even consumerism. The modern world and the modern university believe in progress through human reason, but postmodern thought no longer accepts this metanarrative. What remains is nihilism, or at best a turbulence of relativism. The only stance to take on the world is ironic bemusement. We must struggle to understand what barriers to thinking for oneself such a world creates in our students.

We assume and celebrate the multiversity as a place of free thought. We should not, however, be smug or forget that the space for independent thought must be constantly patrolled and defended. Professors and students have often brought ideological predispositions to their study, which can solidify into a conviction that truth has been found and eventually into intolerance of other orientations. Some critics assert that independent thought is no longer possible within the multiversity because political correctness, they claim, allows only the approved point of view. Those accused of political correctness retort that their demands are not closing down spaces for debate, but rather opening up space for those previously marginalized. Other critics allege that a chilly climate isolates all but those who hold the dominant views of their discipline. And still others argue that patriotic correctness in the global war on terror has silenced independent thought. Many of us take our news and do our reading from sources we know will agree with our preconceptions – we read not to have our thinking challenged but to have it confirmed. All these can be iron cages for our students (and indeed for professors) and barriers to a liberal education.

A second question to ponder in the design of the liberal education minor, very much a question for our age, is why students should study the humanities. We must recognize how threatened are the humanities in our world and how their traditional justifications have been eroded. In the oratorical tradition of the ancient world, literature was the source of values and standards of conduct. In Matthew Arnold's reformulation, 'the best that has been thought and said' provided a counterforce to the philistinism of bourgeois society. For Lionel Trilling, literature could still improve the moral imagination. But these traditions are now exhausted. Literature is not regarded as a moral force;

indeed literature has often been complicit in discourses of domination. Yet we still accept that reading literature must be part of a liberal education. We need a renewed language of justification.

We have almost lost the skill of speaking about literature, and our twenty-first century climate is not hospitable to its cultivation. The skill has atrophied for a long time. Instrumental rationality – the capacity to devise, choose, and implement the most economical means for achieving given ends – guides our living in the world. This has been liberating and allowed magnificent improvement in daily life, but it also flattens and diminishes the world. Charles Taylor called it 'the malaise of modernity.'[25] The university has been always been a place simultaneously celebrating reason and also the value of literature, but things are changing rapidly in the multiversity. Paying higher fees and graduating with higher debts, students become more instrumental. They ask: What do I get for paying this high fee? Will it get me a secure and well-paid job? Donors, both private and corporate, favor science, medicine, and technology over the humanities. Multiversities are now regarded as institutions for producing ideas and people of direct economic benefit. Instrumental reason governs the multiversity's affairs and its view of the world. And it must be said that the humanities departments themselves, taking a postmodern stance to the text, have diminished the pleasures of reading and undermined the traditional justifications for the study of literature.

The renewed justification for reading the humanities must begin from the belief that reason alone is inadequate for complete knowledge of the world and that reason alone is inadequate as the basis for being human. We must start from a view of human nature which recognizes that an autonomous individual possessed of instrumental reason cannot be complete. Humans need to be autonomous, but they also need to be connected to other humans. Reason alone is not the means to connect to others and to understand oneself. The experience of joy and love, of sadness and grief, of honour and dignity, are part of being human, and cannot be approached through reason alone. The multiversity, autonomous and (still somewhat) separated from economic life, surely is a place to articulate this justification by incorporating it into its reflection on a liberal education.

Charles W. Anderson, in his essay on the aims of liberal education and the duties of the citizen, proposes that the task of the humanities 'is to teach us how to go beyond the thin theory of knowledge, to teach us how to extract a fuller measure of meaning from the world, and to provide us with deeper, more explicit, guidance on how to make our way in it.'[26] He quotes the novelist Annie Dillard: 'As symbol, or as the structuring of symbols, art can render intelligible – or at least visible, at least discussable – those wilderness regions which philosophy has abandoned and those hazardous terrains where science's tools do not fit. I mean the rim of knowledge where language falters; and I mean all those areas of human experience, feeling, and thought about which we care so much and know so little; the meaning of all that is before us, of our love for each other, and the forms of freedom in time, and power, and destiny, and all whereof we imagine: grace, perfection, beauty, and the passage of all materials to thoughts and of all ideas to forms.'[27]

David Dyzenhaus, in his essay 'The Case for Public Investment in the Humanities,' offers another forceful justification, using an argument that he characterizes as pragmatic liberalism as opposed to the crude utilitarianism, so dominating today. His argument is eloquently presented in a lengthy quotation from the famous American Judge, Billings Learned Hand, which begins the essay:

> I dare hope why it might now begin to be clearer why I am arguing that an education which includes the 'humanities' is essential to political wisdom. By 'humanities' I especially mean history; but close behind history and of almost, if not quite equal importance are letters, poetry, philosophy, the plastic arts, and music. Most of the issues that mankind sets out to settle, it never does settle. They are not solved because ... they are incapable of solution properly speaking, being concerned with incommensurables. At any rate, even if that be not always true, the opposing parties seldom do agree upon a solution; and the dispute fades into the past unsolved, though perhaps it may be renewed as history, and fought over again. It disappears because it is replaced by some compromise that, although not wholly acceptable to either side, offers a tolerable substitute for victory; and he who would find the substitute needs an endowment as rich as possible in experience, an experience which makes the heart generous and provides the mind with an understanding of the hearts of others.[8]

This endowment is built by reading in the humanities. Justice Hand was writing about the proper preparation to be a lawyer or judge, but Dyzenhaus notes it is also the proper preparation be an excellent citizen. And Dyzenhaus argues that such humane citizens are public goods, the resources of a civilized society, and their creation is necessarily prior to creating a society where we can pursue our self-interest.

Such approaches justifying study in the humanities must be explored en route to designing a liberal education for our age. We need to hear more from our humanities professors. The leaders of the multiversity, as they present the multiversity to the world, have a special obligation to articulate the place of the humanities in a liberal education.

The third question to contemplate in designing the liberal education minor is how much of the *artes liberales* and liberal-free traditions can be utilized in our age. In the mid-1990s, Bruce Kimball was invited to review the practice of liberal education in the United States and at the same time to consider, despite the pre-eminence of the European traditions of orators and philosophers, whether there might be a specifically American theory of liberal education. He presented his analysis in his essay 'Toward Pragmatic Education' in the 1995 volume *The Condition of American Liberal Education: Pragmatism and a Changing Tradition*, and in a follow-up essay in the 1997 volume *Education and Democracy: Reimagining Liberal Learning in America*.[29] He reported that 'a consensus is emerging around some seven points in discussion about liberal education in the United States. These seven points are that liberal education should: first, become more multicultural; second, elevate general education and integration rather than specialization; third, promote the commonweal and citizenship; fourth, regard all "levels" of education as belonging to a common enterprise; fifth, reconceive teaching as stimulating learning and inquiry; sixth, promote the formation of values and the practice of service; and seventh, employ assessment.'[30] He goes on to argue the provocative hypothesis that a new conception of liberal education is emerging in the United States rooted in philosophical pragmatism. After the traditions of the orator and the philosopher, he argues, we must recognize the emergence of a new tradition of liberal education that he calls pragmatic liberal education.

Kimball argues that 'these recent developments are usually discussed as separate responses to particular demographic, economic, or disciplinary changes, and they therefore appear to be unrelated, even disparate. But they may be collectively construed as being "pragmatic," either in the sense of being conceptually rooted in pragmatism or in the sense of being rationalized, justified in principle, by pragmatic conceptions.'[31] Among six points of pragmatism imbuing the new liberal education, he lists: 'that belief and meaning, even truth itself, are fallible and revisable; that an experimental method of inquiry obtains in all science and reflective thought; that belief, meaning, and truth depend on the context and intersubjective judgment of the community in which they are formed; that the purpose of resolving doubts or solving problems is intrinsic to all thought and inquiry; and that all inquiry and thought are evaluative, and all judgments about fact are no different from judgments about value.'[32]

Kimball's hypothesis is provocative and demands our attention as we think about a liberal education for our age. American scholars are by no means in complete agreement that he has characterized the U.S. situation correctly. Perhaps because he was asked to explore whether there is an explicitly American theory of liberal education, Kimball asserts that the new conception of pragmatic liberal education is particularly American, and links it to the thought of American pragmatists John Dewey and William James. However, his assertion of American uniqueness is offered without any analysis of the state of liberal education outside the United States. From an external perspective, most of the themes he identifies – multiculturalism, values, citizenship, and general education – are dominant themes of discussion in much of the Anglo-American world. And most of the philosophical principles that he identifies as American pragmatism are also appearing as deep-rooted intellectual and cultural influences across the Anglo-American world.

Viewed in another way, many of these principles can be known by another name: postmodernism. Louis Menand in a follow-up essay to Kimball's wrote: '"Pragmatism" is Kimball's term for these [and allied] developments. It's a friendly sounding term. "Postmodernism" has, to many ears, a less genial sound; but the developments Kimball calls pragmatic might just as easily be called postmodernist.'[33] Using Menand's term, we may be witnessing the emergence of an ideal of liberal education rooted in postmodern thought.

Whatever our views, we cannot reflect on liberal education in our age without being cognizant of postmodern thought and reflecting on this analysis of Kimball and Menand. It is unlikely we will reach a consensus on one view of liberal education. Indeed, we will continue to draw upon both the *artes liberales* and liberal-free traditions. But we must also be aware of, and draw upon, this emergent third tradition, which, following the title of the second volume on Kimball's work – *Education and Democracy: Re-Imaging Liberal Learning in America* – I shall call, not a pragmatic or postmodern liberal education, but rather a democratic liberal education. Such a liberal education would be designed to serve not just any democracy, but the democracies of the Anglo-American world in the early twenty-first century. It is a liberal education that recognizes globalization and the multicultural diversity of Anglo-American societies, that recognizes that democratic life inherently involves differences and that we must deliberate together as we debate our differences, and finally it is a liberal education that emphasizes democratic citizenship.

Liberal Education and Citizenship

A liberal education, since its beginning in ancient Greece, has had education for citizenship as one of its purposes. I believe that the most important component to include in the liberal education minor is a renewed emphasis on citizenship. My conviction that we should restore an emphasis on citizenship arises from three sources.

The first is that society wants a renewed emphasis on citizenship. In his survey of the American debates about liberal education, Kimball identified several points of consensus: today's liberal education should promote the commonweal and citizenship and promote the formation of values and the practice of service. A survey of Canadian debates about liberal education would have produced the same picture and identified a similar concern about citizenship. Such concerns are also heard in England.

The second source is my belief, discussed in chapter 11, that the multiversity should be conceptualized as an institution of democracy. In its democratic role, the multiversity should provide an undergraduate liberal education which emphasizes citizenship.

The third source is my reading of current writing about democracy by political philosophers and political scientists. When I began to reflect upon the multiversity as an institution of democracy and upon citizenship in liberal education, I turned to this current writing about democracy. There has been an outpouring of writing about democracy over the last fifteen years and several themes stand out. In this literature, there is recognition that globalization is spreading democratic ideals, but there is also a deep concern about the actual practice of democracy in the Anglo-American world. A widely debated reform is to make our democracies more deliberative – democratic legitimacy requires that citizens have the ability and opportunity to participate in effective deliberation about government decisions which affect them. The idea of deliberative democracy and the multiversity's role in democratic deliberation was taken up in chapter 11; here, its relevance is that undergraduate education should prepare students for democratic deliberation. Finally, in this recent literature about democracy, there is great focus on the idea of citizenship. Intriguingly, there is virtually no mention of the university or undergraduate education in this recent political science literature about democracy and citizenship. But when you read this literature with the university and undergraduate education in mind, as I did, the relevance fairly jumps off the pages.

Derek Heater, of the University of Brighton, provides an excellent review of the citizenship literature in his 1999 book *What Is Citizenship?* He notes that other ages have had a 'heightened consciousness about citizenship, often associated with particular states. Fifth to fourth-century BC Athens, first-century BC to first-century AD Rome, late medieval Florence, late eighteenth-century America and France spring obviously to mind.' But the present heightened consciousness is different: 'it is virtually global in its extent.'[34] He attributes our current heightened consciousness about citizenship to the ideas of our age: to the collapse of statism, the information technology revolution, and to globalization and the perhaps-declining role of the nation state. He also attributes the renewed interest in citizenship to the multicultural diversity of nation states and the fact that, despite the dominance of liberal ideals, 'for large numbers of people throughout the world the idea of citizenship is still hollow and meaningless, deprived as they are of virtually all its attributes.'[35] Even in the Anglo-American world, many do not have all the attributes of citizenship. Our age is deeply concerned about the meaning of citizenship, and thus a liberal education minor that reinvigorates the concept of citizenship in undergraduate education will respond to these worries of our time.

Heater notes that the idea of citizenship contains two major traditions: 'the civic republican style, which places its stress on duties, and the liberal style, which emphasizes rights. Now, despite the former's origins in classical antiquity and therefore its longevity, it is the liberal form that has been dominant for the past two centuries and remains so today ... Compared to the republican variant, liberal citizenship is much less demanding on the individual. It involves a loosely committed relationship to the state, a relationship held in place in the main by a set of civic rights, honoured by the state, which otherwise interferes as little as possible in the citizen's life.'[36] The liberal tradition sees one's private life as most important; in contrast the civic republican tradition sees participation in public life as most important – citizens learn to submerge their private interests in a concern with the common good.

In the republican tradition, 'the crucial requirement was that citizens must be possessed of and display *arête*, goodness or virtue.'[37]

In reading about the two traditions, it is striking how the liberal and civic republican traditions of citizenship map almost directly onto Kimball's two traditions of liberal education: the liberal-free ideal and the *artes liberales* ideal. Nothing could better demonstrate how liberal education and citizenship are inseparably connected.

Throughout most of history, citizenship in liberal education has been a republican citizenship: an elite group of citizens, of superior mind and character, are prepared through their studies to lead. The *artes liberales* tradition utilized the civic republican idea of citizenship. Today, for our age, we cannot construct a vision of citizenship solely around the republican tradition. We do not have a consensus around the values that should be the basis for an *artes liberales* liberal education or a consensus around which texts should be read to discover these values. The old canon has been rightly criticized by postmodern thought as too patriarchal and Eurocentric. In all our democratic diversity, we no longer seek to create 'an elite group of citizens, of superior mind and character' to lead us. In our undergraduates, we require less a preparation for elite leadership and more a preparation for democratic citizenship.

There is, however, much to draw upon in the spirit of the civic republican and *artes liberales* traditions. A group of scholars, often labeled communitarians, is working to adapt the republican tradition to our age. They argue that liberal notions of citizenship and liberal-free learning should be tempered; liberal ideas have left us with unrestrained and selfish individualism. The importance of community and the common good has been too much downplayed. The balance between rights and responsibilities has been lost, and needs to be restored. They take from the civic republican tradition a renewed sense of democratic duty as opposed to democratic rights, and a renewed commitment to public life as opposed to private life. Their critique demands our attention, even if we do not fully reject the liberal tradition. We do need to re-explore the ideals of community, individual responsibility, and the common good. This must be part of citizenship in the liberal education for our age.[38]

Many scholars are exploring the current – and contested – meanings of democratic citizenship. Will Kymlicka and Wayne Norman survey this literature in their article 'Return of the Citizen: A Survey of Recent Work on Citizenship Theory.' Throughout much of the post–Second

World War period, the time when the multiversity emerged, citizenship was defined almost entirely in terms of rights, most famously and influentially as set out by T.H. Marshall. Kymlicka and Norman note: 'According to Marshall, citizenship is essentially a matter of ensuring that everyone is treated as a full and equal member of society. And the way to ensure this sense of membership is through according people an increasing number of citizenship rights ... For Marshall, the fullest expression of citizenship requires a liberal-democratic welfare state. By guaranteeing civil, political, and social rights to all, the welfare state ensures that every member of society feels like a full member of society, able to participate in and enjoy the common life of the society.'[39] The U.N. Universal Declaration of Human Rights follows the Marshall tradition. Many criticize this orthodoxy, however; it is too passive a notion of citizenship, it emphasizes rights over responsibilities, it contains little notion of the virtues of a good citizen and how they are to be inculcated, and it contains little obligation to participate in the political process. Others criticize it because it is unable (or unwilling) to accommodate the ethnic and cultural diversity of Anglo-American democratic societies – behind an apparent treatment of all in the same way, it leaves much inequality. Many people are still not full and equal members.

One strand of this current literature on citizenship is especially interested in how political participation in our liberal democracies might be increased and how the civility and public-spiritedness of citizens could be encouraged. Kymlicka and Norman identify several answers to the question of how the challenges to democratic citizenship might be met. One answer comes from liberal virtue theorists. These liberal theorists acknowledge that liberals must share blame for the current imbalance between rights and responsibilities. Liberals placed too much emphasis 'on the justification of rights and the institutions to secure these rights, without attending to the responsibilities of citizens.' Liberal virtue theorists articulate a list of citizenship virtues, including political virtues: a 'capacity to discern and respect the rights of others, willingness to demand only what can be paid for, ability to evaluate the performance of those in office, willingness to engage in public discourse.' According to Kymlicka and Norman, 'it is the last two virtues – the ability to question authority and the willingness to engage in public discourse – which are the most distinctive components of liberal virtue theory.'[40] These capacities of a good citizen have clear and direct implications for undergraduate liberal education. The liberal education minor is well-suited to developing the capacity to question authority and the willingness to engage in public discourse.

Martha Nussbaum's persuasive and passionate *Cultivating Humanity: A Classical Defense of Reform in Liberal Education* offers an insightful examination of liberal education and citizenship in the contemporary American curriculum. Her inspirations are classical writers, particularly the Stoics, but her concerns are modern to the moment. She recognizes that our multiversities are educating citizens and 'we must ask what a good citizen of the present day should be and should know.' She argues that a liberal education 'liberates the mind from the bondage of habit and custom, producing people who can function with sensitivity and alertness as citizens of the whole world. This is what Seneca meant by cultivating humanity.'[41] She acknowledges that scientific understanding and economic understanding are necessary for intelligent citizenship, but chooses to focus on those parts of the liberal education associated with the humanities. She identifies three capacities as 'essential for the cultivation of humanity in today's world.' The first is familiar: the capacity for critical examination of oneself and one's traditions. The second is the capacity to see ourselves not only as citizens of a region or country, but also and 'above all, as human beings bound to all other human beings by ties of recognition and concern.'[42] The third essential capacity of a citizen she calls 'the narrative imagination ... the ability to think what it might be like to be in the shoes of a person different from oneself, to be an intelligent reader of that person's story, and to understand the emotions and wishes and desires that someone so placed might have.'[43] Our students learn to understand others through cultivating a narrative imagination. Rejecting criticisms that multiculturalism in the curriculum has brought a relativism which undermines the core of liberal education, she concludes that in the United States, colleges and universities are developing curricula that cultivate humanity. Surely, one of the basic purposes of the liberal education minor should be this cultivation of humanity.

Much of the current writing about citizenship addresses the issue of identity and difference within a liberal democracy. It struggles to develop a concept of citizenship that is fitted for a multiethnic and multicultural society. Over the last twenty years, new social movements – for example those of women, gays, aboriginals, and racial minorities – have pointed to injustice and discrimination which persists despite universal citizenship. Even when they have enjoyed civil, political, and social rights as individuals, these groups have not felt full members of the community. They have sought and won new rights on the basis of their group difference. Cultural politics became as important as redistributive politics in the welfare state. There is a conflict between citizenship, which is universal, and identity, which is particular, between individual rights and group rights. Some see the conflict as irreconcilable, others are more optimistic, but always there is the anxiety that group rights will destroy community. An increasing number of political scientists and philosophers, whom Kymlicka and Norman call 'cultural pluralists,' argue 'that citizenship must take account of these differences. Cultural pluralists believe that the common rights of citizenship, originally defined by and for white men, cannot accommodate the special needs of minority groups. These groups can only be integrated into the common culture if we adopt what Iris Marion Young calls a conception of "differentiated citizenship." '[44]

These tensions are inescapable in a modern democracy. Isaiah Berlin in his famous essay 'Two Concepts of Liberty' elaborated the now-familiar concepts of negative liberty (freedom from) and positive liberty (freedom to). Citizenship must ensure both negative and positive liberty. In his essay, Berlin also elaborated a less familiar conception of group liberty. 'What oppressed classes or nationalities, as a rule, demand is neither simply unhampered liberty of action for their members, nor, above everything, equality of social and economic opportunity, still less, assignment of a place in a frictionless, organic state devised by the national lawgiver. What they want, as often as not, is simply recognition (of their class or nation, or colour or race) as an independent source of human activity, ... [and until they can act in accord with it, they] are not fully human and not fully free.'[45] Berlin knew that we have to deal with group recognition in a democracy and that it must be part of a conception of citizenship.

These writers lead our thinking away from citizenship conceived as a relationship solely with the nation state and towards cosmopolitan citizenship. In our globalizing world, the concept of cosmopolitan citizenship within a cosmopolitan democracy is receiving increasing attention.

Most of today's students, who have grown up after the fall of the Berlin Wall, after the discourse of universal human rights was widespread, and after the World Wide Web connected the globe, have an easy affinity for the notion of cosmopolitan citizenship. In cosmopolitan citizenship, we have rights not because we belong to a nation state, but because rights are universal. We are all members of the world and as citizens we should respond in ways that reflect the worth and dignity of all human beings. It seems inescapable that the concept of cosmopolitan citizenship must be part of a liberal education today.

If we are to place cosmopolitan citizenship at the center of today's liberal education, it is not without its problems for the multiversity. The nation state supports the multiversity and the nation state remains the institutional structure through which citizens acquire rights and through which they can participate in politics. There is no global government to which a citizen is responsible and over which the citizen can exercise control. Many of the communitarians who seek to reinvigorate the civic republican tradition are antagonistic to cosmopolitan thought, believing that the community of people forming a state must be enhanced. Cosmopolitanism, they argue, can only diminish the only true political community we have – the nation state.

Derek Heater, in *World Citizenship: Cosmopolitan Thinking and Its Opponents*, offers a fine survey of the current literature on cosmopolitan citizenship and the tensions with nation citizenship and nationalism. Heater argues that classical Roman thought, particularly of the Stoics, on which Martha Nussbaum drew as well, was strongly cosmopolitan, but 'enjoined a strict adherence to civic duty alongside their commitment to the cosmopolitan code of conduct.'[46] He states that during the classical periods of cosmopolitan consciousness, 'the separate identities of state citizenship, world citizenship and nationhood were mutually compatible. Co-existing without the felt need for any to obliterate or incorporate any other(s). Let us call this "the classical tradition of compatibility." Then, for about two centuries, between around 1800 and 2000, nationalism absorbed citizenship and effaced world citizenship.' However, Heater argues, 'at the turn of the twentieth century, the conflation of nationalism and citizenship began to loosen and the cosmopolitan ideal started to enjoy a revival in a mood which we may call "the new classicism."'[47] However, we are not yet into this new classical age; there remain many complexities to navigate as we struggle to accommodate both national citizenship and cosmopolitan citizenship within the curriculum of the liberal education minor.

In recent years in the United States, there have been calls to emphasize citizenship in liberal education, most noteworthy in the recent volume *Educating Citizens: Preparing America's Undergraduates for Lives of Moral and Civic Responsibility*.[48] We should be cautious, however. Such initiatives can slip, all too easily, into an old-fashioned civic republicanism inappropriate to our heterogeneous age. Amy Gutmann in her *Democratic Education* reminds us that education in democratic virtue and values, as a process of conscious social reproduction in a democracy, belongs at the primary and secondary level. Multiversities as autonomous institutions best serve democracy as 'institutional sanctuaries of free scholarly inquiry' that protect against the tyranny of ideas. This is the first responsibility of the multiversity in a liberal undergraduate education, even while emphasizing citizenship.

Certain postmodern writers are arguing for a more radical conception of citizenship, and it is in their work that we discover the most vigorous current critique of liberal democracy. They do not seek the overthrow of liberal democracy and 'its replacement by a completely new political form of society, as the traditional idea of revolution entailed, but a radicalization of the democratic tradition.'[49] Chantal Mouffe, for example, argues in *Dimensions of Radical Democracy: Pluralism, Citizenship, Community* that 'the task of rethinking democratic politics is more urgent than ever. For those who refuse to see "really existing" liberal democratic capitalism at the "end of history," radical democracy is the only alternative. If the Left is to learn from the tragic experiences of totalitarianism it has to adopt a different attitude towards liberal democracy, and recognize its strengths as well as reveal its shortcomings. In other words, the objective of the Left should be the extension and deepening of the democratic revolution initiated two hundred years ago.'[50] A radical citizenship would expose 'the illusory and ideological character of so-called '"formal bourgeois democracy"' and then 'take its declared principles literally and force liberal democratic societies to be accountable for their professed ideals.'[51] A juxtaposition of the critical perspective and the liberal perspective should be part of any liberal education.

This critical perspective challenges Marshall's analysis – of the natural evolution from civil, to political, to social rights – in many ways. Marshall's analysis masks the conflicts and the nature of power. For Marshall, civil, political, and social rights are complementary. But social rights establish claims upon the state that require expenditure – on health, or pensions, or universities – and therefore ones that require taxation to pay for. Taxation makes claims upon your income and property and so compromises the civil rights of the taxpayer. Civil and social rights can be in conflict. Also, Marshall does not address the conflict and struggle that have been necessary to extract citizenship rights from the powerful and from the state. Furthermore, the state often acts not for the citizen, but for the powerful. How is citizenship to be understood in such a world? The citizen will often be in conflict with the state, and with other (more powerful) members of the community.

Henry A. Giroux links this critical perspective directly to citizenship and liberal education, and indeed to the university itself. Giroux believes that universities 'represent places that affirm and legitimate existing views of the world, produce new ones, and authorize and shape existing social relations; put simply they are places of moral and social regulation "where a sense of identity, place, and worth is informed and contested through practices which organize knowledge and meaning."[52] The university is a place that produces a particular selection and ordering of narratives and subjectivities. It is a place that is deeply political and unarguably normative.'[53] Giroux sees our liberal democracies as deeply inequitable, dominated by a plutocratic elite who resist any reduction in their power. We do not live in a democracy, but are engaged in a struggle to realize a democracy, he argues, and citizenship means recognizing current reality and engaging in the struggle for democracy. He believes liberal education and citizenship must be recognized as contested terrain and places where power is exerted for moral regulation and control. Attempts to re-establish a traditional curriculum of great books and western civilization, he asserts, are 'nothing more than a rhetorical mask that barely conceals their own highly charged, ideological agenda.'[54] A radical notion of citizenship will recognize the struggle for democracy. For Giroux, education must be seen as 'part of an ongoing struggle to develop forms of knowledge and social practices that not only make students critical thinkers but also empower them to address social problems in order to transform existing political and social inequalities.' Citizenship education can be defined in part as 'an ongoing attempt to develop curricula that [are] critical of the injustices of American society.'[55]

This literature of political philosophers and political scientists is instructive as we reflect upon how to re-design a liberal education for our age – the literature highlights a great concern about the concept of citizenship but also reveals how complex and fraught the concept is in our age. But how, then, are we to move forward and design a liberal education minor? Here, we arrive at the most difficult question of all in designing any liberal education: What should be the content of the courses? It is all well to say the purpose of a liberal education is to develop good citizens, but how is this to be achieved? The majority of the writing about citizenship education has dealt with the curriculum for the secondary schools.[56] The most recent major initiative in the Anglo-American world for curriculum reform was the introduction of a citizenship component into the national curriculum in the United Kingdom following the 1998 report *Education for Citizenship and the Teaching of Democracy in Schools*. But here our focus is on the curriculum in the university, not the secondary school.

Again, the thrust of my proposal is that every multiversity should reflect upon this question of course content, recognizing there will not be one answer. But I will offer a specific suggestion. I would recommend that one of the five courses of the liberal education minor be titled 'Liberal Learning and Citizenship' and be devoted to three closely connected themes: the history and development of the university's role in society, the history and development of liberal education, and the history and development of the concept of citizenship. The supporting argument is that we can endeavor to create liberally educated citizens by having students study the ideas of liberal education and the meanings of citizenship.

This course, 'Liberal Education and Citizenship,' in the liberal education minor needs to draw upon the civic republican tradition with the emphasis on duties, not just the liberal tradition and its emphasis on rights, but it also must incorporate the radical critique of our dominant discourses. The restored emphasis on citizenship in liberal education cannot mean an emphasis on *one* concept of citizenship, so much as an emphasis on the *question* of citizenship. The redesign of a liberal undergraduate education should include a reflection, as it always has, on the principles of a just and satisfying political order, but in our age, citizenship is a highly contested concept. We cannot escape this controversy and be true to our times. In the spirit of Gerald Graff's curriculum advice, captured in the title of his book *Beyond the Culture Wars: How Teaching the Conflicts Can Revitalize American Education*, the citizenship controversy should be part of the curriculum for a liberal education.[57] Where once the content of a liberal education was based on a consensus, on 'the best that has been thought and said;' in our age, a liberal education must confront the controversy.

John McGowan, in his book about intellectuals, *Democracy's Children*, writes: 'the democratic polity is not dependent on agreement; it depends on our continuing to talk to one another ... Intellectual activity is precisely this continuing to talk. By enunciation of my views, I contribute to the ongoing talk that is a crucial part of democratic society.'[58] An undergraduate liberal education minor that directly addresses the concept and controversies of citizenship is ideal practice in this democratic conversation.

Writing for the Public World

The desiderata of a liberal education always include the ability to write well. For example, the purpose of the Harvard core curriculum was to create an educated person. The definition began: 'an educated person must be able to think and write clearly and effectively.' Paul Axelrod's definition of a liberal education included activities designed to cultivate 'effective communication skills.' Frank Rhodes's list of qualities of an educated person included the ability 'to listen, read, observe, and analyse with comprehension and to speak and write with clarity and precision.'[59] In the past, we might have valued grace and elegance in writing; today we value clarity and precision. Nonetheless, the ability to write well is an essential part of being liberally educated.

At present, undergraduate writing is almost exclusively academic writing – the writing of essays in the style and format of a particular academic discipline. The intended audience, implicitly, is others in that discipline. But it is not writing that prepares the students for citizenship. Thus, I have one further proposal for the content of the liberal education minor: in the courses of the liberal education minor, we should augment this academic writing with writing for the public world.

In teaching and assessing academic writing, emphasis is placed on organization, the rigour and creativity of the analysis, and also upon footnotes and citations. The latter are appropriate in academic writing because it is important to situate the essay in the literature of the discipline (which the reader will have read, or could read), and to acknowledge, by appropriate citation, the use of ideas from other sources. Professors are at home with such writing, because writing an undergraduate essay is preparation for writing a graduate thesis, and preparation for writing articles in the academic literature. The undergraduate essay is part of an apprenticeship to enter the research community. Professors have traveled this route and know it well.

Academic writing is enormously important in undergraduate education. It is a structured exercise in disciplined thought. The essay is an exercise in the presentation and defense of one's own ideas and indispensable in a liberal education. A common cause of poor writing is that the student did not really understand the material.

Academic writing, however, is not the only type of writing. The writing that most students will do after graduation will not be academic writing, and most of what they will read, either in their work or for pleasure, will not be academic writing. They will read newspapers, magazines, and books for a general audience, not academic literature. The liberally educated person should be able to write for a general audience, for liberally educated readers. This is the writing that will serve their fitness for the world. The sort of assignment designed to practice this sort of writing is easy to conceive, and it need not be in conflict with the traditional academic writing. For example, after writing an essay on Keynes's macroeconomic theories, or the physics of semiconductors, or Foucault's analysis of prisons, the student could be asked to write an 800-word newspaper or magazine article on the same topic.

This proposal to have undergraduates write for a general audience might seem outside the purview of a professor, and indeed there will need to be explicit especially designed instruction in writing for the public world as part of the curriculum.[60] If the role of the professor as a public intellectual is recognized, however, and if we recall that professors have an obligation to engage the public with the substance of their research, then undergraduate writing for a general audience becomes an apprenticeship for the professorial role as public intellectual. This proposal to augment undergraduate writing is consistent with and complements the call to emphasize the professor's role as public intellectual in a democracy.

Both the student and the professor will be well served by such essays. Gerald Graff believes the esoteric jargon of professorial academic writing is one reason why students who are forced to read it remain 'clueless in academe' and alienated from the culture of argument and ideas. Graff cites the linguist and notable public intellectual, Stephen Pinker, approvingly: 'having to explain an idea in plain English to someone with no stake in the matter is an excellent screen for incoherent or contradictory ideas that somehow have entrenched themselves in a field.'[61] Learning to write for the public world is both excellent academic training and excellent preparation for citizenship.

The Future of the Multiversity: A Prodigal Adaptation?

Let me introduce this final section of the final chapter as I ended the first chapter: 'Many in the multiversity are convinced that the ideas of our age will revolutionize the multiversity, so radically changing its functions that the unbroken history with universities past will be severed. The modern multiversity has many functions, often conflicting and always given shifting emphasis. If the tormenting worry had to be summarized in a single sentence it would be: in postindustrial society of the twenty-first century, the economic functions of the multiversity will flourish and its democratic functions will wither. We must not allow this to happen.'

It would be a prodigal adaptation to our age.

The multiversity must of course adapt to our age. The constrained welfare state, the information technology revolution, postmodern thought, commercialization, and globalization will change the multiversity. No doubt, our age does require that the multiversity be given the explicit mission of serving the economy and of commercializing research, but this risks marginalizing much of what the multiversity does and has stood for. In our age, to prevent the prodigal adaptation, the multiversity should be given another explicit mission: it should contribute to democratic life.

There are many initiatives needed to ensure that the multiversity fulfills its responsibilities to democratic life. The most fundamental initiative would be to incorporate the democratic role into the three parts of academic decision-making: it should be incorporated into the mission; it should be incorporated into academic planning and resource allocation; and it should be incorporated into assessment and accountability.

The first step would be to recognize explicitly this democratic task in the university mission statement: the university recognizes its responsibilities to democratic life and accepts the roles of critic, conscience, and public intellectual. When we choose presidents, senior administrators, or board members, we should look not just for academic leaders, skilled administrators, and adept fundraisers, but also for people who appreciate and would articulate and defend this democratic role. This task should also be part of the responsibility of each faculty and each department. Finally, this task should be an explicit part of the service responsibilities of professors.

Having acknowledged the responsibility of serving democratic life at each level in the multiversity, academic planning and resource allocation can be undertaken to accomplish the task. It will take time, effort, and imagination to work out the implications of this new role for multiversities. There will need to be review and reform of the curriculum – this chapter has offered the suggestion of a liberal education minor. There will need to be changes in student financial assistance to insure access. Chapter 7 discussed how the revolution in information technology offers the multiversity new ways to be critic, conscience, and public intellectual and new ways to support lifelong liberal learning in society. The list of possible initiatives can be easily extended and each multiversity can create its own. Course releases could be made available for special projects related to the democratic mission. New professorships could be established with a mandate to engage the public – for example, Oxford University has the Charles Simonyi Professor of the Public Understanding of Science, currently Richard Dawkins. Granting councils could give more weight to activities as public intellectuals as part of research dissemination. Connections between academic departments and specialized journalists could be enhanced to assist professors in their role as public intellectuals. The only limits are our imagination and the strength of our commitment to this role in democratic life.

Finally, each level should be held accountable for the fulfillment of the task. Board members, presidents, and senior administrators should be assessed for their contribution to and leadership in this democratic task in the multiversity's mandate. When we evaluate departments – conducting an undergraduate program review or a graduate program review – we should evaluate the department's contribution not just in teaching and research, but also to democratic life. And the criteria for hiring, tenuring, promoting, and rewarding professors should recognize these democratic responsibilities, just as we recognize the responsibilities for teaching, research, and service.

The multiversity is an autonomous self-governing institution. This expanded mission could come through government request or through civic conversation as the social contract is renewed, but the multiversity itself must believe in the change. This democratic mission will need to be supported by all parts of the multiversity's governance: boards, senates, presidents and senior administrators, and faculty members.

Will the leadership and governance of our multiversities be able to prevent a prodigal adaptation? Many observers worry about our current structures of governance, fearing they will be unable to adjust creatively to the pressures of our age.

The governance of Anglo-American multiversities is subject to much scrutiny and widely criticized. Something is not right. Richard Chait examines the American scene and reports boiling controversy over resurgent boards eroding faculty authority.[62] Jones, Shanahan, and Goyan report that academic senates in Canada feel themselves less and less influential.[63] Surveys of the British scene lament the decline of collegiality, the rise of managerialism, and government's imposition of audits and assessments.[64]

Another worry is that multiversities, with their present governance, will remain sluggish and unresponsive. Many former presidents, especially from the United States, are sounding this alarm. James Duderstadt, former president of the University of Michigan, states: 'It seems clear that the university of the twenty-first century will require new models of governance.'[65]

Others say multiversities may adjust too fast and too easily to the dizzying pace of change and the flood of new responsibilities and commitments. Harold Shapiro, former president of Princeton University, warns that multiversities 'risk being either overwhelmed by values and commitments that may be inimical to the world of scholarship and learning, and/or being too caught up in the rampant materialism of our age and the incentive structure of private markets.'[66]

The multiversity will require leadership, but not leadership as understood in the corporate or political spheres. The multiversity operates with shared, not hierarchical, governance, and therefore leadership will be required from the boards of governors, from presidents and senior administrators, and from professors. They must bring a new creativity and adaptability but also a renewed commitment to the core values of the university.

There is much writing about the leadership required from presidents and, in recent years, about the leadership required from boards of governors.[67] There is rather less writing about the leadership required from faculty members. On the contrary, a recurring theme is the diminishing collective influence of faculty. But if collegial self-governance is to be preserved, and if the multiversity's adaptation is to be rooted in the realities of the classroom and research, leadership must also come from faculty members. Professors themselves must lead in establishing the democratic mission of the multiversity. In many multiversities, leadership from faculty members has become problematic as faculty members withdraw from service to the university to devote their time and energy to teaching and research. Despite their passionate espousal of collegial self-government, many professors are unaware of the broader issues facing the multiversity and how governance works. Also, although they have a visceral commitment to the values of institutional autonomy and academic freedom, they have only a dim appreciation of the reciprocal responsibilities. Henry Rosovsky sees a glaring weak spot in current internal governance: a decline in civic virtue or citizenship among the professoriate in research universities. Too often professors are absent from campus because of their research and external commitments; they slight their institutional obligations of teaching and service.[68] A code of professional conduct must be part of the reform of governance. Also, if professors are given the formal roles of public intellectual, social critic, conscience, we must also articulate new notions of responsibility in these roles. Does any social criticism fall under this role or only that which emerges from the professor's research? When the criticism is outside their expertise, should professors leave unannounced their multiversity affiliation in public statements? Is involvement in partisan politics to be discouraged? This is new ground, there are many risks, and there is much work to be done.

What of the governance structure itself. Is it robust enough to prevent a prodigal adaptation? Is it capable of meeting the principal challenge to higher education: can the multiversity, as James Duderstadt asked, 'find ways to sustain the most cherished aspects of their core values, while discovering ways to respond vigorously to the opportunities of a rapidly changing world?'[69] Burton Clark, after studying a number of universities in Europe and Britain, offers the most insightful analysis available about governance reform. He writes of 'modern pathways of university transformation that can promote greater university autonomy and bolster university achievement in these turbulent times. These interacting pathways ... can also serve to reaffirm traditional university values.'[70] This is exactly what is needed: governance which can creatively adapt while preserving the ideals of the university.

Unfortunately, Clark describes this reform as creating 'entrepreneurial' universities. For many readers, the choice of the word 'entrepreneurial' will prevent them from seeing the subtle insights of his analysis. The dictionary defines an entrepreneur as 'the owner or manager of a business enterprise who, by risk and initiative, attempts to make profits.'[71] The image of Schumpeter's 'creative destruction' is disturbingly evoked. An entrepreneurial university would be one that has forsaken its historic ideals to regard itself as a risk-taking, market-driven institution, but this is not Burton Clark's meaning.

In using the word 'entrepreneurial,' Clark wants to describe a change in the governance and culture of universities that would respond to the ideas of our age but would also serve to reaffirm traditional values. I have struggled to find an alternate word. 'Enterprising' perhaps comes closest: 'ready to embark on new ventures; full of boldness and initiative.'[72] But this too has business connotations, and more significantly does not reflect the tension between bold initiative and commitment to traditional ideals that the multiversity faces.

After his study of European multiversities that had engaged in successful governance reform, Clark was able to 'tease out' some common elements. The multiversities he studied had been, like multiversities in the Anglo-American world, 'overextended, under-focused; overstressed, underfunded.'[73] Using the terms of this book, they were operating in the constrained welfare state and were suffering from mission drift. In response, these successful multiversities all diversified their funding base, relying less on governments, and all developed a new culture of enterprising self-reliance, what Clark calls an 'entrepreneurial culture.' The organizational pathways for university transformation had three components: a strengthened steering core, an enhanced developmental periphery, and a stimulated academic heartland. Clark's categories are crucial to understanding how governance can change and yet prevent a prodigal adaptation: the steering core, the heartland, and the periphery.

The strengthened steering core often began with a strong-minded president, but was supplemented by new collegial forms of decision-making. The process began with the recognition that the multiversity had to adapt, to move more rapidly, and to be more selective and focused, given limited resources. The new decision-making proved able to make the toughest of all decisions: to provide new funds for strategic priorities by taking funds away from existing activities. 'A strengthened steering core is fully formed when it is able to cross-subsidize from pooled resources ... A vigorous all-university steering core seeks not only to subsidize some new experiments and activities but also to enhance old valuable programs in the academic heartland; an example would be to strengthen departments in the humanities and 'soft' social sciences.'[74] The steering core marries strong presidential leadership with new forms of collegial self-governance. The first cannot succeed without the second.

The steering core assisted in the creation of 'a larger, more complex set of units operating on the periphery of the traditional structure, reaching across old boundaries to link up with outside interests.'[75] These new units were, for example, offices for industrial liaison, technology transfer, and consultancy. These were where research was most applied and where it was commercialized. These units were flexible, the locus for experimentation, and entrepreneurial – in the business sense of entrepreneurial. But Clark's insight here is essential: the new units required of our age are located at the *periphery* of the traditional structure. They do not supercede the disciplinary departments, nor do disciplinary departments forsake their traditional roles.

Even with entrepreneurship and transformation, the *academic heartland* is recognized. 'The roles played by heartland departments in academic innovation cannot be overlooked. These departments are the bedrock keepers of academic norms.' Innovation and entrepreneurship that leads to 'shoddy goods' according to academic norms can set off a vicious circle of declining reputation and difficulty attracting faculty, students, and external donors. 'A strongly pro-active university, as it develops, depends on the acceptance of a new evolving posture by the discipline-led departments which serve as the academic heartland.'[76]

Burton Clark's schema offers a governance structure that can adapt without losing core ideals. The strengthened steering core could lead in adding the democratic responsibilities to the multiversity's mission. The entrepreneurial periphery takes up the task of commercializing research, but the ethos of private knowledge remains at the periphery. The academic heartland retains its traditional functions and takes up the task of revitalizing the liberal education.

The university is an extraordinarily long-lived institution; it has been able to adapt yet able to sustain the ideals that gave it birth. Today, under pressure from the ideas of our age, we risk squandering our inheritance, partly through inattention, partly through intransigence, and partly through prodigal adaptation. We can meet this risk by incorporating into the multiversity a new idea of a university: the university as an institution of democracy. And so, great multiversities will be judged not just by the quality of their research, the learning of their students, and the accomplishments of their graduates, but also by their preparation of students for cosmopolitan citizenship and by their contribution to ensuring that we live in a truly deliberative democracy.

Notes

1. Introduction

1 The characterization of postindustrial society follows Daniel Bell, *The Coming of Post-Industrial Society: A Venture in Social Forecasting*. The volume was originally published in 1973, and was republished in 1976 and 1999. Each edition contains a new foreword by Bell.
2 Bell (1999), 14.
3 Ibid., 10.
4 Bell (1967), 30.
5 Kerr (2001a), 1–7.
6 Duderstadt (2000), 21.
7 In the order cited, the books are Cole, Barber, and Graubard, eds. (1994); Emberley and Newall (1994); Readings (1996); Kolodny (1998); Smith and Webster (1997).
8 Ashby (1966), 3.
9 Pocklington and Tupper (2002), 14.

2. The Idea of a University

1 Kerr (2001a), 115. Clark Kerr's 1963 lectures, 'The Uses of the University,' were delivered at Harvard University in the annual Godkin Lectures on the Essentials of Free Government and Duties of the Citizen. They have been republished four times, each time with new chapters by Kerr.
2 Many authors, particularly when writing about the history of the university, have created a typology of universities. See, e.g., Wolff (1968). Veysey (1965), in *The Emergence of the American University*, divided the 'rival conceptions of the higher learning' into four types: discipline and piety, utility,

research, and liberal culture. Ortega y Gasset's volume *Mission of the University* (a series of lectures delivered at the University of Madrid in 1930) offers a thoughtful perspective. In a preface to the volume, republished in 2001, Clark Kerr (2001b) provides a review of different types of universities, distinguished by their different missions.
3 There are exceptions – universities that focus solely on graduate education and research – but these are few.
4 In this book American multiversities are defined as doctoral/research – extensive universities, according to the *Carnegie Classification 2000*. See chapter 3 for a detailed discussion of this definition of a multiversity.
5 Cardinal Newman in Turner (1996b), 3. The quotations from Cardinal Newman and the portrait of his life are taken from Frank M. Turner, ed. *The Idea of a University: John Henry Newman*. The volume, with its essays, is part of a Yale University Press series, Rethinking the Western Tradition, which 'seeks to address the present debate over the western tradition by reprinting key works of that tradition along with essays that evaluate each text from different perspectives.' Newman's book was first published in 1873.
6 Ibid., 78.
7 Ibid., 109.
8 Ibid., 125.
9 Ibid., 77.
10 Ibid., 89.
11 Ibid., 167.
12 Turner (1996a), 283.
13 Rothblatt (1997), 21. Rothblatt attributes to Coleridge the method used by Newman of examining institutions with respect to their essence.
14 Kroetsch (1989), i.
15 Rothblatt (1997), 3.
16 Ibid., 21.
17 Kimball (1996), 11.
18 Kimball (1986), 37–8.
19 Emberley and Newall (1994), 71–2.
20 Cobban (1975), 8.
21 Newman, in Turner (1996b), 166.
22 Rothblatt (1976), 190.
23 Ibid., 190.
24 Proctor (1988), 24.
25 Newman, in Turner (1996b), 5; also other quotations in this paragraph.
26 The German model was very much the product of continental philosophi-

cal traditions; more than one historian of higher education has noted that many people from other countries who were influenced by this German model had only a superficial understanding of its complexities. See, e.g., Veysey (1965, chapter 3).

27 Liedman (1993), 82.
28 Humboldt (1963), 126.
29 Ibid., 136.
30 Perkin (1984), 30.
31 Ibid., 30.
32 Herman (2001), vii and viii.
33 Sloan (1971), 15.
34 Ibid., 23.
35 Thomas Huxley, in Sanderson (1972), 132.
36 Ibid., 137.
37 Ibid.
38 Ibid.
39 Kimball (1986), 199, 120, and 121; also other quotations in this paragraph.
40 Bissell (1977), 7.
41 Proctor (1988), 3.
42 As quoted in ibid., 19–20.
43 Ibid., 24.
44 Ibid., 13.
45 Bissell (1977), 8; also other quotations in this paragraph.
46 The poem 'Dover Beach' can be found in many anthologies, including that edited by Christopher Ricks (1999), *The Oxford Book of English Verse*, 453–4.
47 Matthew Arnold, in Collini (1993b), 32.
48 Ibid., 14.
49 Ibid., 59–61; also other quotations in this paragraph.
50 Ibid., 81–3; also other quotation in this paragraph.
51 Ibid., 100.
52 Ibid., 22–3.
53 Fussell (1975), 52, 53; also other quotations in this paragraph.
54 Lionel Trilling, as quoted in Proctor (1988), 107.
55 Dahl (2000), 11.
56 Ibid., 69.
57 Rothblatt (1993), 29.
58 Reuben (1996), 11.
59 Dahl (2000), 24.
60 Shils (1989), in Shils (1997a), 250.
61 Ibid., 251.

424 Notes to pages 46–60

62 Ibid., 251.
63 Ibid., 259.
64 Merton (1942).
65 Jencks and Riesman (1968), xiii.

3. The Uses of the Multiversity in Postindustrial Society

1 Duderstadt (2000), 49–50.
2 Kerr (2001a), 7.
3 Kerr (2001a), 103.
4 See Noll (1998) for a discussion of the definition of a research university.
5 In the United States, the word 'college' is often reserved for the undergraduate liberal arts portion of the whole, whereas the whole is called the 'university.' For example, Harvard University has Harvard College and Columbia University has Columbia College. In this book, the term 'university' is used to describe an institution of higher education granting at least bachelor's degrees.
6 Robert Maynard Hutchins, former president of the University of Chicago, as quoted in Kerr (2001a), p.15.
7 Ibid., xi–xii and previous paragraphs.
8 Bell (1999), 12.
9 Ibid., 20.
10 Ibid., 26.
11 Kerr (2001a) in later chapters uses the term research university as synonymous with the multiversity. Noll (1998) defines a research university, and his research universities are the same as Kerr's multiversities.
12 Bush (1945), 5.
13 The statement of purpose retrieved at http://www.nsf.gov/about/glance.jsp.
14 Kerr (2001a), 142.
15 Teich (1998), 91.
16 Multiversities are defined as *Carnegie Classification 2000* doctoral/research universities – extensive. The data are from Carnegie Foundation (2000), 23.
17 Rhodes (1994), 180–1.
18 Graubard (1994), 379.
19 Cohen and Brawer (1996) and Medsker and Tilley (1971) provide a comprehensive picture of the American junior college/community college system.
20 U.S. Department of Education (2001), Table 6, 15.
21 Kerr (1991), xii–xv.
22 Trow (1973).

23 Ibid., 7–8.
24 Harvard University (1945), ix.
25 Bell (1966), 1.
26 Harvard University (1945), 51.
27 Ibid., 52–3.
28 Ibid., 60.
29 McKillop (1994), 563.
30 Ibid., 563.
31 Ibid., 563–4.
32 Bledstein (1976), ix and x.
33 Burrage (1993), 142.
34 Ibid., 143.
35 Perkin (1989), xiii.
36 Ibid., 6.
37 Ibid., 87.
38 See Axelrod (1990).
39 Harvard University (2000–1).
40 Cohen and Noll (1998), 44.
41 Bok (1986), chapter 1: 'The American System of Higher Education,' 8–34.
42 UNESCO (1997), 26.
43 Ibid.
44 Ibid., 29.
45 Carnegie Foundation (2000), Table 6, 21.
46 Ibid., Table 5, 20.
47 In 2006, after the research for this book was completed, the Carnegie Foundation released its 2005 revised classification system. Doctoral-granting institutions were defined as awarding at least 20 doctorates (similar to the 2000 classification). In 2000, there were 261 such institutions; in 2005 there were 283. In the 2005 classification, these doctoral-granting universities were separated into three categories: very high research (96 universities), high research (103 universities), and doctoral/research universities (84 universities). The separation is based on a complex multidimensional index of research activity, rather than a single measure of federal funding (used in classifications before 2000). See Carnegie Foundation (2005).
48 Duderstadt (2000), 47.
49 The data in the paragraph above, and the following paragraph, are taken from the Carnegie Foundation (2000).
50 These brief characterizations of the NRC and the national granting councils are taken from the relevant entries in the *Canadian Encyclopedia* (1985).
51 Pocklington and Tupper (2002), 19.

52 Statistics Canada (2003), 5.
53 The G-10 universities are University of British Columbia, University of Alberta, University of Western Ontario, University of Waterloo, McMaster University, University of Toronto, Queen's University, University of Montreal, McGill University, and Laval University.
54 The two additional universities are University of Calgary and University of Ottawa.
55 The enrolment data are from Statistics Canada (1999), the PhD data from the Canadian Association of Graduate studies (2000), and the Canada Research Chair data are from the CRC website http://www.chairs.gc.ca.
56 The history of English higher education below draws upon Pratt (1997), the papers in Warner and Palfreyman (2001), the papers in Phillips and Furlong (2001b), and Scott (1995).
57 See Sanderson (1972).
58 Phillips and Furlong (2001a), 3 and 4.
59 Rees and Stroud (2001), 72.
60 The English Russell Group universities are University of Birmingham, University of Bristol, University of Cambridge, University of Leeds, University of Liverpool, University of Manchester, University of Newcastle on Tyne, University of Nottingham, University of Oxford, University of Sheffield, University of Southampton, University of Warwick, King's College London, London School of Economics and Political Science, University College London, and the Imperial College of Science, Technology and Medicine.
61 The research grant data are taken from the Higher Education Funding Council for England (2003), retrieved at http://www.hefce.ac.uk/news/hefce/2003/GrantAnn/summary.asp and the enrolment data are taken from the Higher Education Statistics Agency (2003), retrieved at http://www.hesa.ac.uk/holisdocs/pubinfo/student/institution0102.htm.
62 See Oxford's website. http://www.ox.ac.uk/innovation/.

4. The Multiversity and the Welfare State

1 The literature on multiversities does not situate the multiversity within the implementation of the welfare state. There is an extraordinarily fruitful terrain of analysis opened by recognizing the multiversity's connection to the welfare state.
2 See Briggs (1961).
3 Gutmann (1988), 3.
4 Mishra (1984), xi.
5 Mishra (ibid.) defined the welfare state as having two pillars: one due to

Keynes and the other to Beveridge. This definition adds two other pillars: Marshall on social citizenship and progressive taxation.
6 For papers on the development of welfare states, see Flora and Heidenheimer (1981).
7 OECD (1985).
8 Smith [1776] (1937), 669.
9 Ibid., 681.
10 Ibid., 768.
11 Ibid., 727.
12 Ibid., 720.
13 These origins of the welfare state are discussed in Flora and Heidenheimer (1981).
14 Marx and Engels (1848).
15 John Stuart Mill, as quoted in Robbins (1976).
16 Fabian Society (1938).
17 See Huber and Stephens (2001).
18 This is the methodology adopted by Mishra (1984), who subtitled his book Social Thought and Social Change.
19 Keynes (1936), 383.
20 Skidelsky (1996), 2.
21 Ibid., 3.
22 Ibid., 3-4.
23 Ibid., 47 and 46.
24 Richard Nixon, as quoted in ibid., 108.
25 Bell (1999), 20.
26 Harris (1977), 419.
27 Beveridge (1942).
28 University settlement houses were 'places where professional men could live among the poor – not as missionaries but as friends.' 'Its practical objectives were originally threefold: to spread education and culture; to discover facts about social problems; and to enable middle-class people to establish personal friendships with members of the working class.' Harris (1977), 44.
29 Harris (1977), 419.
30 Ibid., 426.
31 Franklin Delano Roosevelt, as quoted in Gutmann (1988), 3.
32 For analysis of the U.S. welfare state see Weir, Orloff, and Skocpol (1988) and Pierson (1999).
33 Mishra (1984), 3.
34 Ibid., 13.

35 Ibid.
36 J.H. Smith (1996), x.
37 Giddens (1996), 65.
38 Marshall (1963), 74.
39 Ibid.
40 Ibid.
41 Ibid., 114 and 115.
42 Bell (1995), 105.
43 This definition is drawn from Manzer (2003, 15), augmented to include the family as a crucial unit.
44 Ibid., 3.
45 Nevitte and Gibbins (1990), 1.
46 More recent work identifies a southern European model and, moving beyond Europe, an Asian or Confucian welfare state.

5. A Social Contract: Tasks, Autonomy, and Academic Freedom

1 Ashby (1966), 293 and 290.
2 Private multiversities do not receive operating grants from government, but do rely on government support for research. Also, they rely heavily on philanthropic support from society.
3 Various authors have, from time to time, described the relationship between the university and society as a social contract. See, e.g., Bok (1982), 5.
4 Menand (1996a), 3.
5 Russell (1993), 7.
6 Council for Aid to Education (1996).
7 Pocklington and Tupper (2002), 4.
8 Russell (1993), 10.
9 Bok (1982), 5–6.
10 As quoted in Russell (1993), 1–2.
11 Bologna Charter (1998).
12 AAUP/ACC (1940).
13 Michiel Horn (1999) in his study of academic freedom in Canada notes that it was 'not a burning question' until the late 1950s. Russell's (1993) survey suggests academic freedom was not a pressing issue in the United Kingdom until the later 1970s, and then the issue was much more the government's interference with university autonomy than the academic freedom of professors.
14 This identification of three issues and their discussion follows Metzger (1955).
15 Ibid., 325.

16 As quoted in ibid., 347.
17 Ibid., 364.
18 Ibid., 365–6.
19 Ibid., 366.
20 Ibid., 386–7.
21 Mrs Leland Stanford, as quoted in ibid., 438–9.
22 Veblen (1965).
23 Halsey and Trow (1971).
24 Henry Rosovsky, as quoted in Kennedy (1997), 139.
25 Ibid., 22.
26 Rosovsky and Ameer (1998), 125.
27 The colleges of Oxford and Cambridge, as independent foundations, have different structures; but there is the same split between the existing professors and an 'external' body responsible for fiscal probity.
28 A full treatment of governance would include study of the role of faculty unions and of students.
29 Kerr (2001a), 15.
30 Duderstadt (2000), 247.
31 In recent years, in some interpretations, academic freedom has also come to include the right to publicly criticize the leadership of the university, without fear of losing your job, and also the right to participate in governance. Both are freedoms that workers in private firms or government do not enjoy. The 1966 revised AAUP mission statement states that AAUP's purpose is to advance academic freedom and shared governance.
32 Smith and Webster (1997), 4.
33 Kennedy (1994), 85.
34 Ibid., 86.
35 Duderstadt (2000), 257.
36 Bottomore (1968), 10.
37 Ibid., 10–11.
38 Ibid., 15.
39 New Zealand (1990). See also Crozier (2000).
40 New Zealand (1990).
41 McGowan (2002), xi.
42 Said (1994), as quoted in Jacoby (2000), 39.
43 Said (1994), xv-xvii.
44 Posner (2003), 17. The discussion, which follows exploring the concept of a public intellectual, draws upon Posner. Posner's book is controversial, and I do not use the term as he does, but his definitional exploration is comprehensive and insightful.

45 Ibid., 18.
46 Snow (1964), 15.
47 Goldfarb (1998), 1.
48 Ibid.
49 Kerr (2001a), 201.

6. The Constrained Welfare State

1 Many authors have tackled the question of what lies ahead; Duderstadt (2000) is a recent example. Delanty (2001), using the literature of sociology and social theory, offers a penetrating and insightful reflection. Although from a very different disciplinary perspective than this book, many of the themes are similar. After completing this work, I came upon a special issue of the journal *Studies in Philosophy and Education* containing the proceedings of a conference on Higher Education, Democracy and Citizenship, held in Sweden. Although within the context of the Swedish experience, the papers address many of themes around the university and democracy that are discussed in this book.
2 This is one area where the elite U.S. private multiversities differ significantly from publicly supported multiversities. The private multiversities do not have to rely on government operating grants; they rely upon fees and endowment revenues. However, the research enterprise of the private multiversity is just as reliant on government support, and the senior administration spends countless hours trying to secure more research funds.
3 OECD (1985).
4 Chrystal and Price (1994) offer an excellent overview of the controversies in macroeconomics.
5 Ibid., 5.
6 It is possible to identify two separate streams of this criticism; one labelled neoconservatism and another labelled neoliberalism. I use a broader-gauged approach and encompass both under the heading of neoliberalism.
7 Sowell (1993), 23.
8 Mishra (1984), 35.
9 See ibid.
10 Kymlicka and Norman (1994), 355–6.
11 Chrystal and Price (1994), 8.
12 OECD (2005).
13 Castells (2000), 1:143.
14 OECD (2003).
15 MIT (2004), 6.

16 Council for Aid to Education (1996), 2.
17 Greenaway and Haynes (2000), 14.
18 Ibid., 29.
19 Ibid.
20 Kolodny (1998), 219–20.
21 Barr (2001), 70.
22 Ibid., 172.
23 Ibid., 174.
24 Ibid., 220.
25 Data are from Council for Aid to Education (2001).
26 Per student endowments are taken from the *Chronicle of Higher Education: Almanac 2003*.
27 Duderstadt (2000), 171.
28 Ibid., 170.
29 University of Toronto (2001).
30 Dearing Committee (1997).
31 DFES (2004).

7. The Information Technology Revolution

1 Dertouzos (1997), 5.
2 Peter F. Drucker, as quoted in a column by Robert Kenzner and Stephen S. Johnson in *Forbes Magazine* (10 March 1997), 122–7.
3 Kerr (2001a), 207.
4 Greenspan, as quoted in Shiller (2000). Shiller attributes the term to Greenspan.
5 The five pillars of information technology are discussed in Dertouzos (1997), 51–4, and in the Appendix, 349–60.
6 Ibid., 350.
7 Negroponte (1996), 14.
8 Dertouzos (1997), 351.
9 Reid (2001), 127. Numerous histories of information technology have been written. Reid's book superbly conveys the excitement of invention and the passion of scientists and engineers, and is a source of much of what follows.
10 Ibid., 127.
11 Ibid., 11.
12 Sir Ieuan Madlock, as quoted in ibid., 23.
13 Ibid., 153.
14 Jorgenson (2001), 6.
15 Abbate (1999), 107.

16 Berners-Lee (1999), 4.
17 Himanen (2001), vii. Himanen calls the spirit of the information age 'the hacker ethic.' I have not used this term because the word hacker is now so misunderstood. Common usage is not Himanen's usage.
18 Data on Internet use are available at http://www.internetworldstats.com/ and also at http://www.whois.sc/internet-statistics/.
19 New research capabilities are developed constantly; an up-to-date report is impossible. A relatively recent survey of the social sciences and humanities is to be found in Burton (2002).
20 See, e.g., Harnad (2003) and http://www.openarchives.org.
21 See, e.g., Willinsky (2002) and the University of British Columbia's Public Knowledge Project at http://www.pkp.ubc.ca.
22 See Scientists for Global Responsibility at http://www.sgr.org.uk/SciencePolicy/.
23 Lessig (2004), 114.
24 Kelly (2006), 45.
25 Lessig (2004).
26 Noble (1997), 7.
27 Negroponte (1996), 150.
28 Dertouzos (1997), 63.
29 Ibid., 59.
30 The most high profile of such failures is Fathom.com, a consortium that included Columbia University and the London School of Economics, among others.
31 Many authors have also forecast, erroneously, that the driving dynamic of the future would be the combination of the technology revolution and the private provision of university education, with devastating consequences for traditional providers. See, e.g., Katz and Associates (1999).
32 Kerr (2001a), 219.
33 The courseware also provides systems for recording student grades and for managing all the administrative aspects of a course.
34 An interesting example, far from the usual scientific material we hear so much about, is the Perseus Digital Library for classical studies. See http://perseus.uchicago.edu.
35 See Heyer and Crowley (1999).
36 Goody and Watt (1963), 344.
37 Ibid.
38 Eisenstein (1983) examines the transition from a culture of scribes to print culture.

Notes to pages 206–30   433

39 Febvre and Martin (1958) emphasize the importance of the rise of universities for the development of the book.
40 Ong (1982), 72.
41 Ibid., 40.
42 Ibid., 45.
43 Innis (1948), in Heyer and Crowley (1999).
44 Schultz (1963), 4.
45 This is the conclusion reached by the University of Illinois (2000), a very clear-eyed look at the pedagogy of online learning.
46 Trow (1997).
47 See University of Phoenix at http://uphoenix.edu/. and Cardean University at http://www.cardean.edu/.
48 National Association of State Universities and Land-Grant Colleges (1999), ix.
49 See http://www.merlot.org/ and http://edusplash.net/.
50 Trow (1997), 297–8.
51 Ibid., 299.
52 Cox (2002), 3.
53 McGann (2001), 7.
54 Alexis de Toqueville, as quoted in Rothblatt (1997), 70. Rothblatt points out that de Toqueville saw past the ancient buildings of Oxford to see archaic educational institutions.
55 Ibid., 62.
56 Ibid., 87.

8. Postmodern Thought

1 Sim (2001a), vii.
2 Ibid.
3 Sim (2001a) in Sim (2001b), 3.
4 Ibid.
5 McGowan (1991), ix.
6 Lyon (1999) offers a fine overview of ideas about postmodernity, with emphasis on the consumerism.
7 Searle (1993), 76.
8 Newman, in Turner (1996b), 77.
9 This delineation closely follows Rosenau (1992).
10 For a forceful discussion of this characterization of Romanticism, see Berlin (1999).

11 The right – conservatives like Edmund Burke – also offered a critique of modernity.
12 Marx and Engels (1848).
13 Weber (1983).
14 Searle (1993).
15 Ibid., 58.
16 Ibid., 60. It should be noted that not all rationalists are realists.
17 Ibid., 61.
18 Ibid.
19 Ibid., 62–3.
20 Ibid., 66.
21 Ibid., 69.
22 Eagleton (1983), 2.
23 Ibid.
24 Bauman (1990), as quoted in Rosenau (1992), xii.
25 See Landow (1997) and McGann (2001).
26 Eagleton (1983), 129.
27 Taylor and Winquist (2001), 101.
28 Foucault (1972), as quoted in ibid., 102.
29 Lyotard (1984), 2.
30 Ibid.
31 Taylor and Winquist (2001), 164–5.
32 Said (2003), 40.
33 Ibid.
34 Ibid., 2.
35 Brooks and Miljan (2003), 7.
36 Rorty (1982), 1.
37 Hartmann (1984), as quoted in Gibbins and Youngman (1996), 131.
38 Harding (1986).
39 Delanty (2001), 145.
40 Lionel Trilling, as quoted in Proctor (1988), 107.
41 Eagleton (1983), 16.
42 Graff (1992), 36–9.
43 Searle (1993), 71.
44 Ibid., 73.
45 Cameron (1994), 19.
46 The metaphor of an intellectual experiment station was associated with the original AAUP.
47 For thoughtful discussions of political correctness in the U.K. context, see Dunant (1994).

48 Menand (1996b), viii.
49 Menand (1996a), 5.
50 Said (1996), 215–16.
51 Rosenau (1992), 3.
52 Smith (1998) offers a comprehensive survey of social science methodology, with emphasis on its linguistic turn in recent years. Rosenau (1992) emphasizes how postmodern thought that developed in literature, linguistics, literary criticism, and philosophy has influenced the social sciences.
53 Carter (1998) has edited a collection of essays exploring the implications of postmodern thought for the welfare state.
54 Sim (2001), 243.
55 Harding (1986), 9.
56 Golinski (1998), back cover.
57 Ibid., ix.
58 Gross and Levitt (1994), 2.
59 Ibid., 3.
60 Ibid., 6.
61 Ibid., 4 and 7.
62 Snow (1964), 15.
63 Ibid., 57.
64 Much of postmodern thought is about the nature of knowledge, and therefore, not surprisingly, there is an important postmodern literature about the nature of the university, including contributions from Lyotard, Derrida, and Habermas, which in their philosophical method are beyond the scope of this book; Delanty (2001) provides a fine analysis and survey of this literature, and see too, Smith and Webster (1997).
65 This is Delanty's (2001, 137) characterization of Peter Scott's (1995, 1997) conclusions.
66 Kerr (2001a), 216 and 228.
67 Said (1996), 224–5.
68 Ibid., 225.

9. Commercialization

1 Etzkowitz and Webster (1998), 21.
2 Evans (2003), 1.
3 Solow (1957).
4 See Axelrod (2002), chapter 3, and citations in that chapter, for data on the rate of return to higher education. See also Greenaway and Haynes (2000) and Barr (2001). For recent reviews of the literature on both the

private and public returns to higher education, see Riddell (2005) and Ripstein (2005).
5 Thomas Jefferson, as quoted in Scherer (1999), 34.
6 Ibid., 27.
7 Romer (1993), 63.
8 Scherer (1999), 34.
9 Ibid., 35.
10 For an accessible discussion of the new economic geography and strategic trade theory, see Krugman (1994).
11 Tajnai (1985), 1.
12 The Stanford model is set out in http://www.netvalley.com/archives/mirrors/tajnai-links.html.
13 Data are from http://www.stanford.edu/group/wellspring/economic/html.
14 Leslie (2000), 48.
15 Brown (2000), xiii and xv.
16 Powell and Owen-Smith (2002), 108.
17 It is noteworthy that much genetic research is very computing intensive and that advances in genetic understanding require advances in computational algorithms and software.
18 Sanderson (1975), 10.
19 Rosenberg and Nelson (1996), 192.
20 Ibid., 195.
21 The quotations are from Bush (1945), *Science – The Endless Frontier*.
22 Slaughter and Leslie (1997), 55.
23 For a review of higher education policy in the United Kingdom, see ibid., 40–3. On research policy, also see Gray (1999) and Stephens (1989).
24 For a review of higher education policy in the United States, see Slaughter and Leslie (1997, 44–52). On research policy, also see Rosenberg and Nelson (1996), Nelson (1993), Guston and Keniston (1994), and Cohen et al. (1998).
25 For a review of higher education policy in Canada, see Slaughter and Leslie (1997, 52–4). On research policy, also see Axelrod (2002, chapter 4), Gu and Whewell (1999), and Fisher, Atkinson-Grosjean, and House (2001).
26 Powell and Owen-Smith (2002), 112.
27 Rosenberg and Nelson (1996), 225.
28 Kerr (2002), 18.
29 Powell and Owen-Smith (2002), 119.
30 Ibid., 152.
31 Merton (1942), 116.
32 Ibid., 118.

33 Ibid., 121 and 123.
34 Metzger (1955), 365–6.
35 Kernan (1987), 49.
36 Michael Dertouzos in foreword to Berners-Lee (1999).
37 Lessig (2001), 52. The story of Linux below is based upon ibid., 50–8.
38 McSherry (2001), 35–40.
39 Powell and Owen-Smith (2002), 113.
40 Slaughter and Leslie (1997), 6–7.
41 For two perspectives on the Human Genome Project, see Zweiger (2001) and Sulston and Ferry (2002).
42 Brint (2002a), 231.
43 Ibid., 241.
44 For example, see Mokyr (1990) and Nelson (1996).
45 Duderstadt (2000), 49.
46 University of Oxford website: http://www.ox.ac.uk/innovation/.
47 Taylor and Winquist (2001), 164–5.

10. Globalization

1 Scott (2000), 3.
2 See Hirst and Thompson (1999).
3 See M'Gonigle and Starke (2006) for a thought-provoking prescription of how the university might be transformed to place it at the forefront of the sustainability movement.
4 Slaughter and Leslie (1997), 1.
5 Currie and Newson (1998) and Odin and Manicas (2004). Not all the literature has this edge so critical of globalization, see also Scott (1998), Breton and Lambert (2003), and Jones, McCarney, and Skolnik (2005).
6 See Huntington (1996) for a more thorough discussion of how social science constructs theories in the context of international relations.
7 See Altbach (2004) for a discussion of globalization and the university with emphasis on the developing world.
8 The treatment below follows Held et al. (1999).
9 See Friedrichs (2001) and references there.
10 Alter (1989), as quoted in Gibbins and Youngman (1996), 171.
11 See Anderson (1983).
12 See Wallach (1996) for a wonderful portrayal of the life of Gertrude Bell, and of the Victorian world of empire, intellect, and ad
13 A.J. Arberry as quoted in ibid., 39.
14 As reproduced in ibid., 375.

15 Altbach (2004), 4.
16 The U.N. International Covenant on Civil and Political Rights (1966) and the U.N. International Covenant on Economic, Social and Cultural Rights (1966), both coming to force in 1976, were adopted to add more covenants to ensure the universal rights were secure.
17 United Nations (1948).
18 Ibid.
19 Scott (2005), 42.
20 Knight (2000), 17.
21 Douglass (2005), 5.
22 See Florida (2002).
23 Smith (2004), 69.
24 Some long-time critics of globalization even proclaim its demise. See Gray (1998) and Saul (2004).
25 Altbach (2004), 22.
26 See in Breton and Lambert (2003), 240.
27 See Douglass (2005) for a discussion of the many countervailing forces to globalization.
28 Fukuyama (1992), xi.
29 Ibid., xii–xxi.
30 Ibid., xx.
31 Friedman (2000), 11.
32 Ibid., 32–3.
33 Ibid., 31.
34 Barber (2001), 4.
35 Ibid.
36 Ibid., 5–6.
37 See http://www.whitehouse.org.
38 Ignatieff (2004a). Quotes are from Ignatieff (2004b).
39 See http://www.campuswatch.org.
40 Huntington (1996), 125.
41 Ibid., 321 and 316.
42 Ibid., 58.
43 Ibid., 58–9.
44 Ibid., 54.
45 Ibid., 112–13 and quoting others sources as in his endnote 25.
46 Readings (1996), 3.
47 Ibid., 11.
48 *Collins English Dictionary*, 21st century ed. (2000).

49 Held (2002), 1.
50 Ibid.
51 McGrew (2002), 275.
52 See He (2002).
53 See McGrew (2002) and He (2002) for a brief discussion and references to criticism of global civil society and cosmopolitan democracy.

11. The Multiversity and Liberal Democracy

1 Ashby (1966), 3.
2 Rothblatt (1997), 21.
3 Governments have other obligations under the social contract which must be part of the renewal discussions, but which cannot be dealt with in this space. For example, some critics argue that governments have abandoned their commitment to support basic science and have politicized research, e.g., in research about climate change. Some charge that this politicization is undermining science itself.
4 There is a close connection between the multiversity taking on the task of an institution of democracy and the internal governance of the multiversity. However, space does not allow exploration of this connection.
5 Wingspread Declaration (1999), 7.
6 Ryan (1998), 57.
7 Ibid., 56.
8 Ibid., 60.
9 The crucial role of the professions was highlighted by the social critic Jane Jacobs (2004) in her last book, *Dark Age Ahead*, in which she identified five pillars of our society, pillars that sustain our culture. One of the pillars is the self-regulation of the learned professions. Jacobs worries that this, like other pillars, is showing serious signs of weakness.
10 Bell (1967), 30.
11 Kerr (2001a), 5.
12 Dahl (2000), 37.
13 Ibid., 37–8.
14 Ibid., 188.
15 See Manzer (2003) for an analysis of the relationship of political ideas to primary and secondary education in the Anglo-American world.
16 Gutmann (1987), 3.
17 Ibid., 50–1.
18 Ibid., 173.

19 Ibid., 174.
20 This three-part framework is drawn in part from the discussion in Beetham (2005).
21 Ibid., 12.
22 Ibid., 13.
23 United Nations (1948).
24 Kerr (2001a), xii.
25 There are several organizations that monitor the state of democracy around the world. Freedom House is a well-known example. (See http://www.freedomhouse.org) None of these include the role of universities in their conception of democracy.
26 Guston and Keniston (1994), 2.
27 Trow (1996).
28 Guston and Keniston (1994), 26.
29 Stokes (1997), 73.
30 Ibid., 74.
31 Ibid., 113.
32 Ibid.
33 Guston (2000a) and (2000b). Guston no longer uses the concept of a social contract to describe the new regime; he argues the contract is gone, to be replaced by something else. I believe the reforms required can best be understood as a *renewal* of the social contract.
34 The national granting council for research in the social sciences in Canada has recently established a class of major grants – the Community University Research Alliance (CURA) – that requires the involvement of the community in all aspects of the research.
35 Proctor (1988), 13.
36 Bloom (2000), 21–2.
37 Humanities and Social Sciences Federation of Canada (2002). Retrieved at: www.hssfc.ca.
38 Arts and Humanities Research Board, England (2004). Retrieved at: www.ahrb.ac.uk.
39 Nussbaum (1995), xiii.
40 Bloom (2000), 22.
41 *Collins English Dictionary* (2000).
42 Metzger (1955), 364.
43 Goldfarb (1998), 3.
44 Hofstadter (1963), 9–10, as quoted in Jacoby (2000), 37.
45 Goldfarb (1998), 7.
46 Ibid., 10.

47 Ibid., 15.
48 Barber (1998).
49 See Michael (2000) for a subtle analysis of public intellectuals in a post-modern era.
50 Many social commentators have made this observation. See Posner (2003) and references there.
51 Said (1994), as quoted in Jacoby (2000), 39.
52 Ibid., 40.
53 Ibid., 52.
54 See, e.g., Beiner (2003), Carter and Stokes (2002b), Benhabib (1996), Mouffe (1992), Bohman and Rehg (1997), and Elster (1998).
55 Pharr and Putnam (2000).
56 Dryzek (2000), 1.
57 Gutmann and Thompson (1996), 1.
58 Ibid., 52.
59 Ibid., 56.
60 McGrew (2002), 275–80. Dryzek (2000) also connects deliberative democracy to transnational democracy.
61 Dryzek (2000), 2.
62 Ibid., 1.

12. A Liberal Education for Our Age

1 Rhodes (1994), 180–1.
2 Ibid., 181.
3 Kerr (2001a), 77–8.
4 Pocklington and Tupper (2002), 6 and 8.
5 Scott (2001a), 186.
6 Whitehead (1968), as quoted in Rhodes (2001), xv.
7 Rhodes (2001), 66.
8 Woodruff (2005), 15.
9 Ibid., 145.
10 Ibid., 148–9.
11 Ibid., 191 and 193.
12 Newman, in Turner (1996b), 77.
13 There are also many interdisciplinary degree programs, but these too, are not designed according to any vision of a liberal education.
14 Mark Pattison, as quoted in Rothblatt (1993), 52.
15 Axelrod (2002), 34–5.
16 Newman, in Turner (1996b), 109.

17 Multiversities might offer the option of an entire degree based upon a conception of a liberal education.
18 Rhodes (1994), 182–3.
19 Katz (1995), p.128.
20 Rothblatt (1993, 61) makes this conjecture for Europe.
21 See Harvard (2005).
22 See ibid. Levine (1978) provides a comprehensive report on the undergraduate curriculum in America, with much attention to general education.
23 Kerr (2001b), xvii.
24 Lyon (1999), 71 and 76.
25 Taylor (1991).
26 Anderson (1993), 136–7.
27 Annie Dillard, as quoted in Anderson (1993), 137.
28 Justice Learned Hand, as quoted in Dyzenhaus (2005), 164.
29 These volumes are Orrill (1995) and Orrill (1997).
30 Kimball (1997), 47.
31 Kimball (1995), 88–9.
32 Ibid., 29.
33 Menand (1995), 141.
34 Heater (1999), 1.
35 Ibid., 3.
36 Ibid., 4.
37 Ibid., 45.
38 See ibid., chapter 2, for a discussion of the communitarian adaptation of civic republicanism.
39 Kymlicka and Norman (1994), 354.
40 Ibid., 365.
41 Nussbaum (1997), 8.
42 Ibid., 9.
43 Ibid., 10–11.
44 Kymlicka and Norman (1994), 370. They cite Young (1989; 1990).
45 Berlin (1969), 156–7.
46 Heater (2002), 37.
47 Ibid., 38.
48 Colby et al. (2003).
49 Mouffe (1992a), 1.
50 Ibid.
51 Ibid., 2.
52 Roger I. Simon, as quoted in Giroux (1992), 120.
53 Ibid.

54 Ibid., 141.
55 Giroux (1989), 9.
56 A major contribution is the work by Callen (1997). The famous Harvard Redbook understood well the distinction, but also that the two levels were intimately connected; it discusses general education at both levels.
57 Readings (1996, 167) makes a similar argument when he asks: 'What can be done with and in a University that, along with the nation-state, is no longer central to the question of common life?' His preference is to think of dissensus over consensus.
58 McGowan (2002), 15.
59 Rhodes (2001), 96.
60 There are classic books intended to help master writing for a general audience; two famous examples are William Strunk and E.B. White, *The Elements of Style* (2000) and William Zinsser, *On Writing Well* (1976). For more advanced students, there is Francis-Noel Thomas and Mark Turner, *Clear and Simple as the Truth: Writing Classic Prose* (1994).
61 Stephen Pinker, as quoted in Graff (2003), 10.
62 Chait (2002).
63 Jones, Shanahan, and Goyan (2001).
64 See, e.g., the list of themes in Warner and Palfreyman (2001), 3–4.
65 Duderstadt (2000), 257.
66 Shapiro (2004). Similar sentiments are expressed by Bowen (2001).
67 For examples, see the activities of the Association of Governing Boards of Universities and Colleges in the United States at http://www.abg.org.
68 Rosovsky (2001), 95.
69 Duderstadt (2000), 21.
70 Clark (2002), 323.
71 *Collins English Dictionary* (2000), 516.
72 Ibid., 515.
73 Charles Vest, as quoted in Clark (2002), 338.
74 Ibid., 330.
75 Ibid., 331.
76 Ibid., 334–5.

References

AAUP/ACC. 1940. *1940 Statement of Principles on Academic Freedom and Tenure with 1970 Interpretive Comments.* Retrieved at http://www.aaup.org/statements/.

Abbate, Janet. 1999. *Inventing the Internet.* Cambridge, MA: MIT Press.

Altbach, Philip G. 2004. 'Globalisation and the University: Myths and Realties in an Unequal World.' *Tertiary Education and Management* 10: 3–25.

Alter, Peter. 1989. *Nationalism.* London: Edward Arnold.

American College Dictionary. 1962. New York: Random House.

Anderson, Benedict. 1983. *Imagined Communities: Reflections on the Origin and Spread of Nationalism.* New York: Verso.

Anderson, Charles W. 1993. *Prescribing the Life of the Mind: An Essay on the Purpose of the University, the Aims of a Liberal Education, the Competence of Citizens, and the Cultivation of Practical Reason.* Madison: University of Wisconsin Press.

Ashby, Eric. 1966. *Universities: British, Indian and African. A Study in the Ecology of Higher Education.* London: Weidenfeld and Nicolson.

Axelrod, Paul. 1990. *Making a Middle Class: Student Life in English Canada during the Thirties.* Montreal: McGill-Queen's University Press.

– 2002. *Values in Conflict: The University, the Marketplace, and the Trials of Liberal Education.* Montreal: McGill-Queen's University Press.

Barber, Benjamin R. [1995] 2001. *Jihad vs McWorld: Terrorism's Challenge to Democracy.* New York: Ballantine.

Barber, Bernard. 1998. *Intellectual Pursuits: Towards an Understanding of Culture.* Lanham, MD: Rowman and Littlefield.

Barr, Nicholas. 2001. *The Welfare State as Piggy Bank: Information, Risk, Uncertainty, and the Role of the State.* Oxford: Oxford University Press.

Bauman, Zygmunt. 1990. 'Philosophical Affinities of Postmodern Sociology.' *Sociological Review* 38(3): 411–44.

Beetham, David. 2005. *Democracy: A Beginner's Guide*. Oxford: Oneworld Publications.

Beiner, Ronald. 2003. *Liberalism, Nationalism, Citizenship: Essays on the Problem of Political Community*. Vancouver: UBC Press.

Bell, Daniel. 1966. *The Reforming of General Education: The Columbia College Experience in a National Setting*. New York: Columbia University Press.

– 1967. 'Notes on the Post-Industrial Society (I).' *Public Interest*, no. 6, 24–35.

– [1973] 1999. *The Coming of Post-Industrial Society: A Venture in Social Forecasting*, 3rd ed. New York: Basic Books.

Bell, David. 1995. 'Political Culture in Canada.' In Michael S. Whittington and Glen Williams, eds., *Canadian Politics in the 1990s*, 105–28. Toronto: Nelson.

Benhabib, Seyla, ed. 1996. *Democracy and Difference: Contesting the Boundaries of the Political*. Princeton: Princeton University Press.

Berlin, Isaiah. 1969. *Four Essays on Liberty*. Oxford: Oxford University Press.

– 1999. *The Roots of Romanticism*. Ed. by Henry Hardy. Princeton: Princeton University Press.

Berners-Lee, Timothy. 1999. *Weaving the Web: The Original Design and Ultimate Destiny of the World Wide Web*. New York: HarperBusiness.

Beveridge, William. 1942. *Social Insurance and Allied Services: Report by Sir William Beveridge*. London: HMSO.

Bissell, Claude T. 1977. *Humanities in the University*. Singapore: FEP International.

Bledstein, Burton J. 1976. *The Culture of Professionalism: The Middle Class and the Development of Higher Education in America*. New York: Norton.

Bloom, Harold. 2000. *How to Read and Why*. New York: Scribner.

Bohman, J., and W. Rehg, eds. 1997. *Deliberative Democracy: Essays on Reason in Politics*. Cambridge, MA: MIT Press.

Bok, Derek. 1982. *Beyond the Ivory Tower: Social Responsibilities of the Modern University*. Cambridge, MA: Harvard University Press.

– 1986. *Higher Learning*. Cambridge, MA: Harvard University Press.

– 2003. *Universities in the Marketplace: The Commercialization of Higher Education*. Princeton: Princeton University Press.

Bologna Charter. 1998. *Magna Charta Universitatum*. Rectors of 18 European Universities. Retrieved at http://www.magna-charta.org.

Bottomore, T.B. 1968. *Critics of Society: Radical Thought in North America*. New York: Pantheon.

Bowen, William G. 2001. *At a Slight Angle to the Universe: The University in a*

Digitized, Commercialized Age. Romanes Lecture for 2000, delivered before the University of Oxford. Princeton: Princeton University Press.

Breton, Gilles, and Michel Lambert, eds. 2003. *Universities and Globalization: Private Linkages, Public Trust.* Paris: UNESCO.

Briggs, A. 1961. 'The Welfare State in Historical Perspective.' *European Journal of Sociology* 2: 221–58.

Brint, Steven. 2002a. 'The Rise of the "Practical Arts."' In Steven Brint, ed., *The Future of the City of Intellect: The Changing American University,* 231–59. Stanford: Stanford University Press.

– ed. 2002b. *The Future of the City of Intellect: The Changing American University.* Stanford: Stanford University Press.

Brooks, Stephen, and Lydia Miljan. 2003. *Public Policy in Canada: An Introduction.* Toronto: Oxford University Press.

Brown, John Seeley. 2000. Foreword. In Martin Kenney, ed., *Understanding Silicon Valley: The Anatomy of an Entrepreneurial Region,* ix–xvi. Stanford: Stanford University Press.

Burrage, Michael. 1993. 'From Practice to School-Based Professional Education: Patterns of Conflict and Accommodation in England, France and the United States.' In Sheldon Rothblatt and Bjorn Wittrock, eds., *The European and American University since 1800: Historical and Sociological Essays,* 142–87. Cambridge: Cambridge University Press.

Burton, Orville Vernon, ed. 2002. *Computing in the Social Sciences and Humanities.* Urbana and Chicago: University of Illinois Press.

Bush, Vannevar. 1945. *Science – The Endless Frontier.* Retrieved at http://www.nsf.gov/od/lpa/nsf50/vbush1945.htm.

Cameron, Deborah. 1994. '"Words, Words, Words": The Power of Language.' In Sarah Dunant, ed., *The War of Words: The Political Correctness Debate,* 15–34. London: Virago.

Callen, Eamonn. 1997. *Creating Citizens: Political Education and Liberal Democracy.* Oxford: Clarendon.

Canadian Association of Graduate Studies. 2000. *32nd Statistical Report.* Ottawa: author.

Canadian Encyclopedia. 1985. Edmonton: Hurtig.

Carnegie Foundation. 2000. *Carnegie Classification 2000: The Carnegie Classification of Institutions of Higher Education.* Retrieved at http://www.carnegie foundation.org/Classification/CIHE2000/.

– 2005. *The Carnegie Classification of Institutions of Higher Education.* Retrieved at http://www.carnegiefoundation.org/classifications/.

Carnochan, W.B. 1993. *The Battleground of the Curriculum.* Stanford: Stanford University Press.

Carter, April, and Geoffrey Stokes. 2002a. Introduction. In April Carter and Geoffrey Stokes, eds., *Democratic Theory Today: Challenges for the 21st Century*, 1–19. London: Polity.

– eds. 2002b. *Democratic Theory Today: Challenges for the 21st Century.* London: Polity.

Carter, John, ed. 1998. *Postmodernity and the Fragmentation of Welfare*. London: Routledge.

Castells, Manuel. 2000. *The Information Age: Economy, Society and Culture*. 3 vols. Malden, MA: Blackwell.

Chait, Richard. 2002. 'The "Academic Revolution" Revisited.' In Steven Brint, ed., *The Future of the City of Intellect: The Changing American University*, 293–321. Stanford: Stanford University Press.

Chronicle of Higher Education. 2003. *Chronicle of Higher Education: Almanac 2003*. Washington: author.

Chrystal, K. Alex, and Simon Price. 1994. *Controversies in Macroeconomics*. 3rd ed. New York: Harvester Wheatsheaf.

Clark, Burton R. 2002. 'University Transformation: Primary Pathways to University Autonomy and Achievement.' In Steven Brint, ed., *The Future of the City of Intellect: The Changing American University*, 322–42. Stanford: Stanford University Press.

Cobban, A.B. 1975. *The Medieval Universities: Their Development and Organization*. London: Methuen.

Cohen, Arthur M., and Florence B. Brawer. 1996. *The American Community College*. 3rd ed. San Francisco: Jossey-Bass.

Cohen, Linda R., and Roger G. Noll. 1998. 'Universities, Constituencies, and the Role of the States.' In Roger G. Noll, ed., *Challenges to Research Universities*, 31–62. Washington, DC: Brookings Institution.

Cohen, Wesley M., Richard Florida, Lucien Randazzese, and John Walsh. 1998. 'Industry and the Academy: Uneasy Partners in the Cause of Technological Advance.' In Roger G. Noll, ed., *Challenges to Research Universities*, 171–99. Washington, DC: Brookings Institution.

Colby, Anne, Thomas Ehrlich, Elizabeth Beaumont, and Jason Stephens. 2003. *Educating Citizens: Preparing America's Undergraduates for Lives of Moral and Civic Responsibility*. San Francisco: Jossey-Bass.

Cole, Jonathan R., Elinor G. Barber, and Stephen R. Graubard, eds. 1994. *The Research University in a Time of Discontent*. Baltimore: Johns Hopkins University Press.

Collini, Stefan. 1993a. Introduction. In Stephan Collini, ed., *Culture and Anarchy: And Other Writings. Matthew Arnold*, ix–xxvi. Cambridge: Cambridge University Press.

– ed. 1996b. *Culture and Anarchy: And Other Writings. Matthew Arnold.* Cambridge: Cambridge University Press.
Collins English Dictionary. 2000. 5th ed. Glasgow: HarperCollins.
Council for Aid to Education. 1996. *Breaking the Social Contract: The Fiscal Crisis in Higher Education.* Retrieved at http://www.rand.org/publications/CAE/CAE100/.
– 2001. *Voluntary Support for Education.* Available at http://www.cae.org/vse/vse2001/.
Cox, Geoffrey. 2002. 'Building a Virtual University.' Retrieved at http://www.cardean.edu/.
Crick, Bernard. 2002. *Democracy: A Very Short Introduction.* Oxford: Oxford University Press.
Crozier, Rob, ed. 2000. *Troubled Times: Academic Freedom in New Zealand.* Palmerston, NZ: Dunmore.
Currie, Jan, and Janice Newson, eds. 1998. *Universities and Globalization: Critical Perspectives.* Thousand Oaks, CA: Sage.
Dahl, Robert A. 2000. *On Democracy.* New Haven: Yale University Press.
Darwin, Charles. 1859. *On the Origin of Species by Means of Natural Selection.* London: John Murray, Albemarle Street.
Dearing Committee. 1997. *Education in the Learning Society.* Report of the U.K. National Committee of Inquiry into Higher Education. London: HMSO.
Delanty, Gerard. 2001. *Challenging Knowledge: The University in the Knowledge Society.* Buckingham, U.K.: Society for Research into Higher Education and Open University Press.
Dertouzos, Michael. 1997. *What Will Be: How the New World of Information Will Change Our Lives.* San Francisco: HarperEdge.
DFES. 2004. *Increasing Voluntary Giving to Higher Education: Task Force Report to Government.* London: Department for Education and Skills. Retrieved at http://www.dfes.gov.uk/hegateway/.
Douglass, John Aubrey. 2005. 'All Globalization Is Local: Countervailing Forces and the Influence on Higher Education Markets.' *Research and Occasional Paper Series: CSHE.1.05.* Center for Studies in Higher Education, University of California, Berkeley. Retrieved at http://cshe.berkely.edu.
Dryzek, John S. 2000. *Deliberative Democracy and Beyond: Liberals, Critics, Contestations.* Oxford: Oxford University Press.
Duderstadt, James J. 2000. *A University for the 21st Century.* Ann Arbor: University of Michigan Press.
Dunant, Sarah, ed. 1994. *The War of Words: The Political Correctness Debate.* London: Virago.
Dyzenhaus, David. 2005. 'The Case for Public Investment in the Humanities.'

In Frank Iacobucci and Carolyn Tuohy, eds., *Taking Public Universities Seriously*, 164–73. Toronto: University of Toronto Press.

Eagleton, Terry. 1983. *Literary Theory: An Introduction*. Oxford: Blackwell.

Eisenstein, Elizabeth L. 1983. *The Printing Revolution in Early Modern Europe*. Cambridge: Cambridge University Press.

Elster, Jon. 1998. *Deliberative Democracy*. Cambridge: Cambridge University Press.

Emberley, Peter C., and Waller R. Newall. 1994. *Bankrupt Education: The Decline of Liberal Education in Canada*. Toronto: University of Toronto Press.

Esping-Andersen, Gosta. 1990. *The Three Worlds of Welfare Capitalism*. Cambridge: Polity.

Etzkowitz, Henry, and Andrew Webster. 1998. 'Entrepreneurial Science: The Second Academic Revolution.' In Henry Etzkowitz, Andrew Webster, and Peter Healey, eds., *Capitalizing Knowledge: New Intersections of Industry and Academia*, 21–46. Albany: State University of New York Press.

Evans, John. 2003. Cited in *The Ontario Business Report*, (Dec./Jan.). Toronto: Ministry of Enterprise, Opportunity and Innovation, Government of Ontario.

Fabian Society. 1938. *Fabianism*. Retrieved at http://www.the-wood.org/socialism/fabianism/.

Febvre, Lucien, and Henri-Jean Martin. 1958. *The Coming of the Book: The Impact of Printing, 1450–1800*. London: Verso.

Fisher, Donald, Janet Atkinson-Grosjean, and Dawn House. 2001. 'Changes in Academy-Industry Relations: The Creation and Development of the Networks of Centres of Excellence.' *Minerva* 39: 299–325.

Flora, Peter, and Arnold J. Heidenheimer, eds. 1981. *The Development of Welfare States in Europe and America*. New Brunswick, NJ: Transaction Books.

Florida, Richard. 2002. *The Rise of the Creative Class: And How It's Transforming Work, Leisure, Community and Everyday Life*. New York: Basic Books.

Foucault, Michel. 1972. *The Archaeology of Knowledge*. Trans. A.M. Sheridan Smith. London: Tavistock.

Freud, Sigmund. 1946. *Civilization and Its Discontents*. London: Hogarth Press and the Institute of Psycho-Analysis. (First published in German in 1940).

Friedman, Thomas L. 2000. *The Lexus and the Olive Tree: Understanding Globalization*. Updated from 1999 ed. New York: Anchor Books.

Friedrichs, Jörg. 2001. 'The Meaning of the New Medievalism.' *European Journal of International Relations* 7(4): 475–501.

Fukuyama, Thomas. 1992. *The End of History and the Last Man*. New York: Penguin.

Fussell, Paul. 1975. *The Great War and Modern Memory.* Oxford: Oxford University Press.
Geiger, Roger L. 1993. *Research and Relevant Knowledge: American Research Universities since World War II.* New York: Oxford University Press.
Gibbins, Roger, and Loleen Youngman. 1996. *Mindscapes: Political Ideologies towards the 21st Century.* Toronto: McGraw-Hill Ryerson.
Giddens, Anthony. 1996. 'T.H. Marshall, the State and Democracy.' In Martin Bulmer and Anthony M. Rees, eds., *Citizenship Today: The Contemporary Relevance of T.H. Marshall*, 65–80. London: UCL Press.
Giroux, Henry A. 1989. *Schooling for Democracy: Critical Pedagogy in the Modern Age.* London: Routledge.
– 1992. 'Liberal Arts Education and the Struggle for Public Life: Dreaming about Democracy.' In Darryl J. Gless and Barbara Herrnstein Smith, eds., *The Politics of Liberal Education*, 119–44. Durham: Duke University Press.
Goldfarb, Jeffrey C. 1998. *Civility and Subversion: The Intellectual in Democratic Society.* Cambridge: Cambridge University Press.
Golinski, Jan. 1998. *Making Natural Knowledge: Constructivism and the History of Science.* Cambridge: Cambridge University Press.
Goody, Jack, and Ian Watt. 1963. 'The Consequences of Literacy.' *Comparative Studies in Society and History* 5: 304–45.
Graff, Gerald. 1992. *Beyond the Culture Wars: How Teaching the Conflicts Can Revitalize American Education.* New York: Norton.
– 2003. *Clueless in Academe: How Schooling Obscures the Life of the Mind.* New Haven: Yale University Press.
Graubard, Stephen R. 1994. 'The Research University: Notes toward a New History.' In Jonathan R. Cole, Elinor G. Barber, and Stephen R. Graubard, eds., *The Research University in a Time of Discontent*, 361–90. Baltimore: Johns Hopkins University Press.
Gray, Harry, ed. 1999. *Universities and the Creation of Wealth.* Buckingham, UK: Society for Research into Higher Education and Open University Press.
Gray, John. 1998. *False Dawn: Delusions of Global Capitalism.* London: Granta Books.
Greenaway, David, and Michelle Haynes. 2000. *Funding Universities to Meet National and International Challenges.* School of Economics Policy Report. Nottingham: University of Nottingham.
Gross, Paul R., and Norman Levitt. 1994. *Higher Superstition: The Academic Left and Its Quarrels with Science.* Baltimore: Johns Hopkins University Press.
Gu, Wulong, and Lori Whewell. 1999. *University Research and the Commercialization of Intellectual Property in Canada.* Ottawa: Industry Canada.

Guston, David H. 2000a. *Between Politics and Science: Assuring the Integrity and Productivity of Research*. Cambridge: Cambridge University Press.
– 2000b. 'Retiring the Social Contract for Science.' *Issues in Science and Technology Online*. Retrieved at http://nap.edu/issues/16.4/p_guston.htm.
Guston, David H., and Kenneth Keniston, eds. 1994. *The Fragile Contract: University Science and the Federal Government*. Cambridge, MA: MIT Press.
Gutmann, Amy. 1987. *Democratic Education*. Princeton: Princeton University Press.
– ed. 1988. *Democracy and the Welfare State*. Princeton: Princeton University Press.
Gutmann, Amy, and Dennis Thompson. 1996. *Democracy and Disagreement*. Cambridge, MA: Belknap Press of Harvard University Press.
Halsey, A.H., and M.A. Trow. 1971. *The British Academics*. Cambridge, MA: Harvard University Press.
Hansen, Alvin Harvey. 1953. *A Guide to Keynes*. New York: McGraw-Hill.
Harding, Sandra. 1986. *The Science Question in Feminism*. Ithaca: Cornell University Press.
Harnad, Stevan. 2003. 'Self-archive unto others …' Retrieved at http://www.universityaffairs.ca.
Harris, Jose. 1977. *William Beveridge: A Biography*. Oxford: Clarendon.
Hartmann, Heidi. 1984. 'The Unhappy Marriage of Marxism and Feminism: Towards a More Progressive Union.' In Alison Jaggar and Paula S. Rosenberg, eds., *Feminist Frameworks: Alternative Theoretical Accounts of the Relations between Men and Women*, 172–89. New York: McGraw-Hill.
Harvard University. 1945. *General Education in a Free Society*. Cambridge: Harvard University Press.
– 2000–1. *Factbook*. Retrieved at http://vpf-web.harvard.edu/factbook/00–01/page16.htm.
– 2005. *Harvard College Curricular Review*. Retrieved at http://www.fas.harvard.edu/curriculum-review/.
He, Baogang. 2002. 'Civil Society and Democracy.' In April Carter and Geoffrey Stokes, eds., *Democratic Theory Today: Challenges for the 21st Century*, 203–27. London: Polity.
Heater, Derek. 1999. *What Is Citizenship?* Oxford: Polity Press.
Heater, Derek. 2002. *World Citizenship: Cosmopolitan Thinking and Its Opponents*. London: Continuum.
Held, David. 2002. 'Globalization and the Future of Democracy.' Retreived at http://www.fathom.com/feature/122000/.
Held, David, Anthony McGrew, David Goldblatt, and Jonathan Perraton. 1999.

Global Transformations: Politics, Economics and Culture. Stanford: Stanford University Press.
Herman, Arthur. 2001. *How the Scots Invented the Modern World.* New York: Three Rivers Press.
Heyer, Paul, and David Crowley. 1999. Introduction. In Paul Heyer and David Crowley, eds., *The Bias of Communication,* ix–xxvi. Toronto: University of Toronto Press.
Himanen, Pekka. 2001. *The Hacker Ethic and the Spirit of the Information Age.* New York: Random House.
Hirsch, Werner Z., and Luc E. Weber, eds. 2001. *Governance in Higher Education: The University in a State of Flux.* London: Economica.
Hirst, Paul, and Grahame Thompson. 1999. *Globalization in Question: The International Economy and the Possibilities of Governance.* Cambridge: Polity.
Hofstadter, Richard. 1955. 'Part One: The Age of the College.' In Richard Hofstadter and Walter P. Metzger, *The Development of Academic Freedom in the United States,* 1–274. New York: Columbia University Press.
– 1963. *Anti-Intellectualism in American Life.* New York: Knopf.
Horn, Michiel. 1999. *Academic Freedom in Canada.* Toronto: University of Toronto Press.
Huber, Evelyne, and John D. Stephens. 2001. *Development and Crisis of the Welfare State: Parties and Policies in Global Markets.* Chicago: University of Chicago Press.
Humboldt, Wilhelm von. 1963. *Humanist without Portfolio: An Anthology of the Writings of Wilhelm von Humboldt.* Trans. Marianne Cowan. Detroit: Wayne State University Press.
Huntington, Samuel P. 1996. *The Clash of Civilizations and the Remaking of the World Order.* New York: Simon and Schuster.
Ignatieff, Michael. 2004a. *The Lesser Evil: Political Ethics in an Age of Terror.* Princeton: Princeton University Press.
– 2004b. 'Terrorism's Other Peril Is How It Transforms Us.' *Globe and Mail,* 17 June, A23.
Innis, Harold, A. [1947] 1999. 'Minerva's Owl.' In Paul Heyer and David Crowley, eds., *The Bias of Communication,* 3–32. Toronto: University of Toronto Press.
– [1948] 1999. 'The Bias of Communication.' In Paul Heyer and David Crowley, eds., *The Bias of Communication,* 33–66. Toronto: University of Toronto Press.
Jacobs, Jane. 1969. *The Economy of Cities.* New York: Vintage.
– 2004. *Dark Age Ahead.* Toronto: Random House.

Jacoby, Russell. 1987. *The Last Intellectuals: American Culture in the Age of Academe*. New York: Basic Books.
– 2000. 'Intellectuals and their Discontents.' *The Hedgehog Review: Critical Reflections on Contemporary Culture* 2(3): 36–52.
Jencks, Christopher, and David Riesman. 1968. *The Academic Revolution*. Garden City, NY: Doubleday.
Jones, Glen, Theresa Shanahan, and Paul Goyan. 2001. 'University Governance in Canadian Higher Education.' *Tertiary Education and Management* 7: 135–48.
Jones, Glen A., Patricia L. McCarney, and Michael L. Skolnik, eds. 2005. *Creating Knowledge, Strengthening Nations: The Changing Role of Higher Education*. Toronto: University of Toronto Press.
Jorgenson, Dale W. 2001. 'Information Technology and the U.S. Economy.' *American Economic Review* 91(1): 1–32.
Katz, Richard N., and associates. 1999. *Dancing with the Devil: Information Technology and the New Competition in Higher Education*. San Francisco: Jossey-Bass.
Katz, Stanley N. 1995. 'Possibilities for Remaking Liberal Education at the Century's End.' In Robert Orrill, ed., *The Condition of American Liberal Education: Pragmatism and a Changing Tradition*, 27–33. New York: College Entrance Examination Board.
Kelly, Kevin. 2006. 'Scan This Book!' *New York Times Magazine*, 14 May, 42–49, and 71.
Kennedy, Donald. 1994. 'Making Choices in the Research University.' In Jonathan R. Cole, Elinor G. Barber, and Stephen R. Graubard, eds., *The Research University in a Time of Discontent*, 85–114. Baltimore: Johns Hopkins University Press.
– 1997. *Academic Duty*. Cambridge: Harvard University Press.
Kenney, Martin. 1986. *Biotechnology: The University-Industrial Complex*. New Haven: Yale University Press.
– ed. 2000. *Understanding Silicon Valley: The Anatomy of an Entrepreneurial Region*. Stanford: Stanford University Press.
Kernan, Alvin. 1987. *Printing Technology, Letters, and Samuel Johnson*. Princeton: Princeton University Press.
Kerr, Clark. 1991. *The Great Transformation in Higher Education, 1960–1980*. Essays collected and ed. by Philip Altbach. Albany: State University of New York Press.
– 2001a. *The Uses of the University*. 5th ed. Cambridge: Harvard University Press.
– 2001b. 'Introduction to the Transaction Edition.' In José Ortega y Gasset, *Mission of the University*, ix–xxvi. New Brunswick, NJ: Transaction Publishers.

- 2002. 'Shock Wave II: An Introduction to the Twenty-First Century.' In Steven Brint, ed., *The Future of the City of Intellect: The Changing American University*, 1–19. Stanford: Stanford University Press.
Keynes, John Maynard. 1936. *The General Theory of Employment Interest and Money*. London: Macmillan.
Kimball, Bruce A. 1986. *Orators and Philosophers: A History of the Idea of Liberal Education*. New York: Teachers College Press.
- 1988. 'The Historical and Cultural Dimensions of the Recent Reports on Undergraduate Education.' *American Journal of Education* 96: 293–322.
- 1995. 'Toward Pragmatic Liberal Education.' In Robert Orrill, ed., *The Condition of American Liberal Education: Pragmatism and a Changing Tradition*, 1–122. New York: College Entrance Examination Board.
- 1996. 'A Historical Perspective.' In Nicholas H. Farnham and Adam Yarmolinsky, eds., *Rethinking Liberal Education*, 11–35. Oxford: Oxford University Press.
- 1997. 'Naming Pragmatic Liberal Education.' In Robert Orrill, ed., *Education and Democracy: Re-imagining Liberal Learning in America*, 45–67. New York: College Entrance Examination Board.
Knight, Jane. 2000. *Progress and Promise: The AUCC Report on Internationalization at Canadian Universities*. Ottawa: Association of Universities and Colleges of Canada.
Kolodny, Annette. 1998. *Failing the Future: A Dean Looks at Higher Education in the Twenty-first Century*. Durham: Duke University Press.
Kroetsch, Robert. 1989. *The Lovely Treachery of Words*. Toronto: Oxford University Press.
Krugman, Paul. 1994. *Peddling Prosperity: Economic Sense and Nonsense in the Age of Diminished Expectations*. New York: Norton.
Kymlicka, Will, and Wayne Norman. 1994. 'Return of the Citizen: A Survey of Recent Work on Citizenship Theory.' *Ethics* 104(2): 352–81.
Landow, George P. 1997. *Hypertext 2.0: The Convergence of Contemporary Critical Theory and Technology*. Baltimore: Johns Hopkins University Press.
Leslie, Stuart W. 2000. 'The Biggest "Angel" of Them All: The Military and the Making of Silicon Valley.' In Martin Kenney, ed., *Understanding Silicon Valley: The Anatomy of an Entrepreneurial Region*, 48–67. Stanford: Stanford University Press.
Lessig, Lawrence. 2001. *The Future of Ideas: The Fate of the Commons in a Connected World*. New York: Random House.
- 2004. *Free Culture: The Nature and Future of Creativity*. New York: Penguin.
Levine, Arthur. 1978. *Handbook on the Undergraduate Curriculum*. San Francisco: Jossey-Bass.

Liedman, Sven-Eric. 1993. 'In Search of Isis: General Education in Germany and Sweden.' In Sheldon Rothblatt and Bjorn Wittrock, eds., *The European and American University since 1800: Historical and Sociological Essays*, 74–106. Cambridge: Cambridge University Press.

Lyon, David. 1999. *Postmodernity*. 2nd ed. Buckingham, UK: Open University Press.

Lyotard, Jean-Francois. 1984. *The Postmodern Condition: A Report on Knowledge*. Trans. Geoff Bennington and Brian Massumi. Manchester: Manchester University Press.

Manzer, Ronald. 2003. *Educational Regimes in Anglo-American Democracies*. Toronto: University of Toronto Press.

Marrou, Henri. 1964. *A History of Education in Antiquity*. Trans. George Lamb. New York: New American Library.

Marshall, T.H. 1963. 'Citizenship and Social Class.' In T.H. Marshall, *Sociology at the Crossroads and Other Essays*, 67–127. London: Heinemann.

Marx, Karl, and Friedrich Engels. 1848. *The Manifesto of the Communist Party*. Retrieved at http://www.marxists.org/archive/marx/works/1848/communist-manifesto/.

McGann, Jerome. 2001. *Radiant Textuality: Literature after the World Wide Web*. New York: Palgrave.

McGowan, John. 1991. *Postmodernism and Its Critics*. Ithaca: Cornell University Press.

– 2002. *Democracy's Children: Intellectuals and the Rise of Cultural Politics*. Ithaca: Cornell University Press.

McGrew, Anthony. 2002. 'Transnational Democracy.' In April Carter and Geoffrey Stokes, eds., *Democratic Theory Today: Challenges for the 21st Century*, 269–94. London: Polity.

McGrew, Anthony, and David Held, eds. 2002. *Governing Globalization: Power Authority, and Global Governance*. Cambridge: Polity.

McKillop, A.B. 1994. *Matters of Mind: The University in Ontario, 1791–1951*. Toronto: University of Toronto Press.

McSherry, Corynne. 2001. *Who Owns Academic Work? Battling for Control of Intellectual Property*. Cambridge, MA: Harvard University Press.

Medsker, Leland L., and Dale Tilley. 1971. *Breaking the Access Barriers: A Profile of Two-Year Colleges*. New York: McGraw-Hill.

Menand, Louis. 1995. 'Marketing Postmodernism.' In Robert Orrill, ed.,*The Condition of American Liberal Education: Pragmatism and a Changing Tradition*, 140–4. New York: College Entrance Examination Board.

– 1996a. 'The Limits of Academic Freedom.' In Louis Menand, ed., *The Future of Academic Freedom*, 3–20. Chicago: University of Chicago Press.

– ed. 1996b. *The Future of Academic Freedom.* Chicago: University of Chicago Press.
Merton, Robert K. 1942. 'Science and Technology in a Democratic Order.' *Journal of Legal and Political Sociology.* Republished as 'The Normative Structure of Science.' In *Sociology of Science*, 267–78. Chicago: University of Chicago Press, 1973.
Metzger, Walter P. 1955. 'Part Two: The Age of the University.' In Richard Hofstadter and Walter P. Metzger, *The Development of Academic Freedom in the United States*, 276–506. New York: Columbia University Press.
M'Gonigle, Michael, and Justine Starke. 2006. *Planet U: Sustaining the World and Reinventing the University.* Gabriola Island, BC: New Society.
Michael, John. 2000. *Anxious Intellects: Academic Professionals, Public Intellectuals, and Enlightenment Values.* Durham: Duke University Press.
Mishra, Ramesh. 1984. *The Welfare State in Crisis: Social Thought and Social Change.* Brighton: Wheatsheaf Books.
MIT. 2004. *A 'Weather Map' of Quality of life @ MIT.* Draft Report. Cambridge, MA: MIT.
Mokyr, Joel. 1990. *The Lever of Riches: Technological Creativity and Economic Progress.* Oxford: Oxford University Press.
Mouffe, Chantal, 1992a. 'Preface: Democratic Politics Today.' In Chantal Mouffe, ed., *Dimensions of Radical Democracy: Pluralism, Citizenship, Community*, 1–14. London: Verso.
– ed. 1992b. *Dimensions of Radical Democracy: Pluralism, Citizenship, Community.* London: Verso.
National Association of State Universities and Land-Grant Colleges. 1999. *Returning to Our Roots: A Learning Society.* A Report of the Kellogg Commission on the Future of State Universities and Land-Grant Colleges. Retrieved at http://www.nasulgc.org/Kellogg/kellogg.htm.
Negroponte, Nicholas. 1996. *Being Digital.* New York: Vintage.
Nelson, Richard R., ed. 1993. *National Innovation Systems: A Comparative Analysis.* New York: Oxford University Press.
– 1996. *The Sources of Economic Growth.* Cambridge, MA: Harvard University Press.
Nevitte, Neil, and Roger Gibbins. 1990. *New Elites in Old States: Ideologies in Anglo-American Democracies.* Toronto: Oxford University Press.
New Zealand. 1990. *Education Amendment Act 1990.* Retrieved at http://rangi.knowledge-basket.co.nz/gpacts/public/text/1990/.
Noble, David. 1997. *Digital Diploma Mills: The Automation of Higher Education.* Retrieved at http://communication.ucsd.edo/dl/.
Noll, Roger G. 1998. 'The American Research University: An Introduction.' In

Roger G. Noll, ed., *Challenges to Research Universities*, 1–30. Washington, D.C.: Brookings Institution.

Nussbaum, Martha. 1995. *Poetic Justice: The Literary Imagination in Public Life*. Boston: Beacon Press.

– 1997. *Cultivating Humanity: A Classical Defense of Reform in Liberal Education*. Cambridge, MA: Harvard University Press.

Odin, Jaishree, and Peter T. Manicas, eds. 2004. *Globalization and Higher Education*. Honolulu: University of Hawai'i Press.

OECD. 1985. *Social Expenditure 1960–1990: Problems of Growth and Control*. Paris: author.

– 2003. *Education at a Glance*. Paris: author.

– 2005. *Social Expenditure Database*. Retrieved at http://www.oecd.org.

Ong, Walter J. 1982. *Orality and Literacy: The Technologizing of the Word*. New York: Methuen.

Orrill, Robert, ed. 1995. *The Condition of American Liberal Education: Pragmatism and a Changing Tradition*. New York: College Entrance Examination Board.

– 1997. *Education and Democracy: Re-Imagining Liberal Learning in America*. New York: College Entrance Examination Board.

Ortega y Gasset, José. [1930] 2001. *Mission of the University*. With a new introduction by Clark Kerr. New Brunswick, NJ: Transaction Publishers.

Perkin, Harold. 1984. 'The Historical Perspective.' In Burton R. Clark, ed., *Perspectives on Higher Education: Eight Disciplinary and Comparative Views*, 17–55. Berkeley: University of California Press.

– 1989. *The Rise of Professional Society: England since 1880*. London: Routledge.

Pharr, Susan J., and Robert Putnam, eds. 2000. *Disaffected Democracies: What's Troubling the Trilateral Countries*. Princeton: Princeton University Press.

Phillips, Robert, and John Furlong. 2001a. 'Introduction and Rationale.' In John Furlong and Robert Phillips, eds., *Education, Reform and the State: Twenty-five Years of Politics, Policy and Practice*, 3–11. London: Routledge/Falmer.

– eds. 2001b. *Education, Reform and the State: Twenty-five Years of Politics, Policy and Practice*. London: Routledge/Falmer.

Pierson, Christopher. 1999. *Beyond the Welfare State? The New Political Economy of Welfare*. 2nd ed. Cambridge, MA: Polity.

Pocklington, Tom, and Allan Tupper. 2002. *No Place to Learn: Why Universities Aren't Working*. Vancouver: UBC Press.

Posner, Richard A. 2003. *Public Intellectuals: A Study of Decline*. Cambridge, MA: Harvard University Press.

Powell, Walter A., and Jason Owen-Smith. 2002. 'The New World of Knowledge Production in the Life Sciences.' In Steven Brint, ed., *The Future of the*

City of Intellect: The Changing American University, 107–30. Stanford: Stanford University Press.
Pratt, J. 1997. *The Polytechnic Experiment, 1965–1992.* Buckingham, UK: Society for Research into higher Education and Open University Press.
Proctor, Robert E. 1988. *Education's Great Amnesia: Reconsidering the Humanities from Petrarch to Freud.* Bloomington: Indiana University Press.
Readings, Bill. 1996. *The University in Ruins.* Cambridge, MA: Harvard University Press.
Rees, Gareth, and Dean Stroud. 2001. 'Creating a Mass System of Higher Education: Participation, the Economy and Citizenship.' In John Furlong and Robert Phillips, eds., *Education, Reform and the State: Twenty-five Years of Politics, Policy and Practice*, 72–86. London: Routledge/Falmer.
Reid, T.R. 2001. *The Chip: How Two Americans Invented the Microchip and Launched a Revolution.* New York: Random House.
Reuben, Julie A. 1996. *The Making of the Modern University: Intellectual Transformation and the Marginalization of Morality.* Chicago: University of Chicago Press.
Rhodes, Frank H.T. 1994. 'The Place of Teaching in the Research University.' In Jonathan R. Cole, Elinor Barber, and Stephen R. Graubard, eds., *The Research University in a Time of Discontent*, 179–89. Baltimore: Johns Hopkins University Press.
– 2001. *The Creation of the Future: The Role of the American University.* Ithaca: Cornell University Press.
Ricks, Christopher, ed., 1999. *The Oxford Book of English Verse.* Oxford: Oxford University Press.
Riddell, W. Craig. 2005. 'The Social Benefits of Education: New Evidence on an Old Question.' In Frank Iacobucci and Carolyn Tuohy, eds., *Taking Public Universities Seriously*, 138–63. Toronto: University of Toronto Press.
Ripstein, Arthur. 2005. 'Public and Private Benefits in Higher Education.' In Frank Iacobucci and Carolyn Tuohy, eds., *Taking Public Universities Seriously*, 498–513. Toronto: University of Toronto Press.
Robbins, Lord. 1976. *Political Economy, Past and Present: A Review of Leading Theories of Economic Policy.* London: Macmillan Press.
Romer, Paul M. 1993. 'Two Strategies for Economic Development: Using Ideas and Producing Ideas.' In *Proceedings of the World Bank Annual Conference on Development Economics 1992*, 63–91. Washington: World Bank.
Rorty, Richard. 1982. *Consequences of Pragmatism.* Minneapolis: University of Minnesota Press.
Rosenau, Pauline Marie.1992. *Post-Modernism and the Social Sciences: Insights, Inroads, and Intrusions.* Princeton: Princeton University Press.

Rosenberg, Nathan, and Richard R. Nelson. 1996. 'American Universities and Technical Advance in Industry.' In Richard R. Nelson, *The Sources of Economic Growth*, 189–229. Cambridge, MA: Harvard University Press.

Rosovsky, Henry. 2001. 'Some Thoughts about University Governance.' In Werner Z. Hirsch and Luc E. Weber, eds., *Governance in Higher Education: The University in a State of Flux*, 94–104. London: Economica.

Rosovsky, Henry, and Inge-Lise Ameer. 1998. 'A Neglected Topic: Professional Conduct of College and University Teachers.' In William G. Bowen and Harold T. Shapiro, eds., *Universities and Their Leadership*, 119–56. Princeton: Princeton University Press.

Rothblatt, Sheldon. 1976. *Tradition and Change in English Liberal Education: An Essay in History and Culture*. London: Faber and Faber.

– 1993. 'The Limbs of Osiris: Liberal Education in the English- Speaking World.' In Sheldon Rothblatt and Bjorn Wittrock, eds., *The European and American University since 1800: Historical and Sociological Essays*, 19–73. Cambridge: Cambridge University Press.

– 1997. *The Modern University and Its Discontents: The Fate of Newman's Legacies in Britain and America*. Cambridge: Cambridge University Press.

Rowntree, Seebohm. 1941. *Poverty and Progress: A Second Social Survey of York*. London: Longmans, Green.

Russell, Conrad. 1993. *Academic Freedom*. London: Routledge.

Ryan, Alan. 1998. *Liberal Anxieties and Liberal Education*. New York: Hill and Wang.

Said, Edward W. 1994. *Representations of the Intellectual: The 1993 Reith Lectures*. New York: Vintage Books.

–1996. 'Identity, Authority, and Freedom: The Potentate and the Traveler.' In Louis Menand, ed., *The Future of Academic Freedom*, 214–28. Chicago: University of Chicago Press.

– 2003. *Orientalism*, 25th anniversary ed. New York: Vintage.

Sanderson, Michael. 1972. *The Universities and British Industry, 1850–1970*. London: Routledge and Kegan Paul.

– ed. 1975. *The Universities in the Nineteenth Century*. London: Routledge and Kegan Paul.

Saul, John Ralston. 2004. 'The Collapse of Globalism and the Rebirth of Nationalism.' *Harper's Magazine* 308 (1846): 33–43.

Scherer, F.M. 1999. *New Perspectives on Economic Growth and Technological Innovation*. Washington, DC: Brookings Institution Press.

Schultz, Theodore. 1963. *The Economic Value of Education*. New York: Columbia University Press.

Scott, Peter. 1995. *The Meanings of Mass Higher Education*. Buckingham, UK: Society for Research into Higher Education and Open University Press.

- 1997. 'The Postmodern University?' In Anthony Smith and Frank Webster, eds., *The Postmodern University? Contested Visions of Higher Education in Society*, 36–47. Buckingham, UK: Society for Research into Higher Education and Open University Press.
- 2000. 'Globalisation and Higher Education: Challenges for the 21st Century.' *Journal of Studies in International Education* (Spring): 3–10.
- 2001a. 'Conclusion: Triumph and Retreat.' In David Warner and David Palfreyman, eds., *The State of UK Higher Education: Managing Change and Diversity*, 186–204. Buckingham, UK: Society for Research into Higher Education and Open University Press.
- 2001b. 'Universities as Organizations and their Governance.' In Werner Z. Hirsch and Luc E. Weber, eds., *Governance in Higher Education: The University in a State of Flux*, 125–42. London: Economica.
- 2005. 'The Opportunities and Threats of Globalization.' In Glen A. Jones, Patricia L. McCarney, and Michael L. Skolnick, eds., *Creating Knowledge, Strengthening Nations: The Changing Role of Higher Education*, 42–55. Toronto: University of Toronto Press.
- ed. 1998. *The Globalization of Higher Education*. Buckingham, UK: Society for Research into Higher Education and Open University Press.

Searle, John R. 1972. 'Two Concepts of Academic Freedom.' In Edmund L. Pincoffs, ed., *The Concept of Academic Freedom*, 86–96. Austin: University of Austin Press.
- 1993. 'Rationality and Realism, What is at Stake?' In Jonathan R. Cole, Elinor Barber, and Stephen R Graubard, eds., *The Research University in a Time of Discontent*, 55–83. Baltimore: Johns Hopkins University Press.

Shapiro, Harold. 2004. Address on receiving the James Madison Medal. Princeton University.

Shiller, Robert J. 2000. *Irrational Exuberance*. Princeton: Princeton University Press.

Shils, Edward. [1989] 1997a. 'The Modern University and Liberal Democracy.' In Shils, *The Calling of Education: The Academic Ethic and Other Essays on Higher Education*. Edited by Steven Grosby, 250–90. Chicago: University of Chicago Press.
- 1997b. *The Calling of Education: The Academic Ethic and Other Essays on Higher Education*. Edited by Steven Grosby. Chicago: University of Chicago Press.

Sim, Stuart. 2001a. 'Postmodernism and Philosophy.' In Stuart Sim, ed., *The Routledge Companion to Postmodernism*, 3–14. London: Routledge.
- ed. 2001b. *The Routledge Companion to Postmodernism*. London: Routledge.

Skidelsky, Robert. 1996. *Keynes*. Oxford: Oxford University Press.

Slaughter, Sheila, and Larry L. Leslie. 1997. *Academic Capitalism: Politics,*

Policies, and the Entrepreneurial University. Baltimore: Johns Hopkins University Press.

Sloan, Douglas. 1971. *The Scottish Enlightenment and the American College Ideal.* New York: Teachers College Press.

Smith, Adam. [1776] 1937. *An Inquiry into the Nature and Causes of the Wealth of Nations.* New York: Modern Library.

Smith, Anthony, and Frank Webster, eds. 1997. *The Postmodern University? Contested Visions of Higher Education in Society.* Buckingham, UK: Society for Research into Higher Education and Open University Press.

Smith, Bruce L.R., and David Korn. 2000. 'Is there a Crisis of Accountability in the American Research University?' *Minerva* 38: 129–45.

Smith, Charles W. 2004. 'Globalization, Higher Education, and Markets.' In Jaishree K. Odin and Peter T. Manicas, eds., *Globalization and Higher Education,* 69–81. Honolulu: University of Hawai'i Press.

Smith, J.H. 1996. Foreword. In Martin Bulmer and Anthony M. Rees, eds., *Citizenship Today: The Contemporary Relevance of T.H. Marshall,* ix–xiii. London: UCL Press.

Smith, Mark J. 1998. *Social Science in Question.* London: Sage.

Snow, C.P. 1964. *The Two Cultures: And a Second Look. An Expanded Version of Two Cultures and the Scientific Revolution.* London: Cambridge University Press.

Solow, Robert M. 1957. 'Technical Change and the Aggregate Production Function.' *Review of Economics and Statistics* 39: 312–20.

Sowell, Thomas. 1993. *Is Reality Optional? And Other Essays.* Stanford: Hoover Institution Press.

Statistics Canada. 1999. *Education Indicators in Canada: Report of the Pan-Canadian Education Indicators Program 1999.* Ottawa: author.

– 2003. *Canada at a Glance.* Ottawa: author.

Stephens, Michael D., ed. 1989. *Universities, Education and the National Economy.* London: Routledge.

Stokes, Donald E. 1997. *Pasteur's Quadrant: Basic Science and Technological Innovation.* Washington, DC: Brookings Institution.

Strunk, William Jr., and E.B. White. [1959] 2000. *The Elements of Style.* 4th ed. New York: Longmans.

Sulston, John, and Georgina Ferry. 2002. *The Common Thread: A Story of Science, Politics, Ethics, and the Human Genome.* London: National Science Academies Press.

Tajnai, Caroline E. 1985. *Fred Terman, the Father of Silicon Valley.* Retrieved at http://www.netvalley.com/archives/.

Tapper, Ted, and David Palfreyman. 2000. *Oxford and the Decline of the Collegiate Tradition.* London: Woburn.

Taylor, Charles. 1991. *The Malaise of Modernity.* CBC Massey Lectures. Toronto: Anansi.

Taylor, Victor E., and Charles E. Winquist, eds. 2001. *Encyclopedia of Postmodernism.* London: Routledge.

Teich, Albert H. 1998. 'The Outlook for Federal Support of University Research.' In Roger G. Noll, ed., *Challenges to Research Universities*, 87–104. Washington, DC: Brookings Institution.

Thomas, Francis-Noel, and Mark Turner. 1994. *Clear and Simple as the Truth: Writing Classic Prose.* Princeton: Princeton University Press.

Tight, Malcolm, ed. 1988. *Academic Freedom and Responsibility.* Milton Keynes, UK: Society for Research into Higher Education and Open University Press.

Trow, Martin. 1973. *Problems in the Transition from Elite to Mass Higher Education.* Washington, DC: Carnegie Commission on Higher Education.

– 1996. 'Trust, Markets and Accountability in Higher Education.' *Higher Education Policy* 9(4), 309–24.

– 1997. 'The Development of Information Technology in American Higher Education.' *Daedalus* 126: 293–314.

Turner, Frank M. 1996a. 'Newman's University and Ours.' In Frank M. Turner, ed., *The Idea of a University: John Henry Newman*, 282–301. New Haven: Yale University Press.

– ed. 1996b. *The Idea of a University: John Henry Newman.* New Haven: Yale University Press.

UNESCO. 1997. *International Standard Classification of Education ISCED 1997.* Retrieved at http://www.unesco.org/education/information/nfsunesco/doc/ised_1997.

United Nations. 1948. *The Universal Declaration of Human Rights.* Retrieved at http://www.un.org/Overview/rights.html.

University of Illinois. 2000. *Teaching at an Internet Distance: The Pedagogy of Online Teaching and Learning.* The Report of a 1998–1999 University of Illinois Faculty Seminar. Retrieved at http://vpaa.uillinois.edu/tid/report/.

University of Toronto. 2001. *University of Toronto National Report 2001.* Toronto: author.

U.S. Department of Education. 2001. *Digest of Educational Statistics 2001.* Washington, DC: National Center for Educational Statistics.

Veblen, Thorstein. [1918] 1965. *The Higher Learning in America: A Memorandum on the Conduct of Universities by Business Men.* New York: A.M. Kelley.

Vest, Charles. 2001. *Disturbing the Educational Universe: Universities in the Digital Age: Dinosaurs or Prometheans?* Report of the President 2000–01. Retrieved at http://web.mit.edu/president/communications/.

Veysey, Laurence R. 1965. *The Emergence of the American University.* Chicago: University of Chicago Press.
Wallach, Janet. 1996. *Desert Queen.* New York: Doubleday.
Warner, David, and David Palfreyman, eds. 2001. *The State of UK Higher Education: Managing Change and Diversity.* Buckingham, UK: Society for Research into Higher Education and Open University Press.
Weber, Max. 1983. *Max Weber on Capitalism, Bureaucracy, and Religion: a Selection of Texts.* Trans. Stanislav Andreski. London: Allen and Unwin.
– [1930] 1992. *The Protestant Ethic and the Spirit of Capitalism.* London: Routledge.
Weir, Margaret, Ann Shola Orloff, and Theda Skocpol. 1988. *The Politics of Social Policy in the United States.* Princeton: Princeton University Press.
Whitehead, Alfred North. 1968. *Modes of Thought.* New York: Free Press.
Willinsky, John. 2002. 'Democracy and Education: The Missing Link May Be Ours.' *Harvard Educational Review* 72(3): 367–92.
Wingspread Declaration. 1999. *Wingspread Declaration on the Civic Responsibilities of Research Universities.* Retreived at http://www.compact.org/civic/Wingspread/.
Wisdom, J.O. 1987. *Challengeability in Modern Science.* Dorset: Blackmore.
Wolff, Robert Paul. 1969. *The Ideal of the University.* Boston: Beacon Press.
Woodruff, Paul. 2005. *First Democracy: The Challenge of an Ancient Idea.* New York: Oxford University Press.
Young, Iris Marion. 1989. 'Polity and Group Difference: A Critique of the Idea of Universal Citizenship.' *Ethics* 99: 250–74.
– 1990. *Justice and the Politics of Difference.* Princeton: Princeton University Press.
Zinsser, William. 1976. *On Writing Well: An Informal Guide to Writing Nonfiction.* New York: Harper and Row.
Zweiger, Gary. 2001. *Transducing the Genome: Information, Anarchy, and Revolution in the Biomedical Sciences.* New York: McGraw-Hill.

Index

AAUP (Association of American University Professors), 119, 121, 125, 249; 'Declaration of Principles,' 119, 121, 125. *See also* academic freedom
academic capitalism, 260, 274, 299
academic duties and responsibilities, 126–8, 137, 282–3, 374, 384
academic freedom, 8, 111–12, 113–14, 118–28, 131, 133, 135, 136, 176, 276, 326–7, 336, 339, 351, 370–2, 376; and Darwinism, 120–2, 326; and postmodern thought, 249–50; and private ideas, 285, 288–9, 361; and tenure, 119, 125; and terrorism, 121, 126, 326–7. *See also* AAUP; autonomy of the university; governance of the multiversity; social contract
academic revolution, 47, 261, 290
accessibility, 5, 31–2, 49, 60, 108, 171–2, 416; and online courses, 210–14; and participation rates, 60, 104, 108, 165, 169, 171, 209, 265; for women, 21–2, 45, 55, 60, 108, 165. *See also* land grant universities; Scottish universities; student assistance; tuition fees; undergraduate education

accountability. *See* social contract
American empire, 324–7
antiglobalization, 307, 309, 311–12, 317–19
archetypes of a university, 18, 23, 43, 47–8, 291, 339. *See also* ideas of a university
Arnold, Matthew, 38–41, 63–4, 134, 230, 234, 243, 244, 342, 345; 'the best that has been thought and said,' 39, 63, 227, 398; *Culture and Anarchy*, 38, 134; on democracy and high ideals, 39, 108–9; 'Dover Beach,' 39–40, 234, 245–6. *See also* humanities; ideas of a university; liberal education; Newman, Cardinal John Henry
Ashby, Eric, 8, 112, 340
autonomy of the university, 8, 111, 113–18, 122, 126, 128, 176–7, 196, 276, 301, 326, 336, 339, 340–1, 351, 355, 358, 361, 371, 376, 416; and institutional neutrality, 117–18. *See also* academic freedom; governance of the multiversity; social contract
Axelrod, Paul, 390, 391, 413

Barber, Benjamin R., 323–4

Barr, Nicholas, 170, 171
Baudrillard, Jean, 239
Bayh-Dole Act, 278
Beetham, David, 348, 352; what is democracy, 348–55
Bell, Daniel, 4, 52, 62, 68, 84, 99, 181, 347. *See also* postindustrial society
Bell, Gertrude, 303–4
Berlin, Isaiah, 249, 408
Berlin Wall, 298, 311, 376, 408
Berners-Lee, Timothy, 189–90, 192, 286, 287
Beveridge, William, 96, 99–101, 149, 151–3. *See also* social expenditures; welfare state
biotechnology, 262, 274, 279–81, 282, 286, 289–90, 294
Bismarck, Otto von, 92
Bledstein, Bernard J., 66
Bloom, Harold, 366–7, 369
Bok, Derek, 117, 260
book, history of, 214–16. *See also* Gutenberg, Johann
Brint, Steven, 291
Bush, George W., 126, 157, 159, 324–5, 327
Bush, Vannevar, 54–5, 57, 97, 271, 275–6, 356, 358; *Science – The Endless Frontier*, 55, 97, 275, 356

Cambridge University, 26, 31, 32, 46, 68, 70, 78, 79, 86, 92, 115, 274
campus, 179, 202, 203, 210–11, 216; as a *place*, 219–21, 383
China, 305, 306, 311, 315, 325, 328
citizens, 5, 43–5, 84–5, 87–8, 213, 345, 349–52, 354, 378–80, 386–7, 392, 400. *See also* citizenship
citizenship, 11, 12, 42, 43, 62–3, 102–3, 109, 154, 161–2, 242, 246, 254, 302, 323, 329–35, 341, 335, 377, 386–7, 392, 394, 399, 400; citizen rights, 352–3; citizen wisdom, 386–7; civic republican versus liberal, 404–6, 409, 412; in classical thought, 24–5; in a re-envisioned liberal education, 403–13; radical citizenship, 410–11, 412. *See also* citizens; cosmopolitan citizenship; democracy; liberal education; Marshall, Thomas H.; U.N. Universal Declaration of Human Rights
civic universities. *See* redbrick universities
civil society, 105, 323, 334, 352–5, 378, 379
Clark, Burton, 418–20
Cold War, 126, 298, 305–6, 310, 311, 320, 321, 324–5, 327, 328, 348
colonialism, 41, 227, 297, 302, 305. *See also* imperialism; postcolonialism
commercialization, 57, 195, 260–3; and the character of our age, 9–11, 141, 146–7, 192, 335; as the dominant discourse, 290–6; public ideas or private ideas, 286–90; of research, 277–86. *See also* economics of ideas; human capital; new growth theory; Silicon Valley
communism, 46, 93–4, 301, 306, 320, 345, 374; in the ethos of science, 46, 284. *See also* Marx, Karl
community colleges, 59–60, 73, 76, 79
computer networks, 182, 187–92, 217–18. *See also* Internet; World Wide Web
constrained welfare state, 83, 146–9, 155–65, 169, 176–9, 209, 263, 317, 341, 342, 357, 381, 415, 419; and the character of our age, 9–11, 141,

146–7, 335. *See also* market fundamentalism; neoliberalism; welfare state
correspondence theory of truth, 233, 243, 251
cosmopolitan citizenship, 408–9, 420. *See also* cosmopolitan democracy; cosmopolitanism
cosmopolitan democracy, 329, 332–5, 370, 379, 408. *See also* cosmopolitan citizenship; cosmopolitanism
cosmopolitanism, 299, 314, 332–5, 370, 373, 409. *See also* cosmopolitan democracy; cosmopolitan citizenship
Crick, Sir Bernard, 348; what is democracy, 348–55
critic and conscience, the university's role as, 133–7, 289, 346, 355, 361, 364, 371, 374, 416–18; in the Education Amendment Act of New Zealand, 135–6; and information technology, 196, 214, 416; risks in the role, 136–7. *See also* public intellectuals; social contract

Dahl, Robert, 43, 348; what is democracy, 348–55
Darwin, Charles, 34, 120–1, 303–4; *On the Origin of Species by Means of Natural Selection*, 120, 303
deconstruction, 236, 253
deliberative democracy, 11, 343, 351, 355, 376–80, 403–4, 420
democracy: definitions, 43, 348–55, 386–7; disillusionment about politics, 377; first democracy and *paideia*, 386–7; and globalization, 323–5; and information technology, 190, 194; institutions of democracy, 343–7, 352–5; role of multiversity, 3–5, 107–10, 343–7; role of university, 42–7; social contract for research in a, 355–70; and undergraduate education, 42, 61–3, 106, 108, 329, 403–13. *See also* citizens; citizenship; cosmopolitan democracy; critic and conscience, the university's role as; deliberative democracy; ideas of a university; public intellectuals
Derrida, Jacques, 224, 236, 293
Dertouzos, Michael, 178–87, 199, 286
digital technology, 183, 186, 195, 286
distance education, 211–14
Drucker, Peter F., 179
Dryzek, John, 377, 379
Duderstadt, James, 6, 48, 74, 131, 133, 174, 293, 417, 418

economics of ideas, 265–8. *See also* intellectual property; public goods
economy: institutions of, 292–6, 341, 347; knowledge-based, 51, 52, 84, 262, 343, 348, 355, 385. *See also* globalization; postindustrial society; unemployment
Enlightenment, 27–8, 31, 35, 44, 78, 90, 134, 222, 253–4, 307, 309, 388; and academic freedom, 119; and postmodern thought, 224–33

Fabian ideals, 95, 98, 108
feminism, 121, 153, 226, 241–2, 245, 247, 252, 254–5, 309, 374
Foucault, Michel, 224, 237, 238, 240, 293, 379, 414
Friedman, Milton, 149
Friedman, Thomas L., 321–2
Fukuyama, Francis, 320–1, 376–7;

and the end of history, 320–1, 323, 348, 376–7
fundraising and donations, 82, 123, 126, 131, 166, 173–7, 296, 330, 335–6, 342, 399

GATS, 318–19
GATT, 306, 311–12
general education. *See* liberal education
General Education in Free Society. See Harvard Redbook
German universities, 27–31, 33, 50; and the economy, 30; and the government, 31, 92, 122; and research, 30, 120; and the role of professors, 29, 122–3. *See also* Humboldt, Wilhelm von; ideas of a university; *lehrfreiheit*; University of Berlin
Giroux, Henri, 411
globalization: definitions, 298, 302–3, 305–6, 309, 310–14; and the character of our age, 9–11, 141, 146–7, 192, 335; and convergence of educational systems, 300, 305; and educational spending, 317–18; and national sovereignty, 316–17. *See also* antiglobalization; cosmopolitan democracy; nation state; Westphalian system
Goldfarb, Jeffery C., 139, 372–4
governance of the multiversity, 8, 111, 128–33, 339, 343, 416–20; board of governors, 121, 128–9, 131, 136, 417; collegial self-governance, 130–1, 339, 417–18, 419; leadership, 115, 118, 130, 132–3, 168, 258, 275, 332, 335–6, 344, 416, 417–18, 419; need for reform, 132–3, 416–20; senate, 129; senior administration, 78, 122, 126–8, 129–31, 310, 336. *See also* academic freedom; autonomy of the university; social contract
graduate education, 3, 8, 29–31, 33, 50, 54, 57–8, 72–83, 123, 330, 361, 364, 381, 384. *See also* multiversities: definitions
Graff, Gerald, 245, 412, 414
grand narrative. *See* metanarrative
Great Depression, 87, 97, 100, 305
Guston, David, 356–7, 360
Gutenberg, Johann, 204, 205
Gutmann, Amy, 88, 350–1, 378, 410

Harvard Redbook, 61–3, 246, 394
Harvard University, 7, 36, 50, 61, 69, 73, 86, 173, 174, 195, 258. *See also* Harvard Redbook
Heater, Derek, 404, 409
Held, David, 333
Hofstadter, Richard, 373
human capital, 68, 164, 263–5, 268, 270, 271, 292, 293, 295, 347; and educational choice, 264–5, 295
humanities: and Christian texts, 37, 44; government support for research in, 56–7, 75–7, 295, 361, 362, 364–70; and hypertext, 189–90, 218, 236; in liberal education, 10, 12, 34, 36–42, 62–4, 95, 109–10, 391, 393, 395, 407; marginalized, 10, 12, 283, 335–6, 341, 365; and postmodern thought, 224–30, 234, 243–7, 340; as a program of education, 37, 366; in Renaissance humanism, 27, 37–8; why study the humanities, 396, 398–401. *See also* Arnold, Matthew; liberal education; Newman, Cardinal John Henry; Orientalism; Proctor, Robert; Trilling, Lionel

Humboldt, Alexander von, 303–4
Humboldt, Wilhelm von, 29, 30, 42, 93, 116, 180, 303
Huntington, Samuel P., 327–8
Huxley, Thomas, 34, 42, 121; on liberal education, 34–5
hypertext, 189–90, 217–18, 236

ideas of a university, 18, 22–3, 33–4, 339; of Cardinal Newman, 19–20, 23, 339, 383; German universities, 29–31, 339; as an institution of democracy, 3, 5, 296, 343–7, 355, 381, 383, 415–20; as an institution of the economy, 291–6, 341, 347; medieval universities, 25, 339; multiversity as conglomerate of, 18, 48–9, 140, 291, 296, 339–43, 420; Scottish universities, 31–3, 339. *See also* archetypes of a university; mission of the multiversity
Ignatieff, Michael, 326, 354
IMF, 306–7, 311–12, 316
imperialism, 41, 239, 297, 299, 301, 310, 324, 334, 354. *See also* American empire, colonialism, postcolonialism, Orientalism
industrial revolution, 17, 21, 93, 178, 197, 204, 274–5
information technology revolution, 178–92; and the character of our age, 9–11, 141, 146–7, 192, 335; and undergraduate teaching, 197–204, 208–21; and the multiversity, 192–7. *See also* online courses
Innis, Harold, 204, 208
integrated circuit, 184, 185
intellectual property, 179, 196, 261, 267–71, 277–8, 284, 286–90, 292–3. *See also* economics of ideas

International Standard Classification of Education, 72–3
internationalization of the multiversity, 309–10, 314–16, 330–1
Internet, 179, 189–93, 204, 216, 220, 286–7, 298, 312, 397

Jacobs, Jane, 271
Jacoby, Russell, 375
Johns Hopkins University, 50

Kant, Immanuel, 28, 29
Keniston, Kenneth, 356–7
Kennedy, Donald, 127, 132–3
Kenny, Martin, 273, 279
Kerr, Clark, 5, 17, 48, 73, 130, 141, 257–8, 347, 396; on the importance of knowledge, 51, 353; and the technologies of teaching, 179–80, 200; and undergraduate education, 382, 396
Keynes, John Maynard, 96–9, 149, 153, 229, 306, 321, 414; and his critics, 149–57; on power of ideas, 96, 229; as public intellectual, 99; and unemployment, 96, 98–9, 105, 149, 155–7, 248, 262. *See also* welfare state
Kimball, Bruce, 24, 35, 388, 401–3. *See also* liberal education
knowledge-based society. *See* economy, postindustrial society
Kymlicka, Will, 405, 406, 408

laboratories, 5, 49, 50, 57, 74, 122, 169, 224, 340, 356, 372, 384; and teaching, 199–203, 207
land grant universities, 50, 122, 212, 275, 277, 302, 339. *See also* Morrill Act; Scottish universities

leadership. *See* governance of the multiversity
learning objects, 215–17
lehrfreiheit, 29, 120, 122–3
Leslie, Larry, 260, 277, 299
Lessig, Lawrence, 195, 196
liberal education: *artes liberales* ideal, 24–5, 40–1, 61, 62, 243, 388–9, 396, 401–2, 405; and the autonomous individual, 23–4, 390, 396–8, 399; and Christian texts, 44, 243, 259; and citizenship, 24–5, 43, 63, 243, 387, 403–13; and its curriculum, 26, 36, 42, 62–3, 228, 331–2, 388–92, 396–402; a liberal education minor, 393–6; liberal-free ideal, 35–6, 40–1, 243, 388, 396, 401–2, 405; and lifelong learning, 211–14, 416; of Cardinal Newman, 19–20, 22, 219; and postmodern thought, 228–9, 243–7; and privilege, 44; re-envisioned in our age, 383, 385–6, 396–403, 411–14, 415–16; versus disciplinary education, 61–4, 389–93; and writing, 390, 391, 413–14. *See also* humanities; undergraduate education
liberalism, 46, 344–5, 350; classical liberalism, 92–4, 149, 152. *See also* neoliberalism; Rawls, John; Ryan, Alan
libraries, 5, 50, 116, 122, 147, 169, 193–6, 220, 365; online, 195, 201–3, 215
lifelong learning, 140, 212–4, 372, 416
linear model of research, 275–6, 358–9, 362, 367. *See also* Bush, Vannevar; Stokes, Donald E.
linguistics, 224, 226, 234–7, 252, 254, 340. *See also* signifier/signified
literacy, 204–8. *See also* orality

London School of Economics and Political Science, 81, 95, 100, 176, 180
Lyotard, Jean-François, 237, 238, 240, 293, 294

market fundamentalism, 152, 160, 314, 316–19, 374. *See also* neoliberalism
Marshall, Thomas H., 96, 102, 149, 161, 308, 329, 353, 406, 410; 'Citizenship and Social Class,' 102, 308; civil citizenship, 102, 308, 329, 410; political citizenship, 102, 308, 329; social citizenship, 88, 96, 102–3, 107–8, 148–9, 154, 161, 171, 242, 254, 294, 308, 329, 346, 353, 410. *See also* citizenship; U.N. Universal Declaration of Human Rights
Marx, Karl, 93, 102, 134, 226, 230, 258, 321; *The Manifesto of the Communist Party*, 93, 134, 231. *See also* communism
Marxism, 102, 226, 231, 245, 252, 253, 309
mass higher education, 5, 60–2, 70, 71, 75, 85, 103, 106, 108, 128, 141, 167, 219, 262, 339, 382–3, 394; in England, 77, 79, 81, 167, 394. *See also* Trow, Martin
Massey Commission, 64, 76
McGowan, John, 137, 226, 412
McLuhan, Marshall, 204, 205
medieval universities, 25–7, 33, 66, 115–16, 301, 339. *See also* ideas of a university; professional education
Menand, Louis, 113, 249, 402
mercantilism, 90–1
Merton, Robert, 46, 284

metanarrative, 238, 243, 245, 253, 294–5, 398
Metcalfe, Robert, 187, 188
Metcalfe's Law, 188, 220
Metzger, Walter, 120, 122, 285, 371
microprocessor, 184, 186
Mill, John Stuart, 92, 94
Mishra, Ramesh, 88, 101
mission of the multiversity, vii, 3, 4, 7, 8, 18–36, 42, 54, 110, 122, 136, 141, 277–8, 290–6, 343–7, 414–20; mission drift, 49, 110, 341–3, 346–7, 365, 386, 397, 419. *See also* ideas of a university
modernity, 27, 28, 32, 222–31, 240, 241, 242, 323
monetarism, 150, 151
Moore, Gordon, 185, 272
Moore's Law, 185, 186, 187, 188, 272
moral philosophy, 26, 32, 90, 95
Morrill Act, 50, 275
multicultural society, 159, 242, 392, 401, 402, 403, 407
multiculturalism, 241–2, 248, 258, 401, 402, 407, 408
multiversities: definitions, 3, 48–50, 51, 54, 72–3, 111; as an American institution, 6, 48, 69–71, 73–5; in the Anglo-American world, 6, 49, 71; in Canada, 71, 75–7; in England, 70, 77–82; as conglomerates of ideas, 18, 48–9, 140, 291, 296, 339–43, 420; hierarchy/ranking, 166–7, 172–3, 175, 315, 331, 336, 381; and deliberative democracy, 378–80; as institutions of democracy, 3, 42, 140, 179, 296, 343–7, 355–6, 378–80, 381, 383, 414, 415–20; as a cosmopolitan institution, 330–5; as institutions of the economy, 291–6, 341, 347; as a powerful institution, 4, 7, 11, 86–7, 107, 109, 115, 262, 299, 340, 347, 376; in the international order, 298, 309, 313, 321; public support for, 6, 7, 112, 317–18, 342; and their role in democracy, 5, 42–3, 107–10, 326, 346–7; and their role in the economy, 262, 267–8, 270–1, 342. *See also* ideas of a university; governance of the multiversity; mission of the multiversity

nation. *See* nation state
nation-building, role of universities in, 33, 41, 64–5, 92–3, 146, 147, 302, 329, 364
nation state, 10, 28, 29, 33, 41, 93, 146, 299, 301–2, 305–6, 310, 322, 323, 329, 330, 332, 334–5, 408, 409; national sovereignty, 10, 147, 297–8, 301, 306–7, 316–17, 323–4, 327–8, 334–5, 404. *See also* citizenship; cosmopolitan citizenship; globalization; Westphalian system
nationalism, 41, 299, 301–2
natural philosophy, 26, 32, 358
Negroponte, Nicholas, 183, 198
Nelson, Ted, 189, 190, 236
neoliberalism, 152–3, 154–5, 157, 164, 254. *See also* liberalism; market fundamentalism
new growth theory, 268–71
Newman, Cardinal John Henry, 19–25, 28, 34, 38, 42, 48, 49, 64, 82, 219, 228, 258–9, 293–4, 339, 341, 383, 389, 391–2; *The Idea of a University*, 19–21, 28, 34. *See also* Arnold, Matthew; humanities; ideas of a university; liberal education
Newton, Isaac, 27, 232, 235, 242, 284

Nietzsche, Friedrich, 226
Noble, David, 197–8, 199, 204
Norman, Wayne, 405, 406, 408
Nussbaum, Martha, vii, 368–9, 407, 409

Ong, Walter, 204, 207–8
online courses: courseware, 202–4, 215–16; hybrid courses, 214–19; improving accessibility, 210–14; and lifelong learning, 212–14; open source software, 287–90; orality, 204–8; quality and cost, 180, 198, 199, 208–10, 216–19. *See also* literacy
Orientalism, 238–9, 254, 303–4, 313, 322
Owen-Smith, Jason, 274, 283, 289
Oxford University, 7, 31, 32, 36, 45, 46, 48, 68, 70, 78, 79, 86, 195, 274, 299, 304; and Cardinal Newman, 21, 219, 294, 383; *literae humaniores* curriculum, 36; as a multiversity, 82, 293–4

part-time education, 80, 108, 211–14, 272
participation rate. *See* accessibility
Perkin, Harold, 68, 101
personal computer (PC), 186, 188, 192, 220
Pocklington, Tom, 382, 421, 425, 428
political correctness, 126, 248–50, 398
political culture, 71, 96, 105–7, 162
polytechnics, 79–81
postcolonialism, 239, 245, 247
postindustrial society, 3, 5, 6, 13, 59, 71, 83, 99, 339; definitions, 4, 52–3, 84; and the multiversity, 50–3, 84, 103, 107, 345, 346; and the professions, 67–9; what lies ahead, 146, 148, 181. *See also* Bell, Daniel; economy; globalization
postmodern condition, 227, 231, 237–8, 373, 397–8
postmodern thought: definitions, 224–31; and academic freedom, 249–50; and the character of our age, 9–11, 141, 146–7, 192, 335; and democracy, 379–80, 410; and liberal education, 42, 228–9, 243–7, 394, 402; and the sciences, 255–6; and the social sciences, 252–4
poststructuralism, 226, 236, 249, 252
Powell, Walter, 274, 283, 289
pragmatism, 226, 240–2, 252, 254, 401–2
Princeton University, 174, 175, 302, 309
private goods, 266–7, 269; ideas as, 284, 286–90, 360, 420. *See also* intellectual property
Proctor, Robert, 27, 37, 366, 368, 395, 398. *See also* humanities; liberal education
professional education: in medieval universities, 25–7, 33, 66; and the middle class, 66; in the multiversity, 3, 8, 18, 66–9, 107, 111, 168, 291, 335, 339, 346, 353; and research, 356, 361–4. *See also* ideas of a university
professions: definition, 66–8; and democracy, 5, 67, 108–9
public goods, 266–7, 269, 400; ideas as, 284, 286–90. *See also* intellectual property
public intellectuals, 5, 99, 110, 137–40, 196, 214, 224, 289, 343, 355, 361, 364, 379, 395, 414, 416, 418; definitions, 137–40, 371–2; in a democ-

racy, 371–6; and information technology, 196, 372–3. *See also* democracy; social contract

Rawls, John, 344, 370
Readings, Bill, 257, 330
realism, 232, 241–2, 251
redbrick universities, 78–9, 302
Renaissance humanism, 27, 45, 222
research universities. *See* multiversities
research: applied, 276–7, 283, 341, 358, 360, 363, 367; basic, 55, 267, 275–7, 283, 341, 358, 360, 363, 367; commercialization of, 277–86; and economic prosperity, 57, 262; and information technology, 193–4, 218; as a public good, 267–8; Canadian government support for, 56, 75–7, 278–9; English government support for, 56, 277–8; U.S. government support for, 55–6, 278; social contract for, 343, 355, 370; social contract for humanities, 364–70; social contract for science, 356–61; social contract for social science, 361–4; versus teaching, 28–31, 50, 53–4, 136, 200, 210, 218, 384. *See also* German universities; ideas of a university; linear model of research; multiversities: definitions; Scottish universities; University of Berlin
Reuben, Julie, 44
Rhodes, Frank, 58, 381, 382, 384–5, 391, 413
Romanticism, 40, 230–1, 258
Romer, Paul, 268, 269–70, 292
Roosevelt, Franklin Delano, 88, 101
Rosovsky, Henry, 127, 128, 418

Rothblatt, Sheldon, 22, 23, 44, 219; idea of a university, 22–3
Russell, Conrad, 114, 116
Russell Group, 81, 173, 331
Ryan, Alan, 344–5, 372

Said, Edward, 138, 238–9, 250, 258–9, 303–4, 375. *See also* public intellectuals: definitions; Orientalism
Sausurre, Ferdinand de, 234–5
Schultz, Theodore, 209
Schumpeter, Joseph, 268, 272, 281, 321–2, 418
Scientific Revolution, 27, 35, 45, 78, 119, 134, 138, 222, 232, 256, 388; and academic freedom, 119
Scott, Peter, 297, 313, 382–3
Scottish universities, 21, 32–4, 43, 49–50, 90, 134, 200, 274, 277, 302, 339. *See also* accessibility; research: applied research; ideas of a university
Searle, John, 232, 236, 247–8, 251; Western Rationalistic Tradition, 146, 222, 232–3, 236, 240, 251, 254
semiconductors, 184–5, 414
seminars, 30, 199, 201–4, 207, 210, 214–15, 216, 218, 224, 372, 383. *See also* laboratories; online courses; teaching
Shils, Edward, 45–6
signifier/signified, 235–7, 239, 242–4, 368. *See also* linguistics; postmodern thought
Silicon Valley, 191, 194–5, 271–4, 282, 286, 322
Slaughter, Sheila, 260, 277, 299
Smith, Adam, 28, 90, 134, 152, 159, 263, 266; *An Inquiry into the Nature and Causes of the Wealth of Nations*,

90, 134, 180, 182, 263; on the role of government, 91, 152, 159; on universities, 91–2
Snow, C.P., 138–9, 256–7
social citizenship. *See* Marshall, Thomas H.
social contract: definitions, 110–15; between multiversity and society, 7, 8, 110–15, 247, 339–43; for research in a democracy, 355–70; renewal, 65, 110, 128, 131, 133, 140–1, 177, 339–43, 345–6, 381, 383; role of multiversity leadership, 115, 118, 133; in a welfare state, 5, 84, 87, 113. *See also* academic freedom; autonomy of the university; ideas of a university; governance of the multiversity
social criticism, 5, 110, 118, 133–5, 371, 224, 418; and information technology, 196. *See also* critic and conscience, the university's role as; public intellectuals
social expenditures, 88–9, 96, 104, 157–9, 163; as share of GDP, 89, 104, 158, 160–2. *See also* welfare state
social science: and ideology, 364, 373–4; methodology, 233, 250–4, 320, 362–4, 393; and postmodern thought, 252–4; research in, 11, 87, 96, 147, 135, 154, 160, 252, 300, 362–4. *See also* social criticism
socialism, 95, 98, 102, 124, 149, 253
Socrates, 23–4, 139, 370, 388
Solow, Robert, 264, 265, 268
Sowell, Thomas, 152, 160
Stanford University, 50, 73, 86, 123–4, 187, 194, 289; and Silicon Valley, 194, 271–4
Stokes, Donald E., 358–61, 363–4;

Pasteur's quadrant, 359–61, 363. *See also* Bush, Vannevar; linear model of research
Stoics, 407, 409
student assistance, 55, 58, 171–2, 265, 342, 416. *See also* accessibility; tuition fees

taxation: and globalization, 317–18; and the welfare state, 89, 96, 103–5, 154, 162, 170–1, 410. *See also* constrained welfare state; tuition fees; welfare state
teaching, 18, 19, 28, 116, 128, 137, 193, 197–204, 207–8, 384–5; components of a course, 201–3; role of the lecture, 30, 122, 199–203, 207–8, 210, 214; technologies of teaching, 178–9, 199, 217; versus research, 28–31, 50, 53–4, 126, 136, 200, 210, 218, 384. *See also* laboratories; orality; online courses; seminars
technology transfer, 278–2, 286, 293, 294, 419–20
tenure, 119, 125, 127, 130, 374, 384. *See also* academic freedom
Terman, Fred, 271–2
terrorism, 126, 213, 324–7, 329. *See also* academic freedom: and terrorism
Thompson, Dennis, 378
transistor, 184, 185, 202
Trilling, Lionel, 41, 244, 393, 398; humanities and the moral life, 41, 244, 398. *See also* humanities; liberal education
Trow, Martin, 60, 125, 211, 215–16
tuition fees, 8, 32, 59, 104, 108, 111, 116, 147, 163, 166–7, 169–74, 264–5, 272, 290, 317, 335, 342, 356, 383. *See*

also accessibility; student assistance
Tupper, Allan, 382, 421, 425, 428
Turner, J.M.W., 40, 180, 182; *The Starry Night*, 40, 180, 182

undergraduate education: benefits of, 59, 165–6, 170; as central task of the multiversity, 12, 18, 58–9, 341, 381–6; in Cardinal Newman's university, 19–25; and democracy, 42, 61, 108–9, 329, 350–1, 383, 394, 403–13; and expenditure restraint, 164–9, 209; in first democracy, 386–7; and information technology, 193, 197–221; and internationalization, 314–15; in the multiversity, 58–66, 339, 384; renewed in our age, 393–414; in the renewed social contract, 140–1, 343, 381; time on campus, 219–20. *See also* accessibility; ideas of the university; liberal education; mass higher education
unemployment, 59, 85, 87–9, 97–9, 150, 151, 155–6, 248, 262, 306, 308. *See also* Great Depression; Keynes, John Maynard; welfare state
United Nations, 306–9
U.N. Universal Declaration of Human Rights, 307–9, 321, 332, 353, 406. *See also* citizenship; Marshall, Thomas H.
universities: and democracy, 43, 45–7, 61; and the economy, 25, 27–8, 30, 31, 274–7, 291–6; and the international order, 297, 300–10; and the nation state, 329–35; origins, 25, 27, 30; as place of culture, 41, 302, 320; postmodern, 256–9. *See also* academic freedom; autonomy of the university, ideas of a university; governance of the multiversity
University of Berlin, 29, 31, 48, 93, 116, 303, 305, 339; and the research ideal, 29–30, 50; and the German government, 93. *See also* ideas of a university; Humboldt, Wilhelm von; German universities
University of Edinburgh, 32, 48
University of Michigan, 48, 50, 73, 174, 195, 299
University of Toronto, 175, 299

Veblen, Thorstein, 124, 318

Weber, Max, 231, 244, 258, 397
welfare state, 87, 95–6, 145–6, 148, 160, 306, 308, 316–20, 329, 332, 339; definitions, 5, 85, 87–90; Anglo-American model, 107; comparing Canada, U.S., and England, 88, 104–5, 167–8; intellectual foundations, 95–105; and the multiversity, 4–5, 85–6, 160; origins in Germany, 92–3; and postmodern thought, 254; as a new social contract, 5, 87, 113. *See also* constrained welfare state; social expenditures
Westphalian system, 301, 305, 307, 310, 329, 334, 335
Woodruff, Paul, 386–7
World Wide Web, 181, 189–92, 195–8, 215, 220, 228, 236, 239, 286, 298, 319, 330, 408. *See also* Berners-Lee, Timothy; hypertext; Internet; Nelson, Ted
World Bank, 306–7, 311–12, 316
WTO, 311, 316, 318

York University, 9, 64